Fodor's

SAN DIEGO

WELCOME TO SAN DIEGO

San Diego is a vacationer's paradise, with year-round temperatures in the seventies and near-constant sunshine. One of America's most family-friendly cities, San Diego is home to LEGOLAND, the New Children's Museum, and the famous San Diego Zoo. Sunbathers and surfers are guaranteed to find their perfect beach, and foodies find delights in artisanal breweries, local bistros, and gourmet restaurants. From the Broadway excitement of La Jolla Playhouse to the European feel of Little Italy to the nouveau-chic of the Gaslamp Quarter, San Diego has something for everyone.

TOP REASONS TO GO

★ **Sun and Surf:** Legendary beaches and surfing in La Jolla, Coronado, and Point Loma.

★ **Golf:** A concentration of beautiful courses with sweeping ocean views and light breezes.

★ **Outdoor Sports:** A perfect climate for biking, hiking, sailing—anything—outdoors.

★ **Family Time:** Fun for all ages at LEGOLAND, Balboa Park, the San Diego Zoo, and more.

★ **Great Eats:** Brewpubs, a wide mix of ethnic cuisines, and modern cafés delight diners.

★ **Shopping:** From hip boutiques and fine Mexican crafts to the upscale Fashion Valley Mall.

Fodor's SAN DIEGO

Editorial: Douglas Stallings, *Editorial Director*; Salwa Jabado and Margaret Kelly, *Senior Editors*; Alexis Kelly, Jacinta O'Halloran, and Amanda Sadlowski, *Editors*; Teddy Minford, *Associate Editor*; Rachael Roth, *Content Manager*

Design: Tina Malaney, *Associate Art Director*

Photography: Jennifer Arnow, *Senior Photo Editor*

Maps: Rebecca Baer, *Senior Map Editor*; David Lindroth and Mark Stroud (Moon Street Cartography), *Cartographers*

Production: Jennifer DePrima, *Editorial Production Manager*; Carrie Parker, *Senior Production Editor*; Elyse Rozelle, *Production Editor*

Business & Operations: Chuck Hoover, *Chief Marketing Officer*; Joy Lai, *Vice President and General Manager*; Stephen Horowitz, *Head of Business Development and Partnerships*

Public Relations: Joe Ewaskiw, *Manager*

Writers: Claire Deeks van der Lee, Marlise Kast-Meyers, Kai Oliver-Kurtin, Archana Ram, Juliana Shallcross, Jeff Terich

Editor: Alexis Kelly

Production Editor: Carrie Parker

Production Design: Liliana Guia

31st Edition

ISBN 978-0-14-754688-3

ISSN 1053–5950

All details in this book are based on information supplied to us at press time. Always confirm information when it matters, especially if you're making a detour to visit a specific place. Fodor's expressly disclaims any liability, loss, or risk, personal or otherwise, that is incurred as a consequence of the use of any of the contents of this book.

PRINTED IN THE UNITED STATES OF AMERICA

10 9 8 7 6 5 4 3 2 1

CONTENTS

Fodor's Features

MAPS

ABOUT THIS GUIDE

Fodor's Recommendations

Everything in this guide is worth doing—we don't cover what isn't—but exceptional sights, hotels, and restaurants are recognized with additional accolades. **Fodor's Choice★** indicates our top recommendations; and **Best Bets** call attention to notable hotels and restaurants in various categories. Care to nominate a new place? Visit Fodors.com/contact-us.

Trip Costs

We list prices wherever possible to help you budget well. Hotel and restaurant price categories from **$** to **$$$$** are noted alongside each recommendation. For hotels, we include the lowest cost of a standard double room in high season. For restaurants, we cite the average price of a main course at dinner or, if dinner isn't served, at lunch. For attractions, we always list adult admission fees; discounts are usually available for children, students, and senior citizens.

Hotels

Our local writers vet every hotel to recommend the best overnights in each price category, from budget to expensive. Unless otherwise specified, you can expect private bath, phone, and TV in your room. For expanded hotel reviews visit Fodors.com.

Top Picks
★ Fodor's Choice

Listings
- Address
- Branch address
- Telephone
- Fax
- Website
- E-mail
- Admission fee
- Open/closed times
- Subway
- Directions or Map coordinates

Hotels & Restaurants
- Hotel
- Number of rooms
- Meal plans
- Restaurant
- Reservations
- Dress code
- No credit cards
- Price

Other
- See also
- Take note
- Golf facilities

Restaurants

Unless we state otherwise, restaurants are open for lunch and dinner daily. We mention dress code only when there's a specific requirement and reservations only when they're essential or not accepted.

Credit Cards

The hotels and restaurants in this guide typically accept credit cards. If not, we'll say so.

EUGENE FODOR

Hungarian-born Eugene Fodor (1905–91) began his travel career as an interpreter on a French cruise ship. The experience inspired him to write *On the Continent* (1936), the first guidebook to receive annual updates and discuss a country's way of life as well as its sights. Fodor later joined the U.S. Army and worked for the OSS in World War II. After the war, he kept up his intelligence work while expanding his guidebook series. During the Cold War, many guides were written by fellow agents who understood the value of insider information. Today's guides continue Fodor's legacy by providing travelers with timely coverage, insider tips, and cultural context.

EXPERIENCE SAN DIEGO

SAN DIEGO TODAY

Although most visitors know little about San Diego beyond its fun-in-the-sun reputation, locals are talking about much more than the surf forecast and their tan lines. Concerns about the city's public infrastructure, budget woes, and homeless population are all topics of local debate. After a tumble during the last recession, housing prices have once again skyrocketed and affordability has become a renewed issue. However, San Diegans have managed to keep the city's overall forecast sunny. Several large companies, including Qualcomm, PETCO, and Bridgepoint Education continue to call San Diego home base. The buzz around San Diego's science and biotech industry continues to grow, along with the flourishing craft beer trade. San Diego has been busy shedding its image as LA's less sophisticated neighbor, and coming into an urban identity of its own. Across the region, residents are embracing new trends in the local art, shopping, dining, and cultural scenes.

Today's San Diego:

Eating well. Once considered somewhat of a culinary wasteland, the San Diego dining scene is enjoying a renaissance. All over town, new and exciting restaurants are popping up, celebrating both the local bounty and the region's diversity. Healthy and fresh California Modern cuisine remains a feature on many menus, while neighboring Baja Mexico has given rise to the new trend of BajaMed, a fusion of Mexican and Mediterranean styles. San Diego's sizable Asian population has introduced everything from dim sum carts to Mongolian hot pot, while local sushi chefs take advantage of San Diego's reputation for some of the finest sea urchin in the world. The locavore trend has become somewhat of an obsession for San Diegans, and many restaurants are happy to highlight how and where they source their ingredients.

Toast of the town. San Diego continues to gain recognition as one of the most exciting beer towns in the nation. Craft brewers creating a buzz include AleSmith, Ballast Point, and Alpine Beer Company, just to name a few, and Stone Brewing Company, creator of the notorious Arrogant Bastard Ale, has several locations. All this enthusiasm for San Diego's suds has given rise to a beer tourism industry, from bus tours of local brewers to large beer-themed

WHAT WE'RE TALKING ABOUT

After years of back and forth over funding and new stadium proposals, Chargers fans learned in early 2017 that their NFL team would be leaving San Diego and heading north to Los Angeles. The Qualcomm Stadium site is already being eyed for redevelopment, including a proposal to bring Major League Soccer to the city. This offers little consolation to Chargers fans feeling abandoned by their beloved Bolts.

The buzz surrounding the San Diego craft beer community is growing louder. The recent sale of local brewery Ballast Point to Constellation Brands for a whopping $1 billion made international headlines, and solidified San Diego's reputation as one of the nation's best beer cities. The sale ignited the aspirations of events such as the popular San Diego Beer Week. There's even an app to help you find the perfect pint: inspired by the local brewing scene, a San Diego couple created the TapHunter website and mobile application, which helps beer lovers find what's on tap and where.

Building for the future, and conserving its past. A drive around San Diego reveals a huge range of architecture, from hip to historic to downright hideous. Urban planning from half a century ago, such as the decision to run Interstate 5 right through Little Italy and Downtown, is hard to undo but other efforts to conserve the city's architectural integrity have been more successful. Downtown's Gaslamp Quarter is the most famous conservation area, but the residential neighborhoods of Uptown, Kensington, and South Park delight early-20th-century architecture buffs with streets full of historically designated homes. Projects making waves in San Diego today include the revitalization of the Embarcadero and the opening of the Liberty Public Market.

Get outside. San Diego's near-perfect climate and gorgeous natural landscape make it hard to find an excuse not to get outside and exercise. In fact, San Diego is home to one of the most active populations in the country. Year-round opportunities to surf, sail, bike, or hike offer something for everyone. On weekends and throughout the summer, beaches and parks teem with locals enjoying the great weather and fresh air. Gas barbecues, bouncy houses, and huge shade tents take the concept of the picnic to a whole new level. So when visitors hailing from harsher climates wonder if San Diegans appreciate how good they have it, the answer is a resounding yes.

---

other local brewers, demonstrating the ability to turn their passion into profit.

San Diego loves its markets, and the newly opened Liberty Public Market is no exception. Housed within Liberty Station, the mixed use redevelopment of the old San Diego Naval Training Center, the market buzzes with residents and tourists alike. Vendors sell fresh meat, seafood, pasta, and other ingredients alongside a variety of prepared foods such as empanadas, gumbo, tostadas, and baked goods. Open seating areas throughout the market make this a popular lunch spot.

WHAT'S WHERE

1 Downtown. Downtown used to be a real downer, a mix of bland office towers and seedy sidewalks after sundown. Preservationists and entrepreneurs saved the day, and now the streets are lined with nightclubs, boutiques, and restaurants, from the glam Gaslamp Quarter (a former red-light district) to the edgier East Village (where Padres fans get their baseball fix at PETCO Park). Also nearby are Seaport Village, the Embarcadero, and trendy yet authentic Little Italy.

2 Balboa Park. In the center of the city, this 1,200-acre patch of greenery is home to world-class museums and performing arts, stunning Spanish colonial revival architecture, and the famed San Diego Zoo. Paths wind around gardens, fountains, and groves of shady trees. It's a sort of Central Park of the west—a leafy getaway for locals, and a must for tourists.

3 Old Town. Before there was a sprawling city, there was an Old Town, home to the remnants of San Diego's—and California's—first permanent European settlement. The former pueblo is now a pedestrian-friendly state historic park, with original and reconstructed buildings and sites, along with a tourist bazaar of souvenir shops, art galleries, and Mexican eateries with margaritas and mariachi aplenty.

4 Uptown. Uptown is a catchall for a cluster of trendy neighborhoods near Downtown and north of Balboa Park. Hillcrest is the heart of the city's gay and lesbian community, while in North Park, a hip and edgy set keeps boutiques, galleries, eateries, and bars hopping. The leafy streets of South Park are lined with older homes, charming shops, and welcoming cafés. Mission Hills is a lovely historic neighborhood between Old Town and Hillcrest, while Mission Valley, northeast of Uptown, is mostly known for office towers and shopping malls.

5 Mission Bay and the Beaches. Home to SeaWorld, Mission Bay also boasts a 4,600-acre aquatic park perfect for boating, jet skiing, swimming, and fishing, plus activities like biking, basketball, and kite flying. It's neighbored by bustling Mission Beach and Pacific Beach, where streets are lined with surf shops, ice-cream stands, and beach bars.

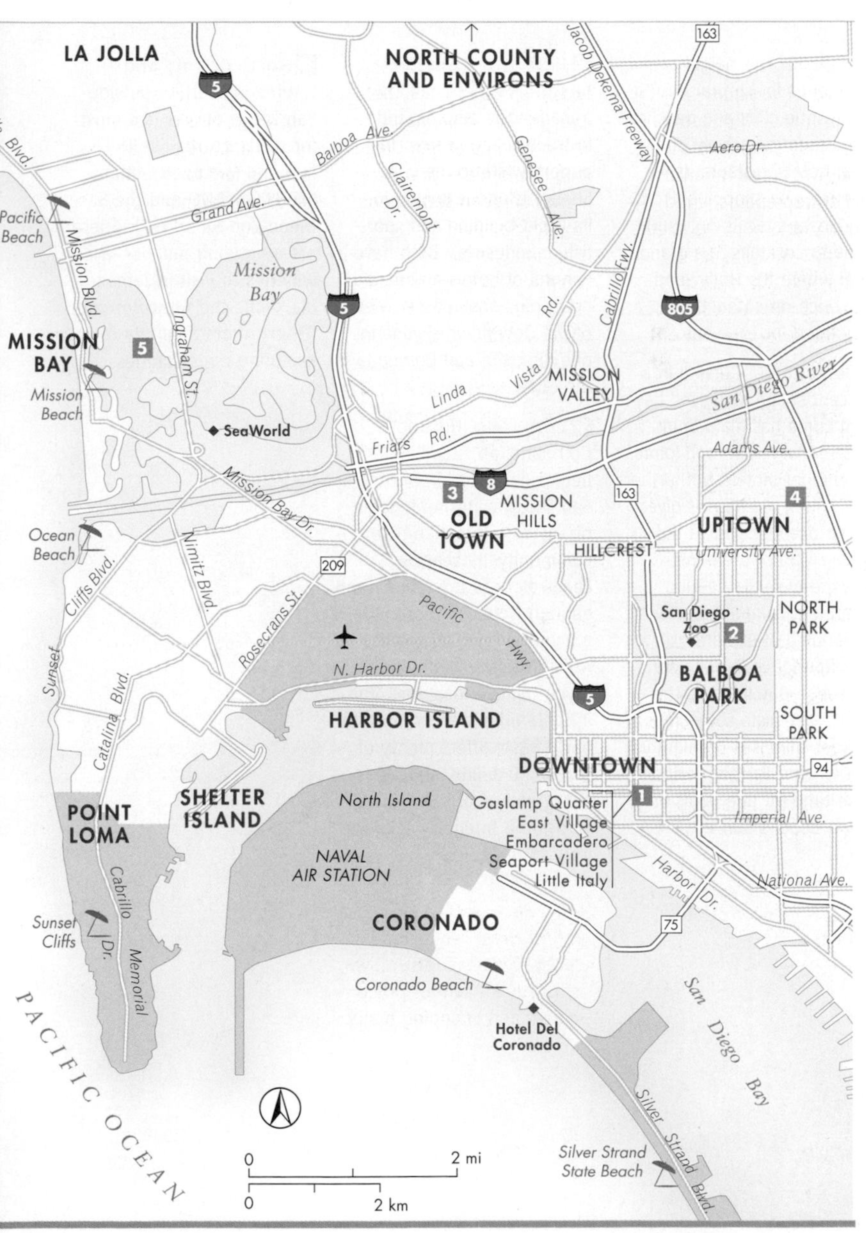
LA JOLLA
NORTH COUNTY AND ENVIRONS
MISSION BAY
MISSION VALLEY
OLD TOWN
MISSION HILLS
UPTOWN
HILLCREST
NORTH PARK
BALBOA PARK
SOUTH PARK
HARBOR ISLAND
DOWNTOWN
Gaslamp Quarter
East Village
Embarcadero
Seaport Village
Little Italy
POINT LOMA
SHELTER ISLAND
CORONADO
North Island
NAVAL AIR STATION
SeaWorld
San Diego Zoo
Hotel Del Coronado
Pacific Beach
Mission Beach
Ocean Beach
Sunset Cliffs
Coronado Beach
Silver Strand State Beach
Mission Bay
San Diego River
San Diego Bay
PACIFIC OCEAN
La Jolla Blvd.
Mission Blvd.
Grand Ave.
Balboa Ave.
Clairemont Dr.
Genesee Ave.
Jacob Dekema Freeway
Cabrillo Fwy.
Aero Dr.
Linda Vista Rd.
Friars Rd.
Ingraham St.
Mission Bay Dr.
Nimitz Blvd.
Sunset Cliffs Blvd.
Rosecrans St.
Catalina Blvd.
Cabrillo Memorial Dr.
Pacific Hwy.
N. Harbor Dr.
Adams Ave.
University Ave.
Imperial Ave.
National Ave.
Harbor Dr.
Silver Strand Blvd.
5
805
8
163
209
94
75
0
2 mi
0
2 km

WHAT'S WHERE

6 La Jolla. This neighborhood lands lavish praise for its picturesque cliffs and beaches, not to mention a bevy of the finest hotels, restaurants, art galleries, and shopping. From Windansea's locals-only surf scene to cocktails at a grand hotel where the Hollywood elite once retreated, there's something for everyone.

7 Point Loma. Curving in a crescent shape along the bay, Point Loma has main drags cluttered with fast-food joints and budget motels, but farther back, grand old houses give way to ocean views. At the southern tip of the peninsula, the majestic Cabrillo Monument commemorates the landing of explorer Juan Rodríguez Cabrillo at San Diego Bay in 1542; the 360-degree vista sometimes includes glimpses of migrating gray whales. Farther north, make time for tide pools at Ocean Beach's Sunset Cliffs.

8 Harbor and Shelter Islands. Harbor Island is a man-made strip of land in the bay across from the airport, while to the west, Shelter Island is known for its yacht-building and sport-fishing industries. Both have a handful of hotels and restaurants, plus unsurpassed views of the Downtown skyline in one direction and Coronado in the other.

9 Coronado. Historic Coronado, an islandlike peninsula across from the San Diego waterfront, came of age as a Victorian resort community. Its seaside centerpiece is the fabled (and gabled) Hotel Del Coronado, a favorite haunt of celebs, A-listers, and—well—ghosts, if you believe local lore. The upscale area, also home to a naval base, offers plenty of shopping, dining, and pleasant stretches of sand. Drive across the bridge or take the ferry to reach it.

10 North County and Environs. Getting outside San Diego proper is a must for beach towns like Del Mar and family attractions like LEGOLAND and the San Diego Zoo Safari Park. There are a growing number of wineries to visit in Temecula, while the Anza-Borrego Desert offers a variety of exploring opportunities.

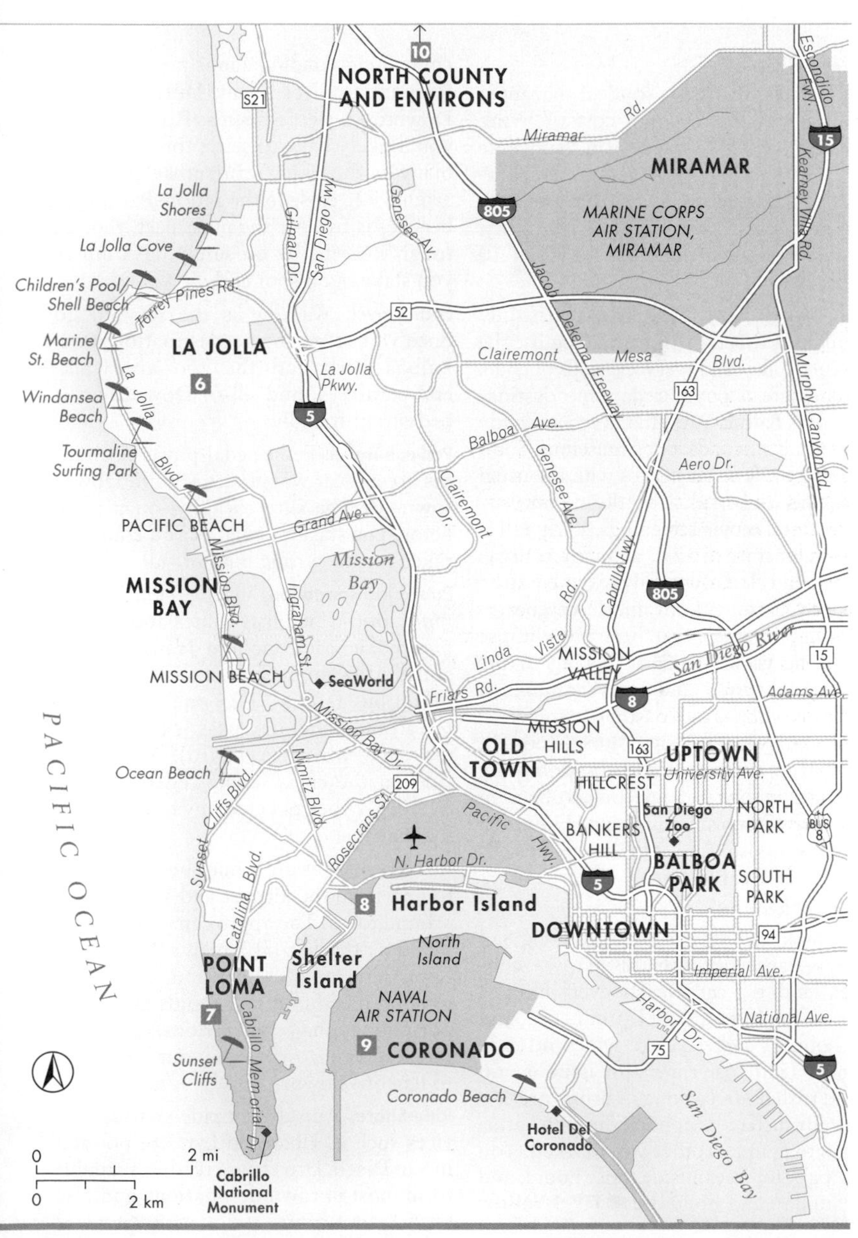

NORTH COUNTY AND ENVIRONS
10
MIRAMAR
MARINE CORPS AIR STATION, MIRAMAR
LA JOLLA
6
La Jolla Shores
La Jolla Cove
Children's Pool/ Shell Beach
Marine St. Beach
Windansea Beach
Tourmaline Surfing Park
PACIFIC BEACH
MISSION BAY
Mission Bay
MISSION BEACH
SeaWorld
Ocean Beach
PACIFIC OCEAN
MISSION VALLEY
MISSION HILLS
OLD TOWN
UPTOWN
HILLCREST
San Diego Zoo
NORTH PARK
BANKERS HILL
BALBOA PARK
SOUTH PARK
DOWNTOWN
8
Harbor Island
Shelter Island
POINT LOMA
7
North Island
NAVAL AIR STATION
9
CORONADO
Coronado Beach
Hotel Del Coronado
Sunset Cliffs
Cabrillo National Monument
San Diego Bay
San Diego River
Miramar Rd.
Escondido Fwy.
Kearney Villa Rd.
Genesee Av.
Gilman Dr.
San Diego Fwy.
Torrey Pines Rd.
Jacob Dekema Freeway
Clairemont Mesa Blvd.
La Jolla Pkwy.
La Jolla Blvd.
Balboa Ave.
Genesee Ave.
Aero Dr.
Murphy Canyon Rd.
Clairemont Dr.
Grand Ave.
Mission Blvd.
Ingraham St.
Cabrillo Fwy.
Linda Vista Rd.
Friars Rd.
Adams Ave.
Mission Bay Dr.
Nimitz Blvd.
Sunset Cliffs Blvd.
Rosecrans St.
Pacific Hwy.
N. Harbor Dr.
Catalina Blvd.
University Ave.
Imperial Ave.
National Ave.
Harbor Dr.
Cabrillo Memorial Dr.
S21
805
52
5
163
15
8
209
94
75
BUS 8
0
2 mi
0
2 km

SAN DIEGO PLANNER

When to Go

San Diego's weather is so ideal that most locals shrug off the high cost of living and relatively low wages as a "sunshine tax." Along the coast, average temperatures range from the mid-60s to the high 70s, with clear skies and low humidity. Annual rainfall is minimal, less than 10 inches per year.

The peak season for sunseekers is July through October. In July and August, the mercury spikes and everyone spills outside. Beaches are a popular daytime destination, as is Balboa Park, thanks to its shady groves and air-conditioned museums. Summer's nightlife scene thrives with the usual bars and clubs, plus outdoor concerts, theater, and movie screenings. Early fall is a pleasant time to visit, as many tourists have already left town and the temperature is nearly perfect. From mid-December to mid-March, whale-watchers can glimpse migrating gray whales frolicking in the Pacific. In spring and early summer, a marine layer hugs the coastline for much or all of the day (locals call it "June Gloom"), which can be dreary and disappointing for those who were expecting to bask in Southern California sunshine. However, wildflowers also blanket the mountainsides and desert in early spring.

Getting Around

Car Travel: To fully explore sprawling San Diego—especially with kids in tow—consider renting a car. Nearly everything of interest can be found off I–5 or I–163, and the county's freeways are wide and easy to use. Traffic isn't a major issue if you avoid rush hour. Parking in urban areas is typically metered, Monday through Saturday, 8 to 6, unless otherwise marked. You may park for free outside those hours, and on Sunday and holidays. **■TIP→ Yellow commercial loading zones are fair game for parking after 6 pm.** During special Downtown events, such as Padres games, you'll likely have to settle for one of the many paid parking structures—they cost around $20 close to the action. Parking at beaches is free for the most part, though tough to come by on sunny days unless you stake out a spot early.

Foot Travel: Walking is the way to go once you've reached a destination area. Balboa Park and the zoo are walkers' paradises, and all of Downtown is pedestrian-friendly.

Pedicab Travel: These pedal-powered chariots are a great way to get around Downtown. Just be sure to agree on a price before you start moving, or you could get taken for the wrong kind of ride.

Public Transportation: Visit 🌐 *www.sdcommute.com*, which lists routes and timetables for the Metropolitan Transit System and North County Transit District. Local/urban bus fare is $2.25 one-way, or $5 for an unlimited day pass (exact change only; pay when you board). A one-way ride on the city's iconic red trolleys is $2.50; get your ticket at any trolley vending machine.

Taxi Travel: Cabs are a fine choice for trips to and from the airport and short jaunts around town. The approximate rates are: $2.80 for the first 1/10 mile, $3 each additional mile, and $24 per hour of waiting time. You can find taxi stands at the airport, hotels, major attractions, and shopping centers. Downtown, your best bet is to flag one down.

Ride-Share: App-driven ride-sharing services such as Uber and Lyft are popular in San Diego. Drivers are readily available from most in-town destinations and also service the airport.

FRED (Free Ride Everywhere Downtown): These open-air electric vehicles offer free rides throughout the Downtown area. Riders can make a pickup request through the FRED app, or simply flag one down.

What to Wear

You won't find a more casual big city. Flip-flops are the favored footwear, shorts and beachy skirts comprise the summer uniform, and designer jeans qualify as dressing up. Dining out warrants a little research; some eateries barely toe the "no shirt, no shoes" rule, while others require more elegant attire.

Safety

San Diego has some sketchy areas, although tourists typically encounter few problems. Downtown can get a little rowdy at night, especially toward 2 am, when bars boot drunken patrons out on the sidewalks. The city also has a large homeless population, who often camp out on shadowy side streets not far from East Village. Most are harmless, aside from the occasional panhandling, but it's safest to stick to well-lighted, busy areas. Certain pockets of Balboa Park are frequented by drug dealers and prostitutes after hours; if you're attending a nighttime theater performance or art event, park nearby or use the valet.

Where to www

Browse these online options for more about what's on.

🌐 *www.fodors.com*, check out the forums on our site for answers to your travel questions and tips.

🌐 *www.sandiego.org* for the San Diego visitor bureau.

🌐 *www.sandiegoreader.com* posts tons of event listings, from big concerts to little community to-dos.

🌐 *www.utsandiego.com* is where the scaled-down *San Diego Union-Tribune* posts all its daily newspaper and original online content, including a searchable entertainment section.

🌐 *www.sdcitybeat.com* for the online version of the alternative weekly *San Diego CityBeat,* a guide to the city's edgier side, from regional politics to hot local bands.

Festivals

Winter: Drawing 100,000 visitors the first Friday and Saturday of December, **Balboa Park December Nights** offers festive carolers, food, music, and dance. The **San Diego Bay Parade of Lights,** also in December, lights up the harbor with boats decked out for the holidays.

January's **Farmers Insurance Open** is the Holy Grail for golf fans; the celeb-heavy tourney has been held at the scenic Torrey Pines Golf Course for decades. In February, the **Mardi Gras** block party in the Gaslamp Quarter invites revelers to let the good times roll.

Spring: **Adams Avenue Unplugged** gives music fans a weekend of free acoustic music, while Little Italy's annual **ArtWalk** showcases local art talent on tent-lined streets.

Summer: The **San Diego County Fair,** the Old Globe's **Summer Shakespeare Festival,** the city's huge **LGBT Pride Festival,** racing season at the **Del Mar Fairgrounds,** and outdoor classical concerts at the **Embarcadero** all take place in summer.

Fall: New on the festival scene, **KAABOO** is a three-day "mix-perience" featuring top music acts, comedians, DJs, artists and celebrity chefs.

SAN DIEGO TOP ATTRACTIONS

D

A

C

B

Balboa Park

(A) Oasis is hardly hyperbole when it comes to describing this 1,200-acre cultural heart of San Diego. Take a peaceful stroll or plan a full day of perusing Balboa Park's many museums, theater spaces, gardens, trails, and playing fields. And don't forget the park's famous San Diego Zoo.

Beaches

(B) San Diego boasts 70 miles of coastline, with beaches for everybody, from pail-and-shovel-toting toddlers to hard-bodied adventurous types—even nudists have their own sheltered spot at Black's Beach. Coronado is a family favorite, twentysomethings soak up some sun at Pacific Beach, and surfers swear by various stretches of shore, including Windansea Beach. Life's a beach, here, literally.

Cabrillo National Monument

(C) On the southern tip of the Point Loma Peninsula, this landmark commemorates the 1542 landing of explorer Juan Rodríguez Cabrillo in San Diego Bay. Unparalleled harbor and skyline views, a military history museum, tidal pools, and an old lighthouse are among the offerings. In winter, you may even catch sight of migrating gray whales along the coast.

Carlsbad Flower Fields

(D) Fifty acres of flowers, mostly ranunculus, bloom in Technicolor hues every March on a hillside perched above the Pacific Ocean. Timing is everything, but if you visit in spring, don't miss this showy display of stunning natural beauty.

G

F

E

La Jolla

First things first: It's pronounced La Hoya. Next you need to know that it's one of the prettiest places in California, a wealthy enclave with a small-town feel and world-class scenic coastline. Visit the Children's Pool, populated by sunbathing seals, or watch locals ride waves at the beach. Then again, you could just shop and nosh the day away.

LEGOLAND California

(E) A whole universe of LEGO fun awaits the pint-size set and their chaperones in Carlsbad, including more than 60 rides and attractions. Especially cool is Miniland USA, scaled-down cities built entirely from LEGO bricks, as well as Pirate Shores and the Egyptian-theme Dune Raiders, a 30-foot racing slide.

San Diego Zoo

(F) One word: pandas. The San Diego Zoo has several of the roly-poly crowd-pleasers. And yes, they're that cute. But the conservation-minded zoo offers much more, from Polar Bear Plunge to oh-so-close encounters of lions, tigers, and bears. Explore the huge, hilly attraction by foot, or take advantage of the guided bus tours, aerial tram, and seated shows. Also a roaring good time: Escondido's Safari Park.

Torrey Pines State Natural Reserve

(G) The nation's rarest pine tree calls this area home, as do the last salt marshes and waterfowl refuges in Southern California. Hikers can wind their way down windswept trails that stretch from the high coastal bluffs to sandy Torrey Pines State Beach below. Panoramic views abound.

TOP EXPERIENCES

Did We Mention the Beach?

If stretching out on the sand with a sunscreen-stained paperback sounds like a snooze, there's always swimming, snorkeling, surfing, diving, and deep-sea fishing. And that's just in the water. On the sand, serve and spike in a friendly beach volleyball pickup or pal around with your pooch at a leash-free dog beach. The truly adventurous should sign up for Over-the-Line, a massive beach softball tourney that takes place every July—the title refers as much to blood alcohol levels as the rules of the game.

Sail Away

So you don't own a historic tall ship. Who says you can't experience the thrill of sailing the seas in high style? Several times a year, the **San Diego Maritime Museum** offers public adventure sails aboard the *Star of India,* the *Californian,* and the HMS *Surprise*. And, on very rare occasions, the ships even stage cannon battle reenactments in the San Diego Bay. *Master and Commander* wannabes, consider it your shot at combat glory.

Culture Vulture

San Diego's artistic scene gets short shrift compared to the city's outdoorsy offerings, which is a shame. Truly top-notch theater dominates the dance cards of local culturati, like **La Jolla Playhouse,** which routinely hosts Broadway-bound shows before they head east. The **Old Globe**—the oldest professional theater in the state—stages everything from Shakespeare to the avant-garde at its cluster of spaces, including the state-of-the-art Conrad Prebys Theatre Center. The **Museum of Contemporary Art San Diego** showcases thought-provoking exhibitions, from regionally focused to international retrospectives, while niche galleries throughout the county cater to the visually curious. And no matter what the season, visitors will find something fetching from area performing-arts staples such as the **San Diego Symphony Orchestra, San Diego Opera,** and **San Diego Ballet.**

Bogey Bliss

Whether you're timid at the tee or an aspiring golf pro, San Diego's wide-ranging golf options will wow you. Never mind the fact that water restrictions have left some greens a little less, er, green. Golfing in San Diego is an experience par none, no matter what your price range and ability. If you can swing the fees, splurge at Carlsbad's **Park Hyatt Resort Aviara** or at the **Rancho Bernardo Resort & Spa.** La Jolla's **Torrey Pines Golf Course,** home to the 2008 U.S. Open and every Buick Invitational (now the Farmers Insurance Open) since 1968, is one of the finest 18-hole public courses in the country, and a more affordable outing. Just be sure to book tee times well in advance.

Sky High

Sometimes, soaring above the earth is the best way to get a sense of its mind-blowing scale—to wit, the colorful hot-air balloons that dot the horizon at sunrise and sunset. Tiny and toylike from the ground, they offer big bird's-eye views to those who take flight. Enjoy a wine and cheese pairing high above the Temecula wine region with **California Dreamin'.** If standing beneath an open flame makes you a basket case, perhaps tandem paragliding will put you in your proper airborne place. At the **Torrey Pines Gliderport,** an instructor handles the hard work. All you have to do is shout in glee as the winged glider climbs and dips above cliff-bordered beaches.

Charge It

When your Visa bill reads like a vacation diary, you know you're a serious shopaholic. Jimmy Choo, Hermès, and Louis Vuitton? That was just an afternoon at **Fashion Valley**! San Diego has options to suit every style of shopper. For unique, edgy scores, scour boutiques in neighborhoods like **Hillcrest, Little Italy,** and **North Park.** Sleek storefronts in **La Jolla** and other well-heeled areas carry all variety of luxury goods, while Downtown's **Westfield Horton Plaza** stocks standard mall fare. For souvenirs—seashells and such—try **Seaport Village,** or browse festive Mexican arts and crafts at Old Town's **Fiesta de Reyes.**

Hang Loose, Dude

Only a grom (a newbie) would say "hang loose," but "dude" is definitely a prominent part of the local surfer's vocabulary (as in, duuuuude). If you have the courage to wriggle into a wetsuit and waddle into knee-deep white water with a big foam board, you might just catch a wave—or at least stand up for a few seconds. Learning to surf is hard work, so your best bet is to take lessons, either private instruction or group-based. Try La Jolla's **Surf Diva Surf School,** geared primarily toward ladies, or Carlsbad's **San Diego Surfing Academy** in North County.

Sample the Fish Tacos

The humble fish taco is a local foodie favorite. Beer-battered and fried or lightly grilled, topped with salsa or white sauce and cabbage, tacos around town appeal to every palate. Sample the different styles from simple storefront restaurants and mobile taco trucks, and be prepared for a heated discussion. The only thing most San Diegans agree on is that fish tacos taste even better with a cold beer.

Spa-tacular

Money may not buy happiness, but it can definitely purchase a day of pampering at one of San Diego's many upscale spas. There's no limit to the luxuriating, from youth-restoring facials to aromatherapy massages that unkink months' worth of muscle aches. If cost is no concern, book a stay at what many consider to be the world's best destination spa, **Golden Door,** or at the historic **Hotel Del Coronado,** a beauty-boosting seaside retreat since the Victorian days.

Skip Town

San Diego's allure extends well beyond its famous coastline. To the east, visitors will find forested mountains and an otherworldly desert landscape. The tiny town of **Julian,** in the Cuyamaca Mountains, charms with olden-day bed-and-breakfasts and ample slices of apple pie. In winter, weather allowing, visitors can even take horse-drawn sleigh rides. In the spring, a stunning 50-acre display of color blooms against the backdrop of the Pacific Ocean at the **Flower Fields at Carlsbad Ranch.** Or, head to Southern California's premium winemaking region, **Temecula,** for award-winning blends, quiet lakes, and citrus and avocado groves.

GREAT ITINERARIES

ONE DAY IN SAN DIEGO

If you've only got 24 hours to spare, start at **Balboa Park,** the cultural heart of San Diego. Stick to El Prado, the main promenade, where you'll pass by peaceful gardens and soaring Spanish colonial revival architecture. Unless you're a serious museum junkie, pick whichever piques your interest—choices range from photography to folk art.

If you're with the family, don't even think of skipping the **San Diego Zoo.** You'll want to spend the better part of your day there, but make an early start of it so you can head for one of San Diego's **beaches** afterward while there's still daylight. Kick back under the late afternoon sun and linger for sunset. Or wander around **Seaport Village** and the **Embarcadero** before grabbing a bite to eat in the **Gaslamp Quarter.**

Alternate plan: Start at **SeaWorld** and end with an ocean-view dinner in **La Jolla.**

FOUR DAYS IN SAN DIEGO

Day 1

The one-day itinerary *above* also works for the first day of an extended visit. If you're staying in North County, though, you may want to bypass the zoo and head for the **San Diego Zoo Safari Park.** Here, you'll see herds of African and Asian animals acting as they would in the wild. Not included in the general admission, but worth it, are the park's "special experiences"—guided photo caravans, behind-the-scenes tours, and the Flightline, a zip line soaring above the animal enclosures.

Another North County option for families with little ones: **LEGOLAND** in Carlsbad.

Note: The San Diego Zoo, the San Diego Safari Park, and LEGOLAND are all-day, wipe-the-kids-out adventures.

Day 2

You might want to ease into your second day with a leisurely breakfast, followed by a 90-minute tour aboard the **SEAL Amphibious Tour,** which departs from Seaport Village daily. The bus-boat hybrid explores picturesque San Diego neighborhoods before rolling right into the water for a cruise around the bay, all with fun-facts narration.

Back on land, you can devote an hour or so to **Seaport Village,** a 14-acre waterfront shopping and dining complex. Meant to look like a 19th-century harbor, Seaport features 4 miles of cobblestone pathways bordered by lush landscaping and water features.

From there, stroll north to the **Embarcadero,** where you'll marvel at the **Maritime Museum's** historic vessels, including the *Star of India* (the world's oldest active sailing ship).

Explore San Diego's military might at the **USS Midway Museum;** the permanently docked aircraft carrier has more than 60 exhibits and 25 restored aircraft.

Spend the rest of your afternoon and evening in **Coronado,** a quick jaunt by ferry or bridge, or walk a few blocks north to the **Gaslamp Quarter,** where the shopping and dining will keep you busy for hours.

Day 3

Set out early enough, and you might snag a parking spot near **La Jolla Cove,** where you can watch sea lions lounging on the beach at the **Children's Pool.** Then head up one block to Prospect Street, where you'll find the vaunted **La Valencia** hotel (called the "Pink Lady" for its blush-hue exterior) and dozens of posh boutiques and galleries.

If you're with kids, head for **La Jolla Shores,** a good beach for swimming and making sand castles, followed by a visit to the **Birch Aquarium** and a bite to eat at the popular **El Pescador Fish Market** (⇨ *See Chapter 8, Where to Eat*).

Once you've refueled, head for **Torrey Pines State Natural Reserve,** where you can hike down the cliffs to the state beach with breathtaking views in every direction. (If you're with small children, the trek might prove too challenging.)

For dinner, swing north to **Del Mar** during racing season, the evening scene is happening.

Day 4

Start the day with a morning visit to **Cabrillo National Monument,** a national park with a number of activities. Learn about 16th-century explorer Juan Rodríguez Cabrillo, take a gentle 2-mile hike on the beautiful Bayside Trail, look around the Old Point Loma Lighthouse, and peer at tide pools. ■ **TIP→ Find out when low tide is before planning your itinerary.**

After Cabrillo, head to **Old Town,** where San Diego's early history comes to carefully reconstructed life. Old Town's Mexican restaurants aren't the city's best, but they're definitely bustling and kid-friendly, and frosty margaritas make an added incentive for grown-ups.

After that, spend a few hours exploring whatever cluster of neighborhoods appeals to you most. If you like casual coastal neighborhoods with a youthful vibe, head to **Pacific, Mission,** or **Ocean Beach,** or venture up to **North County** for an afternoon in **Encinitas,** which epitomizes the old California surf town.

If edgy and artsy are more your thing, check out the hip and ever-changing neighborhoods in **Uptown,** where you'll find super-cool shops, bars, and eateries.

TIPS

■ It's easy to add a theater performance or a concert to any of these days. Some of the city's top venues are in Balboa Park, Downtown, and La Jolla.

■ If you plan to tour many of Balboa Park's museums, buy the **Balboa Park Explorer Pass,** which gets you into 17 attractions for $57, or the **Balboa Park Explorer Combo Pass,** which also gets you into the zoo ($97). Both passes are valid for seven consecutive days. Buy them online or at the **Balboa Park Visitor Center** (*619/239–0512* 🌐 *www.balboapark.org*).

■ The **Trolley** and the **Coaster** are great ways to access foot-friendly neighborhoods up and down the coast. You can head almost anywhere from the **Santa Fe Depot** in Downtown (the cutting-edge Museum of Contemporary Art is next door).

ALTERNATIVES

Adventure junkies might want to ignore the above suggestions and check out the Fodor's Sports and the Outdoors listings in Chapter 13. You can easily fill four days or more with every imaginable outdoor activity, from swimming and surfing to hiking and stand-up paddling. San Diego is an athletic enthusiast's heaven—unless you're a skier.

In **winter,** include more indoor activities—the museums are fantastic—as well as a whale-watching.

In **summer,** check local listings for outdoor concerts, theater, and movie screenings.

LIKE A LOCAL

Just because San Diego has tourist attractions at every turn doesn't mean you shouldn't stray from the beaten path and pretend you're a local for a day.

A Pared-Down Pace

Balboa Park is the city's preferred playground. Visitors with detailed agendas (Museums? Check. Zoo? Check.) often miss out on the sweet spots that keep locals coming back time and again. Grab a map from the visitor center and explore the park's nooks and crannies. Or throw down a blanket on the lawn and laugh at the other tourists with their impossibly long to-do lists.

The Hoppiest Place on Earth

Cold beer seems to suit San Diego's chill personality, which may be why their craft-brewing scene has been lauded as one of the most cutting-edge in the world. You could easily spend an entire day visiting breweries, from the tiny **Alpine Beer Company**—to Escondido and Liberty Station's venerable **Stone Brewing,** which started off as a pet project and now ships nationwide. If a full-fledged beer tour is out of the question, head to **30th Street** in North Park, which is lined with so many brewpubs that it's been nicknamed the "Beer Corridor."

Fill Your Heart with Art

MCASD's **Downtown at Sundown** is a monthly museum party featuring music, drink specials, and food trucks that puts to rest all notions of an artless art scene.

Sunrise, Sunset

The beaches can't be beat, but battling the crazy summer crowds for a spot on the sand is far from relaxing. Take a brisk stroll just after dawn, and savor the views without distraction. Or, find a secluded spot on the cliffs for a more serene sunset.

Break for Breakfast

Even fitness freaks—and San Diegans are among the country's fittest—will agree that a slow-paced morning meal is a lovely start to the weekend, which explains the long lines at any place worth the wait. ⇨ *For full reviews, see Chapter 8, Where to Eat*

The **Mission** has locations in Mission Beach (✉ *3795 Mission Blvd.* ☎ *858/488–9060*), North Park (✉ *2801 University Ave.* ☎ *619/220–8992*), and the East Village (✉ *1250 J St.* ☎ *619/232–7662*). The café food is simple and hearty, ranging from traditional fare (eggs, pancakes) to the Latino-inspired (the Papas Locas or "crazy potatoes" will burn a hole in your tongue).

Hash House A Go Go (✉ *3628 5th Ave., Hillcrest* ☎ *619/298–4646*) specializes in Southern-accented favorites, in large portions. There are a variety of the namesake hashes and eggs Benedict, as well as fluffy pancakes and French toast. Weekends mean long lines, so try to visit during the week.

Kono's Surf Club Café (✉ *704 Garnet Ave.* ☎ *858/483–1669*) in Pacific Beach lures locals with an outdoor patio and ocean views, but the last thing you'll want to do after eating one of Kono's massive breakfast burritos is slip into a bikini. There's a reason for the expression "burrito belly"—but it's a small price to pay for brazenly overindulgent pleasure.

SAN DIEGO WITH KIDS

Beach Fun

A pail and shovel can keep kids entertained for hours at the beach—**Coronado Beach** is especially family-friendly. Be liberal with the sunscreen, even if it's cloudy.

If you're visiting in summer, check out the **Imperial Beach Sun and Sea Festival's** sand castle competition, which usually takes place in late July or early August. There is even a kids' competition.

Drop off the tweens and teens for a morning **surf lesson** and enjoy some guilt-free grown-up time. Or rent bikes for a casual family ride along the **Mission Bay boardwalk.** If that's not enough of an adventure, take your daring offspring on the **Giant Dipper,** an old wooden roller coaster at Mission Bay's **Belmont Park,** also home to a huge arcade.

Top Attractions

LEGOLAND California is a full day of thrills for kids 12 and under, while the **San Diego Zoo** and **San Diego Safari Park** satisfy all age groups and every kind of kid, from the curious (plenty of educational angles) to the boisterous (room to run around and lots of animals to imitate). They even have family sleepover nights in summer.

Winter Sightings

If you're visiting in winter, try a **whale-watching** tour. Even if you don't see any migrating gray whales, the boat ride is fun. La Jolla's **Birch Aquarium** has enough glowing and tentacled creatures to send imaginations plummeting leagues under the sea.

Museums Geared to Kids

An afternoon at the museum might elicit yawns until they spy all the neat stuff at Balboa Park's **San Diego Air and Space Museum,** which celebrates aviation and flight history with exhibitions that include actual planes. The **Reuben H. Fleet Science Center** inspires budding scientists with interactive exhibits and its IMAX dome theater. The **San Diego Model Railroad Museum** features miles and miles of model trains and track, including an incredibly detailed reproduction of the Tehachapi railroad circa 1952.

Downtown's **New Children's Museum** appeals to all age groups; too-cool teens can even retreat to the edgy Teen Studio. With installations geared just for them and dry and wet art-making areas (less mess for you), kids can channel all that excess vacation energy into something productive. While they color and craft, you can admire the museum's ultracontemporary, sustainable architecture.

Take Me Out to the Ball Game

Baseball buffs will have a blast at **PETCO Park,** where the San Diego Padres play all spring and summer. PETCO's Park at the Park, a grassy elevated area outside the stadium, offers stellar center-field views—plus all the action on a big screen—with a sandy play space if your kids get bored after a few innings.

Treating Your Tots

Pacific Beach's yummy **The Baked Bear** (⊠ *4516 Mission Blvd.* 🌐 *www.thebakedbear.com*) offers customized ice-cream sandwiches that are sure to please. Also delish is Hillcrest's **Babycakes** (*3766 5th Ave.* 🌐 *www.babycakessandiego.com*), a stylish spot nestled in an 1889 Craftsman near Balboa Park. Bonus: Babycakes serves beer and wine for weary moms and dads. If toys trump sweet treats, check out the classics at **Geppetto's** (🌐 *www.geppettostoys.com*), a family-run business with nine locations throughout San Diego, including Old Town, La Jolla, and the Fashion Valley Mall.

A WALK THROUGH SAN DIEGO'S PAST

Downtown San Diego is a living tribute to history and revitalization. The Gaslamp Quarter followed up its boomtown years—the late 1800s, when Wyatt Earp ran gambling halls and sailors frequented brothels lining 4th and 5th avenues—with a long stint of seediness, emerging only recently as a glamorous place to live and play. Little Italy, once a bustling fishing village, got a fresh start when the city took its cause to heart.

Where It All Started

Begin at the corner of 4th and Island. This is the location of the 150-year-old **Davis-Horton House,** a saltbox structure shipped around Cape Horn and assembled in the Gaslamp Quarter. Among its famous former residents: Alonzo Horton, the city's founder. Take a tour, keeping a lookout for the house's current resident: a lady ghost.

From there walk a block east to 5th Avenue and head north. Along the way, you'll see some of the 16½-block historic district's best-known Victorian-era commercial beauties, including the Italianate **Marston Building** (at F Street), the **Keating Building,** the **Spencer-Ogden Building,** and the **Old City Hall.** Architecture buffs should pick up a copy of *San Diego's Gaslamp Quarter,* a self-guided tour published by the Historical Society.

At E Street, head back over to 4th Avenue and you'll behold the **Balboa Theatre,** a striking Spanish Renaissance–style building that was constructed in 1923 and restored in 2007. Right next to it is **Westfield Horton Plaza** mall, which opened its doors in 1985. This multilevel mall played a huge role in downtown's revitalization, as entrepreneurs and preservationists realized the value of the Gaslamp Quarter. Pop across Broadway to check out the stately **U.S. Grant Hotel,** built in 1910 by the son of President Ulysses S. Grant.

Art Stop

Follow Broadway west to Kettner Boulevard, where the **Museum of Contemporary Art San Diego (MCASD)** makes a bold statement with its steel-and-glass lines. It's definitely worth a wander, situated in the renovated baggage depot of the 1915 **Santa Fe Depot** (the station itself is also a stunner).

From Fishermen to Fashionistas

From there, head north on Kettner to A Street, make a quick right, and then take a left on India Street. This is the heart of **Little Italy,** which at the turn of the 20th century was a bustling Italian fishing village. The area fell into disarray in the early 1970s due to a decline in the tuna industry and the construction of I–5, which destroyed 35% of the area. In 1996, a group of forward-thinking architects—commissioned by the city—developed new residential, retail, and public areas that coexist beautifully with the neighborhood's historic charms. Now, it's a vibrant urban center with hip eateries, bars, and shops. There are remnants of retro Little Italy, from authentic cafés (check out **Pappalecco,** a popular gelateria) to boccie ball matches played by old-timers at **Amici Park.**

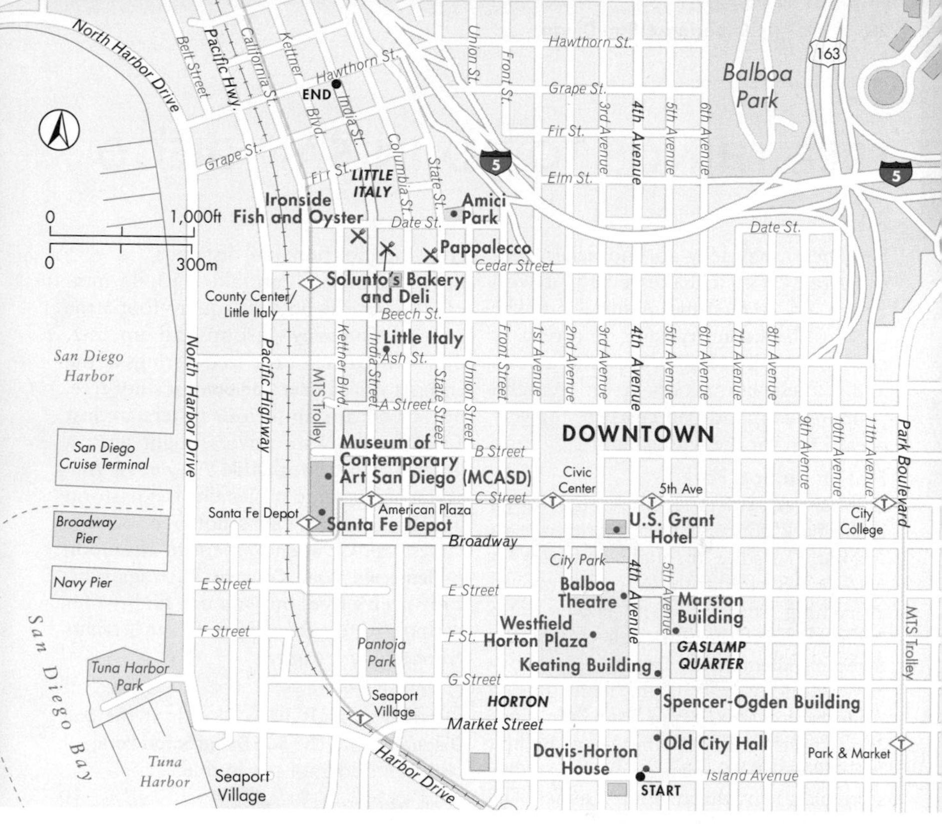

Highlights:	The restored gas lamps that give the Gaslamp its name; the juxtaposition of old and new architecture; Little Italy's sidewalk cafés.
Where to Start:	At the corner of 4th and Island avenues, at the Davis-Horton House. It's a short walk from most Downtown hotels. If you drive, park in a paid lot or at nearby Horton Plaza, which offers three free hours with validation (get your ticket stamped at one of the validation machines).
Length:	About 3 miles and three to four hours round-trip with stops. Take the Orange Line trolley from Santa Fe Depot back if you're tired.
Where to Stop:	From Little Italy follow the same path back or head down Laurel Street to Harbor Drive and wander along the waterfront until you hit Broadway.
Best Time to Go:	Morning or early afternoon.
Worst Time to Go:	During rush hour, when the streets are crowded.
Where to Refuel:	If your stomach is growling, Little Italy is waiting for you like an Italian mamma: mangia, mangia! Try Solunto's Bakery and Deli ✉ *1642 India St.* or Ironside Fish and Oyster ✉ *1654 India St.*

FREE THINGS TO DO IN SAN DIEGO

San Diego may levy an unofficial "sunshine tax," but it makes up for it with plenty of free stuff. Aside from the beaches, backcountry trails, and verdant city parks—all as free as the steadfast sun and endless blue skies—a little careful planning can land you cost-free (or very cheap) fun for the whole family.

Free in Balboa Park

Balboa Park hosts its one-hour **Twilight in the Park** concert series from June to August, Tuesday through Thursday at 6:15 pm. Sit under the stars and take in everything from Dixieland Jazz to Latin salsa. Also at the park, check out the **Spreckels International Organ Festival** concerts Monday at 7:30 pm, from June to August, as well as 2 pm Sunday matinee concerts throughout the year. Balboa Park's **Film in the Garden,** an outdoor movie screening, runs throughout summer. The **Timken Museum of Art** in Balboa Park is free but a donation is suggested.

Free Concerts

The Del Mar Fairgrounds' summertime **4 O'Clock Fridays** series features big-name local and national bands; it's technically free, though you still have to pay a few bucks for racetrack admission.

Also worth catching: Carlsbad's **TGIF Concerts in the Parks,** Friday at 6 pm; **Coronado Summer Concerts in the Park,** Sunday at 6 pm, May through September; **La Jolla Concerts by the Sea,** Sunday at 2 pm, July and August; the **Del Mar Twilight Concert Series,** Tuesday at 7 pm, June through September; and Encinitas' **Sunday Summer Concerts by the Sea,** 3 pm, July and August.

The annual **Adams Avenue Unplugged** festival in spring and **Adams Avenue Street Festival** in September both hit pay dirt: blues, folk, country, jazz, indie, world, and more—all for free.

Free (or Inexpensive) Tastings

Beer aficionados can take a $3, 45-minute tour of the 55,000-square-foot **Stone Brewing Company**—groups fill up fast, maybe because of the free tastings at the end. At **Alpine Beer Company,** it's not free, but it's cheap: up to four tasters are just $1.50 each. Wine lovers might pack a lunch and head for **Orfila Vineyards & Winery,** where picnic tables dot the pastoral landscape—the wine's not free, but the views are. Or spend an entire afternoon in **Temecula Wine Country.** Tastings typically aren't free, but you can find twofer coupons and other discounts at 🌐 *www.temeculawines.org*.

October Freebies

October is Kids Free Month at the **San Diego Zoo** and the **San Diego Safari Park**; all children under 11 get in free.

Free Museums

The **MCASD** is always free for patrons under 25, and for everyone else the third Thursday of the month from 5 to 7 pm.

In February, you can pick up a free **Museum Month Pass** at Macy's that offers half-off admission to 40 museums for the entire month.

Many of San Diego's museums offer a once-a-month free Tuesday, on a rotating schedule (see 🌐 *www.balboapark.org* for the schedule) to San Diego city and county residents and active military, and their families; special exhibitions often require separate admission.

Discounts and Deals

Try **Just My Ticket** (🌐 *www.justmyticket.com*) for deals on last-minute theater, concert, and sporting event tickets, as well as restaurant coupons.

DOWNTOWN

East Village, Embarcadero, Gaslamp Quarter, and Little Italy

Getting Oriented

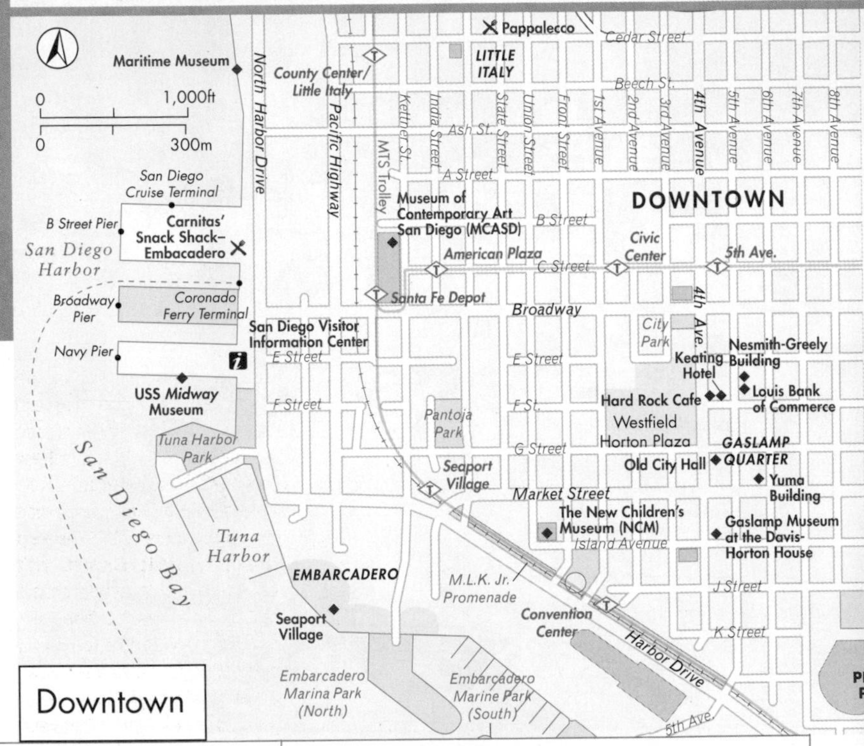

GETTING HERE

It's an easy drive into Downtown, especially from the nearby airport. There are reasonably priced parking lots (about $10 per day) along Harbor Drive, Pacific Highway, and lower Broadway and Market Street. Most restaurants offer valet parking at night, but beware of fees of $15 and up.

If you tire of exploring Downtown on foot, hop aboard a pedicab, hail the Free Ride Everywhere Downtown (FRED) shuttle, or rent a GoCar (three-wheel cars equipped with a GPS-guided audio tour).

TOP REASONS TO GO

Waterfront delights: Stroll along the Embarcadero, explore Seaport Village, or enjoy a harbor cruise.

Contemporary art for all ages: From the stunning galleries of the Museum of Contemporary Art to the clever incorporation of art and play at the New Children's Museum, Downtown is the place for art.

Maritime history: Climb aboard and explore a wide array of vessels from sailing ships to submarines.

Delicious dining: The hip and high-style restaurants of Little Italy, the Gaslamp Quarter and the East Village make Downtown San Diego a diner's delight.

Happening Gaslamp: It's hard to believe this hip neighborhood filled with street art, galleries, restaurants, and buzzing nightlife was once slated for the wrecking ball.

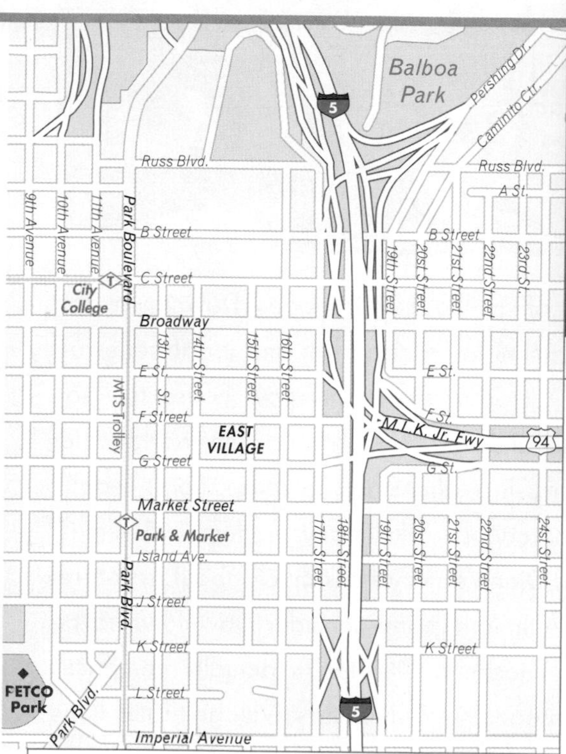

QUICK BITES

Carnitas' Snack Shack - Embarcadero. Indulge in some carnitas tacos, a BLT, or the "Triple Threat" pork sandwich at the Embarcadero outpost of this popular swine-heavy dining spot. ✉ *1004 N. Harbor Dr., Embarcadero* ☎ *619/616–7675* 🌐 *www.carnitassnackshack.com.*

Pappalecco. Kids and adults alike will swoon over the addictive gelato at Pappalecco, while those seeking something savory can choose from a selection of panini and other snacks. ✉ *1602 State St., Little Italy* ☎ *619/238–4590* 🌐 *www.pappalecco.com* 💳 *No credit cards.*

PLANNING YOUR TIME

Most Downtown attractions are open daily, but the Museum of Contemporary Art is closed Wednesday and the New Children's Museum is closed on Tuesday during the school year. For guided tours of the Gaslamp Quarter Historic District, visit on Saturday. A boat trip on the harbor, or at least a hop over to Coronado on the ferry, is a must at any time of year. From December through March, when gray whales migrate between the Pacific Northwest and southern Baja, consider booking a whale-watching excursion from the Broadway Pier.

VISITOR INFORMATION

San Diego Visitor Information Center. This colorful and inviting visitor center is a great resource for information and discounts on hotels, restaurants, and local attractions. ✉ *996 N. Harbor Dr., Embarcadero* ☎ *619/737–2999* 🌐 *www.sandiego.org.*

Sightseeing
★★★★★
Nightlife
★★★★★
Dining
★★★★★
Lodging
★★★★☆
Shopping
★★★★☆

Nearly written off in the 1970s, today Downtown San Diego is a testament to conservation and urban renewal. Once derelict Victorian storefronts now house the hottest restaurants, and the *Star of India,* the world's oldest active sailing ship, almost lost to scrap, floats regally along the Embarcadero. Like many modern U.S. cities, Downtown San Diego's story is as much about its rebirth as its history. Although many consider Downtown to be the 16½-block Gaslamp Quarter, it actually comprises eight neighborhoods, including East Village, Little Italy, and Embarcadero.

GASLAMP QUARTER

Updated by Claire Deeks van der Lee

Considered the liveliest of the Downtown neighborhoods, the Gaslamp Quarter's 4th and 5th avenues are peppered with trendy nightclubs, swanky lounge bars, chic restaurants, and boisterous sports pubs. The Gaslamp has the largest collection of commercial Victorian-style buildings in the country. Despite this, when the move for Downtown redevelopment gained momentum in the 1970s, there was talk of bulldozing them and starting from scratch. In response, concerned history buffs, developers, architects, and artists formed the Gaslamp Quarter Council to clean up and preserve the quarter.

The majority of the quarter's landmark buildings are on 4th and 5th avenues, between Island Avenue and Broadway. If you don't have much time, stroll down 5th Avenue, where highlights include **Louis Bank of Commerce** (No. 835), **Old City Hall** (No. 664), **Nesmith-Greeley** (No. 825), and **Yuma** (No. 631) buildings. The Romanesque Revival **Keating Hotel** at 432 F Street was designed by the same firm that created the famous Hotel Del Coronado, the Victorian grande dame that presides over Coronado's beach. At the corner of 4th Avenue and F Street, peer into the **Hard Rock Cafe,** which occupies a restored turn-of-the-20th-century tavern with a 12-foot mahogany bar and a spectacular stained-glass domed ceiling.

The Gaslamp is a lively place—during baseball season, the streets flood with Padres fans, and festivals, such as Mardi Gras in February, Sham-ROCK on St. Patrick's Day, and Monster Bash in October, keep the party atmosphere going throughout the year.

2

TOP ATTRACTIONS

Gaslamp Museum at the Davis-Horton House. The oldest wooden house in San Diego houses the Gaslamp Quarter Historical Foundation, the district's curator. Before developer Alonzo Horton came to town, Davis, a prominent San Franciscan, had made an unsuccessful attempt to develop the waterfront area. In 1850 he had this prefab saltbox-style house, built in Maine, shipped around Cape Horn and assembled in San Diego (it originally stood at State and Market streets). Ninety-minute walking tours ($20) of the historic district leave from the house on Thursday at 1 pm (summer only) and Saturday at 11 am (year-round). If you can't time your visit with the tour, a self-guided tour map ($2) is available. ✉ *410 Island Ave., at 4th Ave., Gaslamp Quarter* ☎ *619/233–4692* 🌐 *www.gaslampfoundation.org* 🎫 *$5 self-guided, $10 with audio tour* ⏲ *Closed Mon.*

EMBARCADERO

The **Embarcadero** cuts a scenic swath along the harborfront and connects today's Downtown San Diego to its maritime routes. The bustle of Embarcadero comes less these days from the activities of fishing folk than from the throngs of tourists, but this waterfront walkway, stretching from the Convention Center to the Maritime Museum, remains the nautical soul of the city. There are several seafood restaurants here, as well as sea vessels of every variety—cruise ships, ferries, tour boats, and Navy destroyers.

On the north end of the Embarcadero at Ash Street you'll find the **Maritime Museum.** South of it, the **B Street Pier** is used by ships from major cruise lines while tickets for harbor tours and whale-watching trips are sold at the foot of **Broadway Pier.** The terminal for the Coronado Ferry lies in between. Docked at the **Navy Pier** is the decommissioned **USS *Midway*.** At the foot of G Street, **Tuna Harbor** was once the hub of one of San Diego's earliest and most successful industries, commercial tuna fishing. The pleasant Tuna Harbor Park offers a great view of boating on the bay and across to any aircraft carriers docked at the North Island naval base. A few blocks south, **Embarcadero Marina Park North** is an 8-acre extension into the harbor from the center of **Seaport Village.** It's usually full of kite fliers, in-line skaters, and picnickers. Seasonal celebrations, including San Diego's Parade of Lights, the Port of San Diego Big Balloon Parade and the Big Bay July 4 Celebration, are held here and at the similar

Embarcadero Marina Park South. The **San Diego Convention Center,** on Harbor Drive between 1st and 6th avenues, is a waterfront landmark designed by Canadian architect Arthur Erickson. The backdrop of blue sky and sea complements the building's nautical lines. The center often holds trade shows that are open to the public, and tours of the building are available.

A huge revitalization project is under way along the northern Embarcadero. The overhaul seeks to transform the area with large mixed-use development projects, inviting parks, walkways, and public art installations. The redevelopment will eventually head south along the waterfront, with plans under way for a major overhaul of the entire Central Embarcadero and Seaport Village.

TROLLEY DANCES

Every city has street performers, but during the fall in San Diego, the commuter experience comes alive with dance performances at select trolley stops. A partnership between the Jean Isaacs Dance Theater and the city's Metropolitan Transit System, Trolley Dances (🌐 *www.sandiegodancetheater.org/trolleydances2013.html*) combines human movement with the ever-changing scenery of the city as a backdrop. At six different stops, dancers give site-specific performances inspired by their environments, from historic Barrio Logan to the modern Downtown library. Get on the trolley for a tour ($40) to see the performances at each site.

TOP ATTRACTIONS

FAMILY Fodor's Choice ★ **Maritime Museum.** From sailing ships to submarines, the Maritime Museum is a must for anyone with an interest in nautical history. This collection of restored and replica ships affords a fascinating glimpse of San Diego during its heyday as a commercial seaport. The jewel of the collection, the *Star of India,* was built in 1863 and made 21 trips around the world in the late 1800s. Saved from the scrap yard and painstakingly restored, the windjammer is the oldest active iron sailing ship in the world. The newly constructed *San Salvador* is a detailed historic replica of the original ship first sailed into San Diego Bay by explorer Juan Rodriguez Cabrillo back in 1542. And, the popular *HMS Surprise* is a replica of an 18th-century British Royal Navy frigate . The museum's headquarters are on the *Berkeley,* an 1898 steam-driven ferryboat, which served the Southern Pacific Railroad in San Francisco until 1958.

Numerous cruises of San Diego Bay are offered, including a daily 45-minute narrated tour aboard a 1914 pilot boat and 3-hour weekend sails aboard the topsail schooner the *Californian,* the state's official tall ship, and 75-minute tours aboard a historic swift boat, which highlights the city's military connection. Partnering with the museum, the renowned yacht *America* also offers sails on the bay, and whale-watching excursions are available in winter. ✉ *1492 N. Harbor Dr., Embarcadero* ☎ *619/234–9153* 🌐 *www.sdmaritime.org* 🎫 *$16, $5 more for Pilot Boat Bay Cruise.*

Built in 1863, the Maritime Museum's *Star of India* is often considered to be a symbol of San Diego.

Fodor's Choice ★ **Museum of Contemporary Art San Diego (MCASD).** At the Downtown branch of the city's contemporary art museum, explore the works of international and regional artists in a modern, urban space. The Jacobs Building—formerly the baggage building at the historic Santa Fe Depot—features large gallery spaces, high ceilings, and natural lighting, giving artists the flexibility to create large-scale installations. MCASD's collection includes many Pop Art, minimalist, and conceptual works from the 1950s to the present. The museum showcases both established and emerging artists in temporary exhibitions, and has permanent, site-specific commissions by Jenny Holzer and Richard Serra. ✉ *1100 and 1001 Kettner Blvd., Downtown* ☎ *858/454–3541* 🌐 *www.mcasd.org* 🎫 *$10; free 3rd Thurs. of the month 5–7* ⏲ *Closed Wed.*

FAMILY Fodor's Choice ★ **The New Children's Museum (NCM).** The NCM blends contemporary art with unstructured play to create an environment that appeals to children as well as adults. The 50,000-square-foot structure was constructed from recycled building materials, operates on solar energy, and is convection-cooled by an elevator shaft. It also features a nutritious and eco-conscious café. Interactive exhibits include designated areas for toddlers and teens, as well as plenty of activities for the entire family. Several art workshops are offered each day, as well as hands-on studios where visitors are encouraged to create their own art. The studio projects change frequently and the entire museum changes exhibits every 18 to 24 months, so there is always something new to explore. The adjoining 1-acre park and playground is across from the convention center trolley stop. ✉ *200 W. Island Ave., Embarcadero* ☎ *619/233–8792* 🌐 *www.thinkplaycreate.org* 🎫 *$13; 2nd Sun. each month $3* ⏲ *Closed Tues.*

FAMILY **Seaport Village.** You'll find some of the best views of the harbor at Seaport Village, three bustling shopping plazas designed to reflect the New England clapboard, and Spanish Mission architectural styles of early California. On a prime stretch of waterfront the dining, shopping, and entertainment complex connects the harbor with hotel towers and the convention center. Specialty shops offer everything from a kite store and swing emporium to a shop devoted to hot sauces. You can dine at snack bars and restaurants, many with harbor views.

Live music can be heard daily from noon to 4 at the main food court. Additional free concerts take place every Sunday from 1 to 4 at the East Plaza Gazebo. The **Seaport Village Carousel** (rides $3) has 54 animals, hand-carved and hand-painted by Charles Looff in 1895. Across the street, the **Headquarters at Seaport Village** converted the historic police headquarters into several trendsetting shops and restaurants. ✉ *849 W. Harbor Dr., Downtown* ☎ *619/235–4014 office and events hotline* 🌐 *www.seaportvillage.com.*

FAMILY Fodor's Choice ★ **USS Midway Museum.** After 47 years of worldwide service, the retired USS *Midway* began a new tour of duty on the south side of the Navy pier in 2004. Launched in 1945, the 1,001-foot-long ship was the largest in the world for the first 10 years of its existence. The most visible landmark on the north Embarcadero, it now serves as a floating interactive museum—an appropriate addition to the town that is home to one-third of the Pacific fleet and the birthplace of naval aviation. A free audio tour guides you through the massive ship while offering insight from former sailors. As you clamber through passageways and up and down ladder wells, you'll get a feel for how the *Midway*'s 4,500 crew members lived and worked on this "city at sea."

Though the entire tour is impressive, you'll really be wowed when you step out onto the 4-acre flight deck—not only the best place to get an idea of the ship's scale, but also one of the most interesting vantage points for bay and city skyline views. An F-14 Tomcat jet fighter is just one of many vintage aircraft on display. Free guided tours of the bridge and primary flight control, known as "the Island," depart every 10 minutes from the flight deck. Many of the docents stationed throughout the ship served in the Navy, some even on the *Midway*, and they are eager to answer questions or share stories. The museum also offers multiple flight simulators for an additional fee, climb-aboard cockpits, and interactive exhibits focusing on naval aviation. There is a gift shop and a café with pleasant outdoor seating. This is a wildly popular stop, with most visits lasting several hours. ⚠ **Despite efforts to provide accessibility throughout the ship, some areas can only be reached via fairly steep steps; a video tour of these areas is available on the hangar deck.** ✉ *910 N. Harbor Dr., Embarcadero* ☎ *619/544–9600* 🌐 *www.midway.org* 🎫 *$20.*

Home of the San Diego Padres, PETCO Park offers behind-the-scenes tours.

EAST VILLAGE

The most ambitious of the Downtown projects is **East Village,** not far from the Gaslamp Quarter, and encompassing 130 blocks between the railroad tracks up to J Street, and from 6th Avenue east to around 10th Street. Sparking the rebirth of this former warehouse district was the 2004 construction of the San Diego Padres' baseball stadium, **PETCO Park.** The **Urban Art Trail** has added pizzazz to drab city thoroughfares by transforming such things as trash cans and traffic controller boxes into works of art. As the city's largest Downtown neighborhood, East Village is continually broadening its boundaries with its urban design of redbrick cafés, spacious galleries, rooftop bars, sleek hotels, and warehouse restaurants.

TOP ATTRACTIONS

FAMILY **PETCO Park.** PETCO Park is home to the city's major league baseball team, the San Diego Padres. The ballpark is strategically designed to give fans a view of San Diego Bay, the skyline, and Balboa Park. Reflecting San Diego's beauty, the stadium is clad in sandstone from India to evoke the area's cliffs and beaches; the 42,000 seats are dark blue, reminiscent of the ocean, and the exposed steel is painted white to reflect the sails of harbor boats on the bay. The family-friendly lawnlike berm, "Park at the Park," is a popular and affordable place for fans to view the game. Behind-the-scenes guided tours of PETCO, including the press box and the dugout, are offered throughout the year. ✉ *100 Park Blvd., East Village* ☎ *619/795–5011 tour hotline* 🌐 *sandiego.padres.mlb.com* 🎫 *$15 tour.*

LITTLE ITALY

Home to many in San Diego's design community, Little Italy exudes a sense of urban cool. The main thoroughfare, India Street, is filled with lively cafés, chic shops, and many of the city's trendiest restaurants. Little Italy is one of San Diego's most walkable neighborhoods, and a great spot to wander. Art lovers can browse gallery showrooms, while shoppers adore the Fir Street cottages. The neighborhood bustles each Saturday during the wildly popular Mercato farmers' market, *(see Little Italy Mercato in Shopping)* and at special events throughout the year such as Artwalk in spring and FESTA! each fall. Yet the neighborhood is also authentic to its roots and marked by old-country charms: church bells ring on the half hour, and Italians gather daily to play bocce in Amici Park. After an afternoon of gelati and espresso, you may just forget that you're in Southern California.

WESTERN METAL SUPPLY

Initially scheduled for demolition to make room for PETCO Park, the historic Western Metal Supply Co. was instead incorporated into the ballpark and supports the left-field foul pole. Great care was taken to retain the historic nature of the building's exterior despite extensive interior renovations. Built in 1909, the four-story structure originally manufactured wagon wheels and war supplies, and today holds the Padres' Team Store, food and beverage outlets, and rooftop seating.

3

BALBOA PARK AND SAN DIEGO ZOO

Getting Oriented

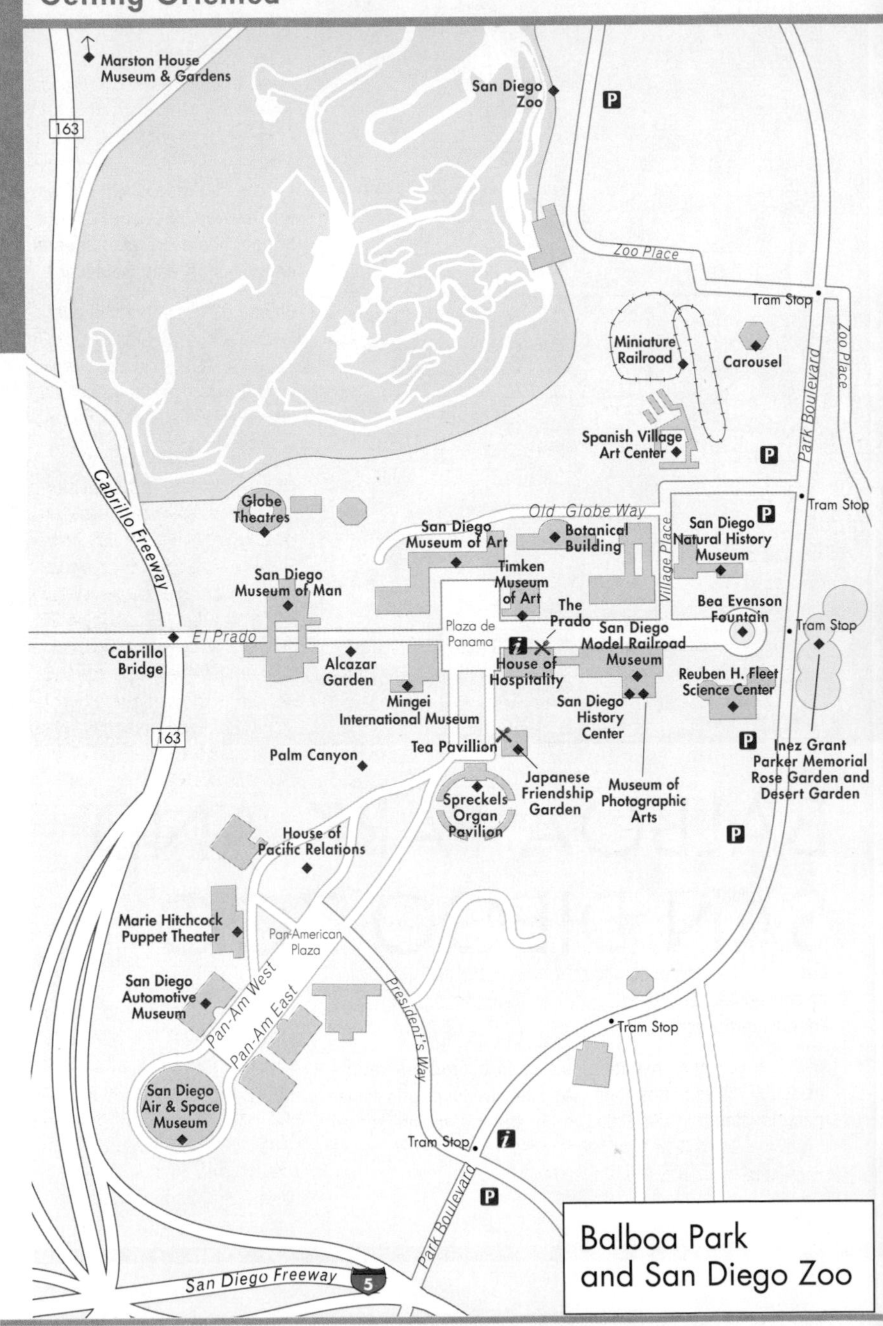

TOP REASONS TO GO

San Diego Zoo: San Diego's best-loved attraction, the world-renowned zoo, is set amid spectacular scenery in the heart of Balboa Park.

Museums galore: Automobiles and spacecraft, international folk art and baroque masters, dinosaur fossils and mummified humans—there is something for everyone at Balboa Park's many museums.

The great outdoors: Escape down a hiking trail, try your hand at a new sport, or just soak in the sunshine from your own stretch of grass. You may even forget you are in the middle of the city.

Gorgeous gardens: From the lush tropical feel of the Botanical Building to the refined design of the Rose Garden, Balboa Park's intricate gardens and landscaping are sure to delight.

Free cultural events: The park is full of freebies, from weekly concerts at the organ pavilion to annual events like Earth Day and December Nights.

QUICK BITES

Quick snacking opportunities abound throughout the park, from cafés tucked in among the museums and grounds, to hot dog, tamale, or ice-cream carts along the walkways and plazas. Good bets include the sushi, noodles, and, of course, tea at the **Tea Pavilion** outside the Japanese Friendship Garden.

The Prado. Enjoy inventive cuisine in a gracious setting inside the House of Hospitality. An extensive lunch and dinner menu is offered in the dining room; casual bites are served in the bar. ✉ *1549 El Prado, Balboa Park* ☎ *619/557–9441* ▭ *No credit cards* ⏲ *No dinner Mon.*

GETTING HERE

Located just north of Downtown, Balboa Park is easily reached from both Interstate 5 and Highway 163. The most spectacular approach is from 6th Avenue over the Cabrillo Bridge. There are also several entrances off Park Boulevard.

Balboa Park is served by public buses, particularly the No. 3, 7, and 120 lines. Taxis can often be found inside the park near the visitor center and lined up outside the zoo.

Although Balboa Park is massive, many of its star attractions are located quite close to each other. That said, exploring the park can lead to a lot of walking, particularly if you throw in a trip to the zoo or take on one of the many hiking trails. The park's free tram service stops at several spots around the park, and can give tired feet a welcome rest at the end of a long day.

VISITOR INFORMATION

House of Hospitality. The visitor center located here is an excellent resource for planning your visit to the park. Check the website before you go or spend a few minutes at the center when you arrive. They also offer a free mobile app with information on sites, special events, and useful tips to help maximize your time. ✉ *1549 El Prado, Balboa Park* ☎ *619/239–0512* 🌐 *www.balboapark.org.*

Sightseeing ★★★★★
Nightlife ★☆☆☆☆
Dining ★★★☆☆
Lodging ☆☆☆☆☆
Shopping ★★★☆☆

Overlooking Downtown and the Pacific Ocean, 1,200-acre Balboa Park is the cultural heart of San Diego. Ranked as one of the world's best parks by the Project for Public Spaces, it's also where you can find most of the city's museums, art galleries, the Tony Award–winning Old Globe Theatre, and the world-famous San Diego Zoo. Often referred to as the "Smithsonian of the West" for its concentration of museums, Balboa Park is also a series of botanical gardens, performance spaces, and outdoor playrooms endeared in the hearts of residents and visitors alike.

Updated by Claire Deeks van der Lee

Thanks to the "Mother of Balboa Park," Kate Sessions, who suggested hiring a landscape architect in 1889, wild and cultivated gardens are an integral part of the park, featuring 350 species of trees. What Balboa Park would have looked like had she left it alone can be seen at Florida Canyon (between the main park and Morley Field, along Park Boulevard)—an arid landscape of sagebrush, cactus, and a few small trees.

In addition, the captivating architecture of Balboa's buildings, fountains, and courtyards gives the park an enchanted feel. Historic buildings dating from San Diego's 1915 Panama–California International Exposition are strung along the park's main east–west thoroughfare, El Prado, which leads from 6th Avenue eastward over the Cabrillo Bridge (formerly the Laurel Street Bridge), the park's official gateway. If you're a cinema fan, many of the buildings may be familiar—Orson Welles used exteriors of several Balboa Park buildings to represent the Xanadu estate of Charles Foster Kane in his 1941 classic, *Citizen Kane*. Prominent among them was the California Building, whose 200-foot tower, housing a 100-carillon bell that tolls the hour, is El Prado's tallest structure. Missing from the black-and-white film, however, was the magnificent blue of its tiled dome shining in the sun.

The parkland across the Cabrillo Bridge, at the west end of El Prado, is set aside for picnics and athletics. Cyclists and skaters zip along Balboa Drive, which leads to the highest spot in the park, Marston Point, overlooking Downtown. At the green beside the bridge, ladies and gents in all-white outfits meet on summer afternoons for lawn-bowling tournaments.

East of Plaza de Panama, El Prado becomes a pedestrian mall and ends at a footbridge that crosses over Park Boulevard, the park's main north–south thoroughfare, to the perfectly tended Rose Garden, which has more than 2,000 rosebushes. In the adjacent Desert Garden, trails wind around cacti and succulents from around the world. Palm Canyon, north of the Spreckels Organ Pavilion, has more than 50 varieties of palms along a shady bridge. Pepper Grove, along Park Boulevard south of the museums, has lots of picnic tables as well as play equipment.

Bankers Hill is a small neighborhood west of Balboa Park, with gorgeous views ranging from Balboa Park's greenery in the east to the San Diego Bay in the west. It's become one of San Diego's hottest restaurant destinations.

BALBOA PARK PLANNER

BEST TIMES TO VISIT

San Diego's ideal climate and sophisticated horticultural planning make visiting Balboa Park a year-round delight. However, summer brings longer opening hours, additional concerts at the Spreckels Organ Pavilion, and the beloved Shakespeare Festival at the Old Globe's outdoor stage. *See the full listing in Chapter 11: Performing Arts.*

OPEN HOURS

Most of the park's museums and attractions are open from 10 or 11 am until 4 or 5 pm, with the zoo opening earlier. Some offer extended hours during the summer. Many of the park's museums are closed on Monday. Balboa Park is beautiful by night, with the buildings along El Prado gorgeously illuminated. The Prado restaurant and the Old Globe Theatre keep this portion of the park from feeling deserted after dark.

PLANNING YOUR TIME

It's impossible to cover all of Balboa Park's museums and attractions in one day, so choose your focus before you head out. If you plan on visiting the San Diego Zoo, expect to spend at least half the day there, leaving no more than a couple of hours to explore Balboa's other attractions afterward. *See the highlighted listing for more information about the San Diego Zoo.* Otherwise, check out these itineraries.

Two Hours: To help maximize your time, rent one of the audio headsets that guide you on a 60-minute tour of the park's history, architecture, and horticulture. Pick a garden of interest to explore or drop down into Palm Canyon. Spend the remainder of your time relaxing in front of the Botanical Building or around the Bea Evenson Fountain.

Half Day: Spend a little more time at the sights above, then select a museum to explore. Alternatively, catch a puppet show at the Marie Hitchcock Theater. Afterward, you might have time for a quick ride on the carousel or a browse around the studios of the Spanish Village Art Center. Cap things off with lunch at Panama 66 in the Sculpture Garden.

Full Day: Consider purchasing a one-day discount pass from the visitor center if you want to tackle several museums. Depending on when you visit, enjoy a free concert at the Spreckels Organ Pavilion, a cultural dance at the House of Pacific Relations International Cottages, or join a guided walking tour. Active types can hit one of the more intensive hiking trails, while others can rest their feet at an IMAX or 3-D movie in the Fleet Center or Natural History Museum, respectively. In the evening, dine at the beautiful Prado restaurant or catch a show at the Old Globe Theatre.

WHAT'S FREE WHEN

Many freebies can be found in Balboa Park, both on a weekly basis and at special times of the year. Free **Ranger Tours** depart from the visitor center Tuesday and Sunday at 11 am providing an overview of the history, architecture, and horticulture of the park. On Saturday at 10 am, volunteers offer a rotating selection of thematic **Offshoot Tours,** also free of charge and departing from the visitor center. If you prefer to explore on your own, head to the visitor center to pick up a free garden tour map.

The free concerts at the **Spreckels Organ Pavilion** take place Sunday afternoons at 2 pm year-round and on Monday evenings in summer. Also at the Speckels Organ Pavilion, the **Twilight in the Park Summer Concert Series** offers various performances Tuesday, Wednesday, and Thursday from 6:15 to 7:15.

The **Timken Museum of Art, Museum of Photographic Arts,** and **San Diego History Center** offer free (a donation is suggested), or pay what you wish admission pricing. Admission to the **House of Pacific Relations International Cottages,** is also free, although they are only open on Sunday. You can explore the studios at the **Spanish Village Art Center** at no charge, although you just might be tempted to purchase a unique souvenir.

A fantastic deal for residents of San Diego County and active-duty military and their families is **Free Tuesdays in the Park,** a rotating schedule of free admission to most of Balboa Park's museums.

The **San Diego Zoo** is free for kids under 12 the whole month of October.

The **December Nights** festival on the first Friday and Saturday of that month includes free admission (and later hours) to most of the Balboa Park museums. The outdoor events during the festival make it something not to miss.

DISCOUNT: EXPLORER PASS

The visitor center offers a selection of Balboa Park Explorer passes that are worth considering if you plan on visiting several museums. The Explorer ($57 adult, $30 children ages 3–12) offers one-time admission to 17 museums and attractions over the course of seven days. If you are also planning on visiting the zoo, the Zoo/Passport Combo might be a good choice ($97 adult, $62 child). A single-day pass includes entry to your choice of 5 out of the 17 options ($46 adult, $27 child).

SHOPPING SPREE

Balboa Park is an excellent place to shop for unique souvenirs and gifts. In addition to the wonderful artwork for sale in Spanish Village, several museums and the visitor center have excellent stores. Of particular note are the shops at the Reuben Fleet Science Center, the Mingei Museum, the Museum of Art, the United Nations Association and, of course, the zoo.

TIPS

Hop aboard the free trams that run every 10 to 20 minutes, 9 am to 6 pm daily, with extended summer hours.

Wear comfortable shoes—you'll end up walking more than you might expect. Bring a sweater or light jacket for the evening drop in temperature.

Don't be afraid to wander off the main drag. Discovering a hidden space of your own is one of the highlights of a trip to Balboa.

If you tire of walking, cruise the Prado on board an Electriquette ($15 per 30 minutes, $25 per hour). These wicker electric carts are replicas of the wildly popular and innovative Electriquettes featured during the 1915 Panama-California Exposition.

Balboa Park is a good bet for the odd rainy day—the museums are nice and dry, and many of the park's buildings are connected by covered walkways.

Make reservations for the Prado restaurant; it's popular with both visitors and locals alike.

If you aren't receiving a discount at one of the museums where San Diego residents get in for free on Tuesday, consider avoiding them on Tuesday, as they can become overcrowded.

Don't overlook the 6th Avenue side of the park, between the Marston House and the Cabrillo Bridge. There are several pathways and open fields that make for a quiet escape.

PARKING

Parking within Balboa Park, including at the zoo, is free. From the Cabrillo Bridge, the first parking area you come to is off El Prado to the right. Don't despair if there are no spaces here; you'll see more lots as you continue along toward Pan American Plaza. Alternatively, you can park at Inspiration Point on the east side of the park, off Presidents Way. Free trams run from Inspiration Point to the visitor center and museums. Valet parking is available outside the House of Hospitality on weekends and on weekday evenings, except Monday.

EXPLORING BALBOA PARK

BALBOA PARK WALK

Although Balboa Park as a whole is huge, many of its top attractions are located within reasonable walking distance. A straight shot across the **Cabrillo Bridge,** through the **Plaza de Panama,** and on to the **Bea Evenson Fountain** will take you past several of the park's architectural gems, including the **House of Hospitality.** Many of the park's museums are housed in the buildings lining the way. This route also encompasses the **Alcazar Garden** and **Botanical Building.** From the fountain, a quick jaunt across the pedestrian footbridge leads you into the **Desert Garden** and the **Inez Grant Parker Memorial Rose Garden.** Back at the fountain, your walking tour can continue by heading north toward the **San Diego Zoo.** This will take you past the **Spanish Village Art Center, Carousel,** and **Miniature Railroad.** Alternatively, double back to the Plaza de Panama and head south toward the **Spreckels Organ Pavilion.** Continuing on from here, a loop will take you past **Palm Canyon,** the **International Cottages,** the **Marie Hitchcock Puppet Theater,** several more museums, and the **Japanese Friendship Garden.**

While the aforementioned routes provide a broad overview, there are several walking opportunities for those seeking more focused explorations of the park. Those wishing to experience the numerous gardens in depth will appreciate the excellent "Gardens of Balboa Park Self-Guided Walk," available free of charge at the visitor center. History and architecture buffs might consider buying a self-guided walking tour pamphlet from the visitor center, or taking the briefer audio tour. Opportunities for hiking abound, from a brief journey through **Palm Canyon** to more strenuous hikes through **Florida Canyon** or on the **Old Bridle Trail.** Stop in the visitor center for maps and guidance before setting out.

TOP ATTRACTIONS

Alcazar Garden. You may feel like royalty here as you rest on the benches by the exquisitely tiled fountains—the garden's highlight—and it's no wonder: the garden's landscaping was inspired by the gardens surrounding the Alcazar Castle in Seville, Spain. The garden is open year-round, allowing for a seasonally shifting color palette. The flower beds, for example, are ever-changing horticultural exhibits featuring more than 7,000 annuals for a nearly perpetual bloom. ✉ *1439 El Prado, Balboa Park* 🌐 *www.balboapark.org.*

Bea Evenson Fountain. A favorite of barefoot children, this fountain shoots cool jets of water upwards of 50 feet. Built in 1972 between the Fleet Center and Natural History Museum, the fountain offers plenty of room to sit and watch the crowds go by. ✉ *Balboa Park* ✣ *East end of El Prado* 🌐 *www.balboapark.org.*

Fodor's Choice ★ **Botanical Building.** The graceful redwood-lath structure, built for the 1915 Panama–California International Exposition, now houses more than 2,000 types of tropical and subtropical plants plus changing seasonal flower displays. Ceiling-high tree ferns shade fragile orchids and feathery bamboo. There are benches beside miniature waterfalls for resting in the shade. The rectangular pond outside, filled with lotuses

Balboa Park is home to gardens and the Spreckels Organ Pavilion, which hosts free concerts every Sunday at 2 pm.

and water lilies that bloom in spring and fall, is popular with photographers. ✉ *1549 El Prado, Balboa Park* ☎ *619/239–0512* 🌐 *www.balboapark.org* 🎫 *Free* 🕒 *Closed Thurs.*

Cabrillo Bridge. The official gateway into Balboa Park soars 120 feet above a canyon floor. Pedestrian-friendly, the 1,500-foot bridge provides inspiring views of the California Tower and El Prado beyond. ■ **TIP→ This is a great spot for photo-capturing a classic image of the park.** ✉ *Balboa Park* ✣ *On El Prado, at 6th Ave. park entrance* 🌐 *www.balboapark.org.*

FAMILY Fodor's Choice ★ **Carousel.** Suspended an arm's length away on this antique merry-go-round is the brass ring that could earn you an extra free ride (it's one of the few carousels in the world that continue this bonus tradition). Hand-carved in 1910, the carousel features colorful murals, big-band music, and bobbing animals including zebras, giraffes, and dragons; real horsehair was used for the tails. ✉ *1889 Zoo Pl., behind zoo parking lot, Balboa Park* ☎ *619/239–0512* 🌐 *www.balboapark.org* 🎫 *$2.75* 🕒 *Closed weekdays Labor Day–mid-June.*

Fodor's Choice ★ **Globe Theatres.** This complex, comprising the Sheryl and Harvey White Theatre, the Lowell Davies Festival Theatre, and the Old Globe Theatre, offers some of the finest theatrical productions in Southern California. Theater classics such as *The Full Monty* and *Dirty Rotten Scoundrels,* both of which later performed on Broadway, premiered on these famed stages. The Old Globe presents a renowned summer Shakespeare Festival with three to four plays in repertory. The theaters, done in a California version of Tudor style, sit between the sculpture garden of the San Diego Museum of Art and the California Tower. ✉ *1363 Old Globe Way, Balboa Park* ☎ *619/234–5623* 🌐 *www.theoldglobe.org* 🕒 *Box office closed Mon.*

CLOSE UP

Balboa's Best Bets

With so much on offer, Balboa Park truly has something for everyone. Here are some best bets based on area of interest.

ARCHITECTURE BUFFS

Bea Evenson Fountain
Cabrillo Bridge
House of Hospitality

ARTS AFICIONADOS

Museum of Photographic Arts
San Diego Museum of Art
Spanish Village Art Center
Spreckels Organ Pavilion
Timken Museum of Art

CULTURAL EXPLORERS

House of Pacific Relations
Mingei International Museum

HISTORY JUNKIES

San Diego History Center
San Diego Museum of Man

KIDS OF ALL AGES

Carousel
Marie Hitchcock Puppet Theater
Miniature Railroad
San Diego Model Railroad Museum
San Diego Zoo

NATURE LOVERS

Alcazar Garden
Botanical Building
Inez Grant Parker Memorial Rose Garden
Japanese Friendship Garden
Palm Canyon

SCIENCE AND TECHNOLOGY GEEKS

Reuben H. Fleet Science Center
San Diego Air & Space Museum
San Diego Automotive Museum

Fodor's Choice ★ **Inez Grant Parker Memorial Rose Garden and Desert Garden.** These neighboring gardens sit just across the Park Boulevard pedestrian bridge and offer gorgeous views over Florida Canyon. The formal rose garden contains 2,500 roses representing nearly 200 varieties; peak bloom is usually in April and May. The adjacent Desert Garden provides a striking contrast, with 2.5 acres of succulents and desert plants seeming to blend into the landscape of the canyon below. ✉ *2525 Park Blvd., Balboa Park* 🌐 *www.balboapark.org.*

Japanese Friendship Garden. A koi pond with a cascading waterfall, a cherry tree grove, and the serene Inamori tea pavilion are highlights of the park's authentic Japanese garden, designed to inspire contemplation and evoke tranquillity. You can wander the various peaceful paths spread over 12 acres, and meditate in the traditional stone and Zen garden. ✉ *2215 Pan American Rd., Balboa Park* ☎ *619/232–2721* 🌐 *www.niwa.org* 🎟 *$10, special exhibits are an additional $4–$5.*

Mingei International Museum. The name "Mingei" comes from the Japanese words *min,* meaning "all people," and *gei,* meaning "art." Thus the museum's name describes what's found under its roof: "art of all people." The Mingei's colorful and creative exhibits of folk art feature toys, pottery, textiles, costumes, jewelry, and curios from around the globe. Traveling and permanent exhibits in the high-ceilinged, light-filled museum include everything from a history of surfboard design and craft to the latest in Japanese ceramics. The gift shop carries items related to major exhibitions as well as artwork from various cultures worldwide, such as Zulu baskets, Turkish ceramics, and Mexican objects. ✉ *House of Charm, 1439 El Prado, Balboa Park* ☎ *619/239–0003* 🌐 *www.mingei.org* 🎟 *$10* 🕓 *Closed Mon.*

Palm Canyon. Enjoy an instant escape from the buildings and concrete of urban life in this Balboa Park oasis. Lush and tropical, with hundreds of palm trees, the 2-acre canyon has a shaded path perfect for those who love walking through nature. ✉ *1549 El Prado, south of House of Charm, Balboa Park.*

FAMILY **Reuben H. Fleet Science Center.** Interactive exhibits here are artfully educational and for all ages: older kids can get hands-on with inventive projects in the Tinkering Studio, while the five-and-under set can be easily entertained with interactive play stations like the Ball Wall and Fire Truck in the center's Kid City. The IMAX Dome Theater, which screens exhilarating nature and science films, was the world's first, as was the Fleet's "NanoSeam" (seamless) dome ceiling that doubles as a planetarium. ✉ *1875 El Prado, Balboa Park* ☎ *619/238–1233* 🌐 *www.rhfleet.org* 🎟 *The Fleet experience includes gallery exhibits and 1 IMAX film $19.95; additional cost for special exhibits or add-on 2nd IMAX film or planetarium show.*

FAMILY Fodor's Choice ★ **San Diego Air & Space Museum.** By day, the streamlined edifice looks like any other structure in the park; at night, outlined in blue neon, the round building appears—appropriately enough—to be a landed UFO. Every available inch of space in the rotunda is filled with exhibits about aviation and aerospace pioneers, including examples of enemy planes from the world wars. In all, there are more than 60 full-size aircraft on the floor and hanging from the rafters. In addition to exhibits from the dawn of flight to the jet age, the museum displays a growing number of space-age exhibits, including the actual *Apollo 9* command module. To test your own skills, you can ride in a two-seat Max Flight simulator or try out the Aerial Combat Experience simulator. Movies in the 3-D/4-D theater are included with admission. ✉ *2001 Pan American Pl., Balboa Park* ☎ *619/234–8291* 🌐 *www.sandiegoairandspace.org* 🎟 *Museum $19.75 (more for special exhibitions); Flight Simulators $5–$8 extra; restoration tour $5 extra and subject to availability.*

Fodor's Choice ★ **San Diego Museum of Art.** Known for its Spanish baroque and Renaissance paintings, including works by El Greco, Goya, Rubens, and van Ruisdael, San Diego's most comprehensive art museum also has strong holdings of South Asian art, Indian miniatures, and contemporary California paintings. The museum's exhibits tend to have broad appeal, and if traveling shows from other cities come to town, you can expect to see them here. Free docent tours are offered throughout the day. An outdoor Sculpture Court and Garden exhibits both traditional and modern pieces. Enjoy the view over a craft beer and some locally sourced food in the adjacent Panama 66 courtyard restaurant.

■ TIP→ The museum hosts "Art After Hours" most Friday nights, with discounted admission 5–8 pm. ✉ *1450 El Prado, Balboa Park* ☎ *619/232–7931* 🌐 *www.sdmart.org* 🎫 *$15; $5 Fri. 5–8 pm; sculpture garden free* 🕓 *Closed Wed.*

HISTORY REVEALED

While demurely posing as a butterfly garden today, the Zoro Garden has a racy history—tucked between the Casa de Balboa and the Fleet Center, this area showcased a nudist colony during the 1935–36 Exposition.

FAMILY Fodor'sChoice ★ **San Diego Museum of Man.** If the facade of this building—the landmark California Building—looks familiar, it's because filmmaker Orson Welles used it and its dramatic tower as the principal features of the Xanadu estate in his 1941 classic, *Citizen Kane*. Closed for 80 years, the tower was recently reopened for public tours. An additional timed ticket and a climb up 125 steps is required, but the effort will be rewarded with spectacular 360-degree views of the coast, Downtown, and the inland mountains. Back inside, exhibits at this highly respected anthropological museum focus on Southwestern, Mexican, and South American cultures. Carved monuments from the Mayan city of Quirigua in Guatemala, cast from the originals in 1914, are particularly impressive. Exhibits might include examples of intricate beadwork from across the Americas, the history of Egyptian mummies, or the lifestyles of the Kumeyaay peoples, Native Americans who live in the San Diego area. ✉ *California Bldg., 1350 El Prado, Balboa Park* ☎ *619/239–2001* 🌐 *www.museumofman.org* 🎫 *$13; special exhibits extra; Tower tickets (including museum admission) $22.50* ☞ *Tower tours are timed-entry and can be booked in advance through website or on arrival at museum.*

FAMILY **San Diego Natural History Museum.** There are 7½ million fossils, dinosaur models, and even live reptiles and other specimens under this roof. Favorite exhibits include the Foucault Pendulum, suspended on a 43-foot cable and designed to demonstrate the Earth's rotation, and *Ocean Oasis*, the world's first large-format film about Baja California and the Sea of Cortés. Permanent exhibits highlight citizen scientists and the regional environment, and traveling exhibits also make a stop here. Included in admission are 3-D films shown at the museum's giant-screen theater. **■ TIP→ Check the website for information about films, lectures, and free guided nature walks.** ✉ *1788 El Prado, Balboa Park* ☎ *619/232–3821* 🌐 *www.sdnhm.org* 🎫 *$19; extra for special exhibits.*

Fodor'sChoice ★ **San Diego Zoo.**

See the highlighted listing in this chapter.

Fodor'sChoice ★ **Spanish Village Art Center.** More than 200 local artists, including glassblowers, enamel workers, woodcarvers, sculptors, painters, jewelers, and photographers work and give demonstrations of their craft on a rotating basis in these red tile–roof studio-galleries that were set up for the 1935–36 exposition in the style of an old Spanish village. The center is a great source for memorable gifts. ✉ *1770 Village Pl., Balboa Park* ☎ *619/233–9050* 🌐 *www.spanishvillageart.com* 🎫 *Free.*

Fodor'sChoice ★ **Spreckels Organ Pavilion.** The 2,400-bench-seat pavilion, dedicated in 1915 by sugar magnates John D. and Adolph B. Spreckels, holds the

DID YOU KNOW?

You can visit Spain without leaving San Diego: the Alcazar Garden was patterned after the Alcazar palace gardens in Seville. Just beyond, the 200-foot California Tower sits atop the Museum of Man.

4,518-pipe Spreckels Organ, the largest outdoor pipe organ in the world. You can hear this impressive instrument at one of the year-round, free, 2 pm Sunday concerts, regularly performed by the city's civic organist and guest artists—a highlight of a visit to Balboa Park. On Monday evenings from late June to mid-August, internationally renowned organists play evening concerts. At Christmastime the park's Christmas tree and life-size Nativity display turn the pavilion into a seasonal wonderland. ✉ *2211 Pan American Rd., Balboa Park* ☎ *619/702–8138* 🌐 *spreckelsorgan.org.*

WORTH NOTING

House of Pacific Relations. This is not really a house but a cluster of red tile–roof stucco cottages representing 34 foreign countries. The word "pacific" refers to the goal of maintaining peace. The cottages, decorated with crafts and pictures, are open Sunday afternoon, when you can chat with transplanted natives and try out different ethnic foods. Folk-song and dance performances are presented on the outdoor stage around 2 pm most weeks—check the schedule at the park visitor center. Across the road from the cottages, but not affiliated with them, is the Spanish colonial–style **United Nations Building.** Inside, the United Nations Association's International Gift Shop, open daily, has reasonably priced crafts, cards, and books. ✉ *2191 Pan American Pl., Balboa Park* ☎ *619/234–0739* 🌐 *www.sdhpr.org* 🎟 *Free, donations accepted.*

FAMILY **Marie Hitchcock Puppet Theater.** Performances incorporate marionettes, hand puppets, rod puppets, shadow puppets, and ventriloquism, while the stories range from traditional fairy tales to folk legends and contemporary puppet plays. Kids stare wide-eyed at the short, energy-filled productions. ✉ *2130 Pan American Pl., Balboa Park* ☎ *619/544–9203* 🌐 *www.balboaparkpuppets.com* 🎟 *$5* ⏲ *Closed Mon. and Tues.*

Marston House Museum & Gardens. George W. Marston (1850–1946), a San Diego pioneer and philanthropist who financed the architectural landscaping of Balboa Park—among his myriad other San Diego civic projects—lived in this 16-room home at the northwest edge of the park. Designed in 1905 by San Diego architects Irving Gill and William Hebbard, it's a classic example of the American Arts and Crafts style, which emphasizes simplicity and functionality of form. On the 5-acre grounds is a lovely English Romantic garden, as interpreted in California. The house may only be visited by guided tour. ■ **TIP→ Call for information about specialty tours of the gardens, historic 7th Ave., and the Bankers Hill neighborhood.** ✉ *3525 7th Ave., Balboa Park* ☎ *619/298–3142* 🌐 *www.marstonhouse.org* 🎟 *$15* ⏲ *Closed Tues.–Thurs.* ☞ *Tours offered every ½ hour and last 40–45 min; last tour is 4 pm.*

FAMILY **Miniature Railroad.** Adjacent to the zoo parking lot and across from the carousel, a pint-size 48-passenger train runs a ½-mile loop through four tree-filled acres of the park. The engine of this rare 1948 model train is one of only 50 left in the world. ✉ *2885 Zoo Pl., Balboa Park* ☎ *619/239–0512* 🎟 *$3* ⏲ *Closed weekdays Sept.–May, except during school holidays.*

Museum of Photographic Arts. World-renowned photographers such as Ansel Adams, Imogen Cunningham, Henri Cartier-Bresson, and Edward Weston are represented in this museum's permanent collection, which

Continued on page 60

Polar bear, San Diego Zoo

LIONS AND TIGERS AND PANDAS: The World-Famous San Diego Zoo

From cuddly pandas and diving polar bears to 6-ton elephants and swinging great apes, San Diego's most famous attraction has it all. Nearly 4,000 animals representing 800 species roam the 100-acre zoo in expertly crafted habitats that replicate the animals' natural environments. While the pandas get top billing, there are plenty of other cool creatures to see here, from teeny-tiny mantella frogs to two-story-tall giraffes. But it's not all just fun and games. Known for its exemplary conservation programs, the zoo educates visitors on how to go green and explains its efforts to protect endangered species.

SAN DIEGO ZOO TOP ATTRACTIONS

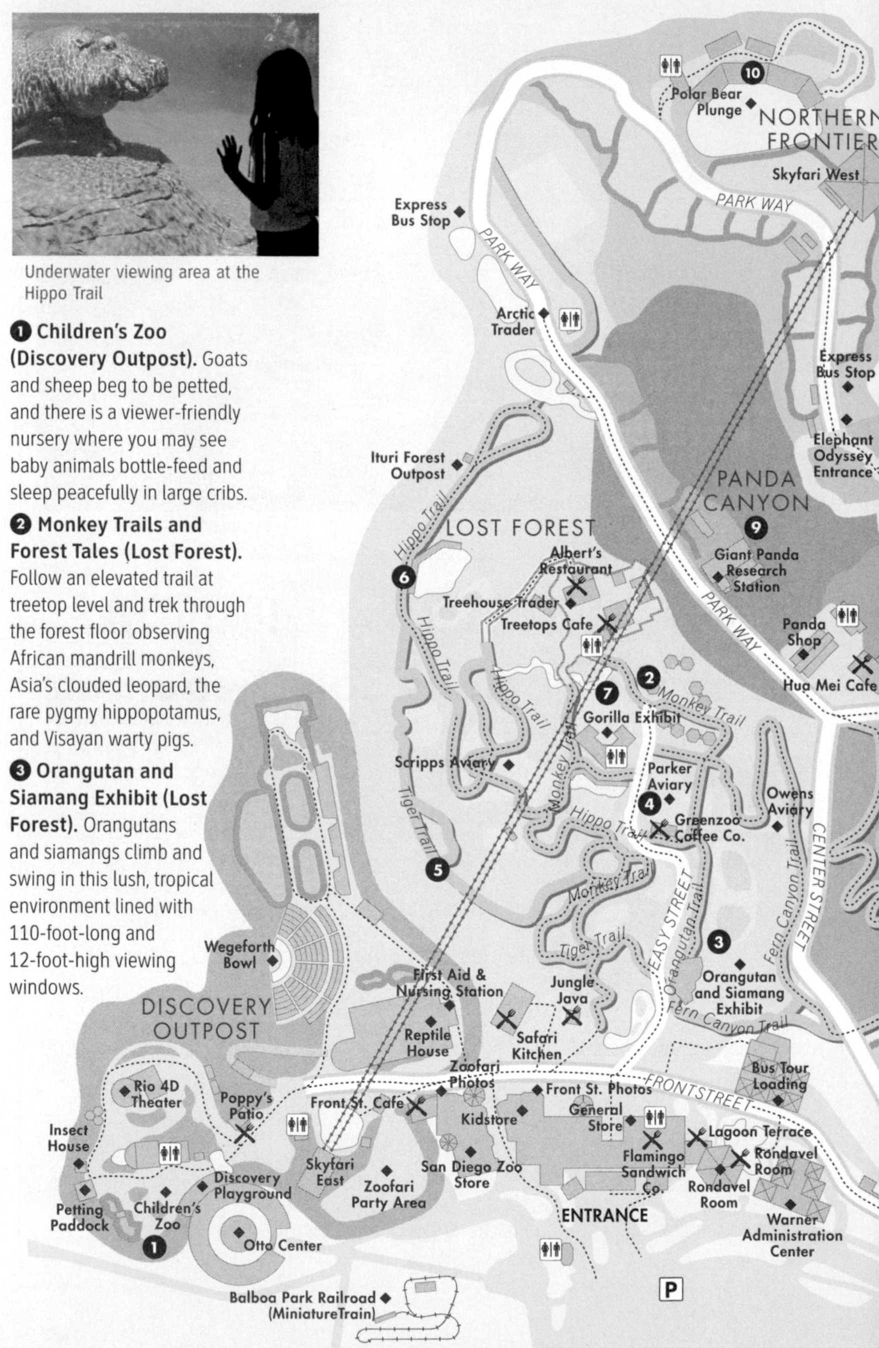

Underwater viewing area at the Hippo Trail

❶ Children's Zoo (Discovery Outpost). Goats and sheep beg to be petted, and there is a viewer-friendly nursery where you may see baby animals bottle-feed and sleep peacefully in large cribs.

❷ Monkey Trails and Forest Tales (Lost Forest). Follow an elevated trail at treetop level and trek through the forest floor observing African mandrill monkeys, Asia's clouded leopard, the rare pygmy hippopotamus, and Visayan warty pigs.

❸ Orangutan and Siamang Exhibit (Lost Forest). Orangutans and siamangs climb and swing in this lush, tropical environment lined with 110-foot-long and 12-foot-high viewing windows.

❹ **Scripps, Parker, and Owens Aviaries (Lost Forest).** Wandering paths climb through the enclosed aviaries where brightly colored tropical birds swoop between branches inches from your face.

❺ **Tiger Trail (Lost Forest).** The mist-shrouded trails of this simulated rainforest wind down a canyon. Tigers, Malayan tapirs, and Argus pheasants wander among the exotic trees and plants.

❻ **Hippo Trail (Lost Forest).** Glimpse huge but surprisingly graceful hippos frolicking in the water through an underwater viewing window and buffalo cavorting with monkeys on dry land.

❼ **Gorilla Exhibit (Lost Forest).** The gorillas live in one of the zoo's bioclimatic zone exhibits modeled on their native habitat with waterfalls, climbing areas, and an open meadow. The sounds of the tropical rain forest emerge from a 144-speaker sound system that plays CDs recorded in Africa.

❽ **Sun Bear Forest (Asian Passage).** Playful beasts claw apart the trees and shrubs that serve as a natural playground for climbing, jumping, and general merrymaking.

❾ **Giant Panda Research Station (Panda Canyon).** An elevated pathway provides visitors with great access

Lories at Owen's Aviary

to the zoo's most famous residents in their side-by-side viewing areas. The adjacent discovery center features lots of information about these endangered animals and the zoo's efforts to protect them.

❿ **Polar Bear Plunge (Polar Rim).** Watch polar bears take a chilly dive from the underwater viewing room. There are also Siberian reindeer, white foxes, and other Arctic creatures here. Kids can learn about the Arctic and climate change through interactive exhibits.

⓫ **Elephant Odyssey.** Get a glimpse of the animals that roamed Southern California 12,000 years ago and meet their living counterparts. The 7.5-acre, multispecies habitat features elephants, California condors, jaguars, and more.

⓬ **Koala Exhibit (Outback).** The San Diego Zoo houses the largest number of koalas outside Australia. Walk through the exhibit for photo ops of these marsupials from Down-Under curled up on their perches or dining on eucalyptus branches.

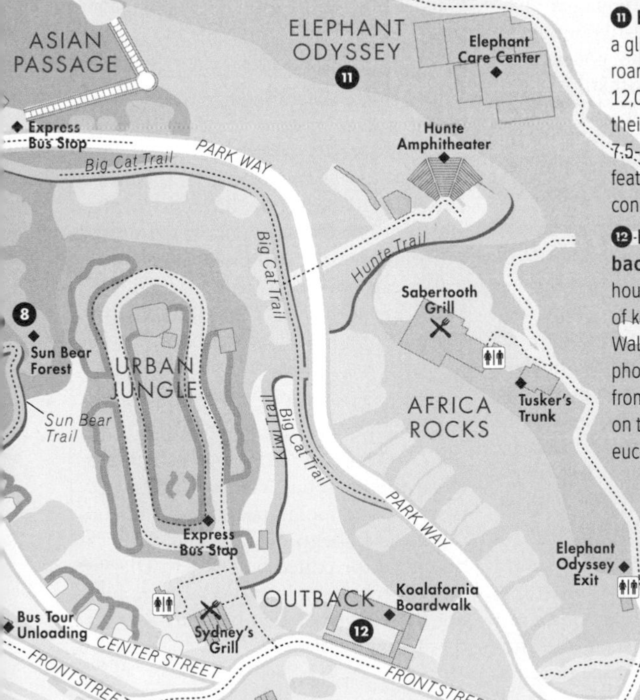

MUST-SEE ANIMALS

❶ GORILLA

This troop of primates engages visitors with their human-like expressions and behavior. The youngsters are sure to delight, especially when hitching a ride on mom's back. Up-close encounters might involve the gorillas using the glass partition as a backrest while peeling cabbage. By dusk the gorillas head inside to their sleeping quarters, so don't save this for your last stop.

❷ ELEPHANT

Asian and African elephants coexist at the San Diego Zoo. The larger African elephant is distinguished by its big flapping ears—shaped like the continent of Africa—which it uses to keep cool. An elephant's trunk has over 40,000 muscles in it—that's more than humans have in their whole body.

❸ GIANT PANDA

The San Diego Zoo is well-known for its giant panda research and conservation efforts, and has had six successful panda births. You'll likely see parents Bai Yun ("White Cloud") and Gao-Gao ("Big-Big") with their youngest baby Xiao Liwu ("little gift").

❹ KOALA

While this collection of critters is one of the cutest in the zoo, don't expect a lot of activity from the koala habitat. These guys spend most of their day curled up asleep in the branches of the eucalyptus tree—they can sleep up to 20 hours a day. Although eucalyptus leaves are poisonous to most animals, bacteria in koalas' stomachs allow them to break down the toxins.

❺ POLAR BEAR

The trio of polar bears is one of the San Diego Zoo's star attractions, and their brand-new exhibit gets you up close and personal. Visitors sometimes worry about polar bears living in the warm San Diego climate, but there is no cause for concern. The San Diego-based bears eat a lean diet, thus reducing their layer of blubber and helping them keep cool.

DID YOU KNOW?

Bamboo is the panda's dietary staple—they can consume 84 pounds of it a day—and the zoo grows 69 species of bamboo to ensure they have plenty of variety.

PLANNING YOUR DAY AT THE ZOO

Left: Main entrance of the San Diego Zoo. Right: Sunbear

PLANNING YOUR TIME

Plan to devote at least a half-day to exploring the zoo, but with so much to see it is easy to stay a full day or more.

If you're on a tight schedule, opt for the guided **35 minute bus tour** that lets you zip through three-quarters of the exhibits. However, lines to board the busses can be long, and you won't get as close to the animals.

Another option is to take the **Skyfari Aerial Tram** to the far end of the park, choose a route, and meander back to the entrance. The Skyfari trip gives a good overview of the zoo's layout and a spectacular view.

The **Elephant Odyssey**, while accessible from two sides of the park, is best entered from just below the Polar Rim. The extremely popular **Panda exhibit** can develop long lines, so get there early.

The zoo offers several entertaining **live shows** daily. Check the website or the back of the map handed out at the zoo entrance for the day's offerings and showtimes.

BEFORE YOU GO

- To avoid ticket lines, purchase and print tickets online using the zoo's Web site.
- To avoid excessive backtracking or a potential meltdown, plan your route along the zoo map before setting out. Try not to get too frustrated if you lose your way, as there are exciting exhibits around every turn and many paths intersect at several points.
- The zoo offers a variety of program extras, including behind-the-scenes tours, backstage pass animal encounters, and sleepover events. Call in advance for pricing and reservations.

AT THE ZOO

- Don't forget to explore at least some of the exhibits on foot—a favorite is the lush Tiger Trail.
- If you visit on the weekend, find out when the Giraffe Experience is taking place. You can purchase leaf-eater biscuits to hand feed the giraffes!
- Splurge a little at the gift shop: your purchases help support zoo programs.
- The zoo rents strollers, wheelchairs, and lockers; it also has a first-aid office, a lost and found, and an ATM.

Fern Canyon, San Diego Zoo

GETTING HERE AND AROUND

The zoo is easy to get to, whether by bus or car.

Bus Travel: Take Bus No. 7 and exit at Park Boulevard and Zoo Place.

Car Travel: From Downtown, take Route 163 north through Balboa Park. Exit at Zoo/Museums (Richmond Street) and follow signs.

Several options help you get around the massive park: express buses loop through the zoo and the Skyfari Aerial Tram will take you from one end to the other. The zoo's topography is fairly hilly, but moving sidewalks lead up the slopes between some exhibits.

QUICK BITES

There is a wide variety of food available for purchase at the zoo from food carts to ethnic restaurants such as the Pan-Asian **Hua Mei Cafe**.

One of the best restaurants is **Albert's**, near the Gorilla exhibit, which features grilled fish, homemade pizza, and fresh pasta along with a full bar.

SERVICE INFORMATION

✉ 2920 Zoo Dr., Balboa Park

☎ 619/234–3153

🌐 www.sandiegozoo.org

Gorilla

SAN DIEGO ZOO SAFARI PARK

About 45 minutes north of the zoo in Escondido, the 1,800-acre San Diego Zoo Safari Park is an extensive wildlife sanctuary where animals roam free—and guests can get close in escorted caravans and on backcountry trails. This park and the zoo operate under the auspices of the San Diego Zoo's nonprofit organization; joint tickets are available.

includes everything from 19th-century daguerreotypes to contemporary photojournalism prints. In addition to selections from its own collection, the museum hosts excellent traveling exhibits. Photos rotate frequently, so call ahead if you're interested in something specific to find out if it is currently on display. ■ **TIP→ MOPA is also known for its film screenings. Check the website for upcoming showings.** ✉ *Casa de Balboa, 1649 El Prado, Balboa Park* ☎ *619/238–7559* 🌐 *www.mopa.org* 🎟 *Pay what you wish pricing* ⏲ *Closed Mon.*

San Diego Automotive Museum. Even if you don't know a choke from a chassis, you're bound to admire the sleek designs of the autos in this impressive museum. On rotating display are gems from the museum's core collection of vintage motorcycles and cars—ranging from a pair of Steve McQueen's dirt bikes and an extremely rare Bizzarrini (only three were ever made), to a 1981 silver Delorean (remember the time machine in *Back to the Future*?)—as well as a series of visiting special exhibits. Be sure to see the *Fabulous Car of Louis Mattar,* which was ingeniously kitted out to set the cross-country endurance record in 1952 (6,320 miles nonstop from San Diego to New York City and back, refueling from a moving gas truck); a video display shows highlights such as Mattar and his co-drivers changing the tire while in motion and pouring a glass of water from the onboard tap. There's also an ongoing automobile restoration program and an extensive automotive research library. ✉ *2080 Pan American Plaza, Balboa Park* ☎ *619/231–2886* 🌐 *www.sdautomuseum.org* 🎟 *$9.*

San Diego History Center. The San Diego Historical Society maintains its research library in the basement of the Casa de Balboa and organizes shows on the first floor. Permanent and rotating exhibits, which are often more lively than you might expect, survey local urban history after 1850, when California entered the Union. A 100-seat theater hosts public lectures, workshops, and educational programs, and a gift shop carries a good selection of books on local history as well as reproductions of old posters and other historical collectibles. ✉ *Casa de Balboa, 1649 El Prado, Balboa Park* ☎ *619/232–6203* 🌐 *www.sandiegohistory.org* 🎟 *Free (donations encouraged).*

FAMILY **San Diego Model Railroad Museum.** When the exhibits at this 27,000-square-foot museum are in operation, you can hear the sounds of chugging engines, screeching brakes, and shrill whistles. Local model railroad clubs built and maintain the four main displays, which represent California railroads in "miniature," with the track laid on scale models of San Diego County terrain. Out back, the Centennial Railway Garden features replicas of the streetcars and scenes of Balboa Park during the 1015 Exposition. The Toy Train Gallery has interactive Lionel exhibit and whimsical vignettes. ✉ *Casa de Balboa, 1649 El Prado, Balboa Park* ☎ *619/696–0199* 🌐 *www.sdmrm.org* 🎟 *$10.75* ⏲ *Closed Mon.*

Timken Museum of Art. Though somewhat out of place architecturally, this small and modern structure, made of travertine imported from Italy, is a jewel box. The museum houses works by major European and American artists as well as a superb collection of Russian icons. ✉ *1500 El Prado, Balboa Park* ☎ *619/239–5548* 🌐 *www.timkenmuseum.org* 🎟 *$10 suggested donation; audio tours $5* ⏲ *Closed Mon.*

OLD TOWN AND UPTOWN

Getting Oriented

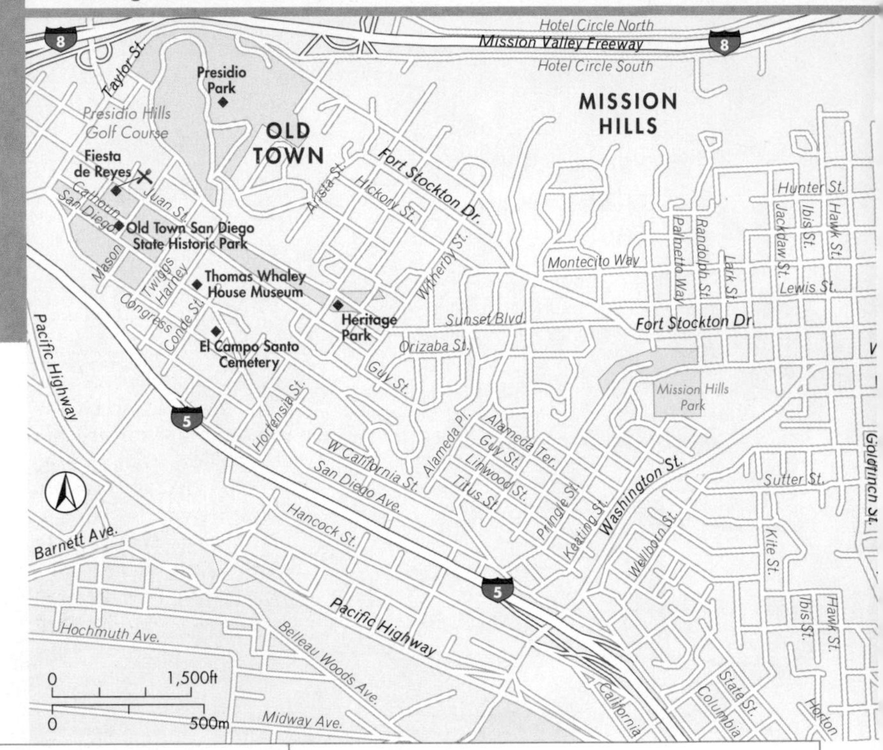

GETTING HERE	TOP REASONS TO GO
Old Town and Uptown are northwest and north of Balboa Park, respectively. Access to Old Town is easy thanks to the nearby Old Town Transit Center. Ten bus lines stop here, as do the San Diego Trolley and the Coaster commuter rail line. Two large parking lots linked to the Old Town Historic Park by an underground pedestrian walkway ease some of the parking congestion. Uptown is best explored by car, although several bus routes do serve the area. Both metered street parking and pay-and-display lots are available.	**Step back in time:** Experience the early days of San Diego, from its beginnings as a remote military outpost and mission to the development of the first town plaza. **Architectural delights:** Take an architectural journey through San Diego's history. Discover the pueblo- and clapboard-style structures of Old Town and the ornate Victorian gems in Heritage Park. Then head up the hill to view wonderfully preserved early-20th-century homes in Uptown. **Scare yourself silly:** A nighttime visit to the Thomas Whaley House Museum, "the most haunted house in America," is sure to give you goose bumps. **Tortillas and margaritas:** Enjoy the convivial atmosphere at one of the many Mexican eateries in Old Town. **Live like a local:** Explore the vibrant shopping, dining, and nightlife of Uptown's unique neighborhoods.

Old Town and Uptown

QUICK BITES

Bread and Cie Café. Its delicious loaves are distributed around town, but visitors can go to the source in Hillcrest. Pastries, soups, salads, sandwiches, and plenty of bread are served in a bustling atmosphere; there's also outdoor seating. ✉ *350 University Ave., Hillcrest* ☎ *619/683–9322* 🌐 *www.breadandcie.com.*

Fiesta de Reyes Snacks. If traveling back in time has left you tired and hungry, Old Town's Fiesta de Reyes has several options for a quick recharge. To the right when you enter from the plaza, La Panaderia serves sweet and savory empanadas, homemade *churros* (strips of fried dough), and hot chocolate. Nibble Chocolate, in the rear of the courtyard, has vegan pastries, specialty coffee drinks, and locally made chocolate. If you're visiting between Friday and Sunday, look for the booth marked Street Tacos for a quick meal. ✉ *4016 Wallace St., Old Town* ☎ *619/297–3100* 🌐 *www.fiestadereyes.com.*

PLANNING YOUR TIME

It takes about two hours to walk through Old Town. Try to time your visit to coincide with one of the daily tours given by costumed park staff. Tours are $10 and depart at 11:30, 1, and 2, from the Robinson-Rose House Visitor Center. If you go to Presidio Park, definitely consider driving up the steep hill from Old Town.

The highlight of an Uptown tour is exploring the heart of Hillcrest, located at the intersection of University and 5th avenues. Plan to drive or catch a bus between neighborhoods, then explore on foot.

FESTIVALS

The Uptown neighborhoods host a variety of events throughout the year. Hillcrest hosts the annual LGBT Pride event every July. In late summer, Cityfest rocks the neighborhood with live music, food stalls, and beer gardens. Old Town celebrates Cinco de Mayo and the Old Town Art Festival held in early fall.

Sightseeing
★★★★☆
Nightlife
★★★★☆
Dining
★★★★★
Lodging
★★☆☆☆
Shopping
★★★★☆

San Diego's Spanish and Mexican roots are most evident in Old Town and the surrounding hillside of Presidio Park. Visitors can experience settlement life in San Diego from Spanish and Mexican rule to the early days of U.S. statehood. Nearby Uptown is composed of several smaller neighborhoods near Downtown and around Balboa Park: the vibrant neighborhoods of Hillcrest, Mission Hills, North Park, and South Park showcase their unique blend of historical charm and modern urban community.

OLD TOWN

Updated by Claire Deeks van der Lee

As the first European settlement in Southern California, **Old Town** began to develop in the 1820s. However, its true beginnings took place on a nearby hillside in 1769 with the establishment of a Spanish military outpost and the first of California's missions, San Diego de Alcalá. In 1774 the hilltop was declared a *presidio reál*, a fortress built by the Spanish empire, and the mission was relocated along the San Diego River. Over time, settlers moved down from the presidio to establish Old Town. A central plaza was laid out, surrounded by adobe and, later, wooden structures. San Diego became an incorporated U.S. city in 1850, with Old Town as its center. In the 1860s, however, the advent of Alonzo Horton's New Town to the southeast caused Old Town to wither. Efforts to preserve the area began early in the 20th century, and Old Town became a state historic park in 1968.

Today Old Town is a lively celebration of history and culture. The **Old Town San Diego State Historic Park** re-creates life during the early settlement, while San Diego Avenue buzzes with art galleries, gift shops, festive restaurants, and open-air stands selling inexpensive Mexican handicrafts.

Dancers perform during the annual Dia de los Muertos celebration at the Fiesta de Reyes plaza in Old Town.

TOP ATTRACTIONS

FAMILY Fodor's Choice ★ **Fiesta de Reyes.** North of San Diego's Old Town Plaza lies the area's unofficial center, built to represent a colonial Mexican plaza. The collection of more than a dozen shops and restaurants around a central courtyard in blossom with magenta bougainvillea, scarlet hibiscus, and other flowers in season reflects what early California might have looked like from 1821 to 1872. Shops are even stocked with items reminiscent of that era. Mariachi bands and folklorico dance groups frequently perform on the plaza stage—check the website for times and upcoming special events. ■ **TIP→ Casa de Reyes is a great stop for a margarita and some chips and guacamole.** ✉ *4016 Wallace St., Old Town* ☎ *619/297–3100* 🌐 *www.fiestadereyes.com.*

Heritage Park. A number of San Diego's important Victorian buildings are the focus of this 7.8-acre park on the Juan Street hill near Harney Street. Among the buildings is Southern California's first synagogue, a one-room classical-revival structure built in 1889 for Congregation Beth Israel. The most interesting of the park's six former residences might be the Sherman-Gilbert House, which has a widow's walk and intricate carving on its decorative trim. It was built for real estate dealer John Sherman in 1887 at the then-exorbitant cost of $20,000—indicating just how profitable the booming housing market could be. All the houses, some of which may seem surprisingly colorful, accurately represent the bright tones of the era. The synagogue and the Senlis Cottage are open to visitors daily from 9 to 5; the latter contains a small exhibit with information on the history and original locations of the houses. The McConaughy House hosts the Coral Tree Tea House and

Old Town Gift Emporium, offering traditional tea service Thursday through Sunday from 11 to 5. Save Our Heritage Organization moved the buildings to this park from their original locations and also restored them. ✉ *2454 Heritage Park Row, Old Town* ☎ *858/565–3600* 🌐 *www.sdparks.org* 🎟 *Free.*

FAMILY Fodor's Choice ★ **Old Town San Diego State Historic Park.** The six square blocks on the site of San Diego's original pueblo are the heart of Old Town. Most of the 20 historic buildings preserved or re-created by the park cluster around **Old Town Plaza,** bounded by Wallace Street on the west, Calhoun Street on the north, Mason Street on the east, and San Diego Avenue on the south. The plaza is a pleasant place to rest, plan your tour of the park, and watch passers-by. San Diego Avenue is closed to vehicle traffic here.

Some of Old Town's buildings were destroyed in a fire in 1872, but after the site became a state historic park in 1968, reconstruction and restoration of the remaining structures began. Five of the original adobes are still intact.

Facing Old Town Plaza, the **Robinson-Rose House** was the original commercial center of Old San Diego, housing railroad offices, law offices, and the first newspaper press. The largest and most elaborate of the original adobe homes, the **Casa de Estudillo** was occupied by members of the Estudillo family until 1887 and later gained popularity for its billing as "Ramona's Marriage Place" based on a popular novel of the time. Albert Seeley, a stagecoach entrepreneur, opened the **Cosmopolitan Hotel** in 1869 as a way station for travelers on the daylong trip south from Los Angeles. Next door to the Cosmopolitan Hotel, the **Seeley Stable** served as San Diego's stagecoach stop in 1867 and was the transportation hub of Old Town until 1887, when trains became the favored mode of travel.

Several reconstructed buildings serve as restaurants or as shops purveying wares reminiscent of those that might have been available in the original Old Town. **Racine & Laramie** a painstakingly reproduced version of San Diego's first cigar store in 1868, is especially interesting.

Pamphlets available at the Robinson-Rose House give details about all the historic houses on the plaza and in its vicinity. Tours of the historic park are offered daily at 11:30, 1, and 2; purchase tickets at the Robinson-Rose House. A free history program is also offered daily in the Seely Stable Theater. ■ **TIP→ The covered wagon located near the intersection of Mason and Calhoun streets provides a great photo op.** ✉ *Visitor center (Robinson-Rose House), 4002 Wallace St., Old Town* ☎ *619/220–5422* 🌐 *www.parks.ca.gov* 🎟 *Free; walking tour $10.*

Presidio Park. The hillsides of the 50-acre green space overlooking Old Town from the north end of Taylor Street are popular with picnickers, and many couples have taken their wedding vows on the park's long stretches of lawn, some of the greenest in San Diego. The park offers a great ocean view from the top, and more than 2 miles of hiking trails below. It's a nice walk from Old Town to the summit if you're in good shape and wearing the right shoes—it should take about half an hour. You can also drive to the top of the park via Presidio Drive, off Taylor Street.

If you walk, look in at the **Presidio Hills Golf Course** on Mason Street. It has an unusual clubhouse that incorporates the ruins of Casa de Carrillo, the town's oldest adobe, constructed in 1820. At the end of Mason Street, veer left on Jackson Street to reach the **presidio ruins,** where adobe walls and a bastion have been built above the foundations of the original fortress and chapel. Also on-site is the 28-foot-high **Serra Cross,** built in 1913 out of brick tiles found in the ruins. Continue up the hill to find the **Junípero Serra Museum,** built at the sight of the original Mission San Diego de Alcalá and often mistaken for the mission. Open weekends, the Serra Museum commemorates the history of the site from the time it was occupied by the Kumeyaay Indians through its Spanish, Mexican, and American periods. Then take Presidio Drive southeast to reach the site of **Fort Stockton,** built to protect Old Town and abandoned by the United States in 1848. Plaques and statues also commemorate the Mormon Battalion, which enlisted here to fight in the battle against Mexico. ✉ *Taylor and Jackson Sts., Old Town* 🌐 *www.sdparks.org.*

AMERICA'S MOST HAUNTED

Built on a former gallows site in 1856, the Whaley House is one of 30 houses designated by the Department of Commerce to be haunted. Legend has it that the house is inhabited by seven spirits, making it the "most haunted house in America." Listen for the sound of heavy footsteps, said to belong to the ghost of Yankee Jim Robinson, a convict hanged on the site in 1852. Less ominous are sightings of the Whaley family's fox terrier scampering about the house.

Thomas Whaley House Museum. A New York entrepreneur, Thomas Whaley came to California during the gold rush. He wanted to provide his East Coast wife with all the comforts of home, so in 1857 he had Southern California's first two-story brick structure built, making it the oldest double-story brick building on the West Coast. The house, which served as the county courthouse and government seat during the 1870s, stands in strong contrast to the Spanish-style adobe residences that surround the nearby historic plaza and marks an early stage of San Diego's "Americanization." A garden out back includes many varieties of prehybrid roses from before 1867. The place is perhaps most famed, however, for the ghosts that are said to inhabit it. You can tour on your own during the day, but must visit by guided tour starting at 5 pm. The evening tours are geared toward the supernatural aspects of the house. They are offered every half hour, with the last tour departing at 9:30 pm, and last about 45 minutes. ✉ *2476 San Diego Ave., Old Town* ☎ *619/297–7511* 🌐 *www.whaleyhouse.org* 🎫 *$8 before 5 pm; $13 after 5 pm* 🕒 *Closed Sept.–May, Wed.*

WORTH NOTING

El Campo Santo cemetery. Now a peaceful stop for visitors to Old Town, the old adobe-wall cemetery established in 1849 was, until 1880, the burial place for many members of Old Town's founding families—as well as for some gamblers and bandits who passed through town. Antonio Garra, a chief who led an uprising of the San Luis Rey Indians, was executed at El Campo Santo in front of the open grave he had been forced to dig for himself. Most of the markers give only approximations of where the people named on them are buried; some of the early settlers laid to rest at El Campo Santo actually reside under San Diego Avenue. ✉ *San Diego Ave. S, between Arista and Ampudia Sts., Old Town.*

HILLCREST

The large retro Hillcrest sign over the intersection of University and 5th avenues makes an excellent landmark at the epicenter of this vibrant section of Uptown. Strolling along University Avenue between 4th and 6th avenues and from Washington Street to Robinson Avenue will reveal a mixture of retail shops and restaurants. National chains such as American Apparel and Pinkberry coexist with local boutiques, bookstores, bars, and coffee shops. A few blocks east, another interesting stretch of stores and restaurants runs along University Avenue to Normal Street. Long established as the center of San Diego's gay community, the neighborhood bustles both day and night with a mixed crowd of shoppers, diners, and partygoers. If you are visiting Hillcrest on Sunday between 9 and 2, be sure to explore the exceptional Hillcrest Farmers Market (⇨ *see Hillcrest in Chapter 14, Shopping*).

MISSION HILLS

The route from Old Town to Hillcrest passes through the historic neighborhood of **Mission Hills** with its delightful examples of early-20th-century architecture. From the top of Presidio Park, take Presidio Drive into the heart of this residential area. A left on Arista Street and a right on Fort Stockton Drive takes you past wonderfully preserved Spanish Revival, Craftsman, and Prairie-style homes, to name a few. Many local residents fine-tune their green thumbs at the **Mission Hills Nursery** (*1525 Ft. Stockton Dr.*), founded in 1910 by Kate Sessions, the "Mother of Balboa Park." Continuing on Fort Stockton Drive, a right on Goldfinch Street leads you to several popular eateries along the neighborhood's burgeoning restaurant row. From there, a left on University Avenue will take you into the Hillcrest section of Uptown.

Founded in 1769, Mission Basilica San Diego de Alcalá was the first of California's 21 Catholic missions.

MISSION VALLEY

Although Mission Valley's charms may not be immediately apparent, it offers many conveniences to visitors and residents alike. One of the area's main attractions is the Fashion Valley mall, with its mix of high-end and mid-range retail stores and dining options, and movie theater. The Mission Basilica San Diego de Alcalá provides a tranquil refuge from the surrounding suburban sprawl.

Fodor's Choice ★ **Mission Basilica San Diego de Alcalá.** It's hard to imagine how remote California's earliest mission must have once been; these days, however, it's accessible by major freeways (I–15 and I–8) and via the San Diego Trolley. The first of a chain of 21 missions stretching northward along the coast, Mission San Diego de Alcalá was established by Father Junípero Serra on Presidio Hill in 1769 and moved to this location in 1774. In 1775, it proved vulnerable to enemy attack, and Padre Luis Jayme, a young friar from Spain, was clubbed to death by the Kumeyaay Indians he had been trying to convert. He was the first of more than a dozen Christians martyred in California. The present church, reconstructed in 1931 following the outline of the 1813 church, is the fifth built on the site. It measures 150 feet long but only 35 feet wide because, without easy means of joining beams, the mission buildings were only as wide as the trees that served as their ceiling supports were tall. Father Jayme is buried in the sanctuary; a small museum named for him documents mission history and exhibits tools and artifacts from the early days; there is also a gift shop. From the peaceful, palm-bedecked gardens out back you can gaze at the 46-foot-high *campanario* (bell tower), the mission's most distinctive feature, with five bells. Mass is celebrated on the weekends. ✉ *10818 San Diego Mission Rd., Mission Valley* ✣ *From I–8 east, exit and turn left on Mission Gorge Rd., then left on Twain Rd.; mission is on right* ☎ *619/281–8449* 🌐 *www.missionsandiego.com* 🎫 *$5.*

NORTH PARK

Named for its location north of Balboa Park, this evolving neighborhood is home to an exciting array of restaurants, bars, and shops. High-end condominiums and local merchants are often cleverly disguised behind historic signage from barbershops, bowling alleys, and theater marquees. The stretch of Ray Street near University Avenue is home to several small galleries, as well as the Ray at Night art walk, held the second Saturday of each month. Just around the corner on University Avenue lies the stunning 1920s-era North Park Theatre. With a steady stream of new openings in the neighborhood, North Park is one of San Diego's top dining and nightlife destinations. Beer enthusiasts won't want to miss the breweries and tasting rooms along the 30th St. Beer Corridor for a chance to sample San Diego's famous ales.

SOUTH PARK

The South Park neighborhood is actually on the east side of Balboa Park, but it's south of North Park, hence the name. The tree-lined neighborhood is largely residential but its collection of interesting galleries, boutiques (⇨ *Specialty Stores in Chapter 14, Shopping*), and restaurants make for a nice stroll.

5

MISSION BAY AND THE BEACHES

Getting Oriented

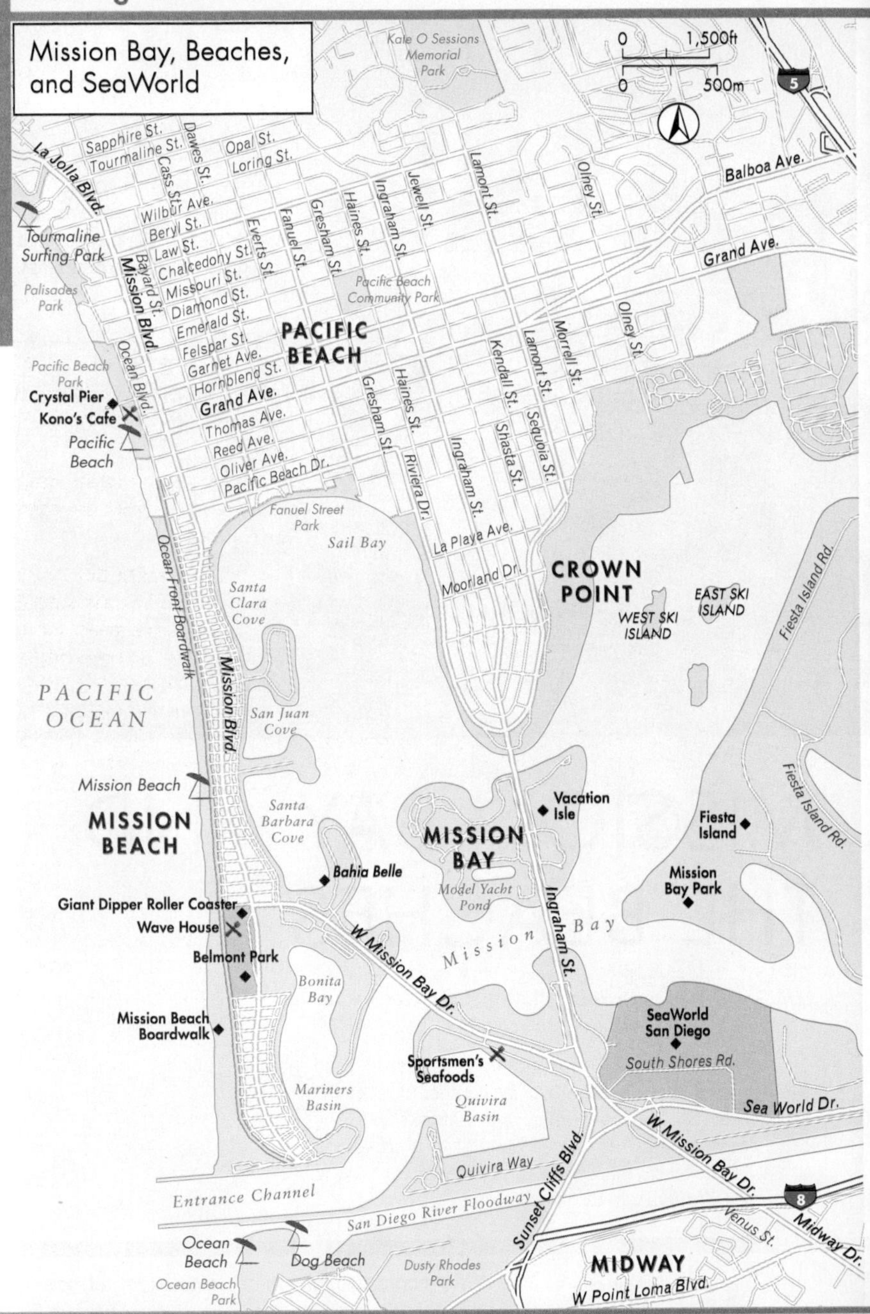

TOP REASONS TO GO

Sun and sand: With sand stretching as far as the eye can see, Mission and Pacific beaches represent the classic Southern California beach experience.

Bustling boardwalk: Twentysomethings partying at the bars, families grilling in front of their vacation homes, and kids playing in the sand—take in the scene with a stroll along the Mission Beach boardwalk.

Bayside delights: A quiet respite from the nearby beaches, Mission Bay is ringed with peaceful pathways, playgrounds, and parks.

Get out on the water: Catch a wave, paddle a kayak, or rev a Jet Ski at this irresistible water-sports playground.

QUICK BITES

There is no shortage of dining options in and around the **Belmont Park** and **WaveHouse** complex, from funnel cakes and hot dogs inside the amusement park, to quick snacks and soda fountain treats at **Dottie's Pop Shop** on the boardwalk. If you have time to sit down for a meal, **Cannonball. Draft,** and the **WaveHouse** are all great spots to take in the scene.

Kono's Cafe. Take in the boardwalk vibe as you wait in line for your breakfast burrito at this legendary spot at the base of Crystal Pier. ✉ *704 Garnet Ave., Pacific Beach* ☎ *858/483–1669* 🌐 *www.konoscafe.com* ⏲ *Closed Thanksgiving and Christmas* ▭ *No credit cards.*

Sportsmen's Seafood. This waterside eatery serves good fish-and-chips, seafood salads, and sandwiches to eat on the inelegant but scenic patio—by the marina, where sportfishing boats depart daily—or to take out to your chosen picnic spot. ✉ *1617 Quivira Rd., Mission Bay* ☎ *619/224–3551* 🌐 *www.sportsmensseafood.com* ▭ *No credit cards.*

GETTING HERE

SeaWorld, Mission Bay, and Mission and Pacific beaches are all served by public bus routes 8 and 9. Many local hotels offer shuttle service to and from SeaWorld. There is a free parking lot at Belmont Park, although it can quickly fill during busy times.

PLANNING YOUR TIME

You may not find a visit to SeaWorld fulfilling unless you spend at least half a day; a full day is recommended.

Belmont Park is open daily, but not all its rides are open year-round.

The Mission Beach Boardwalk and the miles of trails around Mission Bay are great for a leisurely bike ride. On foggy days, particularly in late spring or early summer, the beaches can be overcast in the morning with the fog burning off as the day wears on.

MISSION BAY WARNINGS

Swimmers at Mission Bay should note signs warning about water pollution; on occasions when heavy rains or other events cause pollution, swimming is strongly discouraged.

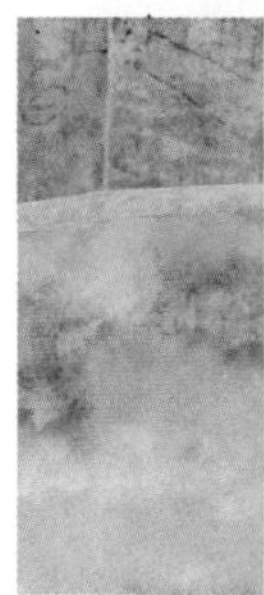

Sightseeing ★★★★☆
Nightlife ★★★☆☆
Dining ★★☆☆☆
Lodging ★★★☆☆
Shopping ★☆☆☆☆

Mission Bay and the surrounding beaches are the aquatic playground of San Diego. The choice of activities available is astonishing, and the perfect weather makes you want to get out there and play. If you're craving downtime after all the activity, there are plenty of peaceful spots to relax and simply soak up the sunshine.

MISSION BAY

Updated by Claire Deeks van der Lee

Mission Bay welcomes visitors with its protected waters and countless opportunities for fun. The 4,600-acre **Mission Bay Park** is the place for water sports like sailing, stand-up paddleboarding, and water-skiing. With 19 miles of beaches and grassy areas, it's also a great place for a picnic. And if you have kids, don't miss **SeaWorld**, one of San Diego's most popular attractions.

TOP ATTRACTIONS

Bahia Belle. At the dock of the Bahia Resort Hotel, on the eastern shores of West Mission Bay Drive, you can board this restored stern-wheeler for a sunset cruise of the bay and a party that continues until the wee hours. There's always music on board, and on Friday and Saturday nights the music is live. You can imbibe at the *Belle*'s full bar, but many revelers like to disembark at the Bahia's sister hotel, the Catamaran Resort, and have a few rounds before reboarding; the boat cruises between the two hotels, which co-own it, stopping to pick up passengers every half hour. Most cruises get a mixed crowd of families, couples, and singles, but cruises after 9:30 pm are adults-only. ✉ *998 W. Mission Bay Dr., Mission Bay* ☎ *858/539–8666* 🌐 *www.sternwheelers.com/cruise.html* 🎟 *$10 for unlimited cruising; free for guests of Bahia and Catamaran hotels* ⏲ *Closed Dec., Jan., and 1st half of Feb.*

Fodor's Choice ★ **Mission Bay Park.** San Diego's monument to sports and fitness, this 4,600-acre aquatic park has 27 miles of shoreline including 19 miles of sandy beaches. Playgrounds and picnic areas abound on the beaches

CLOSE UP

Planning a Day at the Beaches and Bay

A day spent at Mission Bay or the surrounding beaches can be as active or leisurely as you like.

If you want to play in the water, the bay is a great place to kayak, sail, or try some stand-up paddleboarding. If you're into surfing, be sure to check out the waves at **Crystal Pier** in Pacific Beach. A different kind of surfing experience is available at the **WaveHouse** at **Belmont Park,** where the Flow Rider lets you catch a continuous wave.

If you want to keep active on land, the Bayside Walk and Bike Path is a great place to jog or ride along the bay. Beach Cruiser bike rentals are widely available. For a more leisurely stroll and some people-watching, head to the **Mission Beach Boardwalk.** At the south end of Mission Beach try your hand at some typically Californian beach volleyball.

If you'd rather take it easy, just find a spot to lay out your towel anywhere along Mission or Pacific beach and soak up the sun. If you tire of the sand, enjoy a picnic at one of the many grassy spots throughout **Mission Bay Park** or enjoy the view from one of the restaurants at Paradise Point Resort and Spa. As the day winds down, the happy-hour crowd is just heating up along Garnet Avenue in Pacific Beach. Alternatively, head to the Bahia Resort Hotel, where you can catch the ***Bahia Belle*** for a cruise around the bay.

If you are traveling with kids, a day at **SeaWorld** should be high on your list. There is plenty of family fun beyond SeaWorld, too. The protected beaches of the bay are popular spots for youngsters. The well-paved, peaceful Bayside Walk and Bike Path winds past picnic tables, grassy areas, and playgrounds, making it an ideal family spot. For a more lively contrast, cross the street to reach the Mission Beach Boardwalk, a classic boardwalk popular with young, hip surfers. At the south end lies **Belmont Park,** which includes an amusement park, the **WaveHouse,** and the **Giant Dipper** wooden roller coaster.

and low, grassy hills. On weekday evenings, joggers, bikers, and skaters take over. In the daytime, swimmers, water-skiers, paddleboarders, anglers, and boaters—some in single-person kayaks, others in crowded powerboats—vie for space in the water. ✉ *2688 E. Mission Bay Dr., Mission Bay* ✣ *Off I–5 at Exit 22 E. Mission Bay Dr.* ☎ *858/581–7602 park ranger's office* 🌐 *www.sandiego.gov/park-and-recreation* 🎫 *Free.*

FAMILY **SeaWorld San Diego.** Spread over 189 tropically landscaped bayfront acres, SeaWorld is one of the world's largest marine-life amusement parks. The majority of its exhibits are walk-through marine environments like **Shark Encounter,** where guests walk through a 57-foot acrylic tube and come face-to-face with a variety of sharks that call the 280,000-gallon habitat home. **Turtle Reef** offers an incredible up-close encounter with the green sea turtle, while the moving sidewalk at **Penguin Encounter** whisks you through a colony of nearly 300 penguins. The park also wows with its adventure rides like **Journey to**

Trainers at SeaWorld San Diego communicate with dolphins using hand signals and the universal language of play.

Atlantis, with a heart-stopping 60-foot plunge, and **Manta**, a thrilling double-launch coaster. Younger children will enjoy the rides, climbing structures and splash pads at the **Sesame Street Bay of Play**.

SeaWorld is most famous for its large-arena entertainments, but this is an area in transition. A new orca experience debuted in the summer of 2017 that features a nature-inspired backdrop and demonstrates orca behaviors in the wild. This change is part of SeaWorld's efforts to refocus it's orca program toward education and conservation. Other live-entertainment shows feature dolphins, sea otters, and even household pets. Several upgraded animal encounters are available including the Dolphin Interaction Program, which gives guests the chance to interact with SeaWorld's bottlenose dolphins in the water. The hour-long program (20 minutes in the water), during which visitors can feed, touch, and give behavior signals, costs $215. ✉ *500 SeaWorld Dr., near west end of I–8, Mission Bay* ☎ *800/257–4268* 🌐 *www.seaworldparks.com* 🎫 *$90 ages 3 and older; advanced purchase discounts available online; parking $17.*

Vacation Isle. Ingraham Street bisects this island, providing two distinct experiences for visitors. The west side is taken up by the Paradise Point Resort & Spa, but you don't have to be a guest to enjoy the hotel's lushly landscaped grounds and bay-front restaurants. Boaters and jet-skiers congregate near the launch at **Ski Beach** on the east side of the island, where there's a parking lot as well as picnic areas and restrooms. Ski Beach is the site of the annual Bayfair boat races held every September. At the model yacht pond on the south side of the island, children and young-at-heart adults take part year-round in motorized miniature boat races. ✉ *Mission Bay.*

WORTH NOTING

Fiesta Island. The most undeveloped area of Mission Bay Park, this is popular with bird-watchers (there's a large protected nesting site for the California tern at the northern tip of the island) as well as with dog owners, because it's the only place in the park where pets can run free. In July the annual Over-the-Line Tournament, a competition involving a unique local version of softball, attracts thousands of players and oglers. ✉ *Access from East Mission Bay Dr., Mission Bay.*

MISSION BEACH

Heading west on Mission Bay Drive to the ocean, the Giant Dipper roller coaster rises into view, welcoming visitors to the **Belmont Park** amusement park and to **Mission Beach.** Mission Boulevard runs north along a two-block-wide strip embraced by the Pacific Ocean on the west and the bay on the east. Mission Beach is a famous and lively fun zone for families and young people both; if it isn't party time at the moment, it will be five minutes from now. The pathways in this area are lined with vacation homes, many for rent by the week or month. Those fortunate enough to live here year-round have the bay as their front yard, with wide sandy beaches, volleyball courts, and—less of an advantage—an endless stream of sightseers on the sidewalk.

TOP ATTRACTIONS

FAMILY Fodor's Choice ★ **Belmont Park.** The once-abandoned amusement park between the bay and Mission Beach Boardwalk is now a shopping, dining, and recreation complex. Twinkling lights outline the **Giant Dipper,** an antique wooden roller coaster on which screaming thrill-seekers ride more than 2,600 feet of track and 13 hills (riders must be at least 4 feet, 2 inches tall). Created in 1925 and listed on the National Register of Historic Places, this is one of the few old-time roller coasters left in the United States.

Other Belmont Park attractions include miniature golf, laser tag, a video arcade, bumper cars, a tilt-a-whirl, and an antique carousel. The zip line thrills as it soars over the crowds below, while the rock wall challenges both junior climbers and their elders. Belmont Park also has the most consistent wave in the county at the **Wave House,** where the FlowRider provides surfers and bodyboarders a near-perfect simulated wave on which to practice their skills. ✉ *3146 Mission Blvd., Mission Bay* ☎ *858/488–1549 for rides* 🌐 *www.belmontpark.com* 🎟 *Unlimited ride day package $30 for 48 inches and taller, $20 for under 48 inches, some attractions not included in price; individual ride tickets and other ride/attraction combo packages are also available.*

Fodor's Choice ★ **Mission Beach Boardwalk.** The cement pathway lining the sand from the southern end of Mission Beach north to Pacific Beach is always bustling with activity. Cyclists ping the bells on their beach cruisers to pass walkers out for a stroll alongside the oceanfront homes. Vacationers kick back on their patios, while friends play volleyball

BEST BEACHES

The long expanse of sand running from Mission to Pacific Beach is some of the most popular in San Diego with locals and visitors alike. There is an energetic atmosphere among the throngs of beachgoers—the boardwalks bustle with activity, and surf culture reigns supreme.

⇨ *For more information on Mission Bay's Beaches, see Chapter 12: Beaches.*

Mission Beach. The 2-mile stretch of sand that makes up Mission Beach extends north to Belmont Park and draws huge crowds on summer weekends. This is a great place for people-watching along the boardwalk and on the volleyball courts at the southern tip.

Pacific Beach. PB picks up where Mission Beach leaves off and extends north to Crystal Pier. Parking is tough, but the scene on Ocean Front Walk and the party atmosphere may just be worth it.

Tourmaline Surfing Park. Technically part of Pacific Beach, a portion of this stretch of water is designated for surfing only.

in the sand. The activity picks up alongside Belmont Park and the WaveHouse, where people stop to check out the action on the FlowRider wave. ⊠ *Mission Beach* ✣ *Alongside sand from Mission Beach Park to Pacific Beach.*

PACIFIC BEACH

North of Mission Beach is the college-packed party town of **Pacific Beach,** or "PB" as locals call it. The laid-back vibe of this surfer's mecca draws in free-spirited locals who roam the streets on skateboards and beach cruisers, in the local uniform of board shorts, bikinis, and baseball caps. Lining the main strip of Grand and Garnet avenues are tattoo parlors, smoke shops, vintage stores, and coffeehouses. The energy level peaks during happy hour, when PB's cluster of nightclubs, bars, and 150 restaurants open their doors to those ready to party.

TOP ATTRACTION

Fodor's Choice ★ **Crystal Pier.** Stretching out into the ocean from the end of Garnet Avenue, Crystal Pier is Pacific Beach's landmark. A stroll to the end of the pier will likely reveal fishermen hoping for a good catch. Surfers make catches of their own in the waves below. ⊠ *Pacific Beach* ✣ *At end of Garnet Ave.*

6

LA JOLLA

Getting Oriented

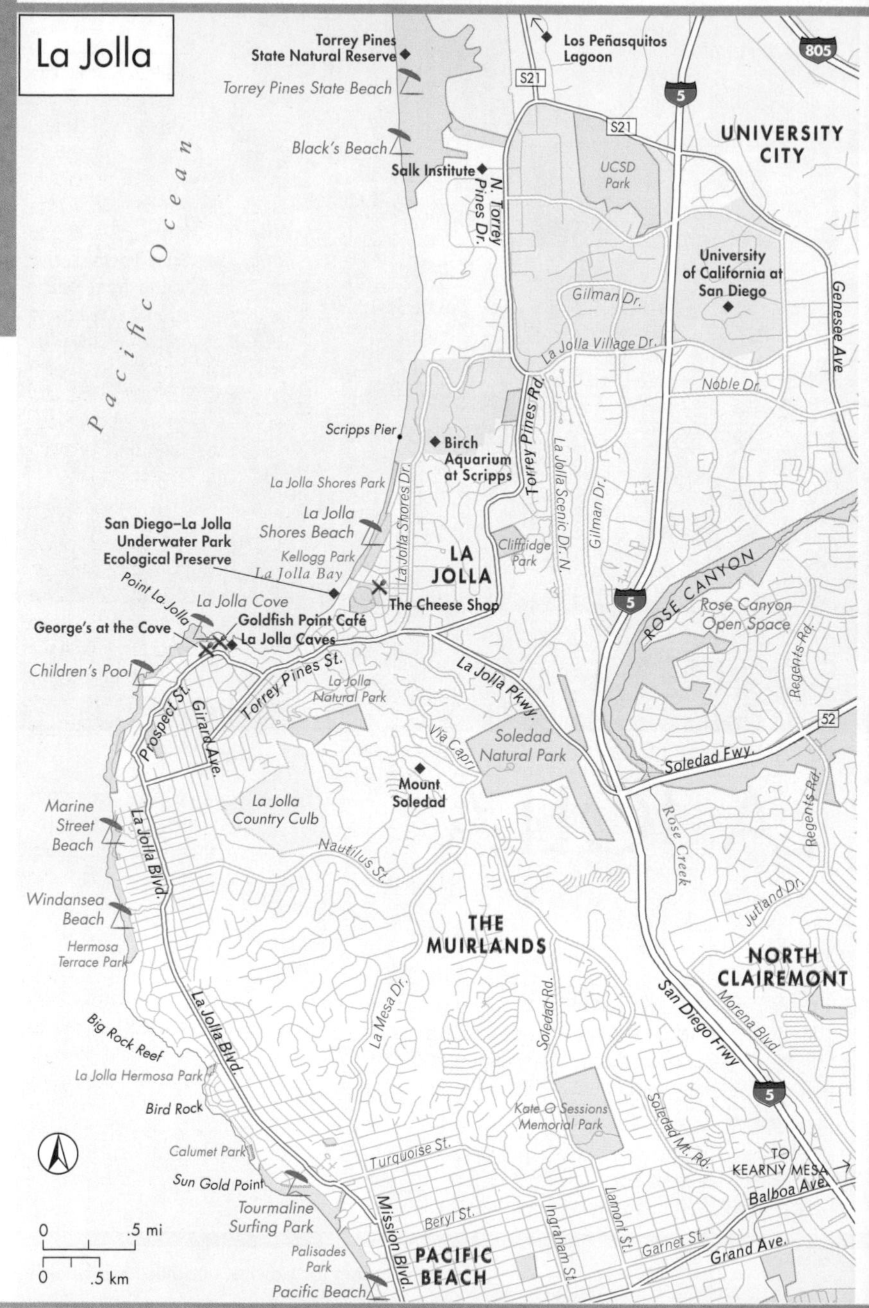

TOP REASONS TO GO

Promenade above the cove: The winding pathways above La Jolla Cove offer stunning views of the surf and sea lions.

Shop 'til you drop: La Jolla's chic boutiques and galleries are San Diego's answer to Rodeo Drive. Watch for celebrities as you browse on Prospect Street and Girard Avenue.

Aquatic adventures: Grab a kayak or scuba gear to explore the San Diego-La Jolla Underwater Park Ecological Preserve.

Luxe living: Visit top-notch spas and restaurants, or gawk at multimillion-dollar mansions and their denizens in Ferraris.

Torrey Pines State Beach and Reserve: Play the links, hike the trails, relax on the beach, or hang glide off the cliffs.

QUICK BITES

The Cheese Shop. Located in the heart of La Jolla Shores, this is a great place to grab a quick lunch or picnic provisions. The sandwiches are excellent, and kids will love the fresh-baked cookies and old-time candy selection. ✉ *2165 Avenida de la Playa* ☎ *858/459–3921* 🌐 *www.cheeseshoplajolla.com* 💳 *No credit cards.*

George's at the Cove. This restaurant complex may be one of the best-known spots in La Jolla for its incredible views of La Jolla Cove. Although the main restaurant, George's California Modern, is an upscale affair, Ocean Terrace on the top level is a great place for a casual meal. Cocktails are inventive and specialties like the Baja fish tacos or Neiman Ranch burger are delicious. ✉ *1250 Prospect St.* ☎ *858/454–4244* 🌐 *www.georgesatthecove.com* 💳 *No credit cards.*

Goldfish Point Café. If you're looking for a casual breakfast or lunch overlooking La Jolla Cove, this café hits the spot without breaking the bank. ✉ *1255 Coast Blvd.* ☎ *858/459–7407* 🌐 *www.goldfishpointcafe.com* 💳 *No credit cards.*

GETTING HERE

If you're traveling north, take the La Jolla Parkway exit off I-5, which veers into Torrey Pines Road, and turn right onto Prospect Street. If you're heading south, take the La Jolla Village Drive exit, which also leads into Torrey Pines Road. For the scenic route, head north from Pacific Beach on La Jolla Boulevard and Camino de la Costa. Signs direct drivers and cyclists past many of La Jolla's famed vistas and coveted homes. As you approach the village, La Jolla Boulevard turns into Prospect Street.

PLANNING YOUR TIME

La Jolla's highlights can be seen in a few hours with a visit to La Jolla Village and the cove followed by a scenic drive along the coast and through Torrey Pines. A day allows for beach time, a hike in Torrey Pines, and some shopping.

The village and La Jolla Cove can be explored on foot, but it's a steep walk between the two. Parking is tough so don't hold out for a better spot.

VISITOR INFORMATION

Find It La Jolla. This kiosk offers information on local events, as well as coupons and discount cards for nearby businesses and attractions. Get the app for information on the go. ✉ *7966 Herschel Ave., La Jolla* 🌐 *www.lajollabluebook.com.*

Sightseeing ★★★★☆
Nightlife ★★☆☆☆
Dining ★★★★☆
Lodging ★★★☆☆
Shopping ★★★★☆

La Jollans have long considered their village to be the Monte Carlo of California, and with good cause. Its coastline curves into natural coves backed by verdant hillsides covered with homes worth millions. La Jolla is both a natural and cultural treasure trove. The upscale shops, galleries, and restaurants of La Jolla Village satisfy the glitterati, while secluded trails, scenic overlooks, and abundant marine life provide balance and refuge.

Updated by Claire Deeks van der Lee

Although **La Jolla** is a neighborhood of the city of San Diego, it has its own postal zone and a coveted sense of class; the ultrarich from around the globe own second homes here and old-money residents maintain friendships with the visiting film stars and royalty who frequent the area's exclusive luxury hotels and private clubs. Development has radically altered the once serene character of the village, but it has gained a cosmopolitan air that makes it a popular vacation resort.

Just off the coast, from La Jolla Cove to La Jolla Shores, lies the 533-acre, world-renowned San Diego-La Jolla Underwater Park Ecological Preserve (⇨ *see Sports and Outdoors, Chapter 13, for more information*).

Native Americans called the site Woholle, or "hole in the mountains," referring to the grottoes that dot the shoreline. The Spaniards changed the name to La Jolla (same pronunciation as La Hoya), "the jewel," which led to the nickname "Jewel City."

TOP ATTRACTIONS

FAMILY **Birch Aquarium at Scripps.** Affiliated with the world-renowned Scripps Institution of Oceanography, this excellent aquarium sits at the end of a signposted drive leading off North Torrey Pines Road and has sweeping views of La Jolla coast below. More than 60 tanks are filled with

BEST BEACHES

Framed in scenic coves and backed by dramatic cliffs, La Jolla's beaches are legendary. Challenging surf breaks, an underwater marine park, and expansive stretches of sand offer something for everyone. Look out over the sparkling waters to see seals frolicking in the surf, or lie back in the sand and watch hang gliders soar overhead.

⇨ *For more information on La Jolla's beaches, see Chapter 12, Beaches.*

Black's Beach. This secluded stretch of sand is considered one of the most beautiful beaches in San Diego. Black's Beach was clothing-optional for many years; although nudity is now prohibited by law, many people still shed their suits whenever the authorities are out of sight.

Children's Pool. This shallow bay was once a great place to bring the kids to swim. Nowadays, it's the best place on the coast to view harbor seals. Good thing kids enjoy that almost as much as playing in the waves.

La Jolla Cove. Truly the jewel of La Jolla, "the Cove" is one of the prettiest spots on the West Coast.

La Jolla Shores. One of the most popular beaches in San Diego, La Jolla Shores features a wide sandy beach and calm waves perfect for swimming and beginner surf lessons.

Torrey Pines State Beach. This popular beach is located just below the Torrey Pines State Reserve. Bring your picnic here after an invigorating hike in the reserve.

Windansea Beach. Incredible views, secluded spots, and world-class waves make this a favorite beach for couples and surfers.

6

colorful saltwater fish, and a 70,000-gallon tank simulates a La Jolla kelp forest. A special exhibit on sea horses features several examples of the species, plus mesmerizing sea dragons and a sea horse nursery. Besides the fish themselves, attractions include interactive educational exhibits based on the institution's ocean-related research and a variety of environmental issues. ✉ *2300 Expedition Way* ☎ *858/534–3474* 🌐 *www.aquarium.ucsd.edu* 🎫 *$18.50.*

FAMILY **La Jolla Caves.** It's a walk of 145 sometimes slippery steps down a tunnel to Sunny Jim, the largest of the caves in La Jolla Cove and the only one reachable by land. This is a one-of-a-kind local attraction, and worth the time if you have a day or two to really enjoy La Jolla. The man-made tunnel took two years to dig, beginning in 1902; later, a shop was built at its entrance. Today the Sunny Jim Cave Store, a throwback to that early shop, is still the entrance to the cave. The shop sells jewelry and watercolors by local artists. ✉ *1325 Coast Blvd. S* ☎ *858/459–0746* 🌐 *www.cavestore.com* 🎫 *$5.*

Fodor's Choice ★ **Torrey Pines State Natural Reserve.** *Pinus torreyana,* the rarest native pine tree in the United States, enjoys a 1,700-acre sanctuary at the northern edge of La Jolla. About 6,000 of these unusual trees, some as tall as 60 feet, grow on the cliffs here. The park is one of only two places in the world (the other is Santa Rosa Island, off Santa Barbara) where the Torrey pine grows naturally. The reserve has several hiking trails

DID YOU KNOW?

Goldfish Point in La Jolla is named after the garibaldi damselfish, which resemble goldfish, found in these waters. The garibaldi is California's official marine fish.

leading to the cliffs, 300 feet above the ocean; trail maps are available at the park station. Wildflowers grow profusely in spring, and the ocean panoramas are always spectacular. When in this upper part of the park, respect the restrictions. Not permitted: picnicking, smoking, leaving the trails, dogs, alcohol, or collecting plant specimens.

You can unwrap your sandwiches, however, at Torrey Pines State Beach, just below the reserve. When the tide is out, it's possible to walk south all the way past the lifeguard towers to Black's Beach over rocky promontories carved by the waves (avoid the bluffs, however; they're unstable). **Los Peñasquitos Lagoon** at the north end of the reserve is one of the many natural estuaries that flow inland between Del Mar and Oceanside. It's a good place to watch shorebirds. Volunteers lead guided nature walks at 10 and 2 on most weekends. ✉ *12600 N. Torrey Pines Rd.* ✢ *N. Torrey Pines Rd. exit off I–5 onto Carmel Valley Rd. going west, then turn left (south) on Coast Hwy. 101* ☎ *858/755–2063* 🌐 *www.torreypine.org* 🎫 *Parking $10–$20, varies by day of week and by season.*

University of California at San Diego. The campus of one of the country's most prestigious research universities spreads over 1,200 acres of coastal canyons and eucalyptus groves, where students and faculty jog, bike, and skateboard to class. If you're interested in contemporary art, check out the **Stuart Collection of Sculpture**—18 thought-provoking, site-specific works by artists such as Nam June Paik, William Wegman, Niki de St. Phalle, Jenny Holzer, and others arrayed around the campus. UCSD's **Price Center** has a well-stocked, two-level bookstore—the largest in San Diego—and a good coffeehouse, Perks. Look for the postmodern **Geisel Library**, named for longtime La Jolla residents Theodor "Dr. Seuss" Geisel and his wife, Audrey. Bring quarters for the parking meters, or cash or a credit card for the parking structures, because free parking is only available on weekends. **■ TIP→ There are two-hour free campus tours for the public Sunday at 2 pm from Gilman Entrance Information Center; reserve online or by calling (858) 534-4414 before noon on Thursday.** ✉ *La Jolla* ✢ *Exit I–5 onto La Jolla Village Dr. going west; take Gilman Dr. off-ramp to right and continue to information kiosk at campus entrance on Gilman Dr.* ☎ *858/534–4414 campus tour information* 🌐 *www.ucsd.edu.*

WORTH NOTING

Mount Soledad. La Jolla's highest spot can be reached by taking Nautilus Street to La Jolla Scenic Drive South, and then turning left. Proceed a few blocks to the park, where parking is plentiful and the views are astounding, unless the day is hazy. The top of the mountain is an excellent vantage point from which to get a sense of San Diego's geography: looking down from here you can see the coast from the county's northern border to the south far beyond downtown. ✉ *6905 La Jolla Scenic Dr. S.*

6

Salk Institute. The world-famous biological-research facility founded by polio vaccine developer Jonas Salk sits on 27 clifftop acres. The twin structures that modernist architect Louis I. Kahn designed in the 1960s in consultation with Dr. Salk used poured concrete and other low-maintenance materials to clever effect. The thrust of the laboratory–office complex is outward toward the Pacific Ocean, an orientation accentuated by a foot-wide "Stream of Life" that flows through the center of a travertine marble courtyard between the buildings. Architects-to-be and building buffs will enjoy the tours of the property; register online in advance. You can, however, stroll at will through the dramatic courtyard during the week—simultaneously monumental and eerie. ■ **TIP→ Architectural tours are offered weekdays at noon (reservations required, see website for details).** ✉ *10010 N. Torrey Pines Rd.* ☎ *858/453–4100* 🌐 *www.salk.edu* 🎫 *Free; $15 for tours* ⏲ *Closed weekends.*

7

POINT LOMA AND CORONADO

with Harbor and Shelter Islands, and Ocean Beach

Getting Oriented

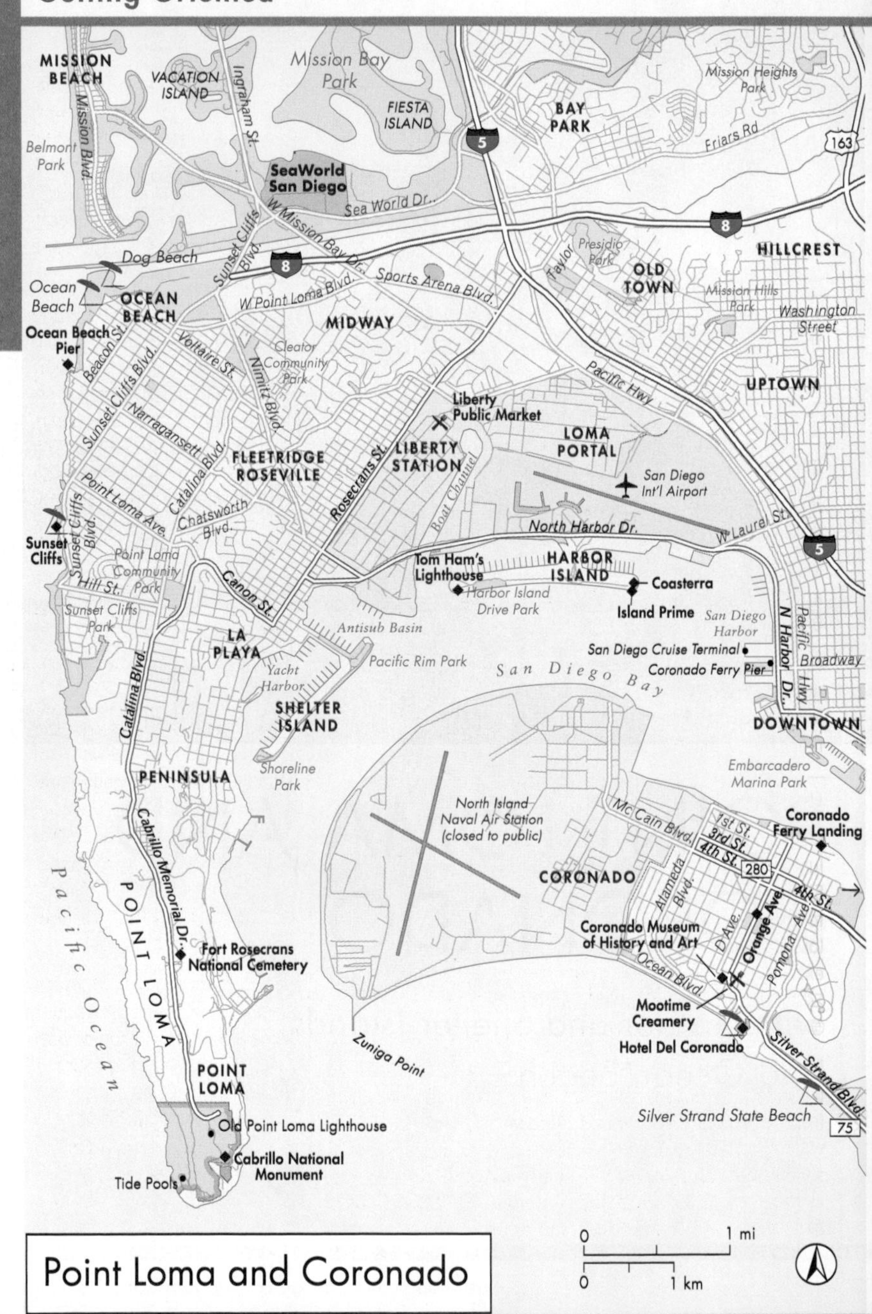

Point Loma and Coronado

TOP REASONS TO GO

Point Loma's panoramic views: Take in the view from the mountains to the ocean at Cabrillo National Monument. Come evening, watch the sun go down at Sunset Cliffs.

The Hotel Del: As the grande dame of San Diego, the historic Hotel Del Coronado charms guests and visitors alike with her graceful architecture and oceanfront setting.

Boating paradise: San Diego's picturesque marinas are filled with sportfishing charters and ultraluxury yachts.

Sandy beaches: The long stretches of sand on Coronado are family-friendly, while Fido will love swimming at Ocean Beach's Dog Beach.

Military might: From the endless rows of white headstones at Fort Rosecrans National Cemetery to the roar of fighter jets over North Island Naval Air Station, San Diego's strong military ties are palpable.

QUICK BITES

Liberty Public Market. This bustling market and food hall is just one of the latest additions to an ever-expanding Liberty Station, the historic mixed-use redevelopment of San Diego's former Naval Training Center. Vendors offer everything from lobster rolls to empanadas, gumbo, or tostadas, making it an excellent place to pop in for a quick but high-quality meal. ✉ *2820 Historic Decatur Rd., Point Loma* ☎ *619/487–9346* 🌐 *www.libertypublicmarket.com.*

Mootime Creamery. For a deliciously sweet pick-me-up, check out the rich ice cream, frozen yogurt, and sorbet made fresh daily on the premises. Dessert nachos made from waffle-cone chips are an unusual addition to an extensive sundae menu. Just look for the statue of Elvis on the sidewalk in front. ✉ *1025 Orange Ave., Coronado* ☎ *619/435–2422* 🌐 *www.mootime.com* 💳 *No credit cards.*

GETTING HERE

Bus 84 serves Cabrillo National Monument on Point Loma, although a transfer is required from Bus 28, near Shelter Island. For Harbor Island, the hearty can walk from the Embarcadero or catch a bus to the airport and walk from there.

Coronado is accessible via the arching blue 2.2-mile-long San Diego–Coronado Bay Bridge, which offers breathtaking views of the harbor and downtown. Alternatively, pedestrians and bikes can reach Coronado via the popular ferry service. Bus 904 meets the ferry and travels as far as Silver Strand State Beach. Bus 901 runs daily between the Gaslamp Quarter and Coronado.

PLANNING YOUR TIME

If you're interested in seeing the tide pools at Cabrillo National Monument, check ahead to find out when low tide will occur. Point Loma Seafoods or Liberty Public Market are good places to find yourself at lunchtime, and Sunset Cliffs Park is where you want to be at sunset.

A leisurely stroll through Coronado takes at least an hour, more if you stop to shop or walk along the family-friendly beaches. Whenever you come, if you're not staying overnight, remember to get back to the dock in time to catch the final ferry out at 9:30 (10:30 on weekends).

CABRILLO NATIONAL MONUMENT

(above) Point Loma from the water, as Cabrillo would have seen it in 1542. (lower right) Old Point Loma Lighthouse stood watch for 36 years. (upper right) Cabrillo's statue adorns the visitor center.

Cabrillo National Monument marks the site of the first European visit to San Diego, made by 16th-century explorer Juan Rodríguez Cabrillo. Cabrillo landed at this spot, which he called San Miguel, on September 15, 1542. Today the 160-acre preserve with its rugged cliffs and shores and outstanding overlooks is one of the most frequently visited of all the national monuments.

Catching sight of a whale from the cliffs of Cabrillo National Monument can be a highlight of a wintertime visit to San Diego. More accessible sea creatures can be seen in the tide pools at the foot of the monument's western cliffs.

On land, trails lead down the hillside through sagebrush and cactus. Overlook points offer spectacular views from the desert mountains to Downtown and beyond. The informative visitor center and the lighthouse give a historical perspective to this once-remote promontory.

SERVICE INFORMATION

The visitor center, located next to the statue of Cabrillo, presents films and lectures about Cabrillo's voyage, the sea-level tide pools, and migrating gray whales.

1800 Cabrillo Memorial Dr., Point Loma ☎ *619/557-5450* 🌐 *www.nps.gov/cabr* $10 per car, $5 per person entering on foot or by bicycle, admission good for 7 days. Park daily 9–5.

A HALF DAY AT CABRILLO NATIONAL MONUMENT

A **statue of Cabrillo** overlooks Downtown from a windy promontory, where people gather to admire the stunning panorama over the bay, from the snowcapped San Bernardino Mountains, 130 miles north, to the hills surrounding Tijuana to the south. The stone figure standing on the bluff looks rugged and dashing, but he is a creation of an artist's imagination—no portraits of Cabrillo are known to exist.

The moderately steep **Bayside Trail,** 2½ miles round-trip, winds through coastal sage scrub, curving under the cliff-top lookouts and taking you ever closer to the bay-front scenery. You cannot reach the beach from this trail and must stick to the path to protect the cliffs from erosion and yourself from thorny plants and snakes—including rattlers. You'll see prickly pear cactus and yucca, fragrant sage, and maybe a lizard, rabbit, or hummingbird. The climb back is long but gradual, leading up to the old lighthouse.

Old Point Loma Lighthouse's oil lamp was first lighted in 1855 and was visible from the sea for 25 miles. Unfortunately, it was too high above the cliffs to guide navigators trapped in Southern California's thick offshore fog. In 1891 a new lighthouse was built 400 feet below. The restored old lighthouse is open to visitors. An exhibit in the Assistant Keepers Quarters next door tells the story of the Old Lighthouse, the daily lives of the keepers, how lighthouses work, and the role they played in the development of early maritime commerce along the West Coast. On the edge of the hill near the old lighthouse sits a refurbished radio room containing displays of U.S. harbor defenses at Point Loma used during World War II.

■ TIP→ Restrooms and water fountains are plentiful, but, except for vending machines at the visitor center, there's no food. Exploring the grounds consumes time and calories; pack a picnic and rest on a bench overlooking the sailboats.

WHALE-WATCHING

The western and southern cliffs of Cabrillo National Monument are prime whale-watching territory. A sheltered **viewing station** has wayside exhibits describing the great gray whales' yearly migration from Baja California to the Bering and Chukchi seas near Alaska. High-powered telescopes help you focus on the whales' water-spouts. Whales are visible on clear days from late December through early March, with the highest concentration in January and February. Note that when the whales return north in spring, they are too far out in the ocean to be seen from the monument.

TIDE POOLS

When the tide is low you can walk on the rocks around saltwater pools filled with starfish, crabs, anemones, octopuses, and hundreds of other sea creatures and plants. Tide pooling is best when the tide is at its lowest, so call ahead or check tide charts online before your visit. Exercise caution on the slippery rocks.

Sightseeing
★★★☆☆
Nightlife
★☆☆☆☆
Dining
★★★☆☆
Lodging
★★★★☆
Shopping
★★★☆☆

Although Coronado is actually an isthmus, easily reached from the mainland if you head north from Imperial Beach, it has always seemed like an island and is often referred to as such. To the west, Point Loma protects the San Diego Bay from the Pacific's tides and waves. Both Coronado and Point Loma have stately homes, sandy beaches, private marinas, and prominent military installations. Nestled between the two, Harbor and Shelter islands owe their existence to dredging in the bay.

POINT LOMA

Updated by Claire Deeks van der Lee

The hilly peninsula of **Point Loma** curves west and south into the Pacific and provides protection for San Diego Bay. Its high elevations and sandy cliffs provide incredible views, and make Point Loma a visible local landmark. Its maritime roots are evident, from its long-time ties to the U.S. Navy to its bustling sport fishing and sailing marinas. The funky community of **Ocean Beach** coexists alongside the stately homes of **Sunset Cliffs** and the honored graves at **Fort Rosecrans National Cemetery.**

TOP ATTRACTIONS

Fodor's Choice ★ **Sunset Cliffs.** As the name suggests, the 60-foot-high bluffs on the western side of Point Loma south of Ocean Beach are a perfect place to watch the sun set over the sea. To view the tide pools along the shore, use the staircase off Sunset Cliffs Boulevard at the foot of Ladera Street.

The dramatic coastline here seems to have been carved out of ancient rock. The impact of the waves is very clear: each year more sections of the cliffs are posted with caution signs. Don't ignore these warnings—it's easy to slip in the crumbling sandstone, and the surf

BEST BEACHES

On Point Loma's beaches surfers and even dogs join in on the fun. The wide beaches and gentle waves of nearby Coronado have been entertaining families for well over a century.

⇨ *For more information on the beaches of Point Loma and Coronado, see Chapter 12: Beaches.*

POINT LOMA

Ocean Beach and Dog Beach. Humans head to the southern Ocean Beach to swim and sunbathe and surfers congregate around the Ocean Beach Pier. The small beach to the north, known as Dog Beach, is one of the few beaches in the country where dogs can play leash-free.

Sunset Cliffs. Popular with surfers and sunbathers seeking privacy among the small coves, this makes for a better viewpoint than swimming beach.

CORONADO

Coronado Beach. The north end of the beach, nearest the Naval Air Station, offers views of fighter jets landing and taking off as well as an off-leash dog area, while the south end has views of the Hotel Del Coronado. This is the widest expanse of beach in San Diego County and is great for families.

Silver Strand State Beach. The stretch of sand that runs along Silver Strand Boulevard from the Hotel Del Coronado to Imperial Beach is a perfect family gathering spot, with restrooms and lifeguards. The shallow shoreline and minimal crowds also make it a popular spot for kitesurfing.

7

can be extremely rough. The small coves and beaches that dot the coastline are popular with surfers drawn to the pounding waves. The homes along the boulevard—pink stucco mansions beside shingled Cape Cod–style cottages—are fine examples of Southern California luxury. ✉ *Sunset Cliffs Blvd., Point Loma.*

WORTH NOTING

Fort Rosecrans National Cemetery. In 1934, 8 of the 1,000 acres set aside for a military reserve in 1852 were designated as a burial site. More than 100,000 people are now interred here; it's impressive to see the rows upon rows of white headstones that overlook both sides of Point Loma just north of the Cabrillo National Monument. Some of those laid to rest at this place were killed in battles that predate California's statehood; the graves of the 17 soldiers and one civilian who died in the 1874 Battle of San Pasqual between troops from Mexico and the United States are marked by a large bronze plaque. Perhaps the most impressive structure in the cemetery is the 75-foot granite obelisk called the Bennington Monument, which commemorates the 66 crew members who died in a boiler explosion and fire on board the USS *Bennington* in 1905. The cemetery, visited by many veterans, is still used for burials. ✉ *Cabrillo Memorial Dr., Point Loma* ☎ *619/553–2084.*

OCEAN BEACH

At the northern end of Point Loma lies the chilled-out, hippyesque town of Ocean Beach, commonly referred to as "OB." The main thoroughfare of this funky neighborhood is dotted with dive bars, coffeehouses, surf shops, and 1960s diners. OB is a magnet for everyone from surfers to musicians and artists. Newport Avenue, generally known for its boisterous bars, is also home to San Diego's largest antiques district. Fans of OB applaud its resistance to "selling out" to upscale development, whereas detractors lament its somewhat scruffy edges.

TOP ATTRACTIONS

Ocean Beach Pier. This T-shape pier is a popular fishing spot and home to the Ocean Beach Pier Café and a small tackle shop. Constructed in 1966, it is the longest concrete pier on the West Coast and a perfect place to take in views of the harbor, ocean, and Point Loma Peninsula. Surfers flock to the waves that break just below. ✉ *1950 Abbott St., Ocean Beach.*

SHELTER ISLAND

In 1950 San Diego's port director decided to raise the shoal that lay off the eastern shore of Point Loma above sea level with the sand and mud dredged up during the course of deepening a ship channel in the 1930s and '40s. The resulting peninsula, **Shelter Island,** became home to several marinas and resorts, many with Polynesian details that still exist today, giving them a retro flair. Shelter Island is the center of San Diego's yacht-building industry, and boats in every stage of construction are visible in its yacht yards. A long sidewalk runs past boat brokerages to the hotels and marinas that line the inner shore, facing Point Loma. On the bay side, fishermen launch their boats and families relax at picnic tables along the grass, where there are fire rings and permanent barbeque grills. Within walking distance is the huge Friendship Bell, given to San Diegans by the people of Yokohama, Japan, in 1960 and the Tunaman's Memorial, a statue commemorating San Diego's once-flourishing fishing industry.

HARBOR ISLAND

Following the successful creation of Shelter Island, in 1961 the U.S. Navy used the residue from digging berths deep enough to accommodate aircraft carriers to build **Harbor Island**, a 1½-mile-long peninsula adjacent to the airport. Restaurants and high-rise hotels dot the inner shore while the bay's shore is lined with pathways, gardens, and scenic picnic spots. A pair of restaurants on the east end point, **Island Prime** and **Coasterra** *(880 Harbor Island Dr., 619/298–6802, 619/814–1300, www.cohnrestaurants.com)* offer killer views of the Downtown skyline. On the west point, the restaurant **Tom Ham's Lighthouse** *(2150 Harbor Island Dr., 619/291–9110, www.tomhamslighthouse.com)* has a U.S. Coast Guard–approved beacon shining from its tower and a sweeping view of San Diego's bayfront.

FERRY TO CORONADO

Coronado Ferry. Fifteen-minute ferries connect two locations along the Downtown San Diego waterfront with the Coronado Ferry Landing. Boats depart on the hour from the Broadway Pier on the Embarcadero and on the half hour from Coronado Ferry Landing to the Embarcadero during operating hours. Between the San Diego Convention Center and the Coronado Ferry Landing, service departs every 30 minutes during operating hours. Buy tickets at the Broadway Pier, 5th Avenue Landing, or Coronado Ferry Landing. To reach the heart of downtown Coronado from the Ferry Landing, you can rent a bike at the landing (or bring one with you), or catch the 904 shuttle bus that runs along Orange Avenue. Ferry service is operated by Flagship Cruises. ✉ *Broadway Pier on the Embarcadero, 990 N. Harbor Dr., San Diego* ☎ *619/234-4111, 619/234-4111* 🌐 *www.flagshipsd.com* 🎫 *Ferry $4.75 each way.*

CORONADO

As if freeze-framed in the 1950s, Coronado's quaint appeal is captured in its old-fashioned storefronts, well-manicured gardens, and charming **Ferry Landing Marketplace.** The streets of Coronado are wide, quiet, and friendly, and many of today's residents live in grand Victorian homes handed down for generations. Naval Air Station North Island was established in 1911 on Coronado's north end, across from Point Loma, and was the site of Charles Lindbergh's departure on the transcontinental flight that preceded his famous solo flight across the Atlantic. Coronado's long relationship with the U.S. Navy have made it an enclave for military personnel; it's said to have more retired admirals per capita than anywhere else in the United States.

TOP ATTRACTIONS

FAMILY **Coronado Ferry Landing.** This collection of shops at Ferry Landing is on a smaller scale than the Embarcadero's Seaport Village, but you do get a great view of the Downtown San Diego skyline. The little bayside shops and restaurants resemble the gingerbread domes of the Hotel Del Coronado. **Bikes and Beyond** (*619/435-7180, www.bikes-and-beyond.com*) rents bikes and surreys, perfect for riding through town and along Coronado's scenic bike path. ✉ *1201 1st St., at B Ave., Coronado* 🌐 *www.coronadoferrylandingshops.com.*

Fodor's Choice ★ **Hotel Del Coronado.** The Del's distinctive red-tile roofs and Victorian gingerbread architecture have served as a set for many movies, political meetings, and extravagant social happenings. It's speculated that the Duke of Windsor may have first met the Duchess of Windsor Wallis Simpson here. Eleven presidents have been guests of the Del, and the film *Some Like It Hot*—starring Marilyn Monroe, Jack Lemmon, and Tony Curtis—used the hotel as a backdrop.

The Hotel Del, as locals call it, was the brainchild of financiers Elisha Spurr Babcock Jr. and H. L. Story, who saw the potential of Coronado's virgin beaches and its view of San Diego's emerging harbor. It opened in 1888 and has been a National Historic Landmark since 1977. The History Gallery displays photos from the Del's early days, and books elaborating on its history are sold, along with logo apparel and gifts, in the hotel's 15-plus shops.

Although the pool area is reserved for hotel guests, several surrounding dining patios make great places to sit back and imagine the scene during the 1920s, when the hotel rocked with good times. Behind the pool area, an attractive shopping arcade features a classic candy shop as well as several fine clothing and accessories stores. A lavish Sunday brunch is served in the Crown Room. During the holidays, the hotel hosts Skating by the Sea, an outdoor beachfront ice-skating rink open to the public. **■ TIP→ Whether or not you're staying at the Del, enjoy a drink at the Sun Deck Bar and Grill in order to gaze out over the ocean—it makes for a great escape.**

Tours of the Del are $20 per person and take place on Monday, Wednesday, and Friday at 10:30, and weekends at 2; reservations are required. ✉ *1500 Orange Ave., at Glorietta Blvd., Coronado* ☎ *619/435–6611, 619/434–7242 tour reservations (through the Coronado Historical Association)* 🌐 *www.hoteldel.com.*

Fodor's Choice ★ **Orange Avenue.** Comprising Coronado's business district and its village-like heart, this avenue is surely one of the most charming spots in Southern California. Slow-paced and very "local" (the city fights against chain stores), it's a blast from the past, although entirely up to date in other respects. The military presence—Coronado is home to the U.S. Navy Sea, Air and Land (SEAL) forces—is reflected in shops selling military gear and places like **McP's Irish Pub,** at No. 1107. A family-friendly stop for a good, all-American meal, it's the unofficial SEALs headquarters. Many clothing boutiques, home-furnishings stores, and upscale restaurants cater to visitors with deep pockets, but you can buy plumbing supplies, too, or get a genuine military haircut at **Crown Barber Shop,** at No. 947. If you need a break, stop for a latte at the sidewalk café of **Bay Books,** San Diego's largest independent bookstore, at No. 1029. ✉ *Orange Ave., near 9th St., Coronado.*

WORTH NOTING

Coronado Museum of History and Art. The neoclassical First Bank of Commerce building, constructed in 1910, holds the headquarters and archives of the Coronado Historical Association, a museum, the Coronado Visitor Center, and the Coronado Museum Store. The museum's collection celebrates Coronado's history with photographs and displays of its formative events and major sights. A guided tour of the area's architecturally and historically significant buildings departs from the museum lobby on Wednesday mornings at 10:30 and costs $15 (reservations required). Alternatively, pick up a self-guided tour in the museum's shop. ✉ *1100 Orange Ave., at Park Pl., Coronado* ☎ *619/435–7242, 619/437–8788 walking tour reservations* 🌐 *www.coronadohistory.org* 🎟 *Free.*

8

WHERE TO EAT

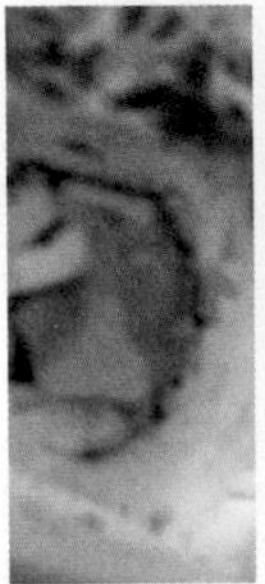

Updated by Archana Ram

San Diego is an up-and-coming culinary destination, thanks to its stunning Pacific Ocean setting, proximity to Mexico, diverse population, and the area's extraordinary farming community. Increasingly the city's veteran top chefs are being joined by a new generation of talented chefs and restaurateurs who are adding stylish restaurants with innovative food and drink programs to the dining scene at a record pace. Yes, visitors still are drawn to the San Diego Zoo and miles of beaches, but now they come for memorable dining experiences as well.

The city's culinary scene got a significant boost when San Diego emerged as one of the world's top craft beer destinations, with artisan breweries and gastropubs now in almost every neighborhood. San Diego also was on the cutting edge of the farm-to-table, Slow Food movement. Local sourcing is possible for everything from seafood to just-picked produce from a host of nationally recognized producers like Chino Farms and Carlsbad Aquafarm. The city's ethnically diverse neighborhoods with their modest eateries offering affordable authentic international cuisines add spice to the dining mix.

San Diego's distinct neighborhoods have their own dining personalities with friendly restaurants and bistros catering to every craving in this sun-blessed city. The trendy Gaslamp Quarter delights visitors looking for a broad range of innovative and international dining and nightlife, while bustling Little Italy offers a mix of affordable Italian fare and posh new eateries. Modern restaurants and cafés thrive in East Village, amid the luxury condos near PETCO Park.

The Uptown neighborhoods centered on Hillcrest—an urbane district with San Francisco flavor—are a mix of bars and independent restaurants, many of which specialize in ethnic cuisine. North Park, in particular, has a happening restaurant and craft beer scene, with just about every kind of cuisine you can think of, and laid-back prices to boot. And scenic La Jolla offers some of the best fine dining in the city with dramatic water views as an added bonus.

SAN DIEGO DINING PLANNER

DINING HOURS

Unless otherwise noted, the restaurants listed in this guide are open daily for lunch and dinner. Lunch is typically served 11:30 am to 2:30 pm, and dinner service in most restaurants begins at 5:30 pm and ends at 10 pm, though a number of establishments serve until 11 pm or later on Friday and Saturday night.

RESERVATIONS

We mention reservations in reviews only when they're essential or not accepted. But reservations are usually a very good idea especially for popular dining spots—reserve as far ahead as you can, and reconfirm when you arrive in town.

WHAT TO WEAR

In San Diego restaurants, generally a "come-as-you-are" attitude prevails. It's a casual city for men and women alike, but going-out dress is generally fashionable and fun, especially for celebratory or upscale dining. Very few dress-up places remain.

CHILDREN

Most San Diego restaurants welcome children and many have special kid's menus with food offerings targeted to younger palates and parent's pocketbooks. Some high-end and bar-oriented establishments may not be appropriate for children—if unsure, call the establishment for confirmation. The restaurants we recommend for families with children are marked with a symbol.

PARKING

With the boom of new apartments and condominiums Downtown and in Little Italy, street parking near many restaurants can be frustrating, especially in the evenings and on weekends. Valet ($5–$15) parking in front of many major restaurants is easy and convenient. Some valet parking is subsidized by restaurants; call ahead for parking offers and suggestions. There are several parking garages and lots throughout Downtown with prices that fluctuate depending on events. Savvy locals use the limited free parking with validation at Downtown's Horton Plaza. For major Downtown events where parking is impossible, consider parking for free at the Old Town transit center and get a quick San Diego Trolley ride to stops in Little Italy, East Village and the Gaslamp Quarter.

SMOKING

Smoking is banned in restaurants in California. The city of San Diego permits smoking on patios, but many restaurants don't allow it. Check before you go.

BEST BETS FOR SAN DIEGO DINING

With hundreds of restaurants from which to choose, how will you decide where to eat? We've selected our favorite restaurants by price, cuisine, and experience in the Best Bets list below. Bon appétit!

By Cuisine

AMERICAN

A.R. Valentien
Bankers Hill Bar and Restaurant
Café Gratitude
Craft & Commerce
Flower Child
Herb & Wood
Jimmy's Famous American Tavern
Rustic Root
Soda & Swine
Trust

ASIAN

Hane Sushi
Harney Sushi
Lanna
Sushi Ota
Tajima
Taka

GASTROPUBS

Panama 66
Slater's 50/50
Stone Brewing Bistro
Waypoint Public

ITALIAN

Bencotto
Bottega Americano
Buona Forchetta
Busalacci's A Modo Mio
Cucina Urbana
Davanti Enoteca
Piacere Mio

LATIN/MEXICAN

The Blind Burro
Carnitas' Snack Shack
Casa Guadalajara
Galaxy Taco
Puesto

SEAFOOD

Coasterra
Eddie V's Prime Seafood
George's at the Cove
Ironside Fish & Oyster
Jake's Del Mar
Point Loma Seafoods
Top of the Market

By Experience

BRUNCH

Bottega Americano
Café Chloe
The Cottage
Cucina Enoteca
Hash House A Go Go
Isabel's Cantina
Jake's Del Mar
The Little Lion
The Mission
Le Parfait Paris
The Patio on Lamont
Snooze
Tom Ham's Lighthouse

COCKTAILS

Bankers Hill Bar and Restaurant
Bottega Americano
Craft & Commerce
Galaxy Taco
The Hake
Herb & Wood
Juniper and Ivy
Prepkitchen
Rustic Root
Searsucker

DINING WITH KIDS

The Blind Burro
Flower Child
Hodad's
Liberty Public Market
Puesto
Slater's 50/50
Stone Brewing Bistro
Tender Greens
Waypoint Public

OUTDOOR DINING

Brockton Villa
Buona Forchetta
Café Chloe
The Crack Shack
Casa Guadalajara
George's at the Cove
Jimmy's Famous American Tavern
Panama66
The Prado

WATER VIEWS

Bali Hai
Coasterra
Eddie V's Prime Seafood
George's at the Cove
Island Prime and C Level
Jake's Del Mar
The Marine Room
Tom Ham's Lighthouse
Top of the Market

WINE LISTS

3rd Corner Wine Shop and Bistro
Cucina Enoteca
Cucina Urbana
George's at the Cove
The Hake
The Patio on Lamont

PRICES

Meals in San Diego popular dining spots can be pricey, especially in areas like La Jolla and the Gaslamp Quarter. Many other restaurants are very affordable or offer extra value with fixed-price menus, early-dining specials and early and late happy hours.

Prices in the reviews are the average cost of a main course at dinner or, if dinner is not served, at lunch.

WHAT IT COSTS

	$	$$	$$$	$$$$
Restaurants	under $18	$18–$27	$28–$35	over $35

Prices are per person for a main course or equivalent combination of smaller plates (e.g., tapas, sushi), excluding 8.75% sales tax.

RESTAURANT REVIEWS

Listed alphabetically within neighborhoods. Use the coordinate (✣ 1: B2) at the end of each listing to locate a site on the San Diego Dining and Lodging Atlas following this chapter.

DOWNTOWN

Downtown San Diego with its gleaming skyscrapers hugs the bayside Embarcadero and embraces some of the city's trendiest neighborhoods including East Village, the Gaslamp Quarter, and Little Italy. It's known around the world for a lively mix of nightlife, fine and casual dining, and ethnic specialty restaurants that reflect the city's multicultural heritage and growing culinary sophistication.

GASLAMP QUARTER

The historic heart of Downtown spread across 4th, 5th, and 6th avenues, the Gaslamp Quarter satisfies foodies, conventioneers, and nightclubbers with a wide choice of eateries and nightlife. Many are pricey, upscale chains and tourist-driven concepts, while others are stylish restaurants or casual gastropubs with local roots, featuring everything from sushi to authentic Mexican and aged steaks.

$$$ ITALIAN ✕ **BiCE Ristorante.** Well-heeled regulars and conventioneers consistently laud this sleek Downtown Italian restaurant. So do its peers in the California Restaurant Association, which in 2014 named it the best Italian fine-dining restaurant in the Gaslamp. "Bee-Chay" is known for its cheese bar, a robust collection of formaggi Italiani personally curated by the chef. **Known for:** extensive cheese bar; $5 happy hour appetizers. *Average main: $34* ✉ *425 Island Ave., Gaslamp Quarter* ☎ *619/239–2423* 🌐 *www.bicesandiego.com* ⏲ *No lunch* ✣ *1:D5.*

$ IRISH ✕ **The Field.** Get your Irish on at this family-run pub imported piece-by-piece from Ireland and reassembled in the Gaslamp Quarter. Home-style meals, traditional brews, and Irish music draw diners here from around the world. **Known for:** traditional Irish breakfast with Irish coffee; live music and televised sports most nights. *$ Average main: $15 ✉ 544 5th Ave., Gaslamp Quarter ☎ 619/232–9840 🌐 www.thefield.com ⊙ No breakfast weekdays ✢ 1:D5.*

$$$ AMERICAN ✕ **Jsix.** Distressed brick walls, rustic wood tables, and vintage waterfront photos suits the restaurant's commitment to modern all-natural coastal cuisine. Start with refreshing cocktails featuring ingredients like chamomile-infused gin and apricot liqueur, and pair it with shareable starters like the lemon-tinged hummus and warm beet salad with Manchego cheese flavored with serrano chili. **Known for:** modern spin on Filipino food; open-air rooftop with skyline views. *$ Average main: $30 ✉ 616 J St., Gaslamp Quarter ☎ 619/531–8744 🌐 www.jsixrestaurant.com ⊙ No lunch ✢ 1:E5.*

$ BAKERY ✕ **Le Parfait Paris.** Two French transplants have brought sleek Parisian style to Downtown San Diego. Rows of eclairs, tarts, croissants, colorful macarons, and the aroma of espresso greet patrons as they enter a minimalist space outfitted with glossy white tables, wooden chairs, and a Euro-chic crowd. **Known for:** traditional French chocolate-almond croissant; extensive macaron selection; dessert-like lavender honey latte. *$ Average main: $10 ✉ 555 G St., Gaslamp ☎ 619/245–4457 🌐 leparfaitparis.com ✢ 1:E4.*

$$$ AMERICAN ✕ **Rustic Root.** Comfort food gets a modern twist at this two-story restaurant, which serves a meat- and seafood-centric lineup downstairs and a slightly different menu on the rooftop that includes ahi poke tacos and fried chicken sliders. The rooftop is the real draw, thanks to whimsical details like rose gold mid-century chairs and animal topiaries. **Known for:** popular weekend brunch with am cocktails; bustling happy hour. *$ Average main: $30 ✉ 535 5th Ave., Gaslamp Quarter ☎ 619/955–5750 🌐 rusticroot.com ⊙ No weekday lunch ✢ 1:E5.*

$$$ AMERICAN ✕ **Searsucker.** Since opened by celebrity chef Brian Malarkey a few years ago, this high-energy flagship restaurant has become the Gaslamp's best for food and energetic atmosphere. Foodies from near and far savor Malarkey's upscale down-home fare like small plates of biscuits with spicy honey, duck fat fries, and shrimp and grits. **Known for:** detailed, home-inspired decor; crispy duck fat fries; late-night menu on Fridays and Saturdays from 11 pm–1 am. *$ Average main: $30 ✉ 611 5th Ave., Gaslamp Quarter ☎ 619/233–7327 🌐 www.searsucker.com ✢ 1:E4.*

$$ JAPANESE ✕ **Taka.** Pristine fish imported from around the world and presented creatively attracts crowds nightly to this intimate Gaslamp restaurant. Take a seat at the bar and watch one of the sushi chefs preparing appetizers, perhaps the monkfish liver with ponzu or spicy tuna tartar. **Known for:** uni sushi topped with wasabi; omakase tasting menu; upscale sake offerings. *$ Average main: $18 ✉ 555 5th Ave., Gaslamp Quarter ☎ 619/338–0555 🌐 www.takasushi.com ⊙ No lunch ✢ 1:E5.*

$$$ FRENCH ✕ **The Westgate Room.** Normandy-born chef Fabrice Hardel oversees the preparation of three meals a day at the Westgate Hotel, writing seasonal menus that mix French and Asian flavors. At dinner you're likely to find specials like grilled salmon with spring onions and shiitake mushrooms, as well as classics like Dover sole meunière and steak frites. **Known for:** opulent Sunday brunch buffet; regal, formal setting. *$ Average main: $29 ✉ Westgate Hotel, 1055 2nd Ave., Gaslamp Quarter ☎ 800/522–1564 🌐 www.westgatehotel.com ✢ 1:D3.*

EAST VILLAGE

Revived with the opening of the San Diego Padres stadium, PETCO Park, this trendy high-rise residential area is an eclectic mix of hip gastropubs, wine bars, and cafés serving everything from French bistro fare to Baja-Mexican, burgers, and artisan-baked bread.

$$ MODERN MEXICAN FAMILY

The Blind Burro. East Village families, baseball fans heading to or from PETCO Park and happy-hour bound singles flock to this airy restaurant with Baja-inspired food and drink. Traditional margaritas get a fresh kick from fruit juices or jalapeno peppers; other libations include sangrias and Mexican beers, all perfect pairings for house-made guacamole, ceviche, or salsas with chips. **Known for:** house margarita with fruit infusions; surf-and-turf Baja-style tacos; gluten-free menu. *Average main: $18 639 J St., East Village 619/795–7880 www.theblindburro.com 1:E5.*

$$ ITALIAN

Bottega Americano. A restaurant and gourmet market converge at this boisterous warehouse-like space that's outfitted in copper light fixtures, intricate tilework, and marble-topped tables. Dining here is as much a treat for the eyes as it is for the stomach, with house-made pastas, freshly shaken cocktails, and Italian meats that double as decor thanks to the open-kitchen culinary stations. **Known for:** shareable meatball trio; salami and cheese bar; all-you-can drink mimosas during brunch. *Average main: $22 1195 Island Ave., East Village 619/255–7800 www.bottegaamericano.com 1:F5.*

$$ FRENCH

Café Chloe. Parisian stylish, jewel-box cozy, and welcoming describe this neighborhood favorite on a busy street in artsy East Village. Surrounded by residential high-rises, hotels, and boutiques, this pretty spot offers French bistro-inspired breakfast, lunch, dinner, and brunch to residents, baseball fans, and courting couples. **Known for:** poached eggs with wild mushrooms on toast; traditional French desserts. *Average main: $22 721 9th Ave., East Village 619/232–3242 www.cafechloe.com 1:E4.*

$$$$ STEAKHOUSE

Cowboy Star. Special-occasion diners, conventioneers on expense accounts, and meat-loving locals haunt this surprisingly intimate dining room for great beef expertly prepared. The wood-and-brick interior has leather accents, Western landscapes, and vintage Old West photos, and servers wear white shirts and stylish denim aprons, all creating a relaxed urban-cowboy ambience. **Known for:** on-site butcher shop selling premium steaks, sausages, and charcuterie; 35-day dry-aged beef. *Average main: $53 640 10th Ave., East Village 619/450–5880 www.cowboystarsd.com No lunch Sat.–Mon. 1:E4.*

$ MEDITERRANEAN

The Kebab Shop. At its five San Diego locations—East Village, Little Italy, Mira Mesa, Mission Valley, and Rancho Bernardo—this fast-food Mediterranean eatery offers a mix of slowly cooked rotisserie meats, grilled to-order seafood, and crispy falafel served on plates of saffron rice or wrapped in grilled flatbread. Fresh tabouli, 10 Mediterranean salads, and baklava desserts round out the meals. **Known for:** rotisserie meats including chicken, beef, and lamb; creamy garlic yogurt sauce. *Average main: $8 630 9th Ave., East Village 619/525–0055 www.thekebabshop.com 1:E4.*

$ AMERICAN

The Mission. Healthy, creative dishes and a friendly staff make this art-filled East Village café a local favorite for breakfast and lunch. Hungry San Diegans wait 30 minutes or more to enjoy fluffy scrambled eggs with chicken apple sausage or strawberry banana pancakes with a side of eggs and bacon. **Known for:** Mexican-influenced breakfast dishes like chilaquiles; French toast made with house-baked cinnamon bread; busy breakfast scene especially on weekends. *$ Average main: $10 ✉ 1250 J St., East Village ☎ 619/232–7662 🌐 www.themissionsd.com ⏲ No dinner ✣ 1:F5.*

SAN DIEGO'S BOUNTY

Sunny San Diego is one of the premier agricultural areas in the country. Visit a farmers' market and have a taste: spring is the season for cherimoyas and strawberries, summer brings peaches and boysenberries, autumn is the time for apples and pears, and winter is abundant with tangerines and grapefruit. There's a different market every day of the week, including the popular Little Italy market. Check the list of farmers' markets around the county at 🌐 *www.sdfarmbureau.org.*

$ JAPANESE

Tajima. With four other locations in the city—Hillcrest, North Park, and two outposts in Kearny Mesa—Tajima has become a favorite source for ramen-hungry San Diegans. Climb into a cozy booth and order a Japanese craft beer or sake before diving into one of the five types of ramen—all of which come in hefty portions with affordable price tags—including an excellent vegan version with spinach noodles. **Known for:** Spicy Sesame Ramen with spicy ground pork and fried garlic; affordable and hefty portions; karaage fried chicken. *$ Average main: $10 ✉ 901 E St., East Village ☎ 619/431–5820 🌐 www.tajimasandiego.com ✣ 1:E4.*

LITTLE ITALY

One of San Diego's oldest and liveliest neighborhoods steeped in the city's Italian and Portuguese fishing culture, Little Italy is known for its bustling nightlife and Italian fine and casual dining mixed with trendy new eateries, dessert destinations, sidewalk cafés, and a few late-night bars.

$$ ITALIAN

Bencotto. The ultramodern Italian eatery with young Milanese owners gets cheers for its design and cuisine from hip Little Italy residents and visitors alike. Diners linger over drinks and house-made pasta at the friendly long bar and more intimate upstairs dining room. **Known for:** mix-and-match pasta entrées; gluten-free pasta options; traditional Italian tiramisu. *$ Average main: $24 ✉ 750 W. Fir St., Little Italy ☎ 619/450–4786 🌐 www.lovebencotto.com ⏲ No lunch Mon. ✣ 1:C2.*

$ VEGETARIAN Fodor's Choice ★

Café Gratitude. Food is served with a side of spiritual enlightenment at this plant-based eatery where friendly, Zen-ed out servers help you navigate the lengthy menu after offering the thoughtful question of the day. All menu items—including the potent wellness shots that can detoxify livers and boost immunity—are named after positive affirmations. **Known for:** bowl entrées with rice or quinoa; wellness tonic drinks; desserts that taste equally delicious without any dairy. *$ Average main: $16 ✉ 1980 Kettner Blvd., Little Italy ☎ 619/736–5077 🌐 www.cafegratitude.com ✣ 1:B2.*

$ AMERICAN FAMILY Fodor's Choice ★ **The Crack Shack.** Next to his successful fine dining restaurant, Juniper and Ivy, celebrity chef Richard Blais has opened this more casual eatery complete with a walk-up counter, picnic-style tables, a bocce ball court, and a giant rooster—a nod to the egg- and chicken-themed menu. Ingredients are sourced from high-quality vendors and used for sandwiches, of which the fried chicken varieties shine, as well as salads and sides like fluffy minibiscuits with a miso-maple butter and a Mexican spin on poutine. **Known for:** Señor Croque fried chicken sandwich with smoked pork belly; biscuits with miso-maple butter; all-outdoor seating with bocce ball court. *Average main: $12 2266 Kettner Blvd., Little Italy 619/795–3299 www.crack-shack.com 1:B1.*

$ MODERN HAWAIIAN **Craft & Commerce.** The redesigned Little Italy restaurant-bar oozes slightly surreal cool. Crammed book shelves line the walls, banquettes and mirrors are scrawled with sayings, and taxidermy appears in odd settings like a lion preying on a hog above the bar. **Known for:** wood-fired cuisine including grilled oysters and fire-roasted eggplant dip; refreshing craft cocktails infused with cucumber, grapefruit, or apple. *Average main: $15 675 W. Beech St., Little Italy 619/269–2202 www.craft-commerce.com 1:C2.*

$$ ITALIAN **Davanti Enoteca.** With its innovative, affordable Italian food, polished service, bustling bar scene and olive tree–shaded patio, this Chicago transplant is right at home in Little Italy. Sip the Davanti Spritz (Aperol, prosecco, and soda) while nibbling on their famous cheesy focaccia sweetened with honey or antipasti cheeses, meats, and olives. **Known for:** build you own Bloody Mary bar during weekend brunch; cheesy focaccia appetizer. *Average main: $18 1655 India St., Little Italy 619/237–9606 www.davantienoteca.com/sandiego No lunch weekends 1:C2.*

8

$ CAFÉ Fodor's Choice ★ **Extraordinary Desserts.** For Paris-perfect cakes and tarts embellished California-style with fresh flowers, head to this sleek, serene branch of Karen Krasne's pastry shop and café. The space with soaring ceilings hosts breakfasts, lunches, and light dinners, accompanied by a wide selection of teas, coffee, organic wines, and craft beers. **Known for:** blueberry coffee cake for breakfast; chocolate dulce de leche cake; housemade dips including onion dip and Parmesan pesto. *Average main: $14 1430 Union St., Little Italy 619/294–7001 www.extraordinarydesserts.com 1:C3.*

$$ AMERICAN **Herb & Wood.** Design lovers will fall for celebrity chef Brian Malarkey's sprawling restaurant, a former art store that has been refashioned into four luxe spaces in one. There's an entryway lounge, outdoor lounge, fireplace-dotted patio, and the main dining room, which is flanked by beaded chandeliers, lush banquettes, and paintings in rich jewel tones. **Known for:** roasted baby carrots with cashew sesame dukkah; soft-as-pillow oxtail gnocchi; the secret menu Parker House rolls topped with Maldon sea salt. *Average main: $20 2210 Kettner Blvd., Little Italy 619/955–8495 www.herbandwood.com No lunch 1:B1.*

$$ SEAFOOD **Ironside Fish & Oyster.** Hundreds of piranhas cover one wall of this soaring, nautically themed dining room dedicated to fresh seafood in all its guises. At the raw bar with its refrigerated metal top, a half dozen

or more varieties of oysters are available for slurping, along with drinks from the booklet size cocktail menu. (During weekday 3–6 happy hour, oysters are just $1 each.) Platters for sampling and sharing—a mix of oysters, shrimp, mussels, and lobster—can be ordered for up to eight people. **Known for:** $1 oysters during weekday happy hour; extensive cocktail menu. *Average main: $24 ✉ 1654 India St., Little Italy ☎ 619/269–3033 🌐 www.ironsidefishandoyster.com ⊕ 1:C2.*

$$$ MODERN AMERICAN

✕ Juniper and Ivy. Celebrity chef Richard Blais's addition to San Diego's restaurant scene fills an open-beamed space with seating for 250 and an open stainless-steel dream kitchen where diners can watch the chef and team in action. Blais sources local farm fresh ingredients for his "left coast cookery" with a molecular gastronomy twist. **Known for:** a California-Baja-inspired Carne Crudo Asada topped with quail eggs; an off-menu "In & Haute" burger; very shareable Yodel chocolate dessert. *Average main: $35 ✉ 2228 Kettner Blvd., Little Italy ☎ 619/269–9036 🌐 www.juniperandivy.com ⏲ Closed for lunch ⊕ 1:B1.*

$$ MODERN AMERICAN Fodor's Choice ★

✕ Prepkitchen Little Italy. Urbanites craving a hip casual setting and gourmet menu pack architectural salvage-styled Prepkitchen Little Italy, tucked upstairs above a busy corner in this thriving neighborhood. With first-date cocktails, after-work brews or birthday champagne, diners relish familiar choices like meatball sandwiches, chops, and pork belly with kimchi brussels. **Known for:** weekend brunch featuring popular chilaquiles dish; bacon-wrapped dates. *Average main: $23 ✉ 1660 India St., Little Italy ☎ 619/398–8383 🌐 www.prepkitchenlittleitaly.com ⊕ 1:C2.*

$$ ARGENTINE

✕ Puerto La Boca. Located on the fringe of Little Italy's bustling restaurant scene, this intimate Argentine steak house is named for a Buenos Aires waterfront neighborhood home to generations of Italian immigrants. The dimly lighted spot may not be as trendy as other dining spots here, but is still a romantic and comfortable destination for visitors and neighborhood regulars. **Known for:** tasty happy hour munchies; Argentinian wines. *Average main: $27 ✉ 2060 India St., Little Italy ☎ 619/577–4959 🌐 www.puertolaboca.com ⊕ 1:C1.*

EMBARCADERO AND MARINA DISTRICT

This walkable Downtown bayfront strip between the iconic County Administration building and the convention center offers visitors access to historic maritime destinations and dining options served up with spectacular views.

$$$ SEAFOOD Fodor's Choice ★

✕ Eddie V's Prime Seafood. Don't be put off by the name, or that it is part of a small chain. This fine-dining restaurant at the Headquarters at Seaport in Downtown has won a devoted following for classic seafood, casual but sophisticated settings, and nightly live jazz. **Known for:** wallet-friendly happy hour deals; indulgent truffled mac and cheese. *Average main: $34 ✉ 789 W. Harbor Dr., Embarcadero ☎ 619/615–0281 🌐 www.eddiev.com ⏲ No lunch ⊕ 1:B5.*

$ MEXICAN Fodor's Choice ★

✕ Puesto. Bold graffiti graphics, chandeliers with tangled telephone wires, and beat-heavy music energize this Downtown eatery that celebrates Mexican street food with a modern twist. Settle into one of the interior rooms or the sunny patio under orange umbrellas to sip margaritas and other specialty cocktails, Baja wines, or fruity Aguas frescas made daily. **Known for:** taco trio plates; unique Parmesan guacamole; fruit-infused margaritas made in-house. *Average main: $16 ✉ 789 W. Harbor Dr., Downtown ☎ 619/233–8880 🌐 www.eat-puesto.com ⊕ 1:B5.*

$$$ SEAFOOD **Top of the Market.** With its bay views from Point Loma to the Coronado Bridge, this upscale seafood house is just right for a memorable evening. The romantic teak-paneled dining room and a deck that sits over the water are popular spots for visitor splurges and locals celebrating special occasions. **Known for:** romantic atmosphere; smoked fish appetizers. *Average main: $35 ✉ 750 N. Harbor Dr., Embarcadero ☎ 619/232-3474 Top of the Market 🌐 www.sdtopofthemarket.com ⊕ 1:A4.*

BALBOA PARK AND BANKERS HILL

This area is defined by the sprawling world-famous park bursting with museums and gardens, but increasingly it is known for an exceptional contemporary dining scene, mostly located in the adjacent neighborhood of Bankers Hill. Choices range from delis, bistros, and trendy ethnic eateries to one of the city's top fine-dining restaurants.

BALBOA PARK

The culinary heart of this museum-filled urban park is the Prado, a stylish sit-down restaurant with a sunny patio. Other dining is limited to museum and zoo food stands, cafés, and food carts.

$ AMERICAN **Panama 66.** Adding a dose of hip to Balboa Park, this gastropub, located adjacent to the San Diego Museum of Art, offers a stylish pit-stop pre-theater or between museum-hopping. Decor is contemporary, with café-style seating, sculptures in the garden, and a view of the California Tower. **Known for:** rotating cocktails pegged to museum exhibits; live music most nights. *Average main: $11 ✉ 1450 El Prado, Balboa Park ☎ 619/696–1966 🌐 www.panama66.com ⊗ No dinner Mon. and Tues. ⊕ 2:E6.*

$$$ ECLECTIC **The Prado at Balboa Park.** Striking Spanish-Moorish details like painted ceilings and wrought-iron chandeliers are only part of the appeal of this lovely restaurant in the historic House of Hospitality. It also makes contemporary fare, friendly service and patio dining available to legions of museum- and theatergoers who come to Balboa Park. **Known for:** post-theater happy hour; Latin-inspired cocktails heavy on rum and citrus juices. *Average main: $28 ✉ 1549 El Prado, Balboa Park ☎ 619/557–9441 🌐 www.pradobalboa.com ⊗ No dinner Mon. ⊕ 2:F6.*

BANKERS HILL

The serene neighborhood west of Balboa Park is lined with upscale condos and some of the city's most enduring restaurants, like the legendary Bertrand at Mister A's. But the eclectic area is also home to French, Asian, and Italian eateries alongside divey bars and sandwich shops.

$$ MODERN AMERICAN Fodor's Choice ★ **Bankers Hill Bar and Restaurant.** The living wall of succulents, hip warehouse interior, and wine bottle chandeliers suit this vibrant restaurant where good times and great eats meet. An after-work crowd joins residents of this quiet stretch of Bankers Hill for happy hour cocktails, craft beers, and well-curated wines served from the zinc bar. **Known**

8

for: popular burger with truffle fries; soft-shell crab lettuce wraps with a vodka-infused batter; living plant wall on the sun-drenched patio. *Average main: $21 ✉ 2202 4th Ave., Bankers Hill ☎ 619/231–0222 ⊕ www.bankershillsd.com ⊙ No lunch ✣ 2:D6.*

$$$$ FRENCH **✕ Bertrand at Mister A's.** For decades, this venerable 12th-floor dining room with panoramic city and bay views has reigned as a celebratory fine-dining destination. Rejuvenated decor and cuisine, plus a popular happy hour, now draw after-work and pretheater crowds for cocktails and bites. **Known for:** affordable happy hour appetizers; tasty mocktail options. *Average main: $39 ✉ 2550 5th Ave., 12th fl., Bankers Hill ☎ 619/239–1377 ⊕ www.asrestaurant.com ✣ 2:D6.*

$$ ITALIAN Fodor's Choice ★ **✕ Cucina Urbana.** Twentysomethings mingle with boomers in this convivial Bankers Hill dining room and bar, one of the most popular restaurants in town. Country-farmhouse decor that mixes rolling pins with modern art looks and feels festive. **Known for:** vasi appetizer platters; seasonal polenta with ragu; ricotta-stuffed zucchini blossoms. *Average main: $20 ✉ 505 Laurel St., Bankers Hill ☎ 619/239–2222 ⊕ www.cucinaurbana.com ⊙ No lunch Sat.–Mon. ✣ 2:E6.*

$$ JAPANESE **✕ Hane Sushi.** An airy room with a sleek red-and-black Japanese aesthetic is the setting for pristine, contemporary sushi by Roger Nakamura, who spent years learning his craft from Yukito Ota of San Diego's beloved Sushi Ota restaurant. Though Hane (pronounced "hah-nay") is trendier than Ota and offers nonsushi options like kobe beef sashimi, sushi purists will be happy with the toro, golden eye snapper, octopus carpaccio, and special delicacies imported from Japan. **Known for:** Japan-sourced dishes like kobe beef sashimi; lunch specials under $15. *Average main: $26 ✉ 2760 5th Ave., Bankers Hill ☎ 619/260–1411 ⊙ Closed Mon. No lunch weekends ✣ 2:D6.*

OLD TOWN AND UPTOWN

With some notable exceptions, historic Old Town celebrates Mexican dining. Nearby, Uptown's diverse communities offers many bars, bistros, and gastropubs, along with ethnic restaurants ranging from Afghan and Indian to Russian and Vietnamese.

OLD TOWN

Touristy, but fun Mexican food reigns here with giant margaritas and heaping dishes of enchiladas, tacos, and carnitas (slow-cooked pork), and you'll also find a few gourmet gems celebrating other cuisines mixed in.

$ MEXICAN **✕ Casa Guadalajara.** It's a fiesta at this vibrant Mexican eatery, dotted with folk art, tile fountains, mariachi music, and a 300-year-old pepper tree that holds court on the charming patio. The menu reads like an encyclopedia of familiar favorites, like nachos, quesdaillas, fajitas, tacos, and enchiladas, along with plenty of vegetarian items—all in hefty portions. **Known for:** weekday happy hour with complimentary appetizers; traditional Mexican breakfast dishes. *Average main: $15 ✉ 4105 Taylor St., Old Town ☎ 619/295–5111 ⊕ www.casaguadalajara.com ✣ 2:A3.*

$ JAPANESE ✕ **Harney Sushi.** One of San Diego's most popular sushi restaurants is set in a sea of touristy Mexican dining spots in the heart of Old Town. Fans young and old flock here for refreshing sangrias, sustainable California-style sushi and modern Asian cuisine served up in a soft-lighted room rocked with DJ-driven R&B and '80s music. **Known for:** creative sushi rolls like the O'sider #55 with New York strip; specialty edamame in flavors like soy truffle and sesame bacon bonito. *Average main: $16 ✉ 3964 Harney St., Old Town ☎ 619/295–3272 www.harneysushi.com No lunch on weekends ✣ 2:A4.*

HILLCREST AND MISSION HILLS

Gay-friendly Hillcrest and the affluent enclave of Mission Hills are meccas for affordable and diverse dining experiences that may begin with hearty breakfasts and span lunches and dinners at trendy neighborhood dining spots before ending at nightclubs and late-night eateries in the wee hours of the morning.

$ SEAFOOD FAMILY ✕ **Blue Water Seafood Market & Grill.** Blame a television segment by Guy Fieri on "Diners, Drive-ins and Dives" for the long lines of fans from around the globe. But it's the fresh seafood cooked to order that keeps them coming back to this no-frills fish market and restaurant. **Known for:** beer-battered cod tacos; classic cioppino plate with mussels and clams, scallops, shrimp, and red snapper. *Average main: $15 ✉ 3667 India St., Mission Hills ☎ 619/497–0914 www.bluewaterseafoodsandiego.com ✣ 2:C5.*

$ CAFÉ ✕ **Bread & Cie.** San Diego's love affair with artisanal bread began when this artsy urban bakery and café opened its doors two decades ago. Owner Charles Kaufman, a former New Yorker and a filmmaker, gave Bread & Cie a sense of theater by putting bread ovens imported from France center stage. **Known for:** crusty black olive bread; traditional afternoon tea. *Average main: $8 ✉ 350 University Ave., Hillcrest ☎ 619/683–9322 www.breadandcie.com No dinner ✣ 2:D4.*

$$ AMERICAN FAMILY ✕ **Hash House A Go Go.** Big caloric portions and long lines are hallmarks of this comfort food destination. During prime weekend brunch hours, hungry regulars from near and far wait an hour or more for an indulgent meal in the crowded (and sometimes noisy) dining room decorated with farm machinery photos. **Known for:** decadent fried chicken eggs Benedict; huge portions perfect for sharing. *Average main: $20 ✉ 3628 5th Ave., Hillcrest ☎ 619/298–4646 www.hashhouseagogo.com No dinner Mon. ✣ 2:D5.*

$ INDIAN ✕ **India Palace.** Among a strip mall with fish tacos, fast-food burgers, and a bakery is this classy space dedicated to North Indian specialties. The dimly lit dining room is peppered with cultural touches like goddess statues and an Indian music soundtrack, with servers who are polite and attentive. **Known for:** chicken tikka masala; sweet mango lassi drink. *Average main: $15 ✉ 694 University Ave., Hillcrest ☎ 619/294–8886 www.indiapalacesd.com ✣ 2:E4.*

8

$ MOROCCAN ✕ **Kous Kous Moroccan Bistro.** With one sip of the bubbly "Moroccan Kiss" cocktail in this room lit with lanterns and draped in desert-hued fabrics, diners are transported to chef-owner Moumen Nouri's motherland. The culinary journey continues with tapas like the B'stila roll stuffed with orange blossom water–scented chicken and cinnamon almonds or classic zaalouk of roasted eggplant flavored with preserved lemons. **Known for:** traditional tagines with chicken, lamb, or vegetables; meatless Monday special. *Average main: $18 3940 4th Ave., Hillcrest 619/295–5560 www.kouskousrestaurant.com No lunch 2:D4.*

$ MEXICAN ✕ **Lucha Libre Gourmet Taco Shop.** Named for a form of Mexican wrestling, this taco shop with its hot-pink walls and shiny booths was famous mostly for its lack of parking until it appeared on the Travel Channel's "Man v. Food." Then long lines of burrito-crazed fans began forming outside the walk-up window for lunch. **Known for:** Tap Me Out taco with fried cheese; Champion nachos with french fries; lively and festive interior seating. *Average main: $7 1810 W. Washington St., Mission Hills 619/296–8226 www.tacosmackdown.com 2:B5.*

$$ MODERN AMERICAN Fodor's Choice ★ ✕ **The Red Door.** Farm-to-table at this cottage-comfy Mission Hills restaurant starts at owners Trish and Tom Watlington's extensive home garden that supplies half the needed produce and herbs. Local organic growers and ranchers add everything else showcased on the constantly changing menu. **Known for:** strong commitment to farm-to-table sourcing; melt-in-your-mouth bone marrow–soaked shrimp; sticky toffee pudding with house-made toffee sauce. *Average main: $23 741 W. Washington St., Mission Hills 619/295–6000 www.thereddoorsd.com/ No lunch weekends 2:C4.*

$ THAI ✕ **Saffron.** Outdoor tables on a narrow sidewalk and inexpensive prices make this and the neighboring Karina's Ceviches & More takeout a standout. The simple menu by Bangkok-born chef-owner Su-Mei Yu has noodle soups; stir-fried noodles with chicken, beef, pork, or shrimp; and a couple of uncommon Vietnamese and Thai-Indian noodle dishes bathed with aromatic sauces: the spicy "Eslam" dish is made of wide rice noodles stir-fried with chicken or tofu in a turmeric sauce. **Known for:** Thai grilled chicken; health-focused dishes like the Brain-Booster Stir-Fry. *Average main: $8 3731 India St., Mission Hills 619/574–7737 www.saffronsandiego.com 2:B5.*

$ VIETNAMESE ✕ **Saigon on Fifth.** This upscale Vietnamese restaurant, open until 3 am, is a favorite for special family gatherings and date nights. It's also where the hipsters go for a steaming hot bowl of pho soup after bar-hopping in Hillcrest. **Known for:** wallet-friendly pho; sophisticated surrounds. *Average main: $16 3900 5th Ave., Hillcrest 619/220–8828 www.saigonon5th.com 2:D4.*

$ AMERICAN ✕ **Snooze.** Bright "Brady Bunch" decor, plus plenty of sunshine and fresh air pouring through windows and skylights are cheery wake-ups for diners at this hip neighborhood haunt for pancakes and lattes. Expect long waits for a table, especially on weekends; free coffee helps the time pass. **Known for:** pineapple upside-down pancakes; half-order Benedicts; boozy brunch drinks. *Average main: $11 3940 5th Ave., Hillcrest 619/500–3344 www.snoozeeatery.com 2:D4.*

$ AMERICAN

✕ **Starlite.** This trendy 21-and-over establishment attracts a diverse and discerning crowd to a somewhat quiet stretch of India Street with its solid seasonal fare and understated mid-century vibe. At the center of the intimate, award-winning interior is a chandelier made of stainless steel tubes cut to reveal soft, twinkling lights. **Known for:** creamy and carb-filled mac and cheese; signature Moscow Mules; late-night dining. *Average main: $15 ✉ 3175 India St., Mission Hills ☎ 619/358–9766 ⊕ www.starlitesandiego.com ✦ 2:C6.*

$$ MODERN AMERICAN Fodor's Choice ★

✕ **Trust.** Old-school wood-fire techniques meet modern architecture in this busy bistro where comic book–style art covers the concrete walls and the bottle-lined bar beckons locals and visitors alike. Dishes feature popular items like the braised oxtail raviolini with horseradish and whipped ricotta, and wood-grilled cauliflower dressed in a curry vinaigrette. **Known for:** five-hour braised oxtail raviolini; roomy outdoor patio. *Average main: $20 ✉ 3752 Park Blvd., Hillcrest ☎ 619/795–6901 ⊕ www.trustrestaurantsd.com ✦ 2:F4.*

NORTH PARK AND SOUTH PARK

Hip gastropubs, community bistros, health-conscious eateries, and soul-satisfying pizza—all often served with the city's acclaimed craft beers—thrive in these artsy, eclectic, and rejuvenated neighborhoods adjacent to Balboa Park.

$ ITALIAN FAMILY Fodor's Choice ★

✕ **Buona Forchetta.** A golden-domed pizza oven, named Sofia after the owner's daughter, delivers authentic Neapolitan-style pizza to fans who often line up for patio tables at this dog- and kid-friendly Italian restaurant in South Park. Slices of classic margherita or truffle-flavored mozzarella and mushroom pizzas make a meal or can be shared, but don't miss the equally delicious appetizers like the tender calamari or succulent artichokes, heaping salads, or fresh pastas, including a hearty lasagna, delicate ravioli, or gnocchi with pesto. **Known for:** house red wine; bubbly Neapolitan-style pizzas; bustling patio. *Average main: $14 ✉ 3001 Beech St., South Park ☎ 619/381–4844 ⊕ www.buonaforchettasd.com ⊙ No lunch Mon. and Tues. ✦ 2:H6.*

$ MODERN MEXICAN

✕ **Carnitas' Snack Shack.** Long lines snake down the block outside this quintessential San Diego dining spot where chef-owner Hanis Cavin serves fast-casual cuisine based on the humble hog. He's so pork-focused that he sports a hog tattoo on his arm and plays with a pet mini-pig named Carnitas. **Known for:** decadent Triple Threat sandwich; casual and roomy outdoor seating. *Average main: $8 ✉ 2632 University Ave., North Park ☎ 619/294–7675 ⊕ www.carnitassnackshack.com ✦ 2:G4.*

$ VEGETARIAN

✕ **Kindred.** Pink paisley wallpaper and marble-topped tables stand among skull prints, Gothic art, and a giant ram head in this busy restaurant-bar—emphasis on the bar. The menu is heavy on beverages, with aperitifs, tropical cocktails, and a group-friendly punch bowl made of gin, curaçao, vermouth, lemon, ginger, pineapple, and sparkling rosé. **Known for:** Memphis BBQ jackfruit sandwich; vegan cheese board. *Average main: $12 ✉ 1503 30th St., South Park ☎ 619/546–9653 ⊕ www.barkindred.com ⊙ No lunch ✦ 2:H6.*

8

$ MIDDLE EASTERN FAMILY Fodor'sChoice ★ **Mama's Bakery & Lebanese Deli.** This small converted house with about 10 tables serves some of the best authentic Lebanese fare in San Diego County. It's not fancy dining. **Known for:** shawarma sandwiches slathered in garlic sauce; sizable selection of Middle Eastern desserts. *Average main: $9 ✉ 4237 Alabama St., North Park ☎ 619/688–0717 🌐 www.mamasbakery.net ⊗ No dinner weekends ✣ 2:F3.*

$ ITALIAN **Piacere Mio.** Fresh homemade pasta served as the diner wants it is the mantra at this coffee shop turned cozy Italian restaurant. Opt for indoor seating, which offers a charming, old-world feel, with warm lighting, wood beam ceilings, and exposed brick. **Known for:** make-it-your-own pasta menu; sizable portions. *Average main: $15 ✉ 1947 Fern St., South Park ☎ 619/794–2543 🌐 www.piaceremiosd.com ✣ 2:H6.*

$$ MODERN AMERICAN **Urban Solace.** Comforts abound at this popular casual North Park eatery with its long bar, communal tables, and covered patio. Regulars who live in this revived neighborhood bustling with galleries, bars, and trendy restaurants flock to chef-owner Matt Gordon's modern comfort food with a Southern accent, all created with all-natural meats and sustainably sourced ingredients. "Not Your Mama's Meatloaf" mixes lamb and pork with figs, almonds, and feta, while pulled chicken is served with buttermilk dumplings and gravy. **Known for:** giant brunch cinnamon rolls with cream cheese frosting; lively bluegrass brunch. *Average main: $24 ✉ 3823 30th St., North Park ☎ 619/295–6464 🌐 www.urbansolace.net ✣ 2:H4.*

$ MODERN AMERICAN FAMILY **Waypoint Public.** Kids romp in their own picket fence–enclosed play area while parents join fellow neighborhood residents in sophisticated meals in this beer-centric casual restaurant. A unique 30-tap system serves up West Coast craft brews; hundreds more from around the world can be had by the bottle. **Known for:** unique 30-tap craft beer setup; kid-friendly ambience. *Average main: $16 ✉ 3794 30th St., North Park ☎ 619/255–8778 🌐 www.waypointpublic.com ⊗ No weekday lunch ✣ 2:H4.*

MISSION BEACH AND PACIFIC BEACH

This sprawling area is all about great views of the water, sandy beaches, and relaxation. Most of the restaurants here are casual spots that diners can visit in T-shirts, shorts, and flip-flops. Food is similarly laid-back. Burgers and tacos are easy to find, but so are sushi, Mexican, and Thai food. Many of the restaurants here are bars at heart.

PACIFIC BEACH

Streets closest to the ocean in San Diego's largest beach community can be party central for visitors and locals who jam-pack a wide range of restaurants and bars reflecting the casual surf and beach culture.

$ ECLECTIC **Isabel's Cantina.** The dragon above the rustic door announces this is no typical cantina. Instead chef and cookbook author Isabel Cruz has blended Asian and Latin fair with a healthy outlook that suits her youthful Pacific Beach clientele. **Known for:** Mexican-inspired breakfast menu; a healthy-meets-boozy pineapple orange kale mimosa. *Average main: $17 ✉ 966 Felspar St., Pacific Beach ☎ 858/272–8400 🌐 www.isabelscantinasd.com ✣ 3:C5.*

CLOSE UP

Talking Tacos

Even though terms like taco, burrito, enchilada, and tostada are as common as macaroni and cheese to San Diegans, don't count on any residents to agree on where to find the best ones. That's because tacos are as individual as spaghetti sauce and come in endless variations from small, authentic Mexico City–style tacos to Cal-Mex versions in crunchy shells topped with cheddar cheese.

The most traditional style of taco features a small soft corn tortilla pressed from corn masa dough and filled with shredded beef, carne asada (roasted beef), braised tongue in green sauce, spicy marinated pork, or deep-fried fish or seafood. Tortillas made from white flour are out there, too, but they're not nearly as tasty.

Garnishes usually include a drizzle of salsa and a squeeze of tart Mexican lime (a small citrus similar to the Key lime that's juicier than the large lime commonly found in the United States), along with chopped cilantro and onion. Whole radishes topped with lime juice and a sprinkle of salt are served on the side.

$ AMERICAN FAMILY

Kono's Surf Club Café. Surfers, bicyclists, and sun worshippers visiting or living in Pacific Beach line up at the counter of this casual seaside café for hearty breakfasts and lunches. Some chow down inside surrounded by surfing decor, while others watch waves crash from the outdoor patio. **Known for:** huge breakfast portions; great people-watching along the boardwalk. *Average main: $7 ✉ 704 Garnet Ave., Pacific Beach ☎ 858/483–1669 No credit cards No dinner ☞ Cash only ⊕ 3:B5.*

8

$ THAI

Lanna. Recipes passed down for generations yield the fresh, vibrant dishes from various regions served at this flower-filled Thai restaurant tucked in a strip mall on the eastern edge of Pacific Beach. Among the house specialties are "Talay Thai," a batter-fried fish fillet topped with a green-apple salad, onions, and cashews; spice-braised duck in a deep, dark, wonderfully fragrant red curry sauce; and "Spicilicious Seafood," a mix of shrimp, squid, mussels, and scallops stir-fried in a chili-garlic sauce. **Known for:** affordable weekday lunch specials; homemade ice cream. *Average main: $16 ✉ 4501 Mission Bay Dr., Pacific Beach ☎ 858/274–8424 ⊕ www.lannathai-cuisine.com ⊕ 3:D4.*

$$ MODERN AMERICAN FAMILY

The Patio on Lamont. Soft breezes blow through the stylish patio of this modern California bistro that straddles a quiet side street in Pacific Beach. Seated beneath a "green wall" of tropical plants, tourists join locals, many with pets in tow, for breakfast, lunch, and dinner, the popular weekday 3 to 6 happy hour and weekend brunch. **Known for:** buzzy brunch scene; plant-filled decor. *Average main: $22 ✉ 4445 Lamont St., Pacific Beach ☎ 858/412–4648 ⊕ www.thepatioonlamont.com ⊕ 3:D5.*

$$ SUSHI Fodor's Choice ★

Sushi Ota. One fan called it "a notch above amazing"—an accolade not expected for a Japanese eatery wedged in a strip mall in Pacific Beach. But it's a destination for lovers of high-quality, superfresh raw fish from around San Diego and abroad. Japanese visitors frequently call for reservations before leaving home. **Known for:** velvety hamachi belly; sea urchin specials. *Average main: $25* *4529 Mission Bay Dr., Pacific Beach* *858/270–5670* *www.sushiota.com* *No lunch Sat.–Mon.* *3:D4.*

LA JOLLA

La Jolla is one of the most scenic and prosperous coastal communities in the county, so it's no surprise that it has some of the area's top culinary gems. Expect five-star meals with Pacific views as well as a few low-key finds.

LA JOLLA

This tony enclave that hugs the ocean from the Bird Rock area to Torrey Pines draws diners from around the world to experience an amazing collection of relaxed fine and casual dining establishments, ranging from classic French bistro fare to California modern cuisine. Ocean-view restaurants along Prospect Street are very popular, but there are many affordable neighborhood favorites that serve tasty food in attractive settings like La Jolla Cove.

$$$$ AMERICAN Fodor's Choice ★

A.R. Valentien. Champions of in-season, fresh-today produce and seafood, executive chef Jeff Jackson and chef de cuisine Kelli Crosson have made this cozy room in the luxurious, Craftsman-style Lodge at Torrey Pines one of San Diego's top fine dining destinations. Their food combinations are simultaneously simple and delightfully inventive—duck breast with celery root risotto; ahi tuna with grapefruit and crispy quinoa; or swordfish with chorizo and charred scallion salsa verde. **Known for:** red-wine braised short rib; creamy chicken liver pâté; patio that overlooks the resort pool and the famed 18th green at Torrey Pines South Course. *Average main: $38* *The Lodge at Torrey Pines, 11480 N. Torrey Pines Rd., La Jolla* *858/777–6635* *www.arvalentien.com* *3:B1.*

$$$ MODERN FRENCH

Bistro du Marche. Formerly known as Tapenade, acclaimed chef Jean Michel Diot has reinvented his La Jolla fixture with a new look but much of the same vibe. The airy dining room, lined with black-and-white photos of France, is comfortable, if not romantic, an ideal setting for the ever-changing menu that emphasizes fresh ingredients sourced from the Sunday farmers' market that holds court in front of the restaurant. **Known for:** French classics like duck confit; poutine and $8 wine during happy hour. *Average main: $30* *7437 Girard Ave., La Jolla* *858/551–7500* *www.bistrodumarche.net* *No lunch Sat.–Tues.* *3:A2.*

$$ AMERICAN

Brockton Villa. One of the few restaurants with a view that's also worth eating at, Brockton Villa is tucked in an historic cottage on a hillside above La Jolla Cove. Food is served all day, but this dining spot excels at brunch and lunch when ocean views are best. **Known for:** prime ocean views; orange-scented Coast French Toast. *Average main: $20* *1235 Coast Blvd., La Jolla* *858/454–7393* *www.brocktonvilla.com* *3:B2.*

$ AMERICAN

Cody's La Jolla. This cozy dining spot in a converted house a block from beautiful La Jolla Cove and Park serves up ocean views and tasty contemporary American fare for well-heeled La Jollans and tourists alike. The atmosphere is laid-back and beach-festive, especially on the front-porch patio cooled by sea breezes. **Known for:** crab cake Benedicts; patio with ocean views. *Average main: $13 8030 Girard Ave., La Jolla 858/459–0040 www.codyslj.com No dinner 3:A2.*

$ AMERICAN **The Cottage.** A cozy beach cottage sets the stage for American comfort food with a California twist at this La Jolla staple. The restaurant serves lunch and dinner, but it's the well-loved daily breakfast that has locals and visitors happily queuing—sometimes up to two hours on weekends. **Known for:** daily breakfast that people line up for; treats for those waiting in line; great patio seating. *Average main: $13 7702 Fay Ave., La Jolla 858/454–8409 www.cottagelajolla.com No dinner Sun. and Mon. 3:A2.*

$ SEAFOOD **El Pescador Fish Market & Restaurant.** This bustling fish market and café in the heart of La Jolla Village has been popular with locals for its superfresh fish for more than 30 years. Order the char-grilled, locally caught halibut, swordfish, or yellowtail on a toasted torta roll to enjoy in-house or to-go for an oceanfront picnic at nearby La Jolla Cove. **Known for:** superfresh fish; bustling on-site fish market. *Average main: $15 634 Pearl St., La Jolla 858/456–2526 www.elpescadorfishmarket.com 3:A2.*

$$ MODERN MEXICAN **Galaxy Taco.** Local chef icon Trey Foshee of George's at the Cove has opened this casual eatery, which focuses on high-quality Mexican food like tacos made from non-GMO heirloom corn with elevated fillings like charred shishito peppers and parsnip chips served in a colorful cantina. Start with shareables like the birria-steamed clams or blue corn quesadilla with sweet potato and arugula before choosing from mains that cover tamales, enchiladas, and a wood-grilled carne asada. **Known for:** housemade, high-end blue corn tortillas; smoky mezcal-cocktails. *Average main: $24 2259 Avenida de la Playa, La Jolla 858/228–5655 www.galaxytaco.com 3:A2.*

$$$$ AMERICAN Fodor's Choice ★ **George's at the Cove.** La Jolla's ocean-view destination restaurant includes three dining areas: California Modern on the bottom floor, the Level2 bar in the middle, and Ocean Terrace on the roof. The sleek main dining rooms presents elegant preparations of seafood, beef, and venison, which star-chef Trey Foshee enlivens with amazing local produce. **Known for:** beef tartare with 67-degree egg; excellent ocean views; attention to detail for special occasion dinners. *Average main: $37 1250 Prospect St., La Jolla 858/454–4244 www.georgesatthecove.com 3:B2.*

$$$ INTERNATIONAL **The Hake.** A 2016 renovation has brought on a new chef, menu, and ocean view at this restaurant situated in pedestrian-friendly La Jolla Village. The clean, elevated design features a custom-made copper bar, spacious terrace, and polished woods. **Known for:** huge windows overlooking La Jolla Cove; global-inspired cuisine including a pork-free opah chorizo. *Average main: $32 1250 Prospect St., La Jolla 858/454–1637 www.thehake.com No lunch 3:B2.*

$$$$ MODERN AMERICAN **The Marine Room.** It's hard to dine closer to the Pacific than at this venerable La Jolla Shores mainstay. Two-story-tall windows capture beachgoers, kayakers, snorkelers, and swooping gulls. **Known for:**

well-priced afternoon happy hours; High Tide breakfast buffet. *Average main: $38 2000 Spindrift Dr., La Jolla 866/644–2351 www.marineroom.com 3:B2.*

$ CAFÉ FAMILY **Michele Coulon Dessertier.** The desserts are magnificent at this small, charming shop in the heart of La Jolla, where dessertier Michele Coulon confects wonders, using organic produce and imported chocolate. Snack on cookies, cupcakes, brownies, chocolate-dipped strawberries, and mini-desserts. **Known for:** Instagram-worthy presentation; the buttercream- and berry-filled Gateau Aileen. *Average main: $12 7556 Fay Ave., Suite D, La Jolla 858/456–5098 www.dessertier.com Closed Sun. No dinner 3:A2.*

$$$ AMERICAN **Nine-Ten.** Accolades continue to roll in for executive chef Jason Knibb—winner of an award of excellence by *Wine Spectator* in 2016—whose seasonal menus for breakfast, lunch, and dinner are magnets for travelers and San Diegans seeking a memorable meal. Located at La Jolla's Grande Colonial Hotel, the space encompasses a cozy ground-floor dining room, bar, and ocean-glimpse, covered patio. **Known for:** juicy Jamaican jerk pork belly; breezy patio with La Jolla Village views. *Average main: $34 Grande Colonial Hotel, 910 Prospect St., La Jolla 858/964–5400 www.nine-ten.com No lunch Sun. 3:A2.*

$ ITALIAN **Osteria Romantica.** Two guys who grew up in Italy founded this cozy La Jolla Shores eatery a decade ago to bring authentic Italian food to residents and visitors of the walkable neighborhood and its nearby beaches. Italian opera plays in the dining room where friendly servers deliver house-made breads, pastas, and sauces. **Known for:** tender lamb pappardelle; cozy Italian vibe. *Average main: $17 2151 Ave. de la Playa, La Jolla 858/551–1221 www.osteriaromantica.com 3:B2.*

$$$ MODERN AMERICAN **Whisknladle.** This hip eatery has won national acclaim for its combination of casual comfort and a menu of ever-changing local fare. In nice weather, request a patio table to enjoy the people-watching along with cocktails like the Earl of Venice with vodka-infused Earl Grey tea or house Sangria. **Known for:** brunch served Friday through Sunday; craft cocktails including their seasonal mimosas. *Average main: $29 1044 Wall St., La Jolla 858/551–7575 www.whisknladle.com No lunch 3:A2.*

POINT LOMA, OCEAN BEACH, AND SHELTER AND HARBOR ISLANDS

Bays, beaches, and cliffs are the stars of these diverse coastal communities, where low-key seafood spots mingle with romantic eateries, quaint bistros, and lively beer bars. Along with Harbor and Shelter Islands, Point Loma caters to sailing enthusiasts, while Ocean Beach has retained its bohemian beach town vibe.

POINT LOMA

Once a neighborhood of tuna-fishing families, this famous peninsula is now a wealthy enclave where residents enjoy charming neighborhood restaurants, and new upscale dining spots clustered in walkable Liberty

Station, and Harbor and Shelter Islands. Although there's some fine dining here, most eateries are casual and cater to laid-back locals, sun-loving tourists, and sailing enthusiasts.

$ CAFÉ FAMILY

Con Pane Rustic Breads & Cafe. The scent of fresh-baked bread whets the appetite of customers at this Liberty Station bakery and café seeking rustic scones or raisin brioche cinnamon rolls for breakfast or one of the hearty lunch sandwiches like almost grilled cheese with melted brie and gorgonzola on warm rosemary olive oil bread. All can be enjoyed inside or on the sunny patio with hot or cold drinks including the house-made lemonade. **Known for:** fluffy raisin brioche cinnamon rolls; sandwiches served in half portions. *Average main: $7 2750 Dewey Rd., Point Loma 619/224–4344 Closed Tues. and Wed. 4:C1.*

$$ AMERICAN

Jimmy's Famous American Tavern. Tucked bayside between Harbor and Shelter islands, Jimmy's (JFAT for short) draws hungry boaters and sea-lovers with its marina views and all-American comfort food. The interior blends lots of varnished wood with industrial-chic I-beams and garage-style doors, plus there's a beach with a patio fire pit. **Known for:** Bloody Marys during weekend brunch; nine types of burgers. *Average main: $21 4990 N. Harbor Dr., Point Loma 619/226–2103 www.j-fat.com 4:B1.*

$ INTERNATIONAL FAMILY Fodor's Choice ★

Liberty Public Market. The city's former Naval Training Center is now home to nearly 30 vendors so even the pickiest of diners will be pleased. Options include tacos and quesadillas at Cecilia's Taqueria; fried rice, pad Thai, and curries at Mama Made Thai; gumbo, fried chicken, jambalaya, and other Southern specialties at Cane Patch Kitchen; smoothies and cold-pressed juices at Fully Loaded; and croissants, eclairs, and macarons at Le Parfait Paris. **Known for:** colossal burgers with creative fillings at Stuffed!; lively kid- and dog-friendly patio. *Average main: $10 2820 Historic Decatur Rd., Liberty Station 619/487–9346 www.libertypublicmarket.com 4:C1.*

$ BARBECUE

Phil's BBQ. During peak hours at San Diego's most popular barbecue, lines can be long for diners craving heaping portions of fall-off-the-bone baby-back ribs, moist pulled pork, or huge, crispy onion rings. The Toro tri-tip sandwich made the 2012 list of America's best sandwiches compiled by Travel Channel celebrity Adam Richman. **Known for:** Toro tri-tip sandwich; tender baby back ribs. *Average main: $15 3750 Sports Arena Blvd., Point Loma 619/226–6333 www.philsbbq.net 4:B1.*

$ SEAFOOD FAMILY Fodor's Choice ★

Point Loma Seafoods. When fishing boats unload their catch there, a seafood restaurant and market earns the right to boast that they offer "The Freshest Thing in Town." At first, mostly sport fishermen came here for tasty just-caught grilled fish on San Francisco–style sourdough bread. But the word got out and now locals and visitors come to enjoy bay views, sunshine, and a greatly expanded menu of seafood dishes. **Known for:** San Francisco-style seafood on sourdough; dockside bay views. *Average main: $13 2805 Emerson St., Point Loma 619/223–1109 www.pointlomaseafoods.com 4:B2.*

$ BURGER FAMILY

Slater's 50/50. Bacon is king at this lively burger, beer, and sports bar in Liberty Station. Founder Scott Slater's signature "designer" patty, half beef and half ground bacon, is topped with a fried egg, cheese,

8

and sauced with chipotle adobo mayonnaise. **Known for:** half-beef and half-ground bacon burgers; extensive craft beer selection. *Average main: $13 2750 Dewey Rd., Point Loma 619/398–2600 www.slaters5050.com 4:C1.*

$ BURGER **Soda & Swine.** Meatballs get a trendy spin at S&S, where the decor blends a gold-wrapped bar and geometric stools with old-time touches like a bakery area fashioned after a vintage storefront. This cozy space is the perfect spot to indulge in comfort food with a twist. **Known for:** mix-and-match meatball menu; housemade pies paired with soft serve. *Average main: $8 2750 Dewey Rd., Liberty Station 619/501–9989 www.sodaandswine.com 4:C1.*

$$ ECLECTIC FAMILY Fodor's Choice ★ **Stone Brewing World Bistro and Gardens.** This 50,000 square-foot monument to beer and good food in Liberty Station is a crowd-pleaser, especially for fans of San Diego's nationally known craft beer scene. Barbecue duck tacos, banh mi sandwiches, and other dishes on the global menu are perfect pairings with on-tap and bottled beers from around the world and Stone's famous IPAs. **Known for:** massive outdoor patio; brew-friendly eats. *Average main: $22 2816 Historic Decatur Rd., Liberty Station 619/269–2100 www.stonelibertystation.com 4:C1.*

$ AMERICAN FAMILY **Tender Greens.** "Farm-fresh ingredients served up with little fuss" is the ethos behind this casual cafeteria-style spot, with additional locations in Liberty Station, La Jolla, Downtown San Diego, and Mission Valley; all are very popular at lunch but the lines move quickly. Expect big salads like seared tuna Niçoise with quail egg, salami with kale, or the Happy Vegan, a mix of farro wheat with cranberry and hazelnuts, quinoa, cucumber, beets, green hummus, and tabbouleh. **Known for:** grass-fed Backyard Steak Salad; casual cafeteria ambience. *Average main: $12 2400 Historic Decatur Rd., Point Loma 619/226–6254 www.tendergreens.com 4:C1.*

OCEAN BEACH

One of the last "real" California beach towns, OB, as locals know it, has one foot in its hippie past and another in gentrified coastal living, which explains why it home to an eclectic group of bars and restaurants, everything from charming wine bars and bistros to Cuban pastries and colossal burgers.

$ CUBAN Fodor's Choice ★ **Azucar.** For a taste of Cuba in San Diego, head to this colorful Ocean Beach bakery where owner Vivian Hernandez Jackson combines her Cuban heritage, Miami childhood, and London culinary training in breakfast and lunch offerings. This friendly café is an ideal stop for a quick bite before shopping or hitting the beach. **Known for:** tangy, citrus-centric desserts; traditional Cuban pastries. *Average main: $7 4820 Newport Ave., Ocean Beach 619/523–2020 www.iloveazucar.com No dinner 4:B1.*

$$ BISTRO **Bo-Beau kitchen + bar.** Ocean Beach is a slightly eccentric beach town, not a place diners would expect to find this warm, romantic bistro that evokes a French farmhouse. The satisfying French-inspired menu of soups, woodstone oven flatbreads, mussels, and other bistro classics is served in cozy dining rooms and a rustic outdoor patio. **Known for:** popular crispy Brussels sprouts with pancetta; Tuesday date night

special. *Average main: $22 ✉ 4996 W. Point Loma Blvd., Ocean Beach ☎ 619/224–2884 🌐 www.cohnrestaurants.com/bobeaukitchenbar ⊗ No lunch ✧ 4:B1.*

$ BURGER FAMILY Fodor's Choice ★ **Hodad's.** Like a little sass with your burger? This funky joint in Ocean Beach delivers plenty along with world-famous bacon-cheeseburgers, fries, onion rings, and shakes. **Known for:** legendary bacon-cheeseburgers and thick-cut onion rings; surf-shack vibe. *Average main: $9 ✉ 5010 Newport Ave., Ocean Beach ☎ 619/224–4623 🌐 www.hodadies.com ✧ 4:B1.*

$ MODERN AMERICAN Fodor's Choice ★ **The Little Lion.** Amid surf shacks and hippie beach bars, this restaurant perched on stunning Sunset Cliffs feels like a hidden European bistro. The sisters who run the show come from a long line of successful local restaurateurs and have brought their passed-down expertise to the simple, healthy menu and thoughtful service. **Known for:** light, healthy breakfast fare; cozy bistro setting. *Average main: $14 ✉ 1424 Sunset Cliffs Blvd., Ocean Beach ☎ 619/756–6921 🌐 www.thelittlelioncafe.com ⊗ Closed Mon.; no dinner Tues., Wed., and Sun. ✧ 4:A1.*

$ PIZZA **Pizza Port.** Rows of picnic tables, surfboard decor, and beer-brewing on-site have made this funky, friendly brewpub a block from the beach a locals' favorite. The nearly dozen brews on tap include a namesake pour and other craft beers that have made San Diego a beer-drinkers destination. **Known for:** namesake Pizza Port beer; beer-friendly menu items. *Average main: $18 ✉ 1956 Bacon St., Ocean Beach ☎ 619/224–4700 🌐 www.pizzaport.com ✧ 4:B1.*

$ BURGER **Raglan Public House.** Inspired by the grass-fed burgers they sampled in New Zealand, the founders of this convivial eatery set out to replicate those same high-quality 'wiches in their Ocean Beach spot. The interior nods to the outdoor-oriented Kiwi country, with surfboards turned into light fixtures, rugby photos, and bodyboards as wall art. **Known for:** grass-fed beef burgers; convivial outdoor patio. *Average main: $13 ✉ 1851 Bacon St., Ocean Beach ☎ 619/794–2304 🌐 www.raglanpublichouse.com ✧ 4:B1.*

$$ WINE BAR **3rd Corner Wine Shop and Bistro.** Enthusiasts from around the world laud this combined wine shop, bar, and cozy California bistro. An amazing array of nicely discounted wines can be purchased to go or enjoyed on premises (with a $5 corkage fee). **Known for:** knowledgeable staff who can offer bottle recommendations; bottomless mimosa Sunday brunch. *Average main: $20 ✉ 2265 Bacon St., Ocean Beach ☎ 619/223–2700 🌐 www.the3rdcorner.com ⊗ Closed Mon. ✧ 4:B1.*

SHELTER ISLAND

Countless yachts and sailboats are berthed at marinas and hotels along this bayfront spit of land where visitors and locals come to picnic, enjoy concerts, and dine at a variety of casual bayside restaurants specializing in fresh seafood.

$$ HAWAIIAN **Bali Hai.** For more than 50 years, generations of San Diegans and visitors have enjoyed this Polynesian-theme icon with its stunning bay and city skyline views. Much of the kitsch has been replaced by contemporary decor, but you'll still spot tikis here and there. **Known for:** potent Bali Hai mai tais; Sunday brunch buffet with a DIY sundae bar. *Average main: $25 ✉ 2230 Shelter Island Dr., Shelter Island ☎ 619/222–1181 🌐 www.balihairestaurant.com ⊗ No lunch Sun. ✧ 4:C2.*

HARBOR ISLAND

The man-made peninsula across from the airport, with its bayside parks, marinas, and hotels, is a popular dining destination for lunches and dinners served with stunning views of San Diego Bay and the city skyline.

$$$ MODERN MEXICAN ✕ **Coasterra.** It took eight years to bring this massive waterfront destination to fruition, but with one of the best skyline views in the city, Coasterra was worth the wait. The space is swathed in murals, intricate light fixtures, breezy outdoor seating, and a cushy interior. **Known for:** extraordinary skyline views; happy hour appetizers. *Average main: $33 ✉ 880 Harbor Island Dr., Harbor Island ☎ 619/814–1300 🌐 www.cohnrestaurants.com/coasterra ⊕ 4:F1.*

$$$$ MODERN AMERICAN ✕ **Island Prime and C Level.** Two restaurants in one share this enviable spot on the shore of Harbor Island: the splurge-worthy Island Prime steak house and the relaxed C Level with a choice terrace. Both venues tempt with unrivaled views of downtown San Diego's skyline. **Known for:** sunset views; popover bread served with jalapeño jelly butter. *Average main: $39 ✉ 880 Harbor Island Dr., Harbor Island ☎ 619/298–6802 🌐 www.cohnrestaurants.com/islandprime ⊗ No lunch at Island Prime ⊕ 4:F1.*

$$$ SEAFOOD ✕ **Tom Ham's Lighthouse.** It's hard to top this longtime Harbor Island restaurant's incredible views across San Diego Bay to the Downtown skyline and Coronado Bridge. Now a new alfresco dining deck and a contemporary seafood-focused menu ensure the dining experience at this working lighthouse doesn't take a backseat to the scenery. **Known for:** bottomless mimosa Sunday brunch; alfresco dining deck with skyline and Coronado bridge views. *Average main: $30 ✉ 2150 Harbor Island Dr., Harbor Island ☎ 619/291–9110 🌐 www.tomhamslighthouse.com ⊗ No lunch Sun. ⊕ 4:D1.*

DINING AND LODGING MAP ATLAS

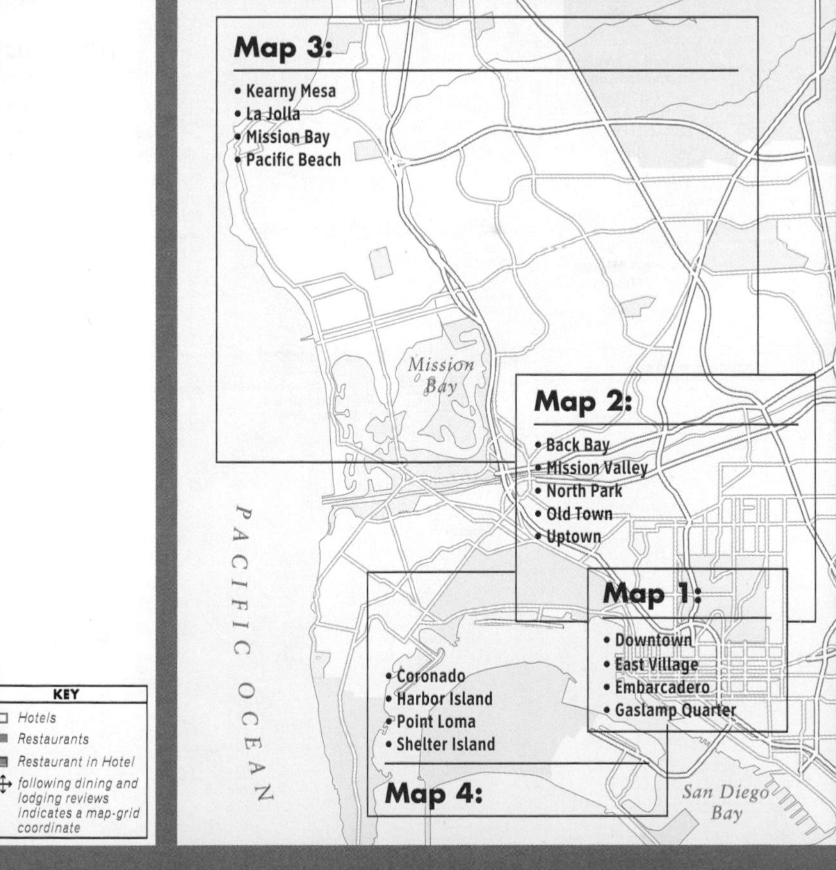

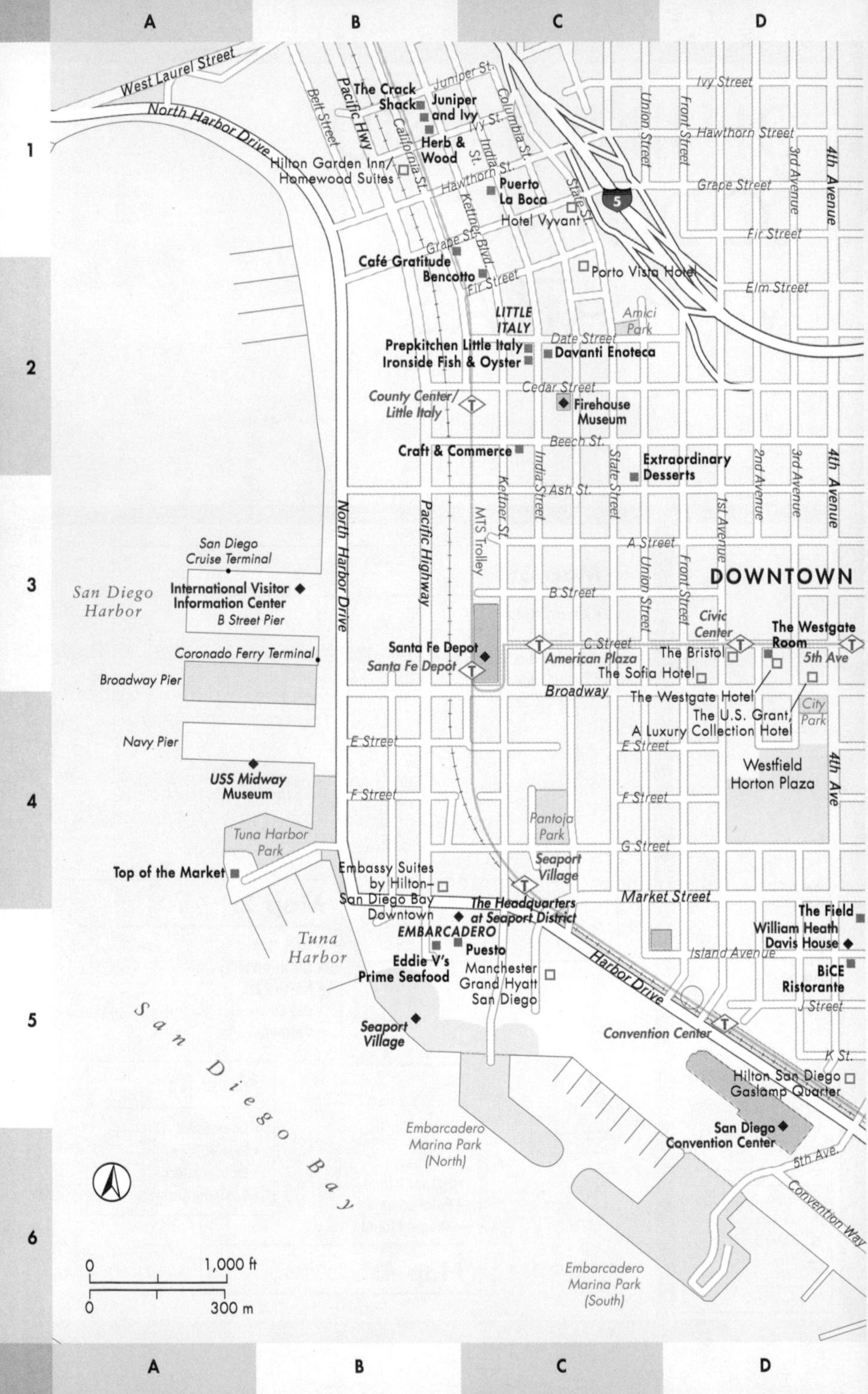

A
B
C
D
1
2
3
4
5
6
West Laurel Street
North Harbor Drive
Belt Street
Pacific Hwy
The Crack Shack
Juniper and Ivy
Herb & Wood
Juniper St.
Ivy St.
California St.
India St.
Columbia St.
Hilton Garden Inn/ Homewood Suites
Hawthorn St.
Puerto La Boca
Kettner Blvd
State St.
Hotel Vyvant
Grape St.
Café Gratitude
Bencotto
Fir Street
Porto Vista Hotel
LITTLE ITALY
Amici Park
Date Street
Prepkitchen Little Italy
Ironside Fish & Oyster
Davanti Enoteca
Cedar Street
County Center/ Little Italy
Firehouse Museum
Beech St.
Craft & Commerce
Extraordinary Desserts
Ash St.
India Street
State Street
Kettner St.
MTS Trolley
Pacific Highway
North Harbor Drive
Ivy Street
Hawthorn Street
Grape Street
Fir Street
Elm Street
Union Street
Front Street
3rd Avenue
4th Avenue
2nd Avenue
1st Avenue
5
A Street
B Street
C Street
DOWNTOWN
Civic Center
The Westgate Room
The Bristol
5th Ave
American Plaza
The Sofia Hotel
Broadway
The Westgate Hotel
The U.S. Grant, A Luxury Collection Hotel
City Park
E Street
Westfield Horton Plaza
4th Ave
F Street
G Street
Market Street
Island Avenue
The Field
William Heath Davis House
BiCE Ristorante
J Street
K St.
San Diego Cruise Terminal
International Visitor Information Center
B Street Pier
San Diego Harbor
Coronado Ferry Terminal
Broadway Pier
Navy Pier
USS Midway Museum
Tuna Harbor Park
Top of the Market
Santa Fe Depot
Santa Fe Depot
Pantoja Park
Seaport Village
Embassy Suites by Hilton–San Diego Bay Downtown
The Headquarters at Seaport District
EMBARCADERO
Puesto
Eddie V's Prime Seafood
Manchester Grand Hyatt San Diego
Tuna Harbor
Harbor Drive
Convention Center
Seaport Village
San Diego Bay
Hilton San Diego Gaslamp Quarter
San Diego Convention Center
5th Ave.
Convention Way
Embarcadero Marina Park (North)
Embarcadero Marina Park (South)
0
1,000 ft
0
300 m

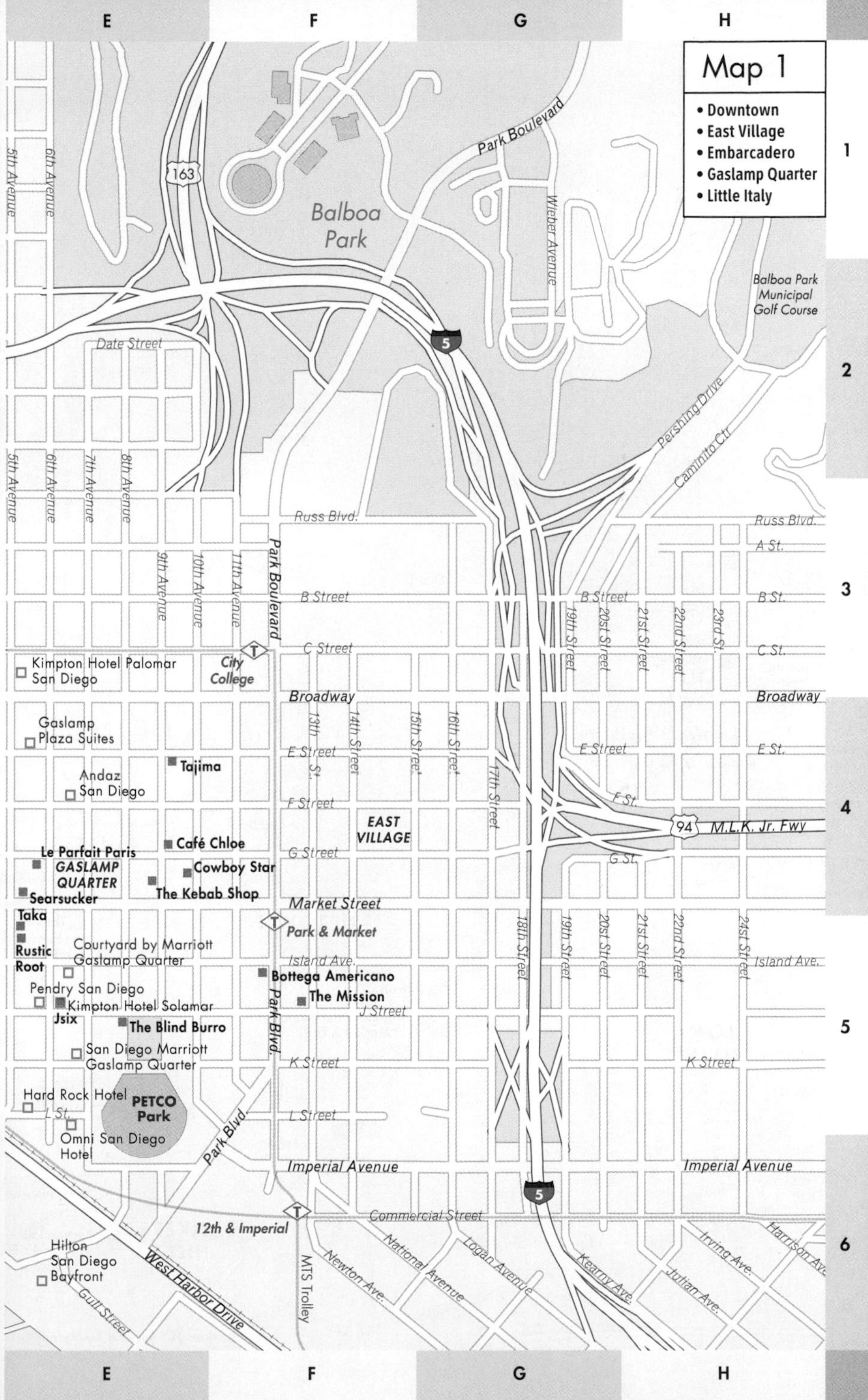

Map 1
• Downtown
• East Village
• Embarcadero
• Gaslamp Quarter
• Little Italy
E
F
G
H
1
2
3
4
5
6
Balboa Park
Park Boulevard
163
5
Wieber Avenue
Balboa Park Municipal Golf Course
Date Street
Pershing Drive
Caminito Ctr.
Russ Blvd.
A St.
B Street
B St.
C Street
C St.
Broadway
E Street
E St.
F Street
F St.
G Street
G St.
Market Street
Island Ave.
J Street
K Street
L Street
L St.
Imperial Avenue
Commercial Street
5th Avenue
6th Avenue
7th Avenue
8th Avenue
9th Avenue
10th Avenue
11th Avenue
13th St.
14th Street
15th Street
16th Street
17th Street
18th Street
19th Street
20st Street
21st Street
22nd Street
23rd St.
24st Street
94
M.L.K. Jr. Fwy
City College
Park & Market
12th & Imperial
EAST VILLAGE
GASLAMP QUARTER
Kimpton Hotel Palomar San Diego
Gaslamp Plaza Suites
Tajima
Andaz San Diego
Café Chloe
Le Parfait Paris
Cowboy Star
The Kebab Shop
Searsucker
Taka
Rustic Root
Courtyard by Marriott Gaslamp Quarter
Pendry San Diego
Kimpton Hotel Solamar
Jsix
The Blind Burro
Bottega Americano
The Mission
Park Blvd.
San Diego Marriott Gaslamp Quarter
Hard Rock Hotel
PETCO Park
Omni San Diego Hotel
Hilton San Diego Bayfront
West Harbor Drive
Gull Street
MTS Trolley
Newton Ave.
National Avenue
Logan Avenue
Kearny Ave.
Julian Ave.
Irving Ave.
Harrison Ave.

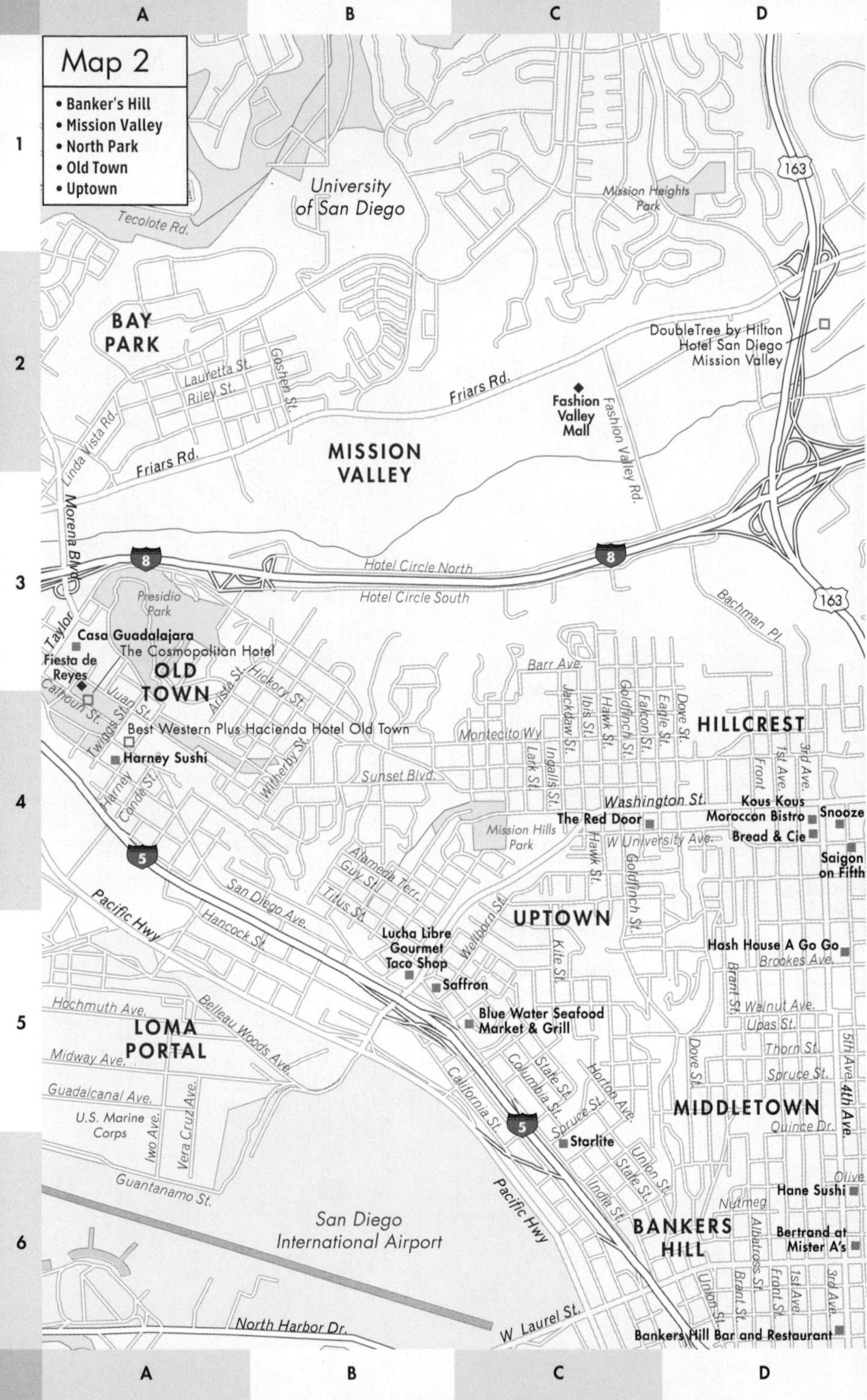

Map 2
• Banker's Hill
• Mission Valley
• North Park
• Old Town
• Uptown
A
B
C
D
1
2
3
4
5
6
University of San Diego
Mission Heights Park
163
Tecolote Rd.
BAY PARK
DoubleTree by Hilton Hotel San Diego Mission Valley
Lauretta St.
Riley St.
Goshen St.
Friars Rd.
Fashion Valley Mall
Linda Vista Rd.
MISSION VALLEY
Fashion Valley Rd.
Morena Blvd.
8
Hotel Circle North
Hotel Circle South
Presidio Park
Bachman Pl.
Taylor
Casa Guadalajara
The Cosmopolitan Hotel
Fiesta de Reyes
OLD TOWN
Hickory St.
Arista St.
Calhoun St.
Juan St.
Barr Ave.
Twiggs St.
Best Western Plus Hacienda Hotel Old Town
Montecito Wy
Jackdaw St.
Ibis St.
Hawk St.
Goldfinch St.
Falcon St.
Eagle St.
Dove St.
HILLCREST
Harney Sushi
Witherby St.
Sunset Blvd.
Lark St.
Ingalls St.
Front
1st Ave.
3rd Ave.
Harney
Conde St.
Washington St.
Kous Kous Moroccan Bistro
Snooze
The Red Door
Mission Hills Park
W University Ave.
Bread & Cie
5
Saigon on Fifth
Alameda Terr.
Guy St.
San Diego Ave.
Titus St.
Pacific Hwy
Hancock St.
UPTOWN
Wellborn St.
Kite St.
Lucha Libre Gourmet Taco Shop
Hash House A Go Go
Brookes Ave.
Brant St.
Saffron
Walnut Ave.
Hochmuth Ave.
Blue Water Seafood Market & Grill
Upas St.
LOMA PORTAL
Belleau Woods Ave.
Thorn St.
Midway Ave.
State St.
Columbia St.
Horton Ave.
5th Ave.
Spruce St.
Guadalcanal Ave.
California St.
Spruce St.
4th Ave.
MIDDLETOWN
U.S. Marine Corps
Iwo Ave.
Vera Cruz Ave.
Quince Dr.
Starlite
Union St.
State St.
Olive
Guantanamo St.
Hane Sushi
India St.
Nutmeg
San Diego International Airport
Pacific Hwy
BANKERS HILL
Albatross St.
Bertrand at Mister A's
Union St.
Brant St.
Front St.
1st Ave.
3rd Ave.
North Harbor Dr.
W Laurel St.
Bankers Hill Bar and Restaurant
A
B
C
D

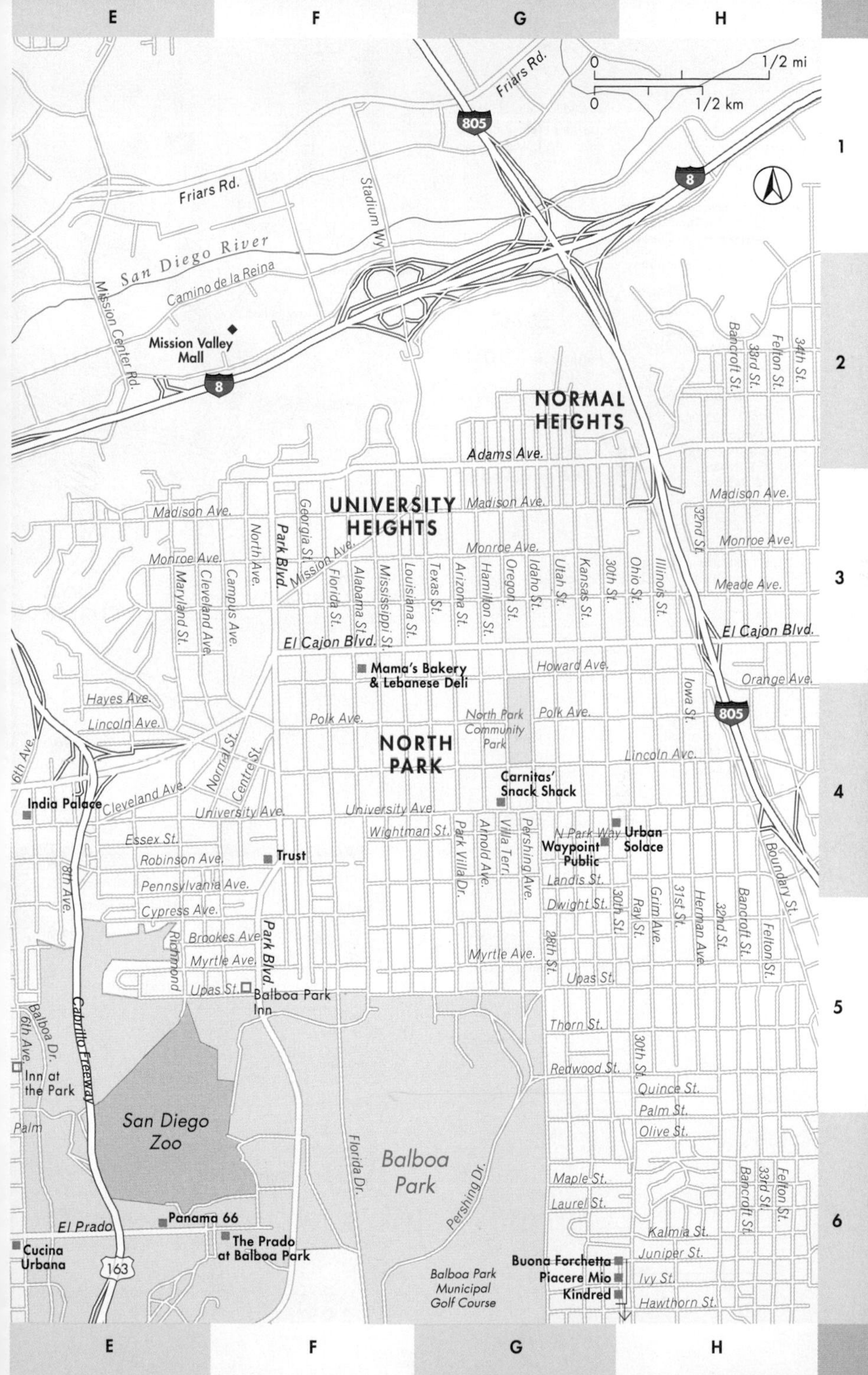
E
F
G
H
1
2
3
4
5
6
0
1/2 mi
0
1/2 km
Friars Rd.
805
8
Friars Rd.
Stadium Wy
San Diego River
Camino de la Reina
Mission Center Rd.
Mission Valley Mall
NORMAL HEIGHTS
Bancroft St.
33rd St.
Felton St.
34th St.
Adams Ave.
UNIVERSITY HEIGHTS
Madison Ave.
Madison Ave.
Madison Ave.
Monroe Ave.
Monroe Ave.
Monroe Ave.
Meade Ave.
32nd St.
Georgia St.
Park Blvd.
North Ave.
Mission Ave.
Maryland St.
Cleveland Ave.
Campus Ave.
Florida St.
Alabama St.
Mississippi St.
Louisiana St.
Texas St.
Arizona St.
Hamilton St.
Oregon St.
Idaho St.
Utah St.
Kansas St.
30th St.
Ohio St.
Illinois St.
El Cajon Blvd.
El Cajon Blvd.
Mama's Bakery & Lebanese Deli
Howard Ave.
Orange Ave.
Iowa St.
Hayes Ave.
Lincoln Ave.
Polk Ave.
North Park Community Park
Polk Ave.
NORTH PARK
Lincoln Ave.
6th Ave.
Normal St.
Centre St.
Cleveland Ave.
Carnitas' Snack Shack
India Palace
University Ave.
University Ave.
Essex St.
Wightman St.
Park Villa Dr.
Arnold Ave.
Villa Terr.
Pershing Ave.
N Park Way
Urban Solace
Waypoint Public
Boundary St.
Robinson Ave.
Trust
8th Ave.
Pennsylvania Ave.
Landis St.
Cypress Ave.
Dwight St.
30th St.
Ray St.
Grim Ave.
31st St.
Herman Ave.
32nd St.
Bancroft St.
Felton St.
Brookes Ave.
Richmond
Park Blvd.
Myrtle Ave.
Myrtle Ave.
28th St.
Upas St.
Upas St.
Balboa Park Inn
Balboa Dr.
6th Ave.
Cabrillo Freeway
Thorn St.
Redwood St.
30th St.
Inn at the Park
Quince St.
Palm St.
Palm
San Diego Zoo
Olive St.
Florida Dr.
Balboa Park
Pershing Dr.
Maple St.
Bancroft St.
33rd St.
Felton St.
Laurel St.
Panama 66
El Prado
The Prado at Balboa Park
Kalmia St.
Cucina Urbana
163
Juniper St.
Buona Forchetta
Piacere Mio
Ivy St.
Balboa Park Municipal Golf Course
Kindred
Hawthorn St.
E
F
G
H

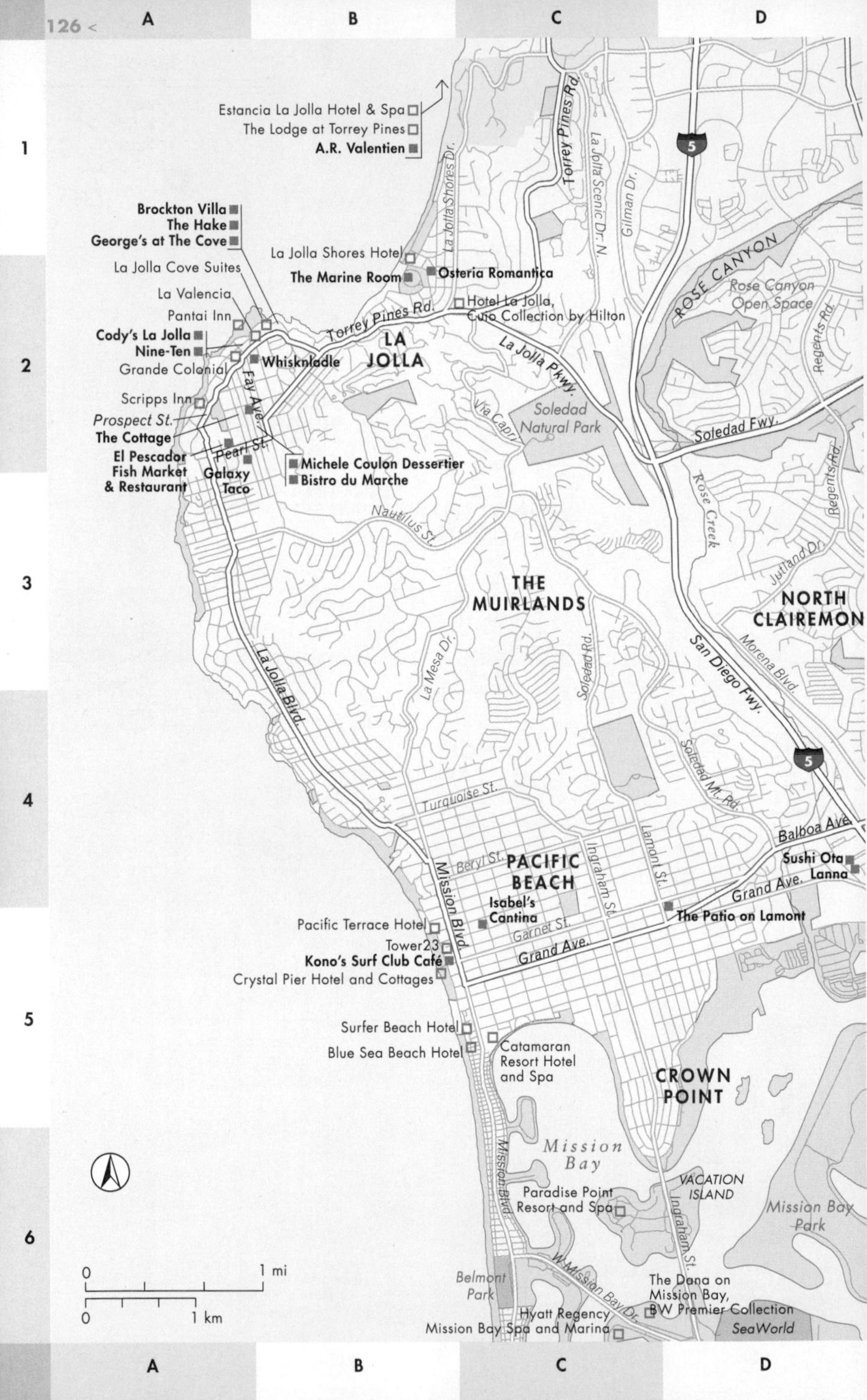
A
B
C
D
1
2
3
4
5
6
Estancia La Jolla Hotel & Spa
The Lodge at Torrey Pines
A.R. Valentien
Brockton Villa
The Hake
George's at The Cove
La Jolla Cove Suites
La Valencia
Pantai Inn
Cody's La Jolla
Nine-Ten
Grande Colonial
Scripps Inn
Prospect St.
The Cottage
El Pescador Fish Market & Restaurant
Galaxy Taco
Pearl St.
Fay Ave.
Whisknladle
La Jolla Shores Hotel
The Marine Room
Osteria Romantica
Hotel La Jolla, Curio Collection by Hilton
Torrey Pines Rd.
LA JOLLA
La Jolla Shores Dr.
La Jolla Scenic Dr. N.
Gilman Dr.
La Jolla Pkwy.
Via Capri
Soledad Natural Park
Michele Coulon Dessertier
Bistro du Marche
Nautilus St.
ROSE CANYON
Rose Canyon Open Space
Regents Rd.
Soledad Fwy.
Rose Creek
Jutland Dr.
NORTH CLAIREMON
THE MUIRLANDS
La Jolla Blvd.
La Mesa Dr.
Soledad Rd.
San Diego Fwy.
Morena Blvd.
Soledad Mt. Rd.
5
Turquoise St.
Balboa Ave.
Sushi Ota
Lanna
Beryl St.
PACIFIC BEACH
Ingraham St.
Lamont St.
Grand Ave.
The Patio on Lamont
Isabel's Cantina
Garnet St.
Mission Blvd.
Pacific Terrace Hotel
Tower23
Kono's Surf Club Café
Crystal Pier Hotel and Cottages
Surfer Beach Hotel
Blue Sea Beach Hotel
Catamaran Resort Hotel and Spa
CROWN POINT
Mission Bay
VACATION ISLAND
Paradise Point Resort and Spa
Mission Bay Park
Belmont Park
W Mission Bay Dr.
The Dana on Mission Bay, BW Premier Collection
Hyatt Regency Mission Bay Spa and Marina
SeaWorld
0
1 mi
0
1 km

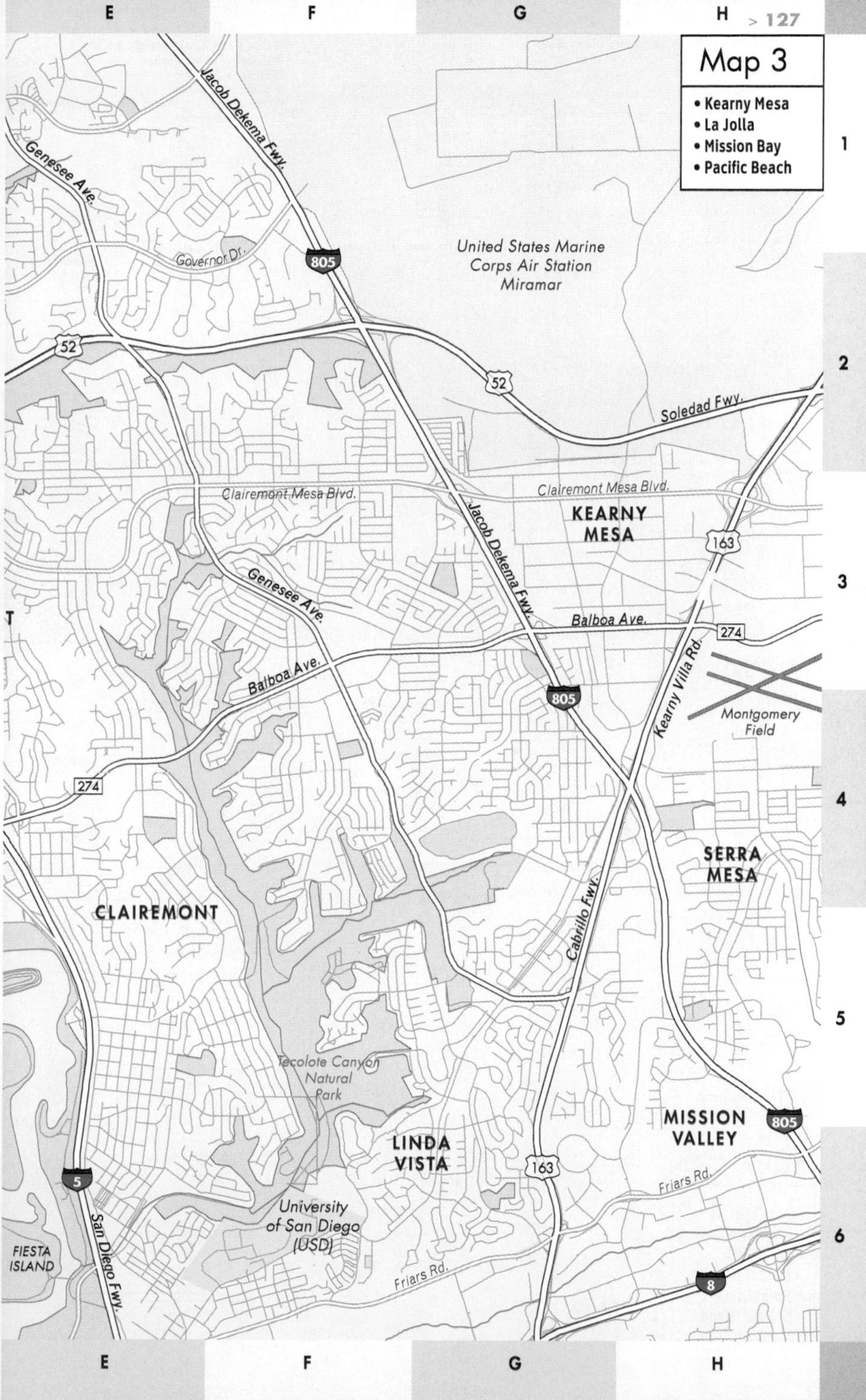

E
F
G
H
Map 3
• Kearny Mesa
• La Jolla
• Mission Bay
• Pacific Beach
1
2
3
4
5
6
Jacob Dekema Fwy.
Genesee Ave.
Governor Dr.
805
United States Marine
Corps Air Station
Miramar
52
52
Soledad Fwy.
Clairemont Mesa Blvd.
Clairemont Mesa Blvd.
KEARNY
MESA
163
Jacob Dekema Fwy.
Genesee Ave.
Balboa Ave.
274
Balboa Ave.
805
Kearny Villa Rd.
Montgomery
Field
274
SERRA
MESA
CLAIREMONT
Cabrillo Fwy.
Tecolote Canyon
Natural
Park
MISSION
VALLEY
805
LINDA
VISTA
163
Friars Rd.
5
University
of San Diego
(USD)
FIESTA
ISLAND
San Diego Fwy.
Friars Rd.
8
E
F
G
H

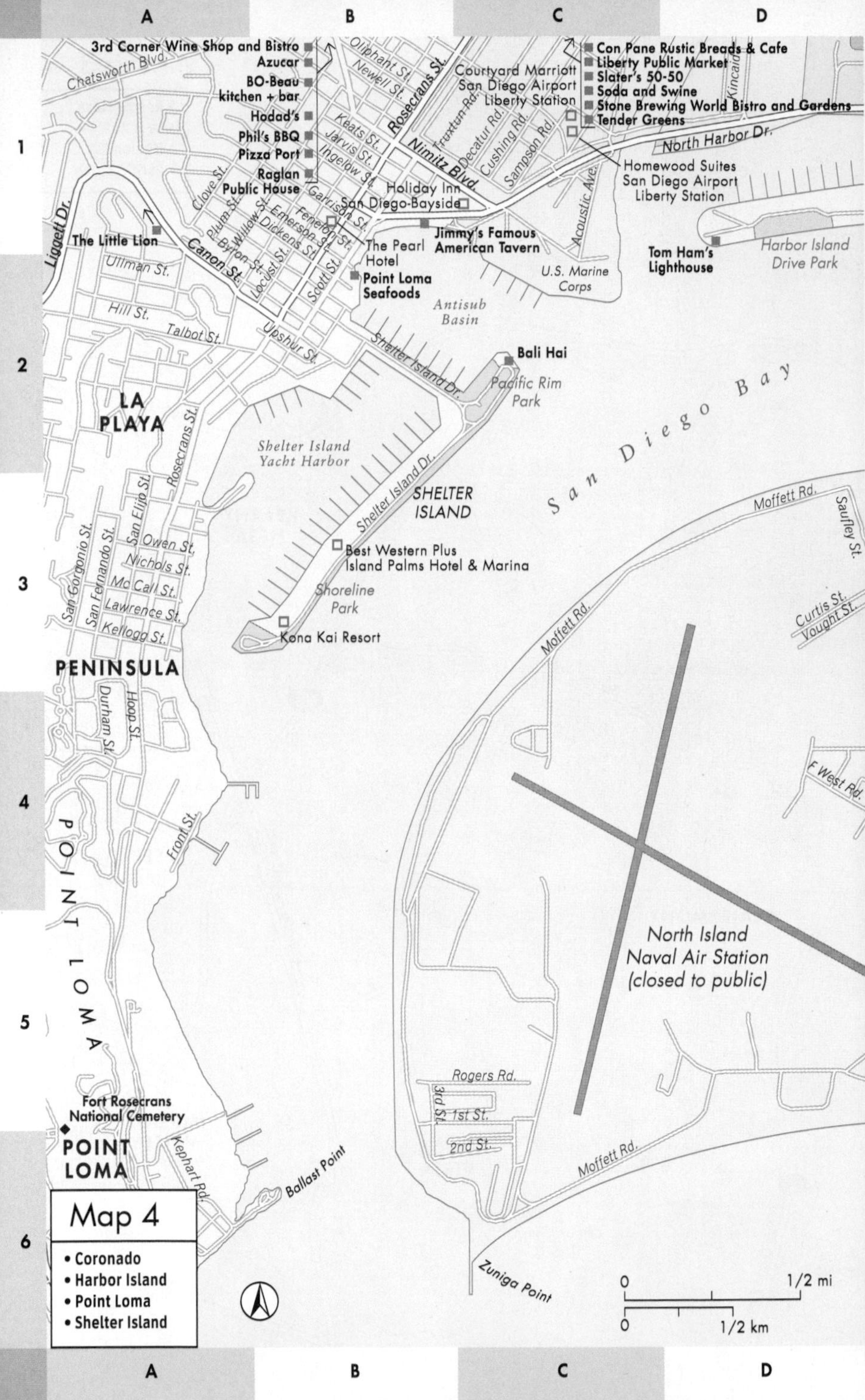
Map 4
• Coronado
• Harbor Island
• Point Loma
• Shelter Island
3rd Corner Wine Shop and Bistro
Azucar
BO-Beau kitchen + bar
Hodad's
Phil's BBQ
Pizza Port
Raglan Public House
The Little Lion
Con Pane Rustic Breads & Cafe
Liberty Public Market
Slater's 50-50
Soda and Swine
Stone Brewing World Bistro and Gardens
Tender Greens
Courtyard Marriott San Diego Airport Liberty Station
Homewood Suites San Diego Airport Liberty Station
Holiday Inn San Diego-Bayside
The Pearl Hotel
Point Loma Seafoods
Jimmy's Famous American Tavern
Tom Ham's Lighthouse
Harbor Island Drive Park
U.S. Marine Corps
Antisub Basin
Bali Hai
Pacific Rim Park
LA PLAYA
Shelter Island Yacht Harbor
SHELTER ISLAND
San Diego Bay
Best Western Plus Island Palms Hotel & Marina
Shoreline Park
Kona Kai Resort
PENINSULA
POINT LOMA
Fort Rosecrans National Cemetery
POINT LOMA
Ballast Point
Zuniga Point
North Island Naval Air Station (closed to public)
Chatsworth Blvd.
Oliphant St.
Newell St.
Rosecrans St.
Nimitz Blvd.
Truxtun Rd.
Decatur Rd.
Cushing Rd.
Sampson Rd.
Kincaid
North Harbor Dr.
Acoustic Ave.
Keats St.
Jarvis St.
Ingelow St.
Garrison St.
Clove St.
Plum St.
Willow St.
Emerson St.
Dickens St.
Byron St.
Locust St.
Fenelon St.
Scott St.
Canon St.
Liggett Dr.
Ullman St.
Hill St.
Talbot St.
Upshur St.
Shelter Island Dr.
Rosecrans St.
San Elijo St.
Owen St.
Nichols St.
McCall St.
Lawrence St.
Kellogg St.
San Gorgonio St.
San Fernando St.
Durham St.
Hoop St.
Front St.
Kephart Rd.
Moffett Rd.
Saufley St.
Curtis St.
Vought St.
F West Rd.
Rogers Rd.
3rd St.
1st St.
2nd St.
0 1/2 mi
0 1/2 km
A B C D
1 2 3 4 5 6

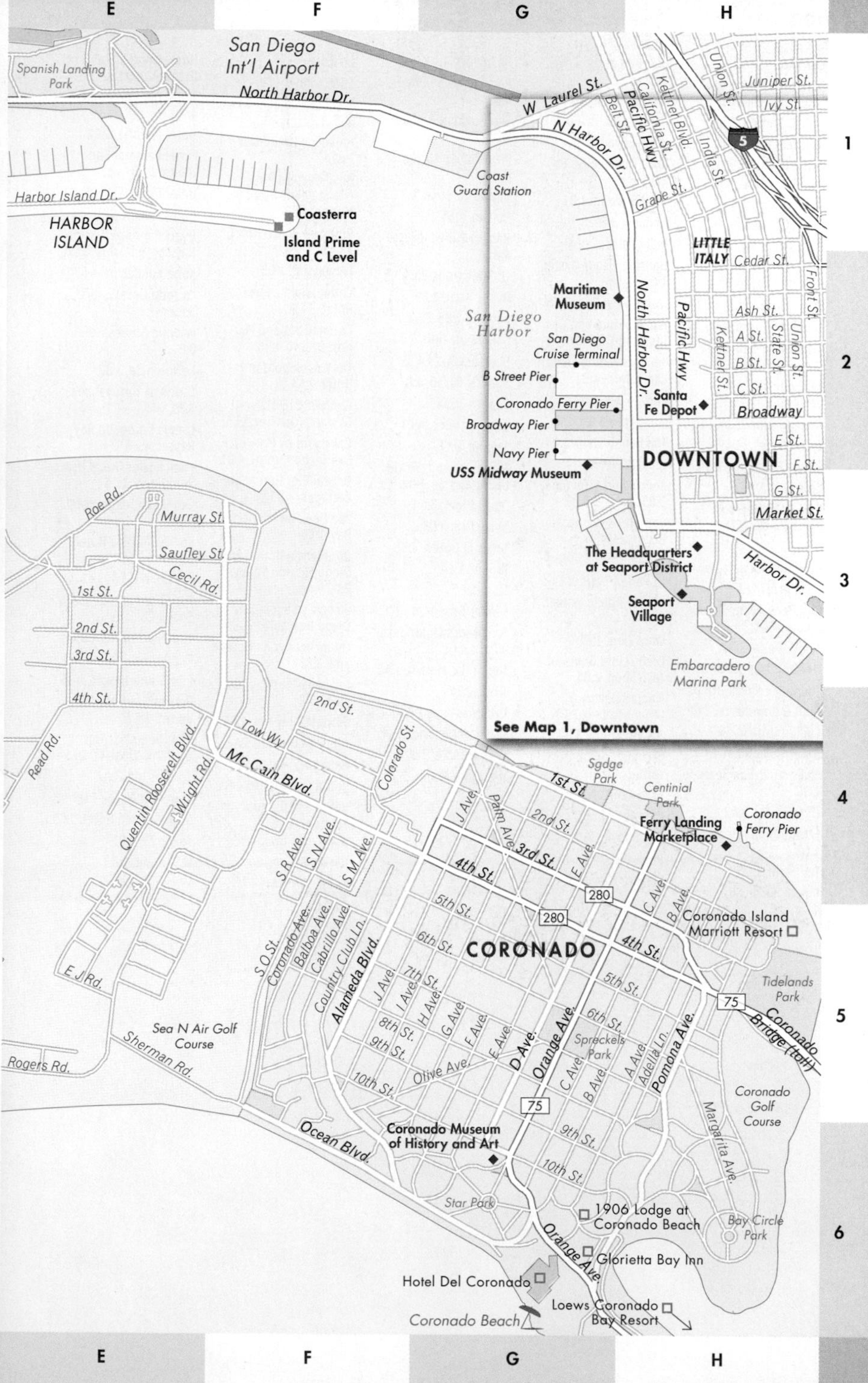

E
F
G
H
1
2
3
4
5
6
San Diego Int'l Airport
Spanish Landing Park
North Harbor Dr.
W Laurel St.
N Harbor Dr.
Belt St.
Pacific Hwy
California St.
Kettner Blvd.
India St.
Union St.
Juniper St.
Ivy St.
5
Harbor Island Dr.
HARBOR ISLAND
Coasterra
Island Prime and C Level
Coast Guard Station
Grape St.
LITTLE ITALY
Cedar St.
Front St.
Maritime Museum
San Diego Harbor
North Harbor Dr.
Pacific Hwy
Ash St.
A St.
B St.
C St.
Kettner St.
State St.
Union St.
San Diego Cruise Terminal
B Street Pier
Coronado Ferry Pier
Broadway Pier
Navy Pier
USS Midway Museum
Santa Fe Depot
Broadway
E St.
F St.
G St.
DOWNTOWN
Market St.
The Headquarters at Seaport District
Harbor Dr.
Seaport Village
Embarcadero Marina Park
See Map 1, Downtown
Roe Rd.
Murray St.
Saufley St.
Cecil Rd.
1st St.
2nd St.
3rd St.
4th St.
2nd St.
Tow Wy
Read Rd.
Quentin Roosevelt Blvd.
Wright Rd.
Mc Cain Blvd.
Colorado St.
Sgdge Park
Centinial Park
1st St.
J Ave.
Palm Ave.
2nd St.
3rd St.
E Ave.
Ferry Landing Marketplace
Coronado Ferry Pier
S R Ave.
S N Ave.
S M Ave.
4th St.
280
280
C Ave.
B Ave.
Coronado Island Marriott Resort
5th St.
6th St.
CORONADO
4th St.
S O St.
Coronado Ave.
Balboa Ave.
Cabrillo Ave.
Country Club Ln.
Alameda Blvd.
J Ave.
7th St.
I Ave.
H Ave.
5th St.
Tidelands Park
75
Coronado Bridge (toll)
E J Rd.
8th St.
9th St.
G Ave.
F Ave.
E Ave.
D Ave.
Orange Ave.
6th St.
Spreckels Park
C Ave.
B Ave.
A Ave.
Adella Ln.
Pomona Ave.
Sea N Air Golf Course
Sherman Rd.
Rogers Rd.
10th St.
Olive Ave.
Coronado Golf Course
75
Margarita Ave.
Ocean Blvd.
Coronado Museum of History and Art
9th St.
10th St.
Star Park
1906 Lodge at Coronado Beach
Bay Circle Park
Orange Ave.
Glorietta Bay Inn
Hotel Del Coronado
Loews Coronado Bay Resort
Coronado Beach
E
F
G
H

Dining

3rd Corner Wine Shop and Bistro, 4:B1
A. R. Valentien, 3:B1
Azucar, 4:B1
Bali Hai, 4:C2
Bankers Hill Bar + Restaurant, 1:D5
Bencotto, 1:C2
Bertrand at Mister A's, 2:D6
BiCE Ristorante, 1:D5
Bistro du Marche, 3:B2
The Blind Burro, 1:E5
Blue Water Seafood Market & Grill, 2:C5
BO-Beau kitchen + bar, 4:B1
Bottega Americano, 1:F5
Bread & Cie, 2:D4
Buona Forchetta, 2:H6
Café Chloe, 1:E4
Café Gratitude, 1:B2
Carnitas' Snack Shack, 2:G4
Casa Guadalajara, 2:A4
Coasterra, 4:F1
Con Pane Rustic Breads & Café, 4:C1
The Cottage, 3:B2
Cowboy Star, 1:E4
The Crack Shack, 1:B1
Craft & Commerce, 1:C2
Cucina Urbana, 2:E6
Davanti Enoteca , 1:C2
Eddie V's Prime Seafood, 1:B5
El Pescador, 3:A2
Extraordinary Desserts, 1:C2
The Field, 1:D5
Galaxy Taco, 3:B2
George's at the Cove, 3:B2
The Hake, 3:B2
Hane Sushi, 2:D6
Harney Sushi, 2:A4
Hash House A Go Go, 2:D5
Herb & Wood, 1:B1
Hodad's, 4:B1
India Palace, 2:E4
Ironside Fish & Oyster, 1:C2
Isabel's Cantina, 3:C5
Island Prime and C Level, 4:F1
Jimmy's Famous American Tavern, 4:B1
Jsix, 1:E5
Juniper and Ivy, 1:B1
The Kebab Shop, 1:E4
Kindred, 2:G6
Kono's Surf Club Café, 3:B5
Kous Kous Moroccan Bistro, 2:D4
Lanna, 3:D4
Le Parfait Paris, 2:E4
Liberty Public Market, 4:C1
Little Lion, 4:B1
Lucha Libre Gourmet Taco Shop, 2:B5
Mama's Bakery & Lebanese Deli, 2:F3
Marine Room, 3:B2
Michele Coulon Dessertier, 3:A2
Nine-Ten, 3:A2
Osteria Romantica, 3:B2
Panama 66, 2:E6
Phil's BBQ, 4:B1
Piacere Mio, 2:G6
Pizza Port, 4:B1
Point Loma Seafoods, 4:B2
The Prado at Balboa Park, 2:F6
Prepkitchen Little Italy, 1:C2
Puerto La Boca, 1:C1
Puesto, 1:B5
Raglan Public House, 4:B1
The Red Door, 2:C4
Rustic Root, 1:E4
Saffron, 2:B5
Saigon on Fifth, 2:D4
Searsucker, 1:E4
Slater's 50/50, 4:C1
Snooze, 2:D4
Soda & Swine, 4:C1
Starlite, 2:C6
Stone Brewing World Bistro and Gardens, 4:C1
Sushi Diner, 3:G4
Sushi Ota, 3:D4
Tacos El Gordo, 4:B6
Tajima, 1:E4
Taka, 1:E5
Tender Greens, 4:C1
Tom Ham's Lighthouse, 4:D1
Top of the Market, 1:A4
Trust, 2:F4
Urban Solace, 2:G4
Waypoint Public, 2:G4
Whisknladle, 3:A2
Westgate Room, 1:D3

Lodging

1906 Lodge, 4:G6
Andaz San Diego, 1:E4
Best Western Plus Hacienda Hotel–Old Town, 2:A4
Best Western Plus Island Palms Hotel & Marina, 4:B3
Blue Sea Beach Hotel, 3:C5
The Bristol, 1:D3
Catamaran Resort Hotel, 3:C5
Coronado Island Marriott Resort, 4:H5
The Cosmopolitan Hotel, 2:A4
Courtyard by Marriott Gaslamp Quarter, 1:E5
Courtyard by Marriott San Diego Airport, 4:C1
Crystal Pier Hotel and Cottages, 3:B5
The Dana on Mission Bay, 3:C6
Doubletree Hotel San Diego Mission Valley, 2:D2
Embassy Suites–San Diego Bay, 1:B4
Estancia La Jolla Hotel & Spa, 3:B1
Gaslamp Plaza Suites, 1:E4
Glorietta Bay Inn, 4:G6
Grande Colonial, 3:A2
Hard Rock Hotel, 1:E5
Hilton Garden Inn, 1:B1
Hilton San Diego Bayfront, 1:E6
Hilton San Diego Gaslamp Quarter, 1:D5
Holiday Inn Bayside, 4:C1
Homewood Suites San Diego Airport, 4:C1
Hotel Del Coronado, 4:G6
Hotel La Jolla, 3:C2
Hotel Palomar San Diego, 1:E3
Hotel Solamar, 1:E5
Hotel Vyvant, 1:C1
Hyatt Regency Mission Bay Spa & Marina, 3:C6
Kona Kai Resort, 4:B3
La Jolla Cove Suites, 3:B2
La Jolla Shores Hotel, 3:B2
La Valencia, 3:B2
Lodge at Torrey Pines, 3:B1
Loews Coronado Bay Resort, 4:H6
Manchester Grand Hyatt San Diego, 1:C5
Omni San Diego Hotel, 1:E6
Pacific Terrace Hotel, 3:B5
Pantai Inn, 3:A2
Paradise Point Resort & Spa, 3:C6
The Pearl Hotel, 4:B1
Pendry San Diego, 1:E5
Pier South Resort, 4:H6
Porto Vista Hotel & Suites, 1:C2
San Diego Marriott Gaslamp Quarter, 1:E5
Scripps Inn, 3:A2
The Sofia Hotel, 1:D3
Surfer Beach Hotel, 3:C5
Tower23, 3:B5
U.S. Grant, 1:D3
Westgate Hotel, 1:D3

9

WHERE TO STAY

Updated by Juliana Shallcross

In San Diego, you could plan a luxurious vacation at the beach, staying at a resort with panoramic ocean views, private balconies, and a full-service spa. Or you could stay Downtown, steps from the bustling Gaslamp Quarter, in a modern hotel featuring lively rooftop pools, complimentary wine receptions, and high-tech entertainment systems. But with some flexibility—maybe opting for a partial-view room a quick drive from the action—it's possible to experience San Diego at half the price.

Sharing the city's postcard-perfect sunny skies are neighborhoods and coastal communities that offer great diversity; San Diego is no longer the sleepy beach town it once was. In action-packed Downtown, luxury hotels cater to solo business travelers and young couples with trendy restaurants and cabana-encircled pools. Budget-friendly options can be found in smaller neighborhoods just outside the Gaslamp Quarter such as Little Italy and Uptown.

You'll need a car if you stay outside Downtown, but the beach communities are rich with lodging options. Across the bridge, Coronado's hotels and resorts offer access to a stretch of glistening white sand that's often recognized as one of the best beaches in the country. La Jolla offers many romantic, upscale ocean-view hotels and some of the area's best restaurants and specialty shopping. But it's easy to find a water view in any price range: surfers make themselves at home at the casual inns and budget stays of Pacific Beach and Mission Bay. If you're planning to fish, check out hotels located near the marinas in Shelter Island, Point Loma, or Coronado.

For families, Uptown, Mission Valley, and Old Town are close to SeaWorld and the San Diego Zoo, offering good-value accommodations with extras like sleeper sofas and video games. Mission Valley is ideal for business travelers; there are plenty of well-known chain hotels with conference space, modern business centers, and kitchenettes for extended stays.

WHERE SHOULD I STAY?

	Neighborhood Vibe	Pros	Cons
Downtown	Downtown's hub is the Gaslamp Quarter, an action-packed area with many hotels, boutiques, restaurants, and clubs. Little Italy and Embarcadero areas are quieter.	Close to food and nightlife options for every age and taste. Quick walk or trolley ride to convention center. Won't need a car to get to many attractions.	Streets can be congested and noisy at night, particularly in the Gaslamp Quarter and East Village. Overnight parking is expensive.
Uptown and Old Town	Quieter area north of Downtown with more budget-friendly hotels. Old Town has a busy stretch of Mexican restaurants and historic sites.	Central location that's close to Balboa Park and major freeways. Good for business travelers. More inexpensive dining options.	Limited nightlife options. Feels more removed from San Diego's beachy vibe. Mission Valley area lacks character; it's filled with malls and car lots.
Mission Bay and the Beaches	Relaxed and casual beachside area with many resorts, golf courses, and parks. Largest man-made aquatic park in the country.	Right on the water. Can splurge on Jet Skis and other water sports or stick to barbecues and public playgrounds. Close to SeaWorld.	Resorts are spaced far apart, and area is somewhat removed from central San Diego. Watch for high resort fees and other not-so-obvious charges.
La Jolla	The "jewel" of San Diego, an affluent coastal area with a small-town atmosphere. Has a range of luxury hotels and a few value choices.	Gorgeous views. Close to or right on the beach. Some of the best seafood restaurants and high-end shopping in the state. Safe area for walking.	Often congested, and parking can be nearly impossible in summer. Very expensive area. Has few hotels that cater to children.
Point Loma, Coronado, and Shelter Island	Areas by the bay have historic and resort hotels, beaches, and tourist-oriented restaurants. Coronado and Point Loma are more residential, home to many military families.	Great views of the city, bay, and beaches. Near the airport. Convenient for boaters. Hotels tend to be family-friendly, with large rooms and pools.	Isolated from the rest of the city; you'll spend significant time commuting to other parts of San Diego, such as La Jolla and Balboa Park.

When your work (or sightseeing) is done, join the trendsetters flocking to Downtown's Gaslamp Quarter for its eateries, lounges, and multilevel clubs that rival L.A.'s stylish scenes.

PLANNING

LODGING STRATEGY

Where should I stay? With hundreds of San Diego hotels in dozens of neighborhoods, it may seem like a daunting question. But fret not—our expert writers and editors have done most of the legwork. The selections here represent the best this sunny paradise has to offer—from the best budget motels to the sleekest boutique hotels. Scan "Best Bets" for our top recommendations by price and experience.

PARKING

Given the distances between attractions and limited public transportation routes, a car is almost a necessity for visitors to San Diego. That being said, a vehicle can significantly add to your expenses if you stay in the ritzier areas. Overnight parking in Coronado, La Jolla, and Downtown's Gaslamp Quarter can be as high as $50 per night; in Uptown and Mission Bay it usually runs $10 to $20.

NEED A RESERVATION?

Book well in advance, especially if you plan to visit in summer, which is the busy season for most hotels. In spring and fall, conventions and sports events can fill every Downtown hotel room. When you make reservations, ask about specials. Several properties in the Hotel Circle area of Mission Valley offer reduced rates and even free tickets to the San Diego Zoo and other attractions. You can save on hotels and attractions by visiting the San Diego Tourism Authority website (🌐 *www.sandiego.org*) for special seasonal offers.

STAYING WITH KIDS

The area is full of hotels suited to a family's budget and/or recreational needs, and many allow kids under 18 to stay free with their parents. You'll find the most choices and diversity in and around Mission Bay, which is close to SeaWorld, beaches, parks, and Old Town.

SERVICES

Downtown hotels once catered primarily to business travelers, though the new boutique hotels are attracting hip leisure travelers to the area, while those at Mission Bay, in coastal locations such as Carlsbad and Encinitas, and at inland resort areas offer golf and other sports facilities, spa services, children's activities, and more. If you're traveling with pets, note that pet policies do change and some hotels require substantial cleaning fees of $50 to $100. At many San Diego hotels, even smoking outdoors is frowned on or prohibited.

PRICES

Note that even in the most expensive areas, you can find affordable rooms. High season is summer, and rates are lowest in fall. If an ocean view is important, request it when booking, but it will cost you.

Prices in the reviews are the lowest cost of a standard double room in high season. For expanded hotel reviews, facilities, and current deals, visit Fodors.com.

WHAT IT COSTS

	$	$$	$$$	$$$$
Hotels	under $161	$161–$230	$231–$300	over $300

Prices are for a standard double room in high (summer) season, excluding 10.5% tax.

HOTEL REVIEWS

Listed alphabetically within neighborhoods. Use the coordinates (⊕ 2:F3) after property names or reviews to locate the property on the San Diego Dining and Lodging Atlas. The first number after the j symbol indicates the map number. Following that is the property's coordinate on the map grid.

DOWNTOWN

Lively Downtown is San Diego's hotel hub, with everything from budget chains to boutique and business hotels. Here's a part of Southern California where you won't need a car; you can walk or take the trolley to Seaport Village, the Embarcadero, Petco Park, the convention center, galleries and coffeehouses, and the Horton Plaza shopping center. Smack in the middle of Downtown is the Gaslamp Quarter where you'll find nightlife options for every night of the week, ranging from gastropubs to clubs with celebrity DJs.

GASLAMP QUARTER

$$$$ HOTEL Fodor's Choice ★ **Andaz San Diego.** The lobby of the luxury, Hyatt-managed Andaz—with its dark, sexy vibe, tall columns wrapped in braided leather, buckets of chilled wine awaiting guests, and welcoming service—pretty much sums up the experience here: high-style stay without the attitude. **Pros:** luxurious rooms; romantic vibe; friendly service. **Cons:** noisy on weekends; not a good choice for families. *Rooms from: $319 ✉ 600 F St., Gaslamp Quarter ☎ 619/849–1234 🌐 www.sandiego.andaz.hyatt.com 159 rooms No meals* ⊕ 1:E4.

$$$ HOTEL **The Bristol.** Mod pop art inspired by artists such as Andy Warhol and Ed Ruscha sets the tone at this casual boutique hotel. **Pros:** modern rooms; centrally located; good value. **Cons:** no restaurant; somewhat seedy area. *Rooms from: $234 ✉ 1055 1st Ave., Gaslamp Quarter ☎ 619/232–6141 🌐 www.thebristolsandiego.com 114 rooms No meals* ⊕ 1:D3.

$$ HOTEL FAMILY **Courtyard Marriott Gaslamp Quarter.** This is not your typical Courtyard by Marriott as the building has a historic past—it was the home of San Diego Trust and Savings Bank in 1928. **Pros:** great lobby bar; can accommodate families; 24-hour market. **Cons:** a little far from convention center and Petco Park; expensive valet parking. *Rooms from: $229 ✉ 530 Broadway, Gaslamp Quarter ☎ 619/446–3000 🌐 www.sandiegocy.com 245 rooms No meals* ⊕ 1:E5.

$$ HOTEL **Gaslamp Plaza Suites.** One of San Diego's first "skyscrapers," this 11-story structure has a central location and a vintage feel. **Pros:** historic building; good location a block from Horton Plaza; well priced. **Cons:** books up early; small, dated rooms. *Rooms from: $200 ✉ 520 E St., Gaslamp Quarter ☎ 619/232–9500, 🌐 www.gaslamp-plaza.com 60 rooms Breakfast* ⊕ 1:E4.

9

$$$ HOTEL Fodor's Choice ★ **Hard Rock Hotel.** Self-billed as a hip playground for rock stars and people who want to party like them, the Hard Rock is near Petco Park overlooking glimmering San Diego Bay. The interior oozes laid-back sophistication, and guest rooms include branded Sleep Like a Rock beds and the option of renting a guitar. **Pros:** central location; energetic scene; luxurious rooms. **Cons:** pricey drinks; some attitude. *Rooms from: $249 ✉ 207 5th Ave., Gaslamp Quarter ☎ 619/702–3000, 866/751–7625 ⊕ www.hardrockhotelsd.com ⇨ 420 rooms 🍴 No meals* ✥ 1:E5.

$$ HOTEL FAMILY **Hilton San Diego Bayfront.** This contemporary 30-story hotel overlooking San Diego Bay strives for a boutique feel. **Pros:** close to the convention center and Petco Park; allergy-friendly rooms available. **Cons:** expensive valet parking; not as family-friendly as other area hotels. *Rooms from: $214 ✉ 1 Park Blvd., Gaslamp Quarter ☎ 619/564–3333 ⊕ www.hiltonsandiegobayfront.com ⇨ 1190 rooms 🍴 No meals* ✥ 1:E6.

$$$ HOTEL **Hilton San Diego Gaslamp Quarter.** The moment you experience the cozy lounge spaces and wood accents of the Hilton's modern and sophisticated lobby, you realize this isn't your run-of-the-mill chain hotel. **Pros:** nice decor; upscale lofts; near restaurants and shops. **Cons:** noisy area; pricey parking; Wi-Fi is free for Hilton's HHonors loyalty program members. *Rooms from: $289 ✉ 401 K St., Gaslamp Quarter ☎ 619/231–4040, 800/445–8667 ⊕ www3.hilton.com/en/hotels/california/hilton-san-diego-gaslamp-quarter-SANGQHF/index.html ⇨ 273 rooms 🍴 No meals* ✥ 1:D5.

$$$ HOTEL **Kimpton Hotel Palomar San Diego.** A few blocks from the heart of the Gaslamp Quarter, this swanky Kimpton hotel features luxurious guest rooms and a popular rooftop lounge. **Pros:** modern rooms; centrally located; complimentary evening wine hour. **Cons:** expensive parking. *Rooms from: $239 ✉ 1047 5th Ave., Gaslamp Quarter ☎ 619/515–3000 ⊕ www.hotelpalomar-sandiego.com ⇨ 211 rooms 🍴 No meals* ✥ 1:E3.

$$$ HOTEL FAMILY Fodor's Choice ★ **Kimpton Hotel Solamar.** Best known for its pool-side rooftop bar, LoungeSix, and stylish lobby decor, Solamar's recently refreshed guest rooms reflect this urban escape's mixture of luxury and fun, with prints galore and subtle nods to San Diego's happy beach culture. **Pros:** great restaurant; attentive service; upscale rooms. **Cons:** busy valet parking; daily facility fee. *Rooms from: $279 ✉ 435 6th Ave., Gaslamp Quarter ☎ 619/819–9500, 877/230–0300 ⊕ www.hotelsolamar.com ⇨ 235 rooms 🍴 No meals* ✥ 1:E5.

$$$ HOTEL **Omni San Diego Hotel.** Business travelers who also want to catch a baseball game flock to this modern masterpiece that occupies the first 21 floors of a 32-story high-rise overlooking Petco Park. **Pros:** great views; good location; modern setting. **Cons:** busy; crowded during baseball season. *Rooms from: $278 ✉ 675 L St., Gaslamp Quarter ☎ 619/231–6664, 800/843–6664 ⊕ www.omnihotels.com ⇨ 511 rooms 🍴 No meals* ✥ 1:E6.

$$$$ HOTEL Fodor's Choice ★ **Pendry San Diego.** Opened in early 2017, the Pendry San Diego is the Gaslamp's newest stunner. **Pros:** well-situated in Gaslamp Quarter; excellent dining options; complimentary coffee in the mornings. **Cons:** pricey room rates; meals are expensive. *Rooms from: $480 ✉ 550 J St., Gaslamp Quarter ☎ 619/738–7000 ⊕ www.pendryhotels.com ⇨ 317 rooms 🍴 No meals* ✥ 1:E5.

$$$ HOTEL **San Diego Marriott Gaslamp Quarter.** The 22-story Marriott sits amid the Gaslamp's restaurants and boutiques, near a trolley station, the convention center, and Petco Park. **Pros:** good views; modern decor; central location. **Cons:** rooftop bar can get rowdy; no pool. *Rooms from: $269 660 K St., Gaslamp Quarter 619/696–0234 www.sandiegogaslamphotel.com 306 rooms No meals* 1:E5.

$$$ HOTEL Fodor's Choice ★ **The Sofia Hotel.** This stylish and centrally located boutique hotel may have small rooms, but it more than compensates with pampering extras like motion-sensor temperature controls, a Zen-like 24-hour yoga studio, an updated lobby, and a brand-new spa suite. **Pros:** upscale amenities; historic building; near shops and restaurants. **Cons:** busy area; small rooms. *Rooms from: $259 150 W. Broadway, Gaslamp Quarter 619/234–9200, 800/826–0009 www.thesofiahotel.com 211 rooms No meals* 1:D3.

$$$$ HOTEL Fodor's Choice ★ **The U.S. Grant, a Luxury Collection Hotel.** The U.S. Grant may be more than a hundred years old (it first opened in 1910) but thanks to a top-to-bottom renovation in 2017, this grand old dame is now one of the most glamorous hotels in Southern California. **Pros:** sophisticated rooms; great location; near shopping and restaurants. **Cons:** street noise can be heard from the guest rooms. *Rooms from: $304 326 Broadway, Gaslamp Quarter 619/232–3121, 800/325–3589 www.usgrant.net 223 rooms, 47 suites No meals* 1:D3.

$$$ HOTEL **The Westgate Hotel.** A modern high-rise near Horton Plaza hides San Diego's most opulent old world–style hotel, featuring a lobby outfitted with bronze sculptures and Baccarat chandeliers. **Pros:** affordable luxury; serene rooftop pool deck. **Cons:** dated guest rooms; mandatory facility fee. *Rooms from: $299 1055 2nd Ave., Gaslamp Quarter 619/238–1818, 800/522–1564 www.westgatehotel.com 223 rooms No meals* 1:D3.

LITTLE ITALY

$$$ HOTEL FAMILY **Hilton Garden Inn/Homewood Suites.** Two brands from Hilton Hotels now share a building in Little Italy two blocks from the bay, giving guests more space to spread out and be relatively within budget. **Pros:** modern guest rooms; plenty of tech conveniences. **Cons:** on a busy block; valet parking only. *Rooms from: $235 2137 Pacific Hwy. 619/696–7000 Homewood Suites, 619/696–6300 Hilton Garden Inn www.sandiegohiltonhotels.com 364 rooms Breakfast* 1:B1.

$ B&B/INN **Hotel Vyvant.** You'll find more amenities at other Downtown hotels but it's hard to beat this property's value and charm. **Pros:** good location; historic property; welcoming staff. **Cons:** some shared baths; no parking. *Rooms from: $139 505 W. Grape St., Little Italy 619/230–1600, 800/518–9930 www.hotelvyvant.com 23 rooms Breakfast* 1:C1.

$ HOTEL **Porto Vista Hotel.** This former budget motel has transformed into a contemporary hotel-motel with modern furnishings, a stylish restaurant and lounge, a fitness center, and even a hair salon. **Pros:** great location in Little Italy; complimentary airport shuttle. **Cons:** can be noisy; rooms need updating. *Rooms from: $160 1835 Columbia St., Little Italy 619/544–0164 www.portovistasd.com 191 rooms No meals* 1:C2.

EMBARCADERO

$$$ HOTEL FAMILY **Embassy Suites by Hilton San Diego Bay Downtown.** The front door of each spacious, contemporary suite here opens out onto a 12-story atrium. **Pros:** harbor-facing rooms have spectacular views; spacious accommodations; good location. **Cons:** busy area; ho-hum decor. *Rooms from: $269 601 Pacific Hwy., Embarcadero 619/239–2400, 800/362–2779 www.sandiegobay.embassysuites.com 341 suites Breakfast* 1:B4.

$$$ HOTEL FAMILY **Manchester Grand Hyatt San Diego.** Primarily a draw for business travelers, this hotel between Seaport Village and the convention center also works well for leisure and family travelers. **Pros:** great views; conference facilities; good location; spacious rooms. **Cons:** lots of convention-goers; some trolley noise. *Rooms from: $259 1 Market Pl., Embarcadero 619/232–1234, 800/233–1234 www.manchester.grand.hyatt.com 1628 rooms No meals* 1:C5.

OLD TOWN AND UPTOWN

San Diego's Uptown area is close to the San Diego Zoo and Balboa Park, and includes the neighborhoods of Hillcrest, Mission Hills, and University Heights. There are few hotels, but the area offers pedestrian-friendly shopping and many of San Diego's venerable craft beer bars and breweries.

Dense with Mexican eateries, Old Town is the place to be for quick and easy access to house-made tortillas. The neighborhood is also home to historic adobe shops and museums. East of Old Town is Mission Valley, a suburban maze of freeways, shopping centers, and Hotel Circle, where many spacious and inexpensive lodging options are located.

OLD TOWN

$$ HOTEL FAMILY **Best Western Plus Hacienda Hotel Old Town.** Perched on a hill in the heart of Old Town, this hotel is known for its expansive courtyards, outdoor fountains, and maze of stairs that connect eight buildings of guest rooms. **Pros:** airport shuttle; well-maintained outdoor areas. **Cons:** some rooms need renovating; complicated layout. *Rooms from: $210 4041 Harney St., Old Town 619/298–4707 www.haciendahotel-oldtown.com 198 rooms No meals* 2:A4.

$ B&B/INN **The Cosmopolitan Hotel.** With antique furniture, pull-chain toilets, and a veranda overlooking Old Town State Historic Park, the Cosmo offers guests a taste of Victorian-era living. **Pros:** historic charm; huge suites. **Cons:** no TVs; limited on-site parking; street noise. *Rooms from: $159 2660 Calhoun St., Old Town 619/297–1874 www.oldtowncosmopolitan.com 10 rooms Breakfast* 2:A4.

MISSION VALLEY

$$$ HOTEL **DoubleTree by Hilton Hotel San Diego Mission Valley.** Near the Fashion Valley shopping mall and adjacent to the Hazard Center—which has a seven-screen movie theater, four major restaurants, and more than 20 shops—the DoubleTree is also convenient to Route 163 and I–8 and there's a San Diego Trolley station within walking distance. **Pros:** stellar service; large rooms; good for fitness buffs. **Cons:** no mini-refrigerators in rooms; unimpressive views. *Rooms from: $235* ✉ *7450 Hazard Center Dr.* ☎ *619/297–5466, 800/222–8733* 🌐 *www.doubletree.com* *300 rooms* *No meals* ✥ 2:D2.

MISSION BAY AND THE BEACHES

Mission Bay, with its beaches, bike trails, boat-launching ramps, golf course, and grassy parks—not to mention SeaWorld—is a haven of hotels and resorts. Smaller hotels, motels, and hostels can be found nearby in Mission Beach and Pacific Beach. These coastal communities are popular among local twentysomethings for the many inexpensive dining and nightlife options. The streets are also filled with surf shops and boutiques for picking up flip-flops, sundresses, and other beachy souvenirs.

MISSION BAY

$$ RESORT FAMILY **The Dana on Mission Bay, BW Premier Collection.** A part of Best Western's BW Premier Collection, this waterfront resort, just down the road from SeaWorld, has an ideal location for active leisure travelers. **Pros:** water views; many outdoor activities. **Cons:** expensive resort fee. *Rooms from: $209* ✉ *1710 W. Mission Bay Dr., Mission Bay* ☎ *619/222–6440, 800/445–3339* 🌐 *www.thedana.com* *271 rooms* *No meals* ✥ 3:C6.

$$$ RESORT FAMILY **Hyatt Regency Mission Bay Spa and Marina.** This modern property has many desirable amenities, including balconies with excellent views of the garden, bay, ocean, or swimming pool courtyard. **Pros:** close proximity to water sports; 120-foot waterslides in pools, plus kiddie slide. **Cons:** daily resort fee; not centrally located. *Rooms from: $299* ✉ *1441 Quivira Rd., Mission Bay* ☎ *619/224–1234, 800/233–1234* 🌐 *www.missionbay.regency.hyatt.com* *429 rooms* *No meals* ✥ 3:C6.

$$$ RESORT FAMILY **Paradise Point Resort and Spa.** Minutes from SeaWorld but hidden in a quiet part of Mission Bay, the beautiful landscape of this 44-acre resort offers plenty of space for families to play and relax. **Pros:** water views; five pools; good service. **Cons:** not centrally located; motel-thin walls; parking and resort fees. *Rooms from: $289* ✉ *1404 Vacation Rd., Mission Bay* ☎ *858/274–4630, 800/344–2626* 🌐 *www.paradisepoint.com* *462 rooms* *No meals* ✥ 3:C6.

9

MISSION BEACH

$$$$ RESORT FAMILY **Catamaran Resort Hotel and Spa.** Tiki torches light the way through grounds thick with tropical foliage to the six two-story buildings and the 14-story high-rise on Mission Bay. The Polynesian theme continues in the guest rooms while the Catamaran Spa offers Hawaiian-style lomilomi massages, ginger-root detox wraps, and starfruit sugar body scrubs. **Pros:** no resort fees; some rooms have bay views; many activities for kids. **Cons:** common areas need renovating; dated room decor. *Rooms from: $349 ✉ 3999 Mission Blvd., Mission Beach ☎ 858/488–1081 🌐 www.catamaranresort.com 310 rooms No meals* ✣ 3:C5.

PACIFIC BEACH

$$$$ HOTEL FAMILY **Blue Sea Beach Hotel.** A modern take on the beachfront motel, the Blue Sea Beach hotel has Pacific Beach's only oceanfront pool. **Pros:** fun lobby; great pool deck. **Cons:** small rooms; can be expensive in peak season. *Rooms from: $471 ✉ 707 Pacific Beach Dr., Pacific Beach ☎ 858/488–4780 🌐 www.blueseabeachhotel.com 126 rooms No meals* ✣ 3:C5.

$$ HOTEL FAMILY **Crystal Pier Hotel and Cottages.** Rustic little oases with a charm all their own, the beachy cottages may lack some of the amenities of comparably priced hotels, but you're paying for character and proximity to the ocean—these lodgings are literally on the pier. **Pros:** ocean views everywhere you look; historic lodgings; free parking. **Cons:** few amenities; reservations fill up fast. *Rooms from: $175 ✉ 4500 Ocean Blvd., Pacific Beach ☎ 800/748–5894 🌐 www.crystalpier.com 30 rooms No meals* ✣ 3:B5.

$$$$ RESORT **Pacific Terrace Hotel.** Travelers love this terrific beachfront hotel and the ocean views from most rooms; it's a perfect place for watching sunsets over the Pacific. **Pros:** beach views; large rooms; friendly service. **Cons:** busy and sometimes noisy area; expensive in peak season. *Rooms from: $549 ✉ 610 Diamond St., Pacific Beach ☎ 858/581–3500, 800/344–3370 🌐 www.pacificterrace.com 73 rooms No meals* ✣ 3:B5.

$$$ HOTEL **Surfer Beach Hotel.** Choose this place for its great location—right on bustling Pacific Beach. **Pros:** beach location; ocean-view rooms; pool. **Cons:** dated rooms; no air-conditioning. *Rooms from: $260 ✉ 711 Pacific Beach Dr., Pacific Beach ☎ 800/820–5772 🌐 www.surferbeachhotel.com 69 rooms No meals* ✣ 3:C5.

$$$$ HOTEL **Tower23.** A neomodern masterpiece with a beachy vibe, this boutique hotel is a favorite of the young and young-at-heart. **Pros:** beach views; central location; hip decor. **Cons:** no pool; busy area. *Rooms from: $399 ✉ 723 Felspar St., Pacific Beach ☎ 858/270–2323 🌐 www.t23hotel.com 44 rooms No meals* ✣ 3:B5.

LA JOLLA

Multimillion-dollar homes line the beaches and hillsides of beautiful and prestigious La Jolla, a community about 20 minutes north of Downtown. La Jolla Shores is a mile-long sandy beach that gets crowded in summer with kayakers, sunbathers, and students in scuba-diving classes. The village—the heart of La Jolla—is chockablock with expensive boutiques, art galleries, restaurants, and a grassy beachfront park that's popular for picnics and weddings.

$$$ RESORT **Estancia La Jolla Hotel & Spa.** With its rambling California mission–style architecture and brilliant gardens, this resort on what once was a famous equestrian ranch exudes rustic elegance. **Pros:** upscale rooms; nice spa; landscaped grounds. **Cons:** mandatory resort fees; not centrally located. *Rooms from: $279* *9700 N. Torrey Pines Rd., La Jolla* *858/550–1000* *www.estancialajolla.com* *210 rooms* *No meals* 3:B1.

$$$$ HOTEL Fodor's Choice ★ **Grande Colonial.** This white wedding cake–style hotel in the heart of La Jolla village has ocean views and charming European details that include chandeliers, mahogany railings, and French doors. **Pros:** great location; superb restaurant. **Cons:** somewhat busy street; no fitness center; valet parking only. *Rooms from: $369* *910 Prospect St., La Jolla* *888/828–5498* *www.thegrandecolonial.com* *93 rooms* *No meals* 3:A2.

$$$ HOTEL **Hotel La Jolla, Curio Collection by Hilton.** This coastal-chic hotel boasts sparkling views of the Pacific and an excellent 11th-floor restaurant, Cusp Dining & Drinks. **Pros:** new rooms; stunning views from the higher floors. **Cons:** tiny gym; valet parking only. *Rooms from: $279* *7955 La Jolla Shores Dr., La Jolla* *858/459–0261* *www.hotel-lajolla.com* *110 rooms* *No meals* 3:C2.

$$$ HOTEL FAMILY **La Jolla Cove Suites.** It may lack the charm of some properties in this exclusive area, but this motel with studios and suites (some with spacious oceanfront balconies) gives its guests the same first-class views of La Jolla Cove at lower rates. **Pros:** good value; ocean views. **Cons:** haphazard layout; busy street. *Rooms from: $280* *1155 Coast Blvd., La Jolla* *858/459–2621* *www.lajollacove.com* *118 rooms* *Breakfast* 3:B2.

$$$$ HOTEL FAMILY **La Jolla Shores Hotel.** One of San Diego's few hotels actually on the beach, this property is part of La Jolla Beach and Tennis Club. **Pros:** on beach; great views. **Cons:** not centrally located; pool can be noisy; three-night minimum in summer. *Rooms from: $319* *8110 Camino del Oro, La Jolla* *858/923–8058, 877/346–6714* *www.ljshoreshotel.com* *128 rooms* *No meals* 3:B2.

$$$$ HOTEL **La Valencia.** This pink Spanish-Mediterranean confection drew Hollywood film stars in the 1930s and '40s with its setting and views of La Jolla Cove; now it draws the Kardashians. **Pros:** upscale rooms; views; near beach. **Cons:** standard rooms are tiny; lots of traffic outside. *Rooms from: $449* *1132 Prospect St., La Jolla* *858/454–0771* *www.lavalencia.com* *114 rooms* *No meals* 3:B2.

$$$$ RESORT Fodor's Choice ★ **The Lodge at Torrey Pines.** This beautiful Craftsman-style lodge sits on a bluff between La Jolla and Del Mar and commands a coastal view. **Pros:** spacious upscale rooms; good service; adjacent the famed Torrey Pines Golf Course. **Cons:** not centrally located; expensive. *Rooms from: $379 ✉ 11480 N. Torrey Pines Rd., La Jolla ☎ 858/453–4420, 888/826–0224 🌐 www.lodgetorreypines.com Two 18-hole championship golf courses 170 rooms No meals* ⊕ 3:B1.

$$$$ HOTEL **Pantai Inn.** Located along La Jolla coastline with ocean views from almost every corner, this sophisticated, Bali-inspired inn offers a mix of studios, one- and two-bedroom suites, and cottages. **Pros:** spacious rooms; ocean views; free parking. **Cons:** no pool; no fitness center; not good for kids. *Rooms from: $380 ✉ 1003 Coast Blvd., La Jolla ☎ 858/224–7600, 855/287–2682 🌐 www.pantai.com 31 rooms Breakfast* ⊕ 3:A2.

$$$$ B&B/INN **Scripps Inn.** You'd be wise to make reservations well in advance for this small, quiet inn tucked away on Coast Boulevard atop Whale Watch Point; its popularity with repeat visitors ensures that it's booked year-round. **Pros:** beach access; intimate feel. **Cons:** daily resort fee; a three-night minimum is required in the summer. *Rooms from: $355 ✉ 555 S. Coast Blvd., La Jolla ☎ 858/454–3391, 888/976–2912 🌐 www.scrippsinn.com 14 rooms No meals* ⊕ 3:A2.

POINT LOMA, CORONADO, AND SHELTER ISLAND

Coronado feels like something out of an earlier, more gracious era, making it a great getaway. The clean white beaches are some of the best in the state, and they're rarely crowded. However, if you plan to see many of San Diego's attractions, you'll spend significant time commuting across the bridge or riding the ferry.

One of two man-made peninsulas between Downtown and Point Loma, Shelter Island has grassy parks, tree-lined paths, and views of Downtown. (The other peninsula, Harbor Island, is less than five minutes from the airport.) Shelter Island is next to Point Loma, a hilly community that's home to Cabrillo National Monument, a naval base, and a growing destination for shopping and dining called Liberty Station.

POINT LOMA

$$$ HOTEL FAMILY **Courtyard Marriott San Diego Airport Liberty Station.** Close to the restaurants and shops of Liberty Station, this family-friendly hotel spares travelers the extra fees charged by most Downtown and coastal lodgings. **Pros:** modern rooms; free airport shuttle; no resort fees. **Cons:** limited views; not much charm or personality. *Rooms from: $279 ✉ 2592 Laning Rd., Point Loma ☎ 619/221–1900, 888/236–2427 🌐 www.marriott.com/sanal 200 rooms No meals* ⊕ 4:C1.

$$ HOTEL FAMILY **Holiday Inn San Diego-Bayside.** If SeaWorld and the San Diego Zoo aren't enough to sap kids of their energy, the outdoor activities at this hotel across from San Diego Bay fishing docks should do the trick. **Pros:** great for kids; close to airport. **Cons:** not centrally located; confusing

layout; might be too kid-friendly for some. *Rooms from: $216* ✉ *4875 N. Harbor Dr., Point Loma* ☎ *619/224–3621, 800/662–8899* 🌐 *www.holinnbayside.com* *291 rooms* *No meals* ✣ 4:C1.

$$$$ HOTEL FAMILY Fodor's Choice ★ **Homewood Suites San Diego Airport Liberty Station.** Families and business travelers will benefit from the space and amenities at this all-suites hotel. **Pros:** complimentary grocery shopping service; close to paths for joggers and bikers. **Cons:** no pets allowed; far from nightlife. *Rooms from: $349* ✉ *2576 Laning Rd., Point Loma* ☎ *619/222–0500* 🌐 *www.homewoodsuites.com* *150 suites* *Breakfast* ✣ 4:C1.

$$$ HOTEL Fodor's Choice ★ **The Pearl Hotel.** This previously vintage motel received a makeover, turning it into a retro-chic hangout decorated with kitschy lamps and original, in-room art by local children. **Pros:** near marina; hip bar/restaurant on-site (dinner only, except for seasonal specials). **Cons:** not centrally located; one bed in rooms. *Rooms from: $233* ✉ *1410 Rosecrans St., Point Loma* ☎ *619/226–6100* 🌐 *www.thepearlsd.com* *23 rooms* *No meals* ✣ 4:B1.

SHELTER ISLAND

$ HOTEL FAMILY **Best Western Plus Island Palms Hotel & Marina.** With tennis courts, two pools, jogging paths, and complimentary bike rentals, this waterfront hotel is a natural fit for fitness enthusiasts. **Pros:** near water; great room views; private marina. **Cons:** confusing layout; can be noisy. *Rooms from: $159* ✉ *2051 Shelter Island Dr., Shelter Island* ☎ *619/222–0561, 800/922–2336* 🌐 *www.islandpalms.com* *227 rooms* *No meals* ✣ 4:B3.

$$$$ RESORT **Kona Kai Resort.** From the moment you walk into the 11-acre Kona Kai Resort at the tip of Shelter Island, you'll instantly feel relaxed, thanks to the lobby's soothing and kitsch-free tropical, which was introduced during a multimillion-dollar renovation in 2014. **Pros:** quiet area; near marina; water views. **Cons:** not centrally located; resort fees; popular for business meetings. *Rooms from: $329* ✉ *1551 Shelter Island Dr., Shelter Island* ☎ *619/221–8000, 800/566–2524* 🌐 *www.resortkonakai.com* *129 rooms* *No meals* ✣ 4:B3.

9

CORONADO

$$$$ RESORT FAMILY Fodor's Choice ★ **Coronado Island Marriott Resort.** Near San Diego Bay, this snazzy hotel has rooms with great Downtown skyline views. **Pros:** spectacular views; on-site spa; close to water taxis. **Cons:** not in downtown Coronado; resort fee. *Rooms from: $329* ✉ *2000 2nd St., Coronado* ☎ *619/435–3000, 800/228–9290* 🌐 *www.marriotthotels.com/sanci* *300 rooms* *No meals* ✣ 4:H5.

$$ HOTEL FAMILY **Glorietta Bay Inn.** The main building on this property is an Edwardian-style mansion built in 1908 for sugar baron John D. Spreckels, who once owned much of Downtown San Diego. **Pros:** great views; friendly staff; close to beach. **Cons:** mansion rooms are small; lots of traffic nearby. *Rooms from: $179* ✉ *1630 Glorietta Blvd., Coronado* ☎ *619/435–3101, 800/283–9383* 🌐 *www.gloriettabayinn.com* *100 rooms* *Breakfast* ✣ 4:G6.

$$$$ RESORT FAMILY Fodor's Choice ★

Hotel Del Coronado. As much of a draw today as it was when it opened in 1888, the Victorian-style "Hotel Del" is always alive with activity, as guests—including U.S. presidents and celebrities—and tourists marvel at the fanciful architecture and ocean views. **Pros:** 17 on-site shops; on the beach; well-rounded spa. **Cons:** some rooms are small; expensive dining; hectic public areas. *Rooms from: $425* *1500 Orange Ave., Coronado* *800/468–3533, 619/435–6611* *www.hoteldel.com* *757 rooms* *No meals* 4:G6.

$$$$ RESORT FAMILY

Loews Coronado Bay Resort. You can park your boat at the 80-slip marina of this romantic retreat set on a secluded 15-acre peninsula on the Silver Strand. **Pros:** great restaurants; lots of activities; all rooms have furnished balconies with water views. **Cons:** far from anything; confusing layout. *Rooms from: $349* *4000 Coronado Bay Rd., Coronado* *619/424–4000, 800/815–6397* *www.loewshotels.com/CoronadoBay* *439 rooms* *No meals* 4:H6.

$$$$ B&B/INN Fodor's Choice ★

1906 Lodge at Coronado Beach. Smaller but no less luxurious than the sprawling beach resorts of Coronado, this lodge—whose name alludes to the main building's former life as a boardinghouse built in 1906—welcomes couples for romantic retreats two blocks from the ocean. **Pros:** most suites feature Jacuzzi tubs, fireplaces, and porches; historic property; free underground parking. **Cons:** too quiet for families; no pool. *Rooms from: $329* *1060 Adella Ave., Coronado* *619/437–1900, 866/435–1906* *www.1906lodge.com* *17 rooms* *Breakfast* 4:G6.

NIGHTLIFE

10

Updated by Jeff Terich

The San Diego nightlife scene is much more diverse and innovative than it was just a decade ago. Back then, options were limited to the pricey singles-heavy dance clubs Downtown, the party-hearty atmosphere of Pacific Beach, and a handful of charmingly musty neighborhood dive bars popular with locals. Today options in San Diego have expanded dramatically, boasting more than 90 craft breweries throughout the county, not to mention several stylish cocktail lounges.

The Gaslamp Quarter is still one of the most popular areas to go for a night on the town. Named for actual gaslights that once provided illumination along its once-seedy streets (it housed a number of gambling halls and brothels), the neighborhood bears only a trace of its debauched roots. Between the Gaslamp and nearby East Village, Downtown San Diego mostly comprises chic nightclubs, tourist-heavy pubs, and a handful of live music venues. Even most of the hotels Downtown have a street-level or rooftop bar—so plan on making it a late night if that's where you intend to bunk. On weekends, parking can be tricky; most lots run about $20, and though there is metered parking (free after 6 pm and all day Sunday), motorists don't give up those coveted spots so easily. Some restaurants and clubs offer valet, though that can get pricey.

Hillcrest is a popular area for LGBT nightlife and culture, whereas just a little bit east of Hillcrest, ever-expanding North Park features a diverse range of bars and lounges that cater to a twenty- and thirtysomething crowd, bolstering its reputation as the city's hipster capital. Nearby Normal Heights is a slightly less pretentious alternative, though whichever of these neighborhoods strikes your fancy, a cab from Downtown will run about the same price: $15

Nightlife along the beaches is more of a mixed bag. Where the scene in Pacific Beach might feel like every week is Spring Break, La Jolla veers toward being more cost-prohibitive. And although Point Loma is often seen as a sleeper neighborhood in terms of nightlife, it's coming into its own with some select destinations.

If your drink involves caffeine and not alcohol, there's no shortage of coffeehouses in San Diego, and some of the better ones in Hillcrest and North Park stay open past midnight. Many of them also serve beer and wine, if the caffeine buzz isn't enough.

PLANNING

THE LOWDOWN

Step outside to smoke. Smoking is strictly outlawed indoors in public places in San Diego, and since 2014 that includes e-cigarettes or vaporizer pens.

What to wear. In the Gaslamp, East Village, and some of North Park's more upscale spots, dress code is strictly enforced: no flip-flops, ballcaps, jerseys, or shorts at any of the city's swankier bars.

Last call for alcohol. The last chance for nightcaps is theoretically 2 am, but most bars stop serving around 1:30. Listen for the bartender's announcement.

WHAT'S GOING ON?

The city's daily paper, *The San Diego Union-Tribune* (🌐 *www.sandiegouniontribune.com*), has up-to-date entertainment listings, as well as the paper's more nightlife-heavy sister site *Pacific San Diego* (🌐 *www.pacificsandiego.com*), which provides event listings and editorial suggestions. San Diego has two alt-weeklies, of which *The Reader* (🌐 *www.sandiegoreader.com*) boasts more extensive online listings. *San Diego CityBeat* (🌐 *sdcitybeat.com*) is more selective with its recommendations, highlighting the edgier and more innovative cultural events.

San Diego magazine (🌐 *www.sandiegomagazine.com*) is a mainstream read for all walks of life; *Riviera* (🌐 *sandiego.modernluxury.com*) is younger, more upscale, and au courant.

NIGHTLIFE BY NEIGHBORHOOD

DOWNTOWN

GASLAMP QUARTER

Partygoers line up behind velvet ropes to dance inside Downtown's most exclusive clubs.

BARS

Altitude Sky Lounge. Location is everything at this sophisticated lounge on the roof of the 22-floor San Diego Marriott Gaslamp Quarter. The views of the Downtown skyline and PETCO Park will give you a natural high. ✉ *660 K St., Gaslamp Quarter* ☎ *619/696–0234* 🌐 *www.sandiegogaslamphotel.com/nightlife/altitude*.

barleymash. This gigantic space can resemble either a raucous club or a sports bar, depending on what night you're there. But the drinks are strong and reasonably priced, and the reclaimed wood decor makes for an intimate atmosphere, even when the DJs are spinning mostly Top 40. ✉ *600 5th Ave., Gaslamp Quarter* ☎ *619/255–7373* 🌐 *www.barleymash.com.*

Hard Rock Hotel. A-list wannabes (and a few real celebs) gather in two bars, the loungey 207 off the lobby and the rooftop Float. The latter's Intervention and Wintervention daytime parties feature some of the world's biggest DJ names, or if you prefer a rock show, head to Maryjane's Underground at 207. Maybe you can't be a rock star, but you might as well party like one. Just be prepared to spend like one, too. ✉ *207 5th Ave., Gaslamp Quarter* ☎ *619/702–3000* 🌐 *hardrockhotelsd.com.*

LOUNGEsix. The trendy poolside bar on the fourth floor of the swank Hotel Solamar is a sexy spot to people-watch while sipping sangria or chili-mango margaritas and noshing on snacks from the "Slow Food" menu. On cool evenings, reserve a cabana or warm up next to one of the roaring fire pits. ✉ *616 J St., Gaslamp Quarter* ☎ *619/531–8744* 🌐 *www.jsixrestaurant.com.*

The Nolen. Panoramic views, warm and welcoming fire pits, and beer-forward "hop-tails" (cocktails that have beer in them) are the attraction at this rooftop destination, situated atop the Courtyard by Marriott San Diego Gaslamp/Convention Center. ✉ *453 6th Ave., Downtown* ☎ *619/796–6536* 🌐 *www.thenolenrooftop.com.*

Prohibition. This underground jazz lounge lives up to its name with a slinky speakeasy style. Red lighting, dark wood, and leather tufted couches provide a cozy 1920s–'30s-inspired backdrop to the live jazz on weekends. ✉ *548 5th Ave., Gaslamp Quarter* ☎ *619/663–5485* 🌐 *prohibitionsd.com.*

Fodor's Choice ★ **Rooftop600 @Andaz.** At this rooftop bar and lounge atop the Andaz hotel, a fashionable crowd sips cocktails poolside while gazing at gorgeous views of the city. Thursday through Saturday, the scene heats up with a DJ spinning dance music, while velvet ropes and VIP bottle service please the A-listers (like Prince Harry) in the crowd. ✉ *600 F St., Gaslamp Quarter* ☎ *619/814–2060* 🌐 *sandiego.andaz.hyatt.com.*

Side Bar. One of San Diego's premier clubs has a "more is more" decor and an attitude to match. Painted birdcages hang from the loft ceiling and DJs spin from inside a giant cage, which also provides sturdy scaffolding for female go-go dancers on weekends. The black-clad chandeliers and mismatched velvet couches (including one that once belonged to Paris Hilton) get an additional visual pop from the nudie paintings lining the walls. Fancy martinis are a must, and if you get hungry after last call, step next door to get some NYC-style pizza at Ciro's, open till 3 am. ✉ *536 Market St., Gaslamp Quarter* ☎ *619/696–0946* 🌐 *www.sidebarsd.com.*

SummerSalt Rooftop Lounge @ Hotel Palomar. The fourth-floor rooftop of the Hotel Palomar remains a go-to spot for posh party people who don't mind dropping big money for a poolside cabana. Note, though, that the music shuts down after midnight. Those looking for a more nuanced and romantic setting should seek out the plush leather couches and craft cocktails at the lobby-side Saltbox bar. ✉ *1047 5th Ave., Gaslamp Quarter* ☎ *619/515–3000* 🌐 *www.hotelpalomar-sandiego.com.*

Tivoli. Rumor has it that Wyatt Earp himself threw back a whiskey or two at the oldest bar in the Gaslamp, way before the walls were lined with neon beer signs. Perhaps old age accounts for the grungy veneer, but that doesn't stop locals from hitting this dive for $9 pitchers of PBR and hot dogs. The jukebox and pool table keep the unruly in check. Is that a spittoon in the corner? ✉ *505 6th Ave., Gaslamp Quarter* ☎ *619/232–6754.*

COMEDY AND CABARET

American Comedy Co. At this underground space modeled after the legendary comedy clubs in New York, there's not a bad seat in the house—which is especially great since the venue pulls in some of the hugest names in stand-up comedy. ✉ *818 6th Ave., Gaslamp Quarter* ☎ *619/795–3858* 🌐 *www.americancomedyco.com.*

DANCE CLUBS

Fluxx. Arguably the hottest club in the Gaslamp, this Vegas-style, multitheme space is packed to the gills on weekends with pretty people dancing to house and electro music and dropping major cash at the bar. ■ **TIP→ Get here early for a lower cover and to avoid the epic lines that snake around the block.** ✉ *500 4th Ave., Gaslamp Quarter* ☎ *619/232–8100* 🌐 *www.fluxxsd.com.*

Omnia. If the bright and flashy spectacle of Omnia feels a little bit more like Las Vegas than San Diego, it might be helpful to know that it actually has a Vegas counterpart. Top international EDM artists make stops here when they come to town, making it a necessary destination for BPM-seeking nightcrawlers. ✉ *454 6th Ave., Downtown* ☎ *619/544–9500.*

Sevilla. For more than two decades, Cafe Sevilla and the Sevilla nightclub have brought a Latin flavor to the Gaslamp Quarter through a mix of contemporary and traditional Spanish and Latin American music. Get fueled up at the tapas bar before venturing downstairs for dancing. Salsa lessons during the week provide an especially memorable experience. ✉ *353 5th Ave., Gaslamp Quarter* ☎ *619/233–5979* 🌐 *sevillanightclub.com.*

PIANO BARS

Fodor'sChoice ★ **Westgate Hotel Plaza Bar.** The old-money surroundings, including leather-upholstered seats, marble tabletops, and a grand piano, supply one of the most elegant and romantic settings for a drink in San Diego. ✉ *1055 2nd Ave., Gaslamp Quarter* ☎ *619/238–1818* 🌐 *www.westgatehotel.com.*

10

ROCK, POP, HIP-HOP, FOLK, AND BLUES CLUBS

House of Blues. The local branch of the renowned music chain is decorated floor to ceiling with colorful folk art and features three different areas to hear music. There's something going on here just about every night of the week, and the gospel brunch on select Sundays is one of the most praiseworthy events in town. Can we get a hallelujah? ✉ *1055 5th Ave., Gaslamp Quarter* ☎ *619/299–2583* 🌐 *www.houseofblues.com.*

WINE BARS

Fodor'sChoice ★ **Vin de Syrah.** This "spirit and wine cellar" sends you down a rabbit hole (or at least down some stairs) to a whimsical spot straight out of Alice in Wonderland. Behind a hidden door (look for a handle in the grass wall), you'll find visual delights (grapevines suspended from the ceiling, vintage jars with flittering "fireflies," cozy chairs nestled around a faux fireplace and pastoral vista) that rival the culinary ones—the wine list is approachable and the charcuterie boards are exquisitely curated. ■ **TIP→ More than just a wine bar, the cocktails are also worth a try.** ✉ *901 5th Ave., Gaslamp Quarter* ☎ *619/234–4166* 🌐 *www.syrahwineparlor.com.*

EAST VILLAGE

This up-and-coming urban hood has upscale style mashed with hip, underground dives.

BARS

Bar Basic. This spot is always bustling, in part because it's *the* place to be seen for Padres fans or anyone else attending events at PETCO Park. True to its name, Basic reliably dishes up simple pleasures: strong drinks and hot, coal-fired pizza. The garage-style doors roll up and keep the industrial-chic former warehouse ventilated during the balmy summer. ✉ *410 10th Ave., East Village* ☎ *619/531–8869* 🌐 *www.barbasic.com.*

Cat Eye Club. Separated from the hectic hustle of East Village by just a short and dimly lit foyer, Cat Eye Club might as well be in an entirely different world. More specifically, it's a trip back to the 1960s, with mid-century modern furnishings, a Wurlitzer jukebox and Rat Pack flicks on regular rotation. Their menu of tiki cocktails ranges from simple sips to punch bowls, or for those who prefer their drinks flashier, the Cradle of Life, garnished with a flaming lime wedge. ✉ *370 7th Ave., East Village* 🌐 *cateyeclubsd.com/.*

East Village Tavern & Bowl. Twelve bowling lanes means no more hauls to the suburbs to channel one's inner Lebowski. Lane rental is pricey during prime times, but reasonable if you consider that some nearby clubs charge a Jackson just for admission, though reservations are definitely recommended. From the expansive bar area you can watch sports on 33 flat screens, and the satellite radio plays an assortment of alt- and classic rock. ✉ *930 Market St., East Village* ☎ *619/677–2695* 🌐 *www.tavernbowl.com.*

Fodor's Choice ★ **Fairweather.** Hidden in plain sight next to PETCO Park, Fairweather is an urban tiki oasis with a top-notch cocktail menu that boasts classics like daiquiris and their signature frozen pina colada alongside modern interpretations of old-school tiki drinks like corpse revivers and mai tais. ■ **TIP→ Come by during Comic-Con in July to view the parade of costumed characters while sipping on a rum refreshment on the balcony.** ✉ *795 J St., 2nd fl., East Village* ☎ *619/255–6507.*

Monkey Paw. What was once a notorious dive bar attracts hipsters and grizzled locals alike for a vast selection of craft beers (some brewed on-site), shuffleboard, and cheesesteaks that hit the spot no matter the hour. ✉ *805 16th St., East Village* ☎ *619/358–9901* 🌐 *www.monkeypawbrewing.com.*

LITTLE ITALY

Amid its arty galleries and boutiques, Little Italy houses several popular open-air beer bars.

BARS

Fodor's Choice ★ **False Idol.** A walk-in refrigerator harbors the secret entrance to this tiki-themed speakeasy, which is attached to Craft & Commerce. Beneath fishing nets full of puffer-fish lights and elaborate tiki-head wall carvings, the knowledgeable staff serves up creative takes on tropical classics with the best selection of rums in town. **■TIP→ The bar fills up quickly, especially on weekends. Make a reservation online a week or more in advance.** ✉ *675 W. Beech St., Little Italy* 🌐 *falseidoltiki.com.*

Fodor's Choice ★ **The Waterfront Bar & Grill.** It isn't really *on* the waterfront, but San Diego's oldest bar was once the hangout of Italian fishermen. Most of the collars are now white, and patrons enjoy an excellent selection of beers, along with chili, burgers, fish-and-chips, and other great-tasting grub, including fish tacos. Get here early, as there's almost always a crowd. ✉ *2044 Kettner Blvd., Little Italy* ☎ *619/232–9656* 🌐 *www.waterfrontbarandgrill.com.*

NIGHT BAY CRUISES

Flagship Cruises and Events. Flagship Cruises welcomes guests aboard with a glass of champagne as a prelude to nightly dinner-dance and holiday cruises. ✉ *990 N. Harbor Dr., Little Italy* ☎ *619/234–4111* 🌐 *www.flagshipsd.com.*

Hornblower Cruises. Take a dinner-dance cruise aboard the *Lord Hornblower*—the trip comes with fabulous views of the San Diego skyline. ✉ *970 N. Harbor Dr., Little Italy* 🌐 *hornblower.com.*

EMBARCADERO

Scenic drinking spots and higher bar tabs overlook tall ships and naval history.

BARS

The Lion's Share. Hemingway would have loved this exquisitely designed brick-and-wood bar that serves up equally exquisite craft cocktails that, while pricey, are definitely made for sipping. The place attracts a sophisticated crowd and is highly recommended for those looking to impress a special someone. ✉ *629 Kettner Blvd., Embarcadero* ☎ *619/564–6924* 🌐 *lionssharesd.com.*

Top of the Hyatt. This lounge at the Manchester Grand Hyatt crowns the tallest waterfront building in California, affording great views of San Diego Bay, including Coronado to the west, Mexico to the south, and Point Loma and La Jolla to the north. It's pricey and pretentious (don't you dare wear flip-flops), but this champagne-centric bar is great for catching a sunset or celebrating an anniversary. ✉ *1 Market Pl., Embarcadero* ☎ *619/232–1234* 🌐 *topofthehyatt.com.*

10

OLD TOWN AND UPTOWN

OLD TOWN

Old-timey saloons lure tourists with margaritas, mezcal, and mariachis.

BARS

The Cosmopolitan. The bar at the Cosmopolitan Hotel in Old Town maintains the old-timey aesthetic of the tourist-heavy neighborhood, complete with servers in period garb and game trophies on the walls. The quality of the cocktails and the friendly atmosphere make this a gem among the rest of the old west kitsch. ✉ *2660 Calhoun St., Old Town* ☎ *619/297–1874* 🌐 *www.oldtowncosmopolitan.com/.*

El Agave Tequileria. The bar of this restaurant named for the cactus whose sap is distilled into tequila stocks hundreds of top-shelf brands that are as sip-worthy as the finest cognac. ✉ *2304 San Diego Ave., Old Town* ☎ *619/220–0692* 🌐 *www.elagave.com.*

HILLCREST

This is San Diego's most active area for LGBT nightlife.

BARS

Nunu's. This retro-cool hangout with stiff cocktails might be one of the most popular bars in très gay Hillcrest, but don't expect a glitzy facade. The intentionally dated decor sits within the tatty walls of a white-brick box that probably hasn't had a face-lift since the LBJ administration. ✉ *3537 5th Ave., Hillcrest* ☎ *619/295–2878.*

COFFEEHOUSES

Fodor's Choice ★ **Extraordinary Desserts.** This café lives up to its name, which explains why there's often a line, despite the ample seating. Paris-trained Karen Krasne turns out award-winning cakes, tortes, and pastries of exceptional beauty. The Japanese-theme patio invites you to linger over yet another coffee drink. A second location is in Little Italy. ✉ *2929 5th Ave., Hillcrest* ☎ *619/294–2132* 🌐 *www.extraordinarydesserts.com.*

GAY NIGHTLIFE

Fodor's Choice ★ **Baja Betty's.** Although it draws plenty of gay customers, the festive and friendly atmosphere is popular with just about everyone in the Hillcrest area (and their pets are welcome, too). The bar staff stocks more than 100 brands of tequila and mixes plenty of fancy cocktails. ✉ *1421 University Ave., Hillcrest* ☎ *619/269–8510* 🌐 *www.bajabettyssd.com.*

Martinis Above Fourth. This swank lounge presents live piano, comedy, and cabaret on weekends to a friendly crowd. Swill cocktails inside or on the patio, and consider a meal afterward in the restaurant serving contemporary American fare. ✉ *3940 4th Ave., 2nd fl., Hillcrest* ☎ *619/400–4500* 🌐 *www.ma4sd.com.*

Rich's. The dancing and music here are some of the best in the city, making Rich's popular not only with gay men but also plenty of lesbians and straight revelers. ✉ *1051 University Ave., Hillcrest* ☎ *619/295–2195* 🌐 *www.richssandiego.com.*

Urban Mo's Bar and Grill. Cowboys gather for line dancing and two-stepping on the wooden dance floor—but be forewarned, yee-hawers, it can get pretty wild on Western nights. There are also Latin, hip-hop, and drag revues but the real allure is in the creative drinks ("Gone Fishing"—served in a fishbowl, for example) and the breezy patio where love (or something like it) is usually in the air. ✉ *308 University Ave., Hillcrest* ☎ *619/491–0400* 🌐 *www.urbanmos.com.*

CLOSE UP

San Diego On Tap

Home to more than 90 breweries, with more opening every year, San Diego's beer culture expands well beyond the breweries; along 30th Street in North Park, on up to Adams Avenue in Normal Heights, there's a sprawl of craft-beer bars and brewpubs. While you can find all styles of beer, many local brewers contend that Double IPA, an India Pale Ale with attitude, is the specialty.

Bars with the best microbrew selection: Blind Lady Ale House, Hamilton's Tavern, Live Wire, O'Brien's, Toronado.

Best fests: Winter Brew Fest in February, Rhythm and Brews in May, Heroes Brew Fest in July, during Comic-Con 🌐 *www.heroesbrewfest.com*, the San Diego Festival of Beers in September 🌐 *www.sdbeerfest.org*, San Diego Beer Week (November 🌐 *www.sdbw.org*), and the Strong Ale Fest (December).

Best way to sample it all: Brewery Tours of San Diego (🌐 *www.brewerytoursofsandiego.com*).

SAN DIEGO'S BEST BREWERIES

AleSmith Brewing Co. This artisanal microbrewery offers tastings at its out-of-the-way locale in the Miramar area. Try the "Kopi Luwak" special edition of AleSmith's popular Speedway Stout brewed with Civet coffee from Indonesia, made from rare and expensive coffee berries that have been eaten—and passed, undigested—by the Asian Palm Civet. Visitors can tour the entire brewery on Saturday at 2 pm. ✉ *9990 Alesmith Ct., Mira Mesa* ☎ *858/549–9888* 🌐 *www.alesmith.com.*

Alpine Brewing Co. Well worth the mountain drive, this family-owned operation may be itty-bitty, but it's also a big champ: brewmaster Pat McIlhenney, a former fire captain, has won national and international kudos for his hopped-up creations and took the title of the fifth-best brewery in the nation from *Beer Advocate*. Tasters are only a buck each, or fill a growler, which holds a half gallon, for future imbibing. If they're on tap, don't pass up Duet, Pure Hoppiness, or Exponential Hoppiness. Alpine recently opened a pub a few doors down where you can taste flights of their various beers. ✉ *2363 Alpine Blvd., Alpine* ☎ *619/445–2337* 🌐 *www.alpinebeerco.com.*

Ballast Point Brewing Co. Until recently, you had to head to the Miramar/Scripps Ranch area for a tasting at Ballast Point, but now there's a local taproom in Little Italy (2215 India Street). There are also plenty of opportunities to sample the beers at local pubs—the Sculpin IPA is outstanding, and for more adventurous drinkers, the much hotter Habanero sculpin is brewed with Habanero peppers. ✉ *10051 Old Grove Rd., Scripps Ranch* ☎ *858/695–2739* 🌐 *www.ballastpoint.com.*

Stone Brewing World Gardens and Bistro. The Big Daddy of San Diego craft brewing was founded by a couple of basement beer tinkerers in 1996; the company now exports its aggressively hoppy beers—instantly identifiable by their leering gargoyle labels—across the nation. Stone's monumental HQ is out of the way, but worth a visit for its tours ($3 includes souvenir glass), vast on-tap selection (not just Stone beers), and hard-to-beat bistro eats. ✉ *1999 Citracado Pkwy., Escondido* ☎ *760/294–7899* 🌐 *www.stonebrewing.com.*

MISSION HILLS

Take your pick between unpretentious pubs or ultrastylish cocktail grottos.

BARS

Aero Club. Named for its proximity to the airport, this watering hole draws in twenty- and thirtysomethings with its pool tables, dominoes, and 20 beers on tap (including a few local brews). Drinks are cheap, which makes this a popular place to fuel up before heading to Downtown. Don't miss the cool fighting warplanes mural. ✉ *3365 India St., Mission Hills* ☎ *619/297–7211* 🌐 *www.aeroclubbar.com.*

Blonde Bar. Images of Deborah Harry and Iggy Pop wallpaper this small but stylish dive. With a rotating cast of DJs and live bands, plus cocktails named for New York and UK punk icons, Blonde Bar is a small taste of 1977 in modern-day San Diego. ✉ *1808 W. Washington St., Mission Hills* 🌐 *www.blondebarsd.com.*

Shakespeare Pub & Grille. This Mission Hills hangout captures all the warmth and camaraderie of a traditional British pub—except here you can enjoy consistently sunny weather on the sprawling patio. The bar hands pour from a long list of imported ales and stouts, and the early hours for big matches make this *the* place to watch soccer. ✉ *3701 India St., Mission Hills* ☎ *619/299–0230* 🌐 *www.shakespearepub.com.*

Fodor's Choice ★ **Starlite.** Bar-goers are dazzled by Starlite's award-winning interior design, which includes rock walls, luxe leather booths, and a massive mirror-mounted chandelier. A hexagonal wood-plank entryway leads to a sunken white bar, where sexy tattooed guys and girls mix creative cocktails, such as the signature Starlite Mule, served in a copper mug. An iPod plays eclectic playlists ranging from old-timey jazz and blues to obscure vintage rock (and DJs are on hand on certain evenings). During warmer months, procuring a spot on the outside wood-decked patio is an art form. ✉ *3175 India St., Mission Hills* ☎ *619/358–9766* 🌐 *www.starlitesandiego.com.*

COFFEEHOUSES

Gelato Vero Caffe. A youthful crowd gathers here for authentic Italian ice cream, espresso, and a second-floor view of the Downtown skyline. The place is usually occupied by regulars who stay for hours at a time. ✉ *3753 India St., Mission Hills* ☎ *619/295–9269.*

NORTH PARK AND SOUTH PARK

Young, hip artist types gather to sip craft beer along the 30th Street corridor.

BARS

Bar Pink. Cheap drinks, loud music, and a hip crowd explain the line that's usually waiting outside this divey bar co-owned by Rocket From the Crypt frontman John "Speedo" Reis. Stop by on Tiki Tuesday for $5 drinks like their signature Sneaky Tiki, and DJs spinning vintage lounge and exotica tunes. ✉ *3829 30th St., North Park* ☎ *619/564–7194* 🌐 *www.barpink.com.*

Fodor's Choice ★ **Hamilton's Tavern.** Affectionately known to its loyal crowd of locals as Hammy's, this bar has one of the best beer lists in town. On the ceiling, lights strung between old beer taps twinkle as bright as the eyes of the suds-lovers who flock here. In between pours, grab something from

Hammy's kitchen—people come from all over for the wings and burgers. ✉ *1521 30th St., South Park* ☎ *619/238–5460* 🌐 *hamiltonstavern.com.*

Kindred. Family-friendly vegan brunch and deceivingly elegant decor are part of the charm of this artfully edgy cocktail bar. The sound system plays metal around the clock while heavily tattooed bartenders shake up potent yet refreshing craft cocktails. For the full experience, try to get a seat next to the four-eyed wolf beast protruding from the wall. ✉ *1503 30th St., South Park* ☎ *619/546–9653* 🌐 *barkindred.com.*

Live Wire. A tried-and-true authentic dive just on the border of the trendy North Park neighborhood lures pierced and tattooed kids in their twenties. A wide-ranging (and very loud) jukebox and TVs screening movies or music videos are the main entertainment, unless you count the people-watching. The cocktails as well as the excellent beers come in pint glasses, so pace yourself; the police lie in wait on nearby side streets. ✉ *2103 El Cajon Blvd., North Park* ☎ *619/291–7450* 🌐 *www.livewirebar.com.*

Red Fox Steak House. Referred to as Red Fox Room by those in the know, this dimly lit lounge is dearly loved by locals, and not just the seniors who flock here to sing Sinatra tunes to tickled ivories and the occasional impromptu horn section. ✉ *2223 El Cajon Blvd., North Park* ☎ *619/297–1313* 🌐 *www.redfoxsd.com.*

Fodor's Choice ★ **Seven Grand.** This whiskey lounge is a swanky addition to an already thriving North Park nightlife scene and a welcome alternative to the neighboring dives and dance clubs. Live jazz, a tranquil atmosphere, and a bourbon-loving craft cocktail list keep locals flocking. ✉ *3054 University Ave., North Park* ☎ *619/269–8820* 🌐 *213hospitality.com.*

Toronado. One of San Diego's favorite gathering spots for hop-heads is named in honor of the San Francisco beer bar of the same name. The beer list—both on tap and by the bottle—is hard to beat. The place can get noisy, but the food—a mix of burgers and American-style comfort food—more than makes up for it. ✉ *4026 30th St., North Park* ☎ *619/282–0452* 🌐 *www.toronadosd.com.*

BREWPUBS

Tiger! Tiger! A communal vibe prevails at this wood, metal, and brick gastropub, where patrons sit at picnic tables to schmooze and sip from one of the dozens of carefully selected craft and micro brews on tap. ✉ *3025 El Cajon Blvd., North Park* ☎ *619/487–0401* 🌐 *www.tiger-tigertavern.com.*

COFFEEHOUSES

Lips. Patrons enjoy their dinner while drag queens entertain (a $3 to $5 per-person cover charge will be added to your check). The place is always a hit for birthdays and bachelorette parties, but fair warning to the conservative—the scene can get raunchy. The motto, "where the men are men and so are the girls," says it all. ✉ *3036 El Cajon Blvd., North Park* ☎ *619/295–7900* 🌐 *lipssd.com.*

DANCE CLUBS

Whistle Stop Bar. Here's a place to get your groove on to indie, electro, and hip-hop, plus live bands on Friday. This tiny-but-banging locals' favorite just a few minutes from downtown gets hot and crowded, and the dance floor is always happening on Saturday. Plus, the cover's usually five bucks. ✉ *2236 Fern St., South Park* ☎ *619/284–6784* 🌐 *whistlestopbar.com.*

NORMAL HEIGHTS

Here beer snobs share barstools with urban hippies, bourbon yuppies, and surly locals.

BARS

Polite Provisions. The look of this cocktail lounge on the border of North Park and Normal Heights is drugstore chic, but the drinks themselves—none of which contain vodka—are much more sophisticated fare, shaken or stirred with house-made bitters and sodas. If you're looking to nosh, the adjoining Soda & Swine serves meatballs right to your table, and the six-hour Monday–Thursday happy hour is a must for those seeking mixology on a budget. ✉ *4696 30th St., Normal Heights* ☎ *619/677–3784* 🌐 *politeprovisions.com/.*

Sycamore Den. The heavy use of wood and stone, and accents like banjos and rifles might give Sycamore Den a masculine vibe, but it's a highly specific, and kitschy one: '70s dads. Though the hipster-pop concept might seem like it was plucked right out of a Tumblr meme, the drinks here are worth the irony, and the calendar is typically filled in with great local, acoustic live bands. ✉ *3391 Adams Ave., Normal Heights* ☎ *619/563–9019* 🌐 *www.sycamoreden.com/.*

Soda Bar. Don't be fooled by the name. Soda is in short supply at this off-the-beaten-path music venue that has earned a reputation as the place to see up-and-coming bands or grab a potent cocktail. ✉ *3615 El Cajon Blvd., Normal Heights* ☎ *619/255–7224* 🌐 *www.sodabarmusic.com.*

COFFEEHOUSES

Lestat's Coffee Shop. One of the few San Diego coffee shops that's open 24 hours a day, this Normal Heights mainstay also has a great selection of baked goods and a neighboring music venue that stages acoustic and comedy acts seven days a week. ✉ *3343 Adams Ave., Normal Heights* ☎ *619/282–0437* 🌐 *www.lestats.com.*

MISSION BAY AND THE BEACHES

MISSION BAY

Here's a seaside spot to glug some suds by the boardwalk after a splash in the Pacific.

NIGHT BAY CRUISES

Bahia Belle. This Mississippi-style stern-wheeler offers relaxing evening cruises along Mission Bay that include cocktails, dancing, karaoke, and live music. Cruises run from Wednesday through Sunday in early summer, daily in July and August, and Friday and Saturday in winter (there are no cruises in December). The $10 fare is less than most nightclub covers, but if you're choosey about the company you keep, remember, these floating bars are known as "booze cruises" for a reason. ✉ *998 W. Mission Bay Dr., Mission Bay* ☎ *858/539–7720* 🌐 *www.bahiahotel.com.*

PACIFIC BEACH

Surfers meet here for happy hour and college students converge to spend their lost weekends.

BARS

JRDN. This contemporary lounge (pronounced "Jordan") occupies the ground floor of Pacific Beach's chicest boutique hotel, Tower23, and offers a more sophisticated vibe in what is a very party-happy neighborhood. Sleek walls of windows and an expansive patio overlook the boardwalk. ✉ *723 Felspar St., Pacific Beach* ☎ *858/270–2323* 🌐 *www.t23hotel.com.*

BREWPUBS

Amplified Ale Works. Pacific Beach often veers between the trendy and the tawdry, so it's refreshing to see a genuine craft brewhouse open up to offer a more casual middle ground. Amplified serves more than a dozen in-house-brewed beers at its scenic outdoor beer garden, with breathtaking ocean views. ✉ *4150 Mission Blvd., No. 208, Pacific Beach* ☎ *858/270–5222* 🌐 *www.amplifiedales.com/.*

SD Tap Room. Beachside locals have been clamoring for an authentic beer bar and certainly got one with this place. Hoppy choices are in the hundreds and the food is better than average bar food. ✉ *1269 Garnet Ave., Pacific Beach* ☎ *858/274–1010* 🌐 *www.sdtaproom.com.*

LA JOLLA

La Jolla has a healthy mixture of laid-back beach bars and upper crust craft-cocktail couture.

BARS

Cusp. The stone walls and modern metal accents along the bar give the impression of Cusp being a dark, intimate lounge, but the panoramic views of La Jolla shores brighten up this chic spot on the 11th floor of Hotel La Jolla. Drop in for live acoustic or jazz music on weekends, or simply sip on one of their signature cocktails during their daily happy hour from 4 to 7. ✉ *7955 La Jolla Shores Dr., La Jolla* ☎ *858/551–3620* 🌐 *www.cusprestaurant.com/.*

George's Level 2. Upstairs from the upscale George's At the Cove is this hip, casual, and somewhat more affordable hangout, which is always buzzing with activity—especially on weekends. Stop in for craft cocktails or bar snacks that rank among La Jolla's best, and with gorgeous ocean views to boot. ✉ *1250 Prospect St., La Jolla* ☎ *858/454–4244* 🌐 *www.georgesatthecove.com/level2.*

COFFEEHOUSES

Living Room Coffee. La Jolla's outpost of this local coffee chain is open until midnight and sports a full bar, which means that customers can spend a pleasant evening sipping a true-blue Irish coffee complete with whiskey at one of the many tables or couches. ✉ *1010 Prospect St., La Jolla* ☎ *858/459–1187* 🌐 *www.livingroomusa.com.*

COMEDY AND CABARET

Comedy Store La Jolla. Like its sister establishment in Hollywood, this club hosts some of the best national touring and local talent. Cover charges range from nothing on open-mike nights to $20 or more for national acts. Seating is at bistro-style tables, and a two-drink minimum applies for all shows. ✉ *916 Pearl St., La Jolla* ☎ *858/454–9176* 🌐 *lajolla.thecomedystore.com.*

POINT LOMA, OCEAN BEACH, AND CORONADO

POINT LOMA

A diverse range of unique watering holes sits amid this sleepy, residential burg.

BARS

Modern Times Beer. Point Loma's funky and unique entry into the craft beer game, Modern Times lives up to its name with innovative design—including a mural made entirely of Post-It notes—simple and stylish take-home six-packs, and a rotating cast of beers on tap with the diversity to please every type of palate. ✉ *3725 Greenwood St., Point Loma* ☎ *619/546–9694* 🌐 *moderntimesbeer.com/.*

The Pearl Hotel. Step into late '60s Palm Springs, with shag carpet, clean lines, and lots of wood accents. The lobby bar is almost as fabulous as the outdoor pool area, where inflatable balls bob in illuminated water and vintage flicks show on a huge screen. And feel free to drink to excess. After 10 pm, when the bar closes, you can stay over at a discounted $79 "play and stay" rate if there are any rooms available. ✉ *1410 Rosecrans St., Point Loma* ☎ *619/226–6100* 🌐 *www.thepearlsd.com.*

OCEAN BEACH

There are hippie hangouts, campy cocktail lounges, and not a dress code in sight.

BARS

Pacific Shores. This bar isn't going for classy with its acid-trip mermaid mural, but hey, it's OB—a surf town populated by leftovers from the '60s, man. A laid-back but see-and-be-seen crowd congregates here for relatively inexpensive drinks (no beers on tap, though), pool games, and pop and rock tunes on the jukebox. ✉ *4927 Newport Ave., Ocean Beach* ☎ *619/223–7549.*

SHELTER ISLAND

The island combines tiki kitsch and mid-century charm, with one of the city's best concert destinations.

ROCK, POP, HIP-HOP, FOLK, AND BLUES CLUBS

Humphrey's by the Bay. From June through September this dining and drinking oasis surrounded by water hosts the city's best outdoor jazz, folk, and light-rock concert series and is the stomping ground of such musicians as the Cowboy Junkies and Chris Isaak. The rest of the year the music moves indoors for first-rate jazz, blues, and more. ✉ *2241 Shelter Island Dr., Shelter Island* ☎ *619/224–3577* 🌐 *www.humphreysconcerts.com.*

PERFORMING ARTS

Updated by Jeff Terich

A diverse and sophisticated arts scene probably isn't the first thing that visitors—or even locals—associate with San Diego. It's a destination for those who seek out its perennial sunshine, gorgeous beaches, and beautiful scenery. Even those within the arts scene readily admit their fiercest competition is the beach! But just a little to the right of the Pacific Ocean, there are some amazing and diverse artistic offerings to prove that San Diego can hold its own.

The theater scene in San Diego may not have the commercial appeal that Broadway does, but it more than makes up for it with talent. In fact, a long list of Broadway-bound productions started right here, including *Jersey Boys,* The Who's *Tommy, Dirty Rotten Scoundrels,* and *Memphis.*

Balboa Park's Old Globe Theatre is modeled after the Shakespearian Globe Theatre in England, and hosts both an annual Shakespeare Festival as well as contemporary plays. A little bit north is La Jolla Playhouse, which was founded by Gregory Peck in 1947, and has hosted dozens of world-premiere productions, in addition to star actors like Laura Linney and Neil Patrick Harris. The playhouse has also launched the Without Walls initiative, which places theater in a new context by removing the theater entirely.

Music also has a major presence in San Diego, courtesy of the world-class San Diego Opera, which performs major works by Puccini and Mozart, and the San Diego Symphony, which caters to a diverse audience thanks to both its classical concerts and its more accessible Summer Pops series.

There's always something new and exciting happening with visual arts in San Diego. No longer limited to a collector's market, younger urban artists are making in-roads with warehouse gallery spaces in Barrio Logan, while galleries in La Jolla and Little Italy showcase bold works of contemporary art on their walls. The annual San Diego Art Prize highlights rising figures in the visual arts realm, and in the field of architecture, Orchids and Onions honors the best and worst in structural design—and with a sense of humor at that.

TOP ARTS EXPERIENCES

Arts free-for-all: Summertime means free concerts, movies, and theater throughout the county.

Puppet strings: Your kids might not care for Shakespeare at The Old Globe, but you can introduce them to great acting at Balboa Park's Marie Hitchcock Puppet Theater.

Gallery gathering: Before you visit, scour gallery websites or places like *www.sdcitybeat.com* for upcoming openings, which usually include a spread of sips and snacks—and art, of course.

San Diego Film Festival: This five-day festival in September is a must for film lovers and celebrity spotters—a day pass will get you into some of San Diego's most glamorous parties.

PERFORMING ARTS PLANNER

TICKETS

Plan ahead and buy tickets early—ideally around the same time that you book your hotel. Not that you can't find an outlet that sells day-of-show tickets, but you'll run the risk of paying a grossly inflated price, and might not end up with good seats.

Arts Tix. You can buy advance tickets, many at half price, to theater, music, and dance events at Arts Tix. ✉ *Box Office, 4th Ave. and E St., Gaslamp Quarter* ☎ *858/381–5595* 🌐 *www.sdartstix.com.*

Ticketmaster. Ticketmaster sells tickets to many performances, as well as to select museum exhibitions. Service charges vary according to the event, and most tickets are nonrefundable. ☎ *800/745–3000* 🌐 *www.ticketmaster.com.*

DANCE

Whether you fancy *rond de jambes* or something a bit more modern, San Diego's scene is *en pointe* for dance fans.

California Ballet Company. The company performs high-quality contemporary and classical works September–May at the **Civic Theatre** . The *Nutcracker* is staged annually around the holiday season. ✉ *San Diego Civic Theatre, 1100 3rd Ave., Downtown* ☎ *619/560–5676* 🌐 *www.californiaballet.org.*

City Ballet. The ballet holds performances at the **Spreckels Theatre** and a few other area venues from November through May. At Christmastime, they dance a mean *Nutcracker*. ✉ *Spreckels Theatre, 121 Broadway #600, Downtown* ☎ *858/274–6058* 🌐 *www.cityballet.org.*

Malashock Dance. The city's esteemed modern dance company presents edgy, intriguing works at venues throughout the city; Malashock has often collaborated on performances with the San Diego Opera, the San Diego Symphony, and other major cultural institutions. ✉ *2650 Truxtun Rd., Suite 104, Point Loma* ☎ *619/260–1622* 🌐 *www.malashockdance.org.*

San Diego Dance Theater. The company has earned serious kudos for its diverse company and provocative programming, including Mexican waltzes and its annual "Trolley Dances," which take place at various trolley stops throughout San Diego. Other performances are held at venues around the city. ✉ *2650 Truxtun Rd., Suite 108* ☎ *619/225–1803* 🌐 *www.sandiegodancetheater.org*.

FILM

Cinephiles won't be left reeling by the unexpectedly diverse cinematic riches in San Diego, from indoor and outdoor theaters to a variety of seasonal film festivals.

Landmark Theatres. Known for first-run foreign, art, American independent, and documentary offerings, Landmark operates three theaters in the San Diego area including La Jolla Village Cinemas, a modern multiplex set in a shopping center. **Hillcrest Cinemas** (3965 5th Avenue, Hillcrest) is a posh multiplex right in the middle of Uptown's action. **Ken Cinema** (4061 Adams Avenue, Kensington) is considered by many to be the last bastion of true avant-garde film in San Diego. It plays a roster of art and revival films that changes regularly (many programs are double bills). ☎ *619/298–2904* 🌐 *www.landmarktheatres.com*.

San Diego Film Festival. Usually held in late September, this festival screens local, national, and international entries at the **Gaslamp Theater** (*701 5th Ave., Gaslamp Quarter*), as well as the **Museum of Contemporary Art-La Jolla** (*700 Prospect St., La Jolla*). The city's glitterati—as well as a few Hollywood celebs—love to rub shoulders at the fest's films, panels, and finale fête. ✉ *2683 Via de la Valle, No. G210, Del Mar* ☎ *619/818–2221* 🌐 *sdfilmfest.com*.

GALLERIES

The gallery scene in San Diego comprises a broad canvas, ranging from certified works of fine art to more accessible pieces by contemporary up-and-comers.

FAMILY **Barracks 15 & 16 at NTC Liberty Station.** The former Naval Training Center at Liberty Station has been transformed into an eclectic and family-friendly alternative to the more avant garde arts scene in San Diego. Galleries include the Mexican-theme works at **Casa Valencia Baja** and innovative photography at **Outside the Lens**—just look for the giant Polaroid camera replica. ✉ *2750 Historic Decatur Rd., Point Loma* ☎ *619/573–9300* 🌐 *www.NTCLibertyStation.com*.

Glashaus. A prominent fixture in the up-and-coming Barrio Logan arts district, this repurposed warehouse space plays host to exhibitions from local artists as well as housing several artists' studios. And yes, there is actual blown-glass art on display, in addition to a wide variety of other disciplines. ✉ *1815 Main St., Suite B, Barrio Logan* 🌐 *theglashaus.com*.

Fodor's Choice ★ **Museum of Contemporary Art San Diego** (*MCASD*). Centrally located in Downtown between a trolley stop and the train station, MCASD has built up a reputation for being the premier site for cutting-edge visual art in San Diego. ■ **TIP→ Every third Thursday is "Downtown at Sundown," which brings together visual and performance arts as musicians and DJs perform outside the museum while patrons are treated to beer, cocktails, and other refreshments.** ✉ *1100 Kettner Blvd., Downtown* ☎ *858/434–3541* 🌐 *www.mcasd.org.*

Quint Gallery. For more than 30 years, art lovers and museum directors have snagged new pieces from established locals as well as international contemporary artists at this revered gallery. If you're in town at the time of one of the gallery's openings, you can schmooze with San Diego art royalty. ✉ *5171 Santa Fe St., Bay Park* ☎ *858/454–3409* 🌐 *quintgallery.com.*

Shane Bowden Gallery. This up-and-coming gallery in La Jolla's art community features the cutting edge, surrealist paintings and silkscreen art of Shane Bowden in a modern, minimalist setting. ✉ *7655 Girard Ave., La Jolla* ☎ *858/729–9880* 🌐 *shanebowden.com.*

The Stuart Collection @ UCSD. Less a gallery than an open-air scavenger hunt for some of the city's most impressive works of visual art, the Stuart Collection—located on campus at UCSD—boasts a number of must-see, and sometimes massive, pieces by some of the biggest names in contemporary art, including Jenny Holzer, John Baldessari, and Robert Irwin. ✉ *UCSD, 9500 Gilman Dr., La Jolla* 🌐 *stuartcollection.ucsd.edu/.*

Thumbprint Gallery. This quaint little gallery brings a little edge to otherwise sleepy La Jolla, showing off some of the best lowbrow and street artists in the city. This is a great place to purchase something truly unique for a low price. ✉ *920 Kline St., La Jolla* ☎ *858/354–6294* 🌐 *www.thumbprintgallerysd.com.*

MUSIC

From its world-class symphony and opera to the sharp array of theaters that host live music, San Diego's musical offerings will have you returning for an encore performance.

Balboa Theatre. This renovated theater offers a variety of performances including ballet, music, plays, and even stand-up comedy. In addition to architectural splendor, the space offers unsurpassed sound . ✉ *868 4th Ave., Gaslamp Quarter* ☎ *619/570–1100* 🌐 *www.sandiegotheatres.org.*

Cal Coast Credit Union Open Air Theatre. Top-name rock, reggae, and popular artists give summer concerts under the stars at this theater in the middle of the San Diego State University campus. ✉ *San Diego State University, 5500 Campanile Dr., College Area* ☎ *619/594–7315.*

Fodor's Choice ★ **Copley Symphony Hall.** The great acoustics here are surpassed only by the incredible Spanish baroque interior. Not just the home of the San Diego Symphony Orchestra, the renovated 2,200-seat 1920s-era theater has also hosted major stars like Elvis Costello, Leonard Cohen, and Sting. ✉ *750 B St., Downtown* ☎ *619/235–0804* 🌐 *www.sandiegosymphony.org.*

Humphreys Concerts by the Bay. This waterfront, outdoor venue stages intimate shows from big-name national acts from April into October. There's not a bad seat in the house, but those who don't want to pay the sometimes-high ticket prices can catch the concert by renting a canoe or boat and parking it in the adjacent bay for a one-of-a-kind view. ✉ *2241 Shelter Island Dr., Point Loma* ☎ *619/224–3577* 🌐 *humphreysconcerts.com.*

The Irenic. Housed inside the Mission Gathering church, which still hosts service on Sunday, the Irenic backs up its sacred atmosphere with immaculate sound. The card tables in the back selling canned beers may give the venue a humble, D.I.Y. feel, but these hallowed walls play host to top-notch touring musical acts and performing artists. Can we have a Hallelujah? ✉ *3090 Polk Ave., North Park* 🌐 *theirenic.com/.*

La Jolla Athenaeum Music & Arts Library. The Athenaeum is a membership-supported, nonprofit library with an exceptional collection of books, periodicals, CDs, and other media related to arts and music. It also hosts intimate jazz, chamber music, and the occasional folk concert throughout the year. ✉ *1008 Wall St., La Jolla* ☎ *858/454–5872* 🌐 *ljathenaeum.org.*

The Loft at UCSD. This quaint, comfortable performance space inside the Price Center on the University of California San Diego campus hosts intimate music concerts, spoken word programs, film screenings, and culinary events. ✉ *Price Center East, 9500 Gilman Dr., 4th fl., La Jolla* ☎ *858/534–1959* 🌐 *theloft.ucsd.edu.*

Observatory North Park. Formerly North Park Theatre, the Observatory North Park has more than 85 years of history inside its ornate and beautiful walls, even though it was closed for quite a few of them. But in its newly renovated state, it's a top-tier destination for touring musical acts, ranging from comedians like John Waters and bands like Beach House. ✉ *2891 University Ave., North Park* ☎ *619/239–8836* 🌐 *www.observatorysd.com/.*

San Diego Opera. Drawing international performers, the opera's season runs January–April. Past performances have included *Die Fledermaus, Faust, Idomeneo,* and *La Bohème,* plus solo concerts by such talents as Renee Fleming. ✉ *Civic Theatre, 1100 3rd Ave., Downtown* ☎ *619/533–7000* 🌐 *www.sdopera.com.*

San Diego Symphony Orchestra. The orchestra's events include classical concerts and summer and winter pops, nearly all of them at Copley Symphony Hall. The outdoor Summer Pops series is held on the Embarcadero, on North Harbor Drive beyond the convention center. ✉ *Box office, 750 B St., Downtown* ☎ *619/235–0804* 🌐 *www.sandiegosymphony.org.*

Sleep Train Amphitheatre. The largest concert venue in town, the amphitheater can accommodate 20,000 concertgoers with reserved seats and lawn seating. It presents top-selling national and international acts during its late-spring to late-summer season. ✉ *2050 Entertainment Circle, Chula Vista* ☎ *619/671–3500* 🌐 *www.sleeptrain.com/about-sleep-train-amphitheatre-chula-vista.html.*

Spreckels Organ Pavilion. Home of a giant outdoor pipe organ donated to the city, the beautiful Spanish baroque pavilion hosts concerts by a rotating lineup of guest organists on most Sunday afternoons and on Monday evenings in summer. Local military bands, gospel groups, and barbershop quartets also perform here. All shows are free. ✉ *2211 Pan American Rd. E, Balboa Park* ☎ *619/702–8138* 🌐 *spreckelsorgan.org.*

Spreckels Theatre. A landmark theater erected in 1912, the Spreckels hosts comedy, dance, theater, and concerts. Good acoustics and old-time elegance make this a favorite local venue. ✉ *121 Broadway, , Suite 600, Downtown* ☎ *619/235–9500* 🌐 *www.spreckels.net.*

Valley View Casino Center. Big-name concerts are held at this historic arena with room for 13,000-plus fans. ✉ *3500 Sports Arena Blvd.* ☎ *619/224–4171* 🌐 *valleyviewcasinocenter.com.*

Viejas Arena. Located on the San Diego State campus, the Viejas Arena attracts big-name musical and comedy acts to its 12,500-person facility. ✉ *San Diego State University, 5500 Canyon Crest Dr., College Area* ☎ *619/594–7315.*

THEATER

More than a few Tony-winning Broadway productions have been launched at San Diego theaters; The Old Globe and La Jolla Playhouse are just two stars in the city's large ensemble.

Coronado Playhouse. This cabaret-type theater near the Hotel Del Coronado stages regular dramatic and musical performances. ✉ *1835 Strand Way, Coronado* ☎ *619/435–4856* 🌐 *www.coronadoplayhouse.com.*

Cygnet's Old Town Theatre. A 248-seat theater operated by Cygnet Theatre Company, this is one of the more interesting small San Diego theater groups. Catch local takes on edgy classics like *Sweeney Todd* and *Little Shop of Horrors.* ✉ *4040 Twiggs St., Old Town* ☎ *619/337–1525* 🌐 *www.cygnettheatre.com.*

Diversionary Theatre. San Diego's premier gay and lesbian company presents a range of original works that focus on LGBT themes. ✉ *4545 Park Blvd., Suite 101, University Heights* ☎ *619/220–0097* 🌐 *www.diversionary.org.*

Horton Grand Theatre. After being home to the long running Triple Espresso, the Horton Grand Theatre hosts productions from the likes of San Diego Musical Theatre as well as Intrepid Theatre Company, whose shows include *Who's Afraid of Virginia Woolf?* and *Woody Guthrie's American Song.* ✉ *Hahn Cosmopolitan Theatre, 444 4th Ave., Gaslamp Quarter* ☎ *760/295–7541.*

Ion Theatre Company. The little theater company that could, most of Ion's unique and sometimes controversial productions now take place in the quaint BLKBOX Theatre in Hillcrest and have included productions of *Gypsy* and *Topdog/Underdog.* ✉ *3704 6th Ave., Hillcrest* ☎ *619/600–5020* 🌐 *iontheatre.com.*

Fodor's Choice ★ **La Jolla Playhouse.** Under the artistic direction of Christopher Ashley, the playhouse presents exciting and innovative plays and musicals on three stages. Many Broadway shows—among them *Memphis, Tommy,* and *Jersey Boys*—have previewed here before their East Coast premieres. Its Without Walls program also ensures that the productions aren't limited to the playhouse, having put on site-specific shows in places like outdoor art spaces, cars, and even the ocean. ✉ *University of California at San Diego, 2910 La Jolla Village Dr., La Jolla* ☎ *858/550–1010* 🌐 *www.lajollaplayhouse.org.*

Lamb's Players Theatre. The theater's regular season of five mostly uplifting productions runs from February through November. It also stages an original musical, *Festival of Christmas,* in December. The company has two performance spaces, the one used for most productions in Coronado, and the Horton Grand Theatre in the Gaslamp Quarter. ✉ *1142 Orange Ave., Coronado* ☎ *619/437–6000* 🌐 *www.lambsplayers.org.*

Marie Hitchcock Puppet Theater. Amateur and professional puppeteers and ventriloquists entertain here five days a week. The cost is just a few dollars for adults and children alike. If you feel cramped in the 200-seat theater, don't worry; the shows rarely run longer than a half hour. ✉ *2130 Pan American Plaza, Balboa Park* ☎ *619/544–9203* 🌐 *www.balboaparkpuppets.com.*

Mo`olelo Performing Arts Company. Staging three productions over the year at the 10th Avenue Theatre in Downtown, this company is committed to performances by newer playwrights as well as more obscure works by old masters. ✉ *930 10th Ave., Downtown* ☎ *619/231–4137* 🌐 *moolelo.net.*

North Coast Repertory Theatre. A diverse mix of comic and dramatic works is shown in the 194-seat space. The emphasis is on contemporary productions, but the theater has been known to stage some classics, too. ✉ *987 Lomas Santa Fe Dr., Suite D, Solana Beach* ☎ *858/481–1055* 🌐 *www.northcoastrep.org.*

Fodor's Choice ★ **The Old Globe.** This complex, comprising the Sheryl and Harvey White Theatre, the Lowell Davies Festival Theatre, and the Old Globe Theatre, offers some of the finest theatrical productions in Southern California. Theater classics such as *The Full Monty* and *Dirty Rotten Scoundrels,* both of which went on to Broadway, premiered on these famed stages. The Old Globe presents the family-friendly *How the Grinch Stole Christmas* around the holidays, as well as a renowned summer Shakespeare Festival with three to four plays in repertory. ✉ *1363 Old Globe Way, Balboa Park* ☎ *619/234–5623* 🌐 *www.oldglobe.org.*

San Diego Civic Theatre. The home of the San Diego Opera, the Civic Theatre is the city's largest performing arts venue, with musicals, theatrical productions, and concerts held throughout the year. ✉ *1100 3rd Ave., Downtown* ☎ *619/570–1100* 🌐 *www.sandiegotheatres.org.*

BEACHES

SAN DIEGO'S BEST BEACHES

In San Diego you're never far from a coastal breeze, the sting of saltwater on your face, or the feeling of soft sand squishing between your toes.

(above) Pacific Beach is the place to party. (lower right) Sea lions at the Children's Pool. (upper right) The U.S. Open Sandcastle Competition at Imperial Beach takes place annually in July or August.

This unique Southern California city, known for its easygoing charm, has 70-plus miles of pristine coastline, and the beaches here can rival any in Hawaii or the Mediterranean in terms of beauty and variety. There are beaches backed by dramatic, sheer cliffs, wide, straight stretches, and exotic coves with palm trees and shimmering blue water. Surfing and surf culture dominate some beaches, but nonsurfers can appreciate the delights of snorkeling or stand-up paddling in calmer waters. Each beach charms in a different way. Most beaches are family-friendly, but some attract more specific crowds. **Ocean Beach** has a bohemian feel, while **Pacific Beach** is a magnet for partiers. The North County lays claim to some of the choicest surfing spots, and **Black's Beach** attracts a smattering of nudists.

BEACH BONFIRE

Just because the sun went down doesn't mean it's time to go home. Nothing compares to sitting around a crackling fire as the evening breeze ushers in whiffs of the sea. Fires are allowed only in fire rings, which you can find at **Ocean Beach, Mission Beach, Pacific Beach,** and **Coronado Beach.** Revelers snap up ring slots quickly in summer; stake your claim early by filling one with wood and setting your gear nearby.

BEST BEACHES FOR ...

OCEAN VIEWS

The view at **Sunset Cliffs** in Point Loma is dramatic and heart-achingly beautiful. Look for the few picnic tables that are positioned near the edge of the cliffs. **Torrey Pines State Natural Reserve** also provides fantastic views from its 300-foot-high cliffs.

ROMANCE

For a beautiful secluded spot, head to the lone shacklike hut that's nestled among the rocks at La Jolla's **Windansea Beach.** At **Fletcher Cove** in Solana Beach, look for the single bench overlooking the sea at the beach entrance.

KIDS

Despite its name, the **Children's Pool** isn't a great spot to take your kids to swim, but they'll love watching the seals and sea lions that populate its waters. **La Jolla Shores** is popular for the gentle waves in its swimmer's section, and **Mission Bay's** serene inlets make for shallow swimming pools.

OCEAN WALK

The Hotel Del Coronado on **Coronado Beach** makes the perfect backdrop to a walk along silky sand stretching toward the horizon. **Silver Strand** and **Imperial Beach** are also lovely.

AFTER-BEACH DRINKS

Pacific Beach's Garnet Street is home to the neighborhood's liveliest bars. College students head to Garnet on Friday and Saturday nights; at other times, it's more laid-back.

BEST BEACH EATS

The Baked Bear. This new build-your-own ice cream–sandwich shop a block from Pacific Beach is a local favorite thanks to its homemade cookies and diverse array of ice-cream flavors, from birthday cake to peanut butter fudge. ✉ *4516 Mission Blvd., Suite C, Pacific Beach* ☎ *858/886–7433* 🌐 *www.thebakedbear.com.*

Ki's Restaurant. Surfers love this organic café across the street from Cardiff State Beach for its wide array of healthy items as well as juices and smoothies. The Japanese ahi wrap with spicy wasabi sauce is a must-order. ✉ *2591 S. Coast Hwy. 101, North County* ☎ *760/436–5236* 🌐 *www.kisrestaurant.com.*

Pizza Port. One of five branches, the Pizza Port in Solana Beach is prized by North County locals. They head to this combination pizzeria-brewery for original pies like the seafood-laden Pizza Solana as well as house-brewed stout and cream ales. ✉ *135 N. Hwy. 101, Solana Beach* ☎ *858/481–7332* 🌐 *www.pizzaport.com.*

LA JOLLA'S BEACHES AND BEYOND

La Jolla (pronounced La Hoya) means "the jewel" in Spanish and appropriately describes this small, affluent village and its beaches. Some beautiful coastline can be found here, as well as an elegant upscale atmosphere.

(above) La Jolla is synonymous with beautiful vistas. (lower right) The view from Coast Highway 101 in Carlsbad is spectacular. (upper right) Hike down to the beach from Torrey Pines.

Between North County and the Mission and South bays, La Jolla is easily accessible from Downtown San Diego and North County. It's worth renting a car so you can sample the different beaches along the coast. The town's trademark million-dollar homes won't disappoint either—their cliffside locations make them an attractive backdrop to the brilliant views of the sea below. Downtown La Jolla is more commercialized, with high-end stores great for browsing. La Jolla Shores, a mile-long beach, lies in the more residential area to the north. Above all, the beach and cove are La Jolla's prime charms—the cove's seals and underwater kelp beds are big draws for kayakers and nature lovers.

IN THE BUFF

Some people just don't like tan lines. Black's Beach is one of the largest clothing-optional beaches in the United States. The chances of running into naked beachgoers of all ages are higher at the north end, and Black's is properly secluded and difficult to get to.

COAST HIGHWAY 101

The portion of Coast Highway 101 that runs south from North County into La Jolla is one of San Diego's best drives. Start at South Carlsbad beach at Tamarack Avenue and continue through Leucadia, Encinitas, Cardiff, Solana Beach, Del Mar, and, finally, La Jolla. Any turn west will take you toward the beach. The drive offers intermittent glimpses of the sea; views from Carlsbad and Cardiff are especially beautiful. The grand finale is at Torrey Pines, where the waves roll into the misty, high-bluffed beach.

THE CLIFFS AT TORREY PINES

The ocean views from the 300-foot-high sandstone cliffs atop Torrey Pines State Natural Reserve are vast and exquisite. To reach the cliffs, hike one of the short trails that leads from the visitor center. Perch along the sandy edge, and let your legs dangle. You may even see dolphins swimming along the shore or surfers riding a break.

SEALS AT THE CHILDREN'S POOL

This small protected beach has become one of San Diego's most contentious issues. Originally constructed to provide children a safe place to swim, over the last two decades much of La Jolla's harbor seal population has made itself at home on the sandy beach protected by a seawall. In the late '90s swimmers were told to avoid the pools due to concerns about water contamination and out of concern for the animals; in 2004, one irked swimmer took legal action, claiming that the pool is for children and snorkelers—not for the seals. Animal rights groups argued that the seals should be protected in their chosen habitat. In 2014 the San Diego City Council voted to close the beach entirely to beachgoers during the five-month pupping season.

LA JOLLA COVE WALK AND SHOP

If you're not keen on dipping your toes in the water (or even the sand, for that matter), head over to La Jolla Cove, an ideal spot for strolling and shopping with a view. Park at any of the available metered spaces on Girard Avenue in Downtown La Jolla and browse the Arcade Building, built in the Spanish Mission style. Make your way toward the cove by following the signs, or simply walk toward any patches of ocean you see.

WATER SPORTS

One of the most popular water activities is kayaking along the caves and snorkeling among the kelp beds near the cove at the Underwater Ecological Reserve. Kayak rental shops offer special outings that include moonlight kayaking and the chance to dive among the leopard sharks that roam La Jolla's waters. Don't worry; the sharks are harmless.

Updated by Marlise Kast-Myers

California's entire coastline enchants, but the state's southernmost region stands apart when it comes to sand, surf, and sea. Step out of the car and onto the beach to immediately savor its allure: smell the fresh salty air, feel the plush sand at your feet, hear waves breaking from the shore, and take in breathtaking vistas.

San Diego's sandstone bluffs offer spectacular views of the Pacific as a palette of blues and greens: there are distant indigo depths, emerald coves closer to shore, and finally, the mint-green swirls of the foamy surf.

San Diego's beaches have a different vibe from their northern counterparts in Orange County and glitzy Los Angeles. San Diego is more laid-back and less of a scene. Cyclists whiz by as surfers saunter toward the waves and sunbathers relax in the sun, be it July or November.

Whether you're seeking a safe place to take the kids or a hot spot to work on your tan, there's a beach here that's just right for you. La Jolla Shores and Mission Bay both have gentle waves and shallow waters that provide safer swimming for kids; whereas the high swells at Black's and Swami's attract surfers worldwide. If you're looking for dramatic ocean views, Torrey Pines State Beach and Sunset Cliffs provide a desertlike chaparral backdrop, with craggy cliffs overlooking the ocean below. Beaches farther south in Coronado and Silver Strand have longer stretches of sand that are perfect for a contemplative stroll or a brisk jog. Then there are those secluded, sandy enclaves that you may happen upon on a scenic drive down Highway 101.

Beach reviews are listed geographically from south to north.

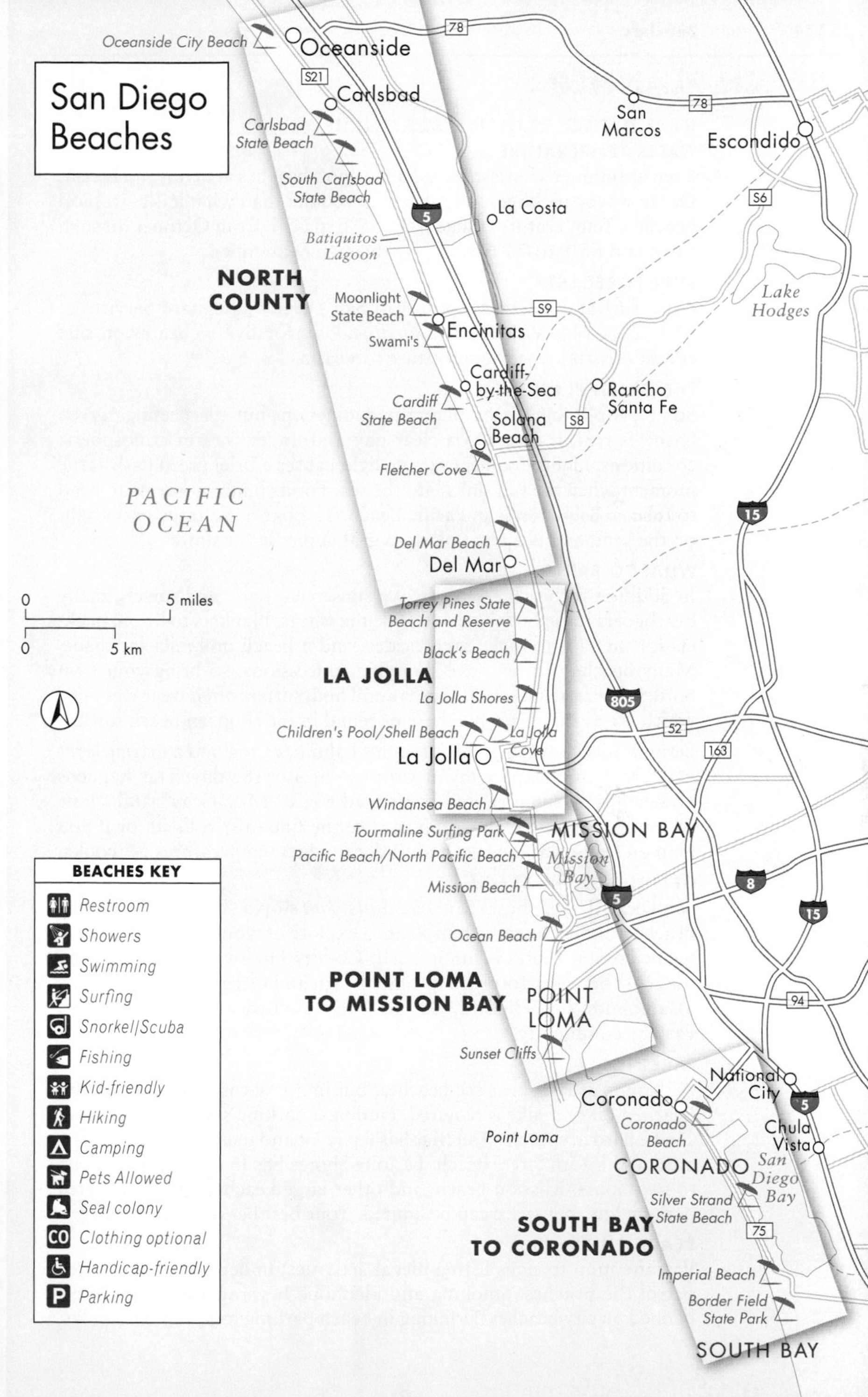

San Diego Beaches
Oceanside City Beach
Oceanside
Carlsbad
Carlsbad State Beach
South Carlsbad State Beach
La Costa
Batiquitos Lagoon
NORTH COUNTY
Moonlight State Beach
Encinitas
Swami's
Cardiff-by-the-Sea
Cardiff State Beach
Solana Beach
Fletcher Cove
Rancho Santa Fe
San Marcos
Escondido
Lake Hodges
PACIFIC OCEAN
Del Mar Beach
Del Mar
Torrey Pines State Beach and Reserve
Black's Beach
LA JOLLA
La Jolla Shores
Children's Pool/Shell Beach
La Jolla Cove
La Jolla
Windansea Beach
Tourmaline Surfing Park
Pacific Beach/North Pacific Beach
Mission Beach
MISSION BAY
Mission Bay
Ocean Beach
POINT LOMA TO MISSION BAY
POINT LOMA
Sunset Cliffs
Point Loma
Coronado
Coronado Beach
CORONADO
National City
Chula Vista
San Diego Bay
Silver Strand State Beach
SOUTH BAY TO CORONADO
Imperial Beach
Border Field State Park
SOUTH BAY
0 5 miles
0 5 km
BEACHES KEY
Restroom
Showers
Swimming
Surfing
Snorkel/Scuba
Fishing
Kid-friendly
Hiking
Camping
Pets Allowed
Seal colony
Clothing optional
Handicap-friendly
Parking

BEACH PLANNER

SAN DIEGO BEACHES PLANNER

WATER TEMPERATURE

Even at summer's hottest peak, San Diego's beaches are cool and breezy. Ocean waves are large, and the water is colder than what it is at tropical beaches. Temperatures range from 55°F to 65°F from October through June, and 65°F to 73°F from July through September.

SURF FORECAST

For a surf and weather report, call San Diego's Lifeguard Services at *619/221–8824*. Visit *www.surfline.com.* for live webcams on surf conditions and water temperature forecasts.

THE GREEN FLASH

Some people think it's a phony phenomenon, but the fleeting "green flash" is real, if rare. On a clear day and under certain atmospheric conditions, higher-frequency green light causes a brief green flash at the moment when the sun sinks into the sea. For a chance at seeing it, head to **Lahaina Beach House** in Pacific Beach. The bar has a large patio right on the sand and is a great place to grab a pitcher at sunset.

WHAT TO BRING

In addition to beach essentials like sunscreen, hats, and towels, many beachgoers bring bodyboards to ride the waves, blankets to lie on, buckets for the kids to make sand castles, and a beach umbrella for shade. Many beaches do not have shoreline concessions, so bring your own bottles of water and snacks. Surfers and bodysurfers often wear wet suits, which are available for purchase or rental in the shops in beach towns.

Despite Southern California's famous balminess, fog and a marine layer may creep in unexpectedly at various parts of the day. This happens often in early summer, and is referred to as "May Gray" and "June Gloom." Bring a light sweater in case the fine mist rolls in, or if you plan on staying at the beach until dark, when temperatures get cooler.

GETTING TO THE BEACH

San Diego Transit buses *www.sdmts.com* stop a short walk from the beaches, but it's better to rent a car to explore on your own. Driving the scenic coastal routes is fun in itself. County Highway S21 runs along the coast between Torrey Pines State Beach and Oceanside, although its local names (Old Highway 101 or Coast Highway 101, for example) vary by community.

PARKING

Parking is usually near the beaches, but in a few cases, such as Black's Beach, a bit of a hike is required. Finding a parking spot near the ocean can be hard in summer. Del Mar has a pay lot and metered street parking around the 15th Street Beach. La Jolla Shores has free street parking up to two hours. Mission Beach, and other large beaches have unmetered parking lots, but space can be limited. Your best bet is to arrive early.

BEACH RULES

Pay attention to signs listing illegal activities; undercover police often patrol the beaches. Smoking and alcoholic beverages are completely banned on city beaches. Drinking in beach parking lots, on boardwalks, and in landscaped areas is also illegal. Glass containers are not permitted on beaches, cliffs, and walkways, or in park areas and adjacent parking lots. Littering is not tolerated, and skateboarding is prohibited at some beaches. Fires are allowed only in fire rings or elevated barbecue grills. Although it may be tempting to take a sea creature from a tide pool as a souvenir, it may upset the delicate ecological balance, and it's illegal, too.

SAFETY

Year-round, lifeguards are stationed at nine permanent stations from Sunset Cliffs to Black's Beach. All other beaches are covered by roving patrols in the winter, and seasonal towers in the summer. When swimming in the ocean be aware of rip currents, which are common in California shores. If you are caught in one, don't panic. Swim parallel to the shore until you can reach land without resistance. To be safe, go swimming near lifeguard towers where you will be visible.

Few beaches have lockers to keep your belongings secure. If you're going to the beach solo and plan on going in the water, leave your wallet out of sight in your car.

POLLUTION

San Diego's beaches are well maintained and very clean during summertime, when rainfall is infrequent. Beaches along San Diego County's northern cities are typically cleaner than ones farther south. Pollution is generally worse near river mouths and storm-drain outlets, especially after heavy rainfall. Call San Diego's Lifeguard Services at *619/221–8824* for a recorded message that includes pollution reports along with surfing and diving conditions. The Heal the Bay organization (🌐 *www.healthebay.org*) monitors and grades California coastal water conditions yearly.

BEACH CAMPING

Overnight camping is not allowed on any San Diego city beach, but there are campgrounds at some state beaches (*800/444–7275 for reservations* 🌐 *www.reserveamerica.com*) throughout the county.

DOG BEACHES

Leashed dogs are permitted on most San Diego beaches and adjacent parks from 6 pm to 9 am; they can run unleashed anytime at Dog Beach at the north end of Ocean Beach and, from the day after Labor Day through June 14, at Dog Beach at the rivermouth in Del Mar. In Mission Bay near SeaWorld, there's an off-leash dog park on Fiesta Island where dogs can splash in the calm water.

RED TIDE

When sporadic algae blooms turn coastal waters a reddish-brown hue, San Diegans know the "red tide" has arrived. Environmentalists may see it as a bane to healthy ocean life, but the phenomenon is welcomed as a chance to witness ocean phosphorescence. The phytoplankton that causes the discoloration is unsightly only until nightfall. After dark, the algae-rich waters crash against the sand, inciting bioluminescent plankton to emit a bluish-green neon light. The result is a marvelous display of glow-in-the-dark waves. California's red tide typically occurs between April and August.

BEACHES BY NEIGHBORHOOD

SOUTH BAY TO CORONADO

SOUTH BAY

Border Field State Park. San Diego's southernmost beach lies within Border Field State Park, an area with sand dunes and salt marshes favored by horseback riders and hikers. The Tijuana River Estuary, designated as a Wetland of National Importance, is a haven for endangered birds. The beach has soft sand, but due to the amount of debris and seaweed that washes up on the shore, it's not a particularly good place for sunbathing. You're better off going for a long walk or picnicking at one of the Monument Mesa sites, which offer scenic ocean views, barbecue grills, and shaded areas. Flooding in winter often restricts access, but normally the park is open to pedestrians, hikers, and equestrians on weekdays. Because of state budget cuts, motorized vehicles are permitted only on weekends and holidays. **Beware:** Swimming and wading are discouraged due to inshore holes and rip currents, and because no lifeguards are on duty. After heavy rains, runoff from the Tijuana River and nearby ranches can pollute the water, leading to occasional beach closures. Bring snacks and drinking water because the closest place to buy food is 5 miles away in Imperial Beach. **Amenities:** parking (fee), toilets. **Best for:** solitude, walking. ✉ *Monument Rd., 15 miles south of San Diego* ✣ *Exit I–5 at Dairy Mart Rd. and head west along Monument Rd. for about 5 miles* ☎ *619/575–3613* 🌐 *www.parks.ca.gov* 🎫 *$5 per vehicle.*

FAMILY **Imperial Beach.** More and more people from around the country are discovering this once sleepy stretch of sand thanks to the Pier South Autograph Collection hotel right on the beach. The 4-mile-long beach is a great place for long walks and bird-watching—more than 370 species can be spotted here. There are year-round lifeguards, two parks with covered picnic areas, two playgrounds, and volleyball and basketball courts. Sea 180, the restaurant at the Pier South Resort, serves Baja-Med cuisine steps from the surf. The wooden fishing pier has views of Mexico to the south and Point Loma to the north. In July the beach is the site of the Sun & Sea Festival sand castle competition, and the Dog Surfing Competition. **Amenities:** lifeguards, food and drink, parking (fee), showers, toilets. **Best for:** surfing, swimming, walking. ✉ *Seacoast Dr. at Evergreen Ave., beach extends from Carnation Ave. to Imperial Beach Blvd., parking at Seacoast Dr. and Palm Ave.* ✣ *From I–5, take Palm Ave. west until it hits beach* ☎ *619/595–3954* 🌐 *www.parks.ca.gov* 🎫 *Parking $2 a day.*

CORONADO

FAMILY Fodor's Choice ★ **Coronado Beach.** This wide beach is one of San Diego's most picturesque thanks to its soft white sand and sparkly blue water. The historic Hotel Del Coronado serves as a backdrop, and it's perfect for sunbathing, people-watching, and Frisbee tossing. The beach has limited surf, but it's great for bodyboarding and swimming. Exercisers might include Navy SEAL teams or other military units that conduct training runs on beaches in and around Coronado. There are picnic tables, grills, and popular fire rings, but don't bring lacquered wood or pallets. Only natural wood is allowed for burning. There's also a dog beach on the north end. There's free parking along Ocean Boulevard, though it's often hard to snag a space. **Amenities:** food and drink, lifeguards, showers, toilets. **Best for:** walking, swimming. ✉ *Ocean Blvd., between S. O St. and Orange Ave., Coronado* ⊕ *From the San Diego–Coronado bridge, turn left on Orange Ave. and follow signs.*

FAMILY **Silver Strand State Beach.** This quiet beach on a narrow sand-spit allows visitors a unique opportunity to experience both the Pacific Ocean and the San Diego Bay. The 2½ miles of ocean side is great for surfing and other water sports while the bay side, accessible via foot tunnel under Highway 75, has calmer, warmer water and great views of the San Diego skyline. Lifeguards and rangers are on duty year-round, and there are places for biking, volleyball, and fishing. Picnic tables, grills, and fire pits are available in summer, and the Silver Strand Beach Cafe is open Memorial Day through Labor Day. The beach is close to Loews Coronado Bay Resort and the Coronado Cays, an exclusive community popular with yacht owners. You can reserve RV sites ($65 beach; $50 inland) online (*www.reserveamerica.com*). Three day-use parking lots provide room for 800 cars. **Amenities:** food and drink, lifeguards, parking (fee), showers, toilets. **Best for:** walking, swimming, surfing. ✉ *5000 Hwy. 75, Coronado* ⊕ *4½ miles south of city of Coronado* ☎ *619/435–5184* 🌐 *www.parks.ca.gov/silverstrand* 🎫 *Parking $10, motorhome $30.*

POINT LOMA, MISSION BAY, AND LA JOLLA

POINT LOMA

Ocean Beach. This mile-long beach south of Mission Bay's channel is the place to get a slice of vintage SoCal beach culture. It's likely you'll see VW vans in the parking lot near the Ocean Beach Pier. The wide beach is popular with volleyball players, sunbathers, and surfers. The municipal pier at the southern end extends a ½ mile out to sea where you can fish without a valid California fishing license. There's a café about halfway out, and taco shops, bars, and restaurants can be found on the streets near the beach. Swimmers should beware of strong rip currents around the main lifeguard tower, where lifeguards are on duty year-round. One of Ocean Beach's most popular features is the Dog Beach at the northern end, where canine's can run freely and splash in the waves 24 hours a day. For shade, picnic areas with barbecues, and a paved path, check out Robb Field, across from Dog Beach. **Amenities:** lifeguards, parking (no fee), showers, toilets. **Best for:** surfing, swimming, walking. ✉ *Newport Ave. at Abbott St., Ocean Beach* ⊕ *7 miles from Downtown San Diego* 🌐 *www.sandiego.gov.*

Sunset Cliffs. As the name would suggest this natural park near Point Loma Nazerene University is one of the best places in San Diego to watch the sunset thanks to its cliff-top location and expansive ocean views. Some limited beach access is accessible via an extremely steep

The grassy palm-lined park above La Jolla Cove is great for picnics.

stairway at the foot of Ladera Street. Beware of the treacherous cliff trails and pay attention to warning signs. The cliffs are very unstable and several fatalities have occurred over the last few years. If you're going to make your way to the narrow beach below, it's best to go at low tide when the southern end, near Cabrillo Point, reveals tide pools teeming with small sea creatures. Farther north the waves lure surfers, and Osprey Point offers good fishing off the rocks. Keep your eyes peeled for migrating California gray whales during the winter months. Check WaveCast (*www.wavecast.com/tides*) for tide schedules. **Amenities:** parking (no fee). **Best for:** solitude, sunset, surfing. ✉ *Sunset Cliffs Blvd., between Ladera St. and Adair St., Point Loma* 🌐 *www.sunsetcliffs.info*.

MISSION BAY

FAMILY **Mission Beach.** With a roller coaster, artificial wave park, and hot dog stands, this 2-mile-long beach has a carnival vibe and is the closest thing you'll find to Coney Island on the West Coast. It's lively year-round but draws a huge crowd on hot summer days. A wide boardwalk paralleling the beach is popular with walkers, joggers, skateboarders, and bicyclists. To escape the crowds, head to South Mission Beach. It attracts surfers, swimmers, and scantily clad volleyball players, who often play competitive pickup games on the courts near the north jetty. The water near the Belmont Park roller coaster can be a bit rough but makes for good bodyboarding and bodysurfing. For free parking, you can try for a spot on the street, but your best bets are the two big lots at Belmont Park. **Amenities:** lifeguards, parking (no fee), showers, toilets. **Best for:** swimming, surfing, walking. ✉ *3000 Mission Blvd.,*

Mission Bay ✢ Parking near roller coaster at West Mission Bay Dr. 🌐 www.sandiego.gov/lifeguards/beaches/mb.shtml.

Pacific Beach/North Pacific Beach. This beach, known for attracting a young college-age crowd and surfers, runs from the northern end of Mission Beach to Crystal Pier. The scene here is lively on weekends, with nearby restaurants, beach bars, and nightclubs providing a party atmosphere. In P.B. (as the local call it) Sundays are known as "Sunday Funday," and pub crawls can last all day. So although drinking is no longer allowed on the beach, it's still likely you'll see people who have had one too many. The mood changes just north of the pier at North Pacific Beach, which attracts families and surfers. Although not quite pillowy, the sand at both beaches is nice and soft, which makes for great sunbathing and sand-castle building. ■ **TIP→ Kelp and flies can be problem on this stretch, so choose your spot wisely.** Parking at Pacific Beach can also be a challenge. A few coveted free angle parking spaces are available along the boardwalk, but you'll most likely have to look for spots in the surrounding neighborhood. If you're staying at nearby Pacific Terrace Hotel, you can simply walk to the beach. **Amenities:** food and drink, lifeguards, parking (no fee), showers, toilets. **Best for:** partiers, swimming, surfing. ✉ *4500 Ocean Blvd., Pacific Beach* 🌐 *www.sandiego.gov/lifeguards/beaches/pb.shtml.*

SNACK TIP

Trader Joe's. On your way to Pacific Beach? Head to Trader Joe's for sandwiches, sandwich fixings, chips, dried fruits, nuts, beverages, and tasty cheeses. ✉ *1640 Garnet Ave., Pacific Beach* ☎ *858/581–9101* 🌐 *www.traderjoes.com.*

Tourmaline Surfing Park. Offering slow waves and frequent winds, this is one of the most popular beaches for surfers. For windsurfing and kiteboarding, it's only sailable with northwest winds. The 175-space parking lot at the foot of Tourmaline Street normally fills to capacity by midday. Just like Pacific Beach, Tourmaline has soft, tawny-colored sand, but when the tide is in the beach becomes quite narrow, making finding a good sunbathing spot a bit of a challenge. **Amenities:** seasonal lifeguards, parking (no fee), showers, toilets. **Best for:** windsurfing, surfing. ✉ *600 Tourmaline St., Pacific Beach.*

LA JOLLA

FAMILY **Children's Pool.** Due to the groups of harbor seals that have claimed it as their own, this shallow cove, protected by a seawall, is closed to the public for the winter pupping season, December 15 through May 15. People may access its calm, protected waters the other seven months of the year, however, and the beach's small waves make it an ideal place for children to splash and play. Adults will appreciate the view. Because of its location at the tip of La Jolla Peninsula, you can actually look east to get unmatched panoramic views of the coastline and ocean. The area just outside the pool is popular with scuba divers, who explore the offshore reef when the surf is calm. Although you may not be able to go down on the beach during the winter months, it's still worth a peak. It's fun to watch the seals and their pups from above. ■ **TIP→ Limited free parking is available along Coast Boulevard.** **Amenities:** lifeguards, showers, toilets, parking (no fee). **Best for:** walking, scuba diving. ✉ *850 Coast Blvd., La Jolla* 🌐 *www.sandiego.gov/lifeguards/beaches/pool.shtml.*

FAMILY Fodor's Choice ★ **La Jolla Cove.** This shimmering blue-green inlet surrounded by cliffs is what first attracted everyone to La Jolla, from Native Americans to the glitterati. "The Cove," as locals refer to it, beyond where Girard Avenue dead-ends into Coast Boulevard, is marked by towering palms that line a promenade where people strolling in designer clothes are as common as Frisbee throwers. Ellen Browning Scripps Park sits atop cliffs formed by the incessant pounding of the waves and offers a great spot for picnics with a view. The Cove has beautiful white sand that is a bit course near the water's edge, but the beach is still a great place for sunbathing and lounging. At low tide, the pools and cliff caves are a destination for explorers. With visibility at 30-plus feet, this is the best place in San Diego for snorkeling, where bright-orange Garibaldi fish and other marine life populate the waters of the **San Diego–La Jolla Underwater Park Ecological Reserve.** From above water, it's not uncommon to spot sea lions and birds basking on the rocks, or dolphin fins just offshore. The cove is also a favorite of rough-water swimmers, while the area just north is best for kayakers wanting to explore the Seven La Jolla Sea Caves. **Amenities:** lifeguards, showers, toilets. **Best for:** snorkeling, swimming, walking. ✉ *1100 Coast Blvd., east of Ellen Browning Scripps Park, La Jolla* 🌐 *www.sandiego.gov/lifeguards/beaches/cove.shtml.*

FAMILY **La Jolla Shores.** This is one of San Diego's most popular beaches due to its wide sandy shore, gentle waves, and incredible views of La Jolla Peninsula. There's also a large grassy park, and adjacent to La Jolla Shores lies the **San Diego La Jolla Underwater Park Ecological Reserve,** 6,000 acres of protected ocean bottom and tide lands. The white powdery sand at La Jolla Sands is some of San Diego's best, and several surf and scuba schools teach here. Kayaks can also be rented nearby. A concrete boardwalk parallels the beach, and a boat launch for small vessels lies 300 yards south of the lifeguard station at Avenida de Playa. Arrive early to get a parking spot in the lot near Kellogg Park at the foot of Calle Frescota. Street parking is limited to one or two hours. **Amenities:** lifeguards, parking (no fee), showers, toilets. **Best for:** surfing, swimming, walking. ✉ *8200 Camino del Oro, in front of Kellogg Park, La Jolla* ↔ *2 miles north of downtown La Jolla* 🌐 *www.sandiego.gov/lifeguards/beaches/shores.shtml.*

Shell Beach. The small cove north of the Children's Pool remains remarkably under the radar and is typically less crowded than nearby beaches like La Jolla Cove and La Jolla Shores. The secluded beach is accessible by stairs and has clear water and tidepools. The reef comes all the way up to the shore, making it a less-than-ideal spot for swimming, but children love to wade in the shallow water. Step with caution, as rocks can be extremely slippery. As the name would imply, tiny shells make up the sand near the water's edge. It's beautiful but coarse and can be hard on people's feet. Your visit is better spent exploring than sunning. The exposed rocks off the coast have been designated a protected habitat for sea lions; you can watch them frolic in the water. Picnic tables, showers, and toilets are available near the cove. **Amenities:** none. **Best for:** solitude. ✉ *Coast Blvd., La Jolla* ✣ *North of Children's Pool and south of Ellen Browning Scripps Park.*

Fodor's Choice ★ **Torrey Pines State Beach and Reserve.** With sandstone cliffs and hiking trails adjacent to the beach rather than urban development, Torrey Pines State Beach feels far away from the SoCal sprawl. The beach and reserve encompasses 1,600 acres of sandstone cliffs and deep ravines, and a network of meandering trails lead to the wide, pristine beach below. Along the way enjoy the rare Torrey pine trees, found only here and on Santa Rosa Island, offshore. Guides conduct free tours of the nature preserve on weekends. Torrey Pines tends to get crowded in summer, but you'll find more isolated spots heading south under the cliffs leading to Black's Beach. Smooth rocks often wash up on stretches of the beach making it a challenge, at times, to go barefoot. If you can find a patch that is clear of debris, you'll encounter the nice soft, golden sand San Diego is known for. There is a paid parking lot at the entrance to the park but also look for free angle parking along N. Torrey Pines Road. **Amenities:** lifeguards, parking (fee), showers, toilets. **Best for:** swimming, surfing, walking. ✉ *12600 N. Torrey Pines Rd.* ☎ *858/755–2063* 🌐 *www.torreypine.org* *Parking $15 per vehicle.*

Fodor's Choice ★ **Windansea Beach.** With its rocky shoreline and strong shore break, Windansea stands out among San Diego beaches for its dramatic natural beauty. It's one of the best surf spots in San Diego County. Professional surfers love the unusual A-frame waves the reef break here creates. Although the large sandstone rocks that dot the beach might sound like a hindrance, they actually serve as protective barriers from the wind, making this one of the best beaches in San Diego for sunbathing. The beach's palm-covered surf shack is a protected historical landmark, and a seat here at sunset may just be one of the most romantic spots on the West Coast. The name Windansea comes from a hotel that burned down in the late 1940s. You can usually find nearby street parking. **Amenities:** seasonal lifeguards, toilet. **Best for:** sunset, surfing, solitude. ✉ *Neptune Pl. at Nautilus St., La Jolla* 🌐 *www.sandiego.gov/lifeguards/beaches/windan.shtml.*

NORTH COUNTY BEACHES

DEL MAR

FAMILY **Del Mar Beach.** This famously clean 2-mile-long beach is the perfect place for long barefoot walks and sunbathing due to its extremely fine, soft sand and lack of seaweed and other debris. Del Mar Beach is also a great place for families. It has year-round lifeguards and areas clearly marked for swimming and surfing. Depending on the swell, you may see surfers at the 15th Street surf break, right below two coastal parks, Powerhouse and Seagrove; volleyball players love the courts at the beach's far North end. The section of beach south of 15th is lined with cliffs and tends to be less crowded than Main Beach, which extends from 15th north to 29th. Leashed dogs are permitted on most sections of the beach, except Main Beach, where they are prohibited from June 15 through the Tuesday after Labor Day. For the rest of the year, dogs may run under voice control at North Beach, just north of the River Mouth, also known locally as Dog Beach. Food, shopping, and hotels including L'Auberge Del Mar, are near Del Mar Beach. Parking costs from $1.50 to $3 per hour at meters and pay lots on Coast Boulevard and along Camino Del Mar. **Amenities:** food and drink, lifeguards, parking (fee), showers, toilets. **Best for:** swimming, walking. ✉ *Main Beach, 1700 Coast Blvd., North Beach 3200–3300 Camino Del Mar, Del Mar* ☎ *858/755–1556* 🌐 *www.delmar.ca.us/203/Beaches-Parks.*

SOLANA BEACH

Fletcher Cove. Most of the beaches in the little city of Solana Beach are nestled under cliffs, and access is limited to private stairways. However, at the west end of Lomas Santa Fe Drive, where it turns into Plaza Street, there's an entrance to this small beach, along with parking lot, picnic area, playground, and restrooms. The softest sand can be found by the cliffs and it gets a bit courser as you near the water's edge. During low tide it's an easy walk under the cliffs to nearby beaches, but high tide can make some of the beach impassable. At the northern end of town there are also restrooms, a pay lot, and easy beach access. The City of Solana Beach and the Belly Up Tavern often host free summer concerts at Fletcher Cove (*www.cityofsolanabeach.org*) and there are plenty of great restaurants nearby on Highway 101 and on Cedros Avenue. Tides and surf conditions are posted at a kiosk by this parking lot. **Amenities:** lifeguards, parking (no fee), showers, toilets. **Best for:** surfing, solitude, swimming, walking. ✉ *Plaza St. at S. Sierra Ave., Solana Beach.*

CARDIFF-BY-THE-SEA

Cardiff State Beach. A reef break draws surfers to this beach, popularly known as George's, and there are great cafés and restaurants nearby, such as Las Olas and Ki's. Stones run along the highway but then give way to a nice swath of sand. A walk south provides access to some of Solana Beach's secluded coves. ■ **TIP→ Pay attention to the incoming tide, or you may have to wade or swim back to the parking lot.** The beach begins at the parking lot immediately north of the cliffs at Solana Beach. Your best bet for a nearby coastal hotel is Cardiff by the Sea Lodge. **Amenities:** lifeguards, parking (fee), showers, toilets. **Best for:** surfing, swimming. ✉ *Hwy. 101 (Rte. S21), Cardiff-by-the-Sea* ✣ *1 mile south of Cardiff* ☎ *760/753–5091* 🌐 *www.parks.ca.gov* 🎫 *$10 per vehicle; $15 peak weekends/holidays.*

ENCINITAS

Moonlight State Beach. Its large parking areas, many facilities, and proximity to the quaint coastal town of Encinitas make this beach tucked into a break in the cliffs a great getaway. The volleyball courts on the northern end attract many competent players, and professionals can be spotted surfing the break known locally as "D

Street." Moonlight is easily accessible from the Encinitas Coaster train station and Coast Highway 101, which runs right through town and is lined with great shops, restaurants and bars. Whole Foods in downtown Encinitas (*www.wholefoodsmarket.com*) is a great place to stop for picnic fixings before heading to the beach. There's a large free parking lot near the corner of 3rd and B Street. **Amenities:** food and drink, lifeguards, parking (no fee), showers, toilets. **Best for:** sunset, surfing, swimming. ✉ *399 C St., Encinitas* ✣ *To get to beach from I–5, take Encinitas Blvd. west until it ends* 🌐 *www.parks.ca.gov*.

Swami's. The palms and the golden lotus-flower domes of the nearby Self-Realization Fellowship temple and ashram earned this picturesque beach, also a top surfing spot, its name. Extreme low tides expose tide pools that harbor anemones, starfish, and other sea life. The only access is by a long stairway leading down from the cliff-top Swami's Seaside Park, where there's free parking. A shower is at the base of the steps. On big winter swells, the bluffs are lined with gawkers watching the area's best surfers take on—and be taken down by—some of the county's best big waves. The beach has flat, packed sand and can accumulate seaweed and some flies, so if laying out is your main objective you might want to head north to Moonlight Beach. Offshore, divers do their thing at North County's underwater park, Encinitas Marine Life Refuge. The small park next to the Swami's parking lot offers shade trees, picnic tables, barbecues, and clean bathrooms. Across the street is the cheerful Swami's Cafe, where surfers refuel postsurf. **Amenities:** lifeguards, parking (no fee), showers, toilets. **Best for:** snorkeling, surfing, swimming. ✉ *1298 S. Coast Hwy. 101 (Rte. S21), Encinitas* ✣ *1 mile north of Cardiff.*

CARLSBAD

South Carlsbad State Beach/Carlsbad State Beach. There are fine street- and beach-level promenades at Carlsbad State Beach, where people come to surf and swim at Ponto and Tamarack Beaches. On the bluff, there's overnight camping for self-contained RVs (*800/444–7275*) and tents (from $30). Farther north at the foot of Tamarack Avenue is Carlsbad State Beach. You can't camp here, but there's fishing and jogging trails and the beach has separate swimming and surfing sections. In summer, the south swell creates good surf when other San Diego beaches are bereft. The cement walkway that borders the beach continues into downtown Carlsbad, which has plenty of restaurants. Carlsbad State Beach has a paid parking lot on Tamarack Ave and at South Ponto. **Amenities:** lifeguards, parking (fee), showers, toilets. **Best for:** walking, swimming, surfing. ✉ *South Carlsbad Beach, 7201 Carlsbad Blvd., Carlsbad Beach; Tamarack Ave. at Carlsbad Blvd., Carlsbad* ☎ *760/438–3143* 🌐 *www.parks.ca.gov* 🎟 *$15 per vehicle.*

OCEANSIDE

Oceanside City Beach. This long, straight beach is popular with swimmers, surfers, and U.S. Marines from nearby Camp Pendleton. The impressive wooden Oceanside Pier extends a quarter of a mile into the ocean, and there's a '50s style diner called Ruby's at the end. The sand here is a bit course, and smaller rocks can be found in some sections, but due to its width (a quarter mile from street to surf near 1200 N. Pacific Street) nice patches can almost always be found. There is surfing around the pier, but the waves are bigger and better just north at Oceanside Harbor, which gets a south swell in the summer. Pay lots and meters are located around the pier and also in the Oceanside Harbor area. A free two-hour lot can be found east of the pay lots on Harbor Drive South. There are plenty of shops and restaurants along Oceanside Harbor Village. Families love the kid-friendly Buccaneer Beach, just south of the pier across from Buccaneer Beach Park. This area has free parking, a café, restrooms, showers, and lifeguards on duty in summer. **Amenities:** seasonal lifeguards, food and drink, parking (fee), toilets, showers. **Best for:** surfing, swimming, walking. ⊠ *200 N. the Strand, Oceanside* *$8 parking.*

13

SPORTS AND THE OUTDOORS

SURFING SAN DIEGO

Head to a San Diego beach on any given day and chances are you'll see a group of surfers in the water, patiently waiting to catch a memorable wave.

(above) La Jolla Shores is a good beach for beginner surfers. (lower right) Surfer at the end of a good ride. (upper right) Instructors at Surf Diva Surf School cater to women.

Surfing may have originated in Hawaii, but modern surfing culture is inextricably linked to the Southern California lifestyle. From the Malibu setting of *Gidget* to the surf-city sounds of Jan and Dean and the Beach Boys, and TV's *Laguna Beach* and *The OC*, the entertainment industry brought a California version of surfing to the landlocked, and in the process created an enduring mystique.

San Diego surfing in particular is unique. Underwater kelp beds help keep waves intact, preventing the choppiness that surfers bemoan. Santa Ana winds that begin to arrive in fall and throughout early winter bring coveted offshore winds that contribute to morning and evening "glass" (the stillness of the water that encourages smooth waves).

BEST TIME TO GO

The biggest swells usually occur in winter, but good-size waves can form year-round. Generally, swells come from the north in winter and from the south in summer. Certain breaks are better on different swells. In winter, try beaches like Swami's or Black's Beach that can hold large swells without closing out. Summer spots are La Jolla's Windansea and nearby Tourmaline Surfing Park.

TYPES OF BREAKS

Beach break: Waves that break over sandbars and the seafloor and are usually tamer and consistently long, thus typically the best type for beginners, with the exception of Black's Beach, which is legendary for its uniquely large, fast, and punchy beach breaks. **La Jolla Shores, Mission Beach,** and **Pacific Beach** are destinations for gentler, more forgiving waves.

Point break: Created as waves that hit a point jutting into the ocean. Surfers then peel down the wave it creates. With the right conditions, this can create very consistent waves. **Swami's** has an excellent point break.

Reef break: Waves break as they hit a reef. It can create great (but dangerous) surf. There's a good chance of getting smashed and scraped over extremely sharp coral or rocks. Many of San Diego's best breaks occur thanks to underwater reefs, as at **San Elijo, La Jolla Cove,** and **Windansea.**

SAN DIEGO SURF FINDER

Get a closer view of surfers doing their thing from any municipal pier, such as at **Oceanside, Pacific,** and **Mission beaches.** The high bluffs of **Black's Beach** are also excellent points to watch surfers.

Swami's: Famous for its point break and beautiful waters.

Black's Beach: This strand below the cliffs is where to go for beach breaks. Serious surfers carry their boards down the narrow, steep trails to reach the beach.

Windansea Beach: A dual beach for surf and romance. Known for its reef breaks.

Tourmaline Surfing Park: Windsurfers and surfers share Tourmaline's smooth waves.

La Jolla Shores: First-timers head here for more modest waves.

SURF SLANG

Barrel: The area created when a wave breaks onto itself in a curl.

Close out: When a wave breaks all at once, rather than breaking steadily in one direction.

Cutback: The most basic turn; executed to maintain position close to the barrel.

Dropping in: A severe breach of etiquette wherein a second surfer joins the wave later and cuts off the original rider.

Goofy foot: Having a right-foot-forward stance on the surfboard.

Grom: An affectionate term for those sun-bleached kids with tiny surfboards.

Hollow: Barrels big enough to create a tube that a surfer can ride within—also called the green room.

Lineup: A group of surfers waiting beyond the whitewash for waves.

Turtle roll: When a surfer rolls over on the surfboard, going underwater and holding the board upside down to bypass the crashing waves.

Updated by Marlise Kast-Myers

With average daily temperatures of 70.5°F, San Diego is built for outdoor activities year-round. As you'd expect, the ocean is one of San Diego's most popular natural attractions. Surfers, swimmers, kayakers, divers, snorkelers, and paddleboarders have 70 miles of shorefront to explore. What might surprise you is there is also great hiking, horseback riding, rock-climbing, biking, and more.

The possibilities for outdoor activity really are endless and evidence of San Diego's outdoorsy spirit is apparent everywhere; you'll likely see runners swarming the waterfront and Balboa Park, groups of surfers bobbing in the water at dawn, hang gliders swooping off sandstone cliffs, and white sails gliding gracefully along the shore. Outdoor enthusiasts are as much a part of San Diego's landscape as the sea, sand, and hills, and if you want to get in on the action, it's easy. Companies offering kayak and snorkeling tours and rentals are prevalent, especially in the beach communities of La Jolla, Mission Beach, and on Coronado. If you want to learn to surf, sign up for a lesson at one of the many surf schools in La Jolla or rent a board in Mission Beach and go out on your own. If sightseeing is more your style you can head out on a fishing or whale-watching excursion aboard a charter boat or take a sunset stroll on a wide, sandy beach. At the end of the day at any beach in the county, you'll surely see a local ritual: everyone stops what they're doing to watch the sun's orange orb slip silently into the blue-gray Pacific.

SPORTS AND THE OUTDOORS PLANNER

SAN DIEGO BY THE SEASONS

San Diego has miles of beaches and bays, numerous lakes, mountains, and deserts to explore. With balmy average temperatures and less than a foot of rain per year, the lure to go play outside is hard to resist. That said, Southern California isn't as seasonless as some claim. Although the weather is generally mild and sunny year-round, the seasons do bring different outdoor activities.

TOP OUTDOOR EXPERIENCES

Kayak La Jolla's caves: Join a tour to explore the seven caves off La Jolla Cove; you can see lots of wildlife, including seals, sea lions, and maybe leopard sharks and dolphins.

Bike the boardwalk: Rent a beach cruiser and pedal along the Mission Bay boardwalk. You'll be in good company among the scene-making muscle men and ladies in bikinis.

Catch a wave: Surf La Jolla Cove's famous reef breaks or watch the surfers at Swami's from the Self-Realization Fellowship's meditation gardens on the cliffs above.

Horseback ride in the surf: San Diego Beach Rides offers sunset horseback rides in Border Field State Park.

Hit the links: With so many courses in San Diego, there's sure to be something for every golfer. Add to that the perfect weather and sweeping views of the ocean and it's tee time.

Summer is the best time to plan your trip from an outdoor activities point of view (this is peak tourist season for a reason). San Diego's proximity to the ocean offers an almost endless selection of water activities. Rent kayaks at La Jolla Cove, take a charter boat off Point Loma for deep-sea tuna fishing, or simply hit the beach and go for a swim. Action Sport Rentals, operating out of the Bahia Resort at Mission Bay, offers paddleboards and sailboat rentals to help you enjoy the shimmering bay. Visitors planning a trip in early summer should be aware of the phenomenon known as "May Gray and June Gloom," when fog often blankets the coast in the morning. Things usually clear up by the afternoon, but occasionally the fog lasts all day, making a trip to the beach a damp and chilly affair.

The temperature begins to cool down for winter, but before it does, Santa Ana winds usher a warm dry spell throughout Southern California through the **fall.** It's the perfect time to shoot 18 holes at the Park Hyatt Aviara in Carlsbad, or take a hike at the Bayside Trail at Cabrillo National Monument—fall's cloudless skies allow for a crisp, clear vision of the Pacific. And although the foliage in San Diego doesn't turn into burnished reds and golds, you can appreciate the rare species of evergreen at Torrey Pines State Reserve.

Winter in California is hardly bitter or harsh, but the weather certainly gets too cold for water sports. Serious surfers love the breaks best in winter, when the swells are high. Thick wet suits are a must, because water temperatures can drop into the mid-50s. Black's Beach continues to be one of the most challenging surfing beaches in San Diego. Winter is also when gray whales migrate to warmer waters. Charter boats offer whale-watching trips between December and March. View the whales with San Diego Harbor Excursion or with one of the more intimate sailboat charters offered around town. Sunsets can be particularly spectacular during the winter months.

In **spring,** wildflowers begin to appear in the desert and at the 50 acres of flower fields at the Carlsbad Ranch. At its peak, Southern California's largest bulb farm is abloom with thousands of Giant Tecolote ranunculus.

If you're interested in something sportier, Escondido's lakes are filled with bass, bluegill, and catfish waiting to be hooked.

PARTICIPATION SPORTS

BALLOONING

Enjoy views of the Pacific Ocean, the mountains, and the coastline south to Mexico and north to San Clemente from a hot-air balloon at sunrise or sunset; most excursions include beverages and snacks, too. The conditions are perfect: wide-open spaces and just enough wind to breeze you through them.

California Dreamin'. Head here for hot-air balloon rides, specializing in Temecula wine country flights and Del Mar sunset coastal excursions. ✉ *33133 Vista del Monte Rd., Temecula* ☎ *800/373–3359* 🌐 *www.californiadreamin.com* 🎫 *From $178.*

BICYCLING

San Diego offers bountiful opportunities for bikers, from casual boardwalk cruises to strenuous rides into the hills. The mild climate makes biking in San Diego a year-round delight. Bike culture is respected here, and visitors are often impressed with the miles of designated bike lanes running alongside city streets and coastal roads throughout the county.

BIKE PATHS

Lomas Santa Fe Drive. Experienced cyclists follow this route in Solana Beach east into Rancho Santa Fe, perhaps even continuing east on Del Dios Highway, past Lake Hodges, to Escondido. These roads can be narrow and winding in spots.

Mission Beach Boardwalk. A ride here is a great way to take in a classic California scene. Keep in mind this route is more for cruising than hardcore cycling, as the gawkers and crowds often slow foot- and bike traffic to a crawl. ✉ *Mission Beach.*

Route S21 (*Coast Highway 101*). On many summer days, Route S21, aka Old Highway 101, from La Jolla to Oceanside looks like a freeway for cyclists. About 24 miles long, it's easily the most popular and scenic bike route around, never straying far from the beach. Although the terrain is fairly easy, the long, steep Torrey Pines grade is famous for weeding out the weak. Another Darwinian challenge is dodging slow-moving pedestrians and cars pulling over to park in towns like Encinitas and Del Mar. ✉ *La Jolla.*

San Luis Rey River Trail. Paralleling the San Luis Rey River, this 7.2-mile (one-way) paved trail starts in Oceanside and ends at the beach near the Harbor. Void of traffic lights and motorized traffic, the bike path is relatively flat and is a fun way to reach the coast. ✉ *North Santa Fe Ave. and Hwy. 76, Oceanside.*

THE GREAT WIDE OPEN

An $8.50 round-trip ferry ride transports you and your bike from Downtown San Diego to hyperflat, supercruisable Coronado, with a wide, flat beach, the historic Hotel Del Coronado (an unbeatable background for photos), and the beautifully manicured gardens of its many residential streets.

13

BIKE TOURS AND RENTALS

Bike & Kayak Tours. This bike and kayak outfitter, with locations in La Jolla and on Coronado, is your one-stop shop for biking and kayaking fun. It offers bike rentals and tours like La Jolla Freefall tour that starts at Mt. Soledad, La Jolla's highest point, and continues down the mountain, past mansions, and along the coastline. Bike & Kayak Tours also offers a hotel delivery service, via which they drop off bikes right at your doorstep. ✉ *2158 Ave. De La Playa, La Jolla* ☎ *858/454–1010* 🌐 *bikeandkayaktours.com* 🎫 *Tours from $49; bike rentals from $29.*

The Bike Revolution. Choose from a wide array of rentals, from road bikes to cruisers, and embark on a ride along the Downtown waterfront, up the hill to Balboa Park, or hop on the ferry to Coronado Island for a leisurely ride around the idyllic island. ✉ *522 6th Ave., Downtown* ☎ *619/564–4843* 🌐 *www.thebikerevolution.com* 🎫 *From $20.*

Cheap Rentals. One block from the boardwalk, this place has good daily and weekly prices for surfboards, paddleboards, kayaks, snorkel gear, skateboards, ice chests, umbrellas, chairs, and bike rentals, including beach cruisers, tandems, hybrids, and two-wheeled baby carriers. Kids bikes are also available. Demand is high during the busy season (May through September), so call to reserve equipment ahead of time. ✉ *3689 Mission Blvd., Mission Beach* ☎ *858/488–9070, 800/941–7761* 🌐 *www.cheap-rentals.com* 🎫 *From $12.*

Hike Bike Kayak Adventures. This outfitter offers a wide range of guided bike tours, from easy excursions around Mission Bay and Coronado Island to slightly more rigorous trips through coastal La Jolla. Tours last up to 2½ hours. The company also rents kayaks, paddleboards, and snorkel gear. ✉ *2222 Ave. de la Playa, La Jolla* ☎ *858/551–9510* 🌐 *www.hikebikekayak.com* 🎫 *From $40.*

Holland's Bicycles. This is a great bike rental source on Coronado Island, so you can ride the Silver Strand Bike Path on an electric bike, beach cruiser, road bike, or tandem. ✉ *977 Orange Ave., Coronado* ☎ *619/435–3153* 🌐 *www.hollandsbicycles.com* 🎫 *From $25.*

Wheel Fun Rentals. Surreys, cruisers, mountain bikes, tandems, among other two-, three-, and four-wheeled contraptions, are available at the Downtown Holiday Inn and a number of other locations around San Diego; call or visit the website for details. ✉ *1355 N. Harbor Dr., Downtown* ☎ *619/342–7244* 🌐 *www.wheelfunrentals.com* 🎫 *From $32.*

DIVING AND SNORKELING

The kelp forests and protected marine areas off the San Diego coast are easily accessible and offer divers ample opportunities to explore. Classes are available for beginners, while experienced divers will appreciate the challenges of local wreck and canyon dives. Water temperatures can be chilly, so check with a local outfitter for the appropriate gear before setting out.

San Diego City Lifeguard Service. Call this hotline for prerecorded, up-to-date diving information and conditions. ☎ *619/221–8824* 🌐 *www.sandiego.gov/lifeguards.*

DIVE SITES

The HMCS *Yukon,* a decommissioned Canadian warship, was intentionally sunk off Mission Beach to create the main diving destination in San Diego. A mishap caused the ship to settle on its side, creating a surreal, M.C. Escher–esque diving environment. This is a technical dive and should be attempted only by experienced divers; even diving instructors have become disoriented inside the wreck, and a few have even died trying to explore it.

Diving enthusiasts the world over come to San Diego to snorkel and scuba dive off La Jolla at the San Diego–La Jolla Underwater Park Ecological Preserve. Because all sea life is protected here, this 533-acre preserve (all of La Jolla Cove to La Jolla Shores) is the best place to see large lobster, sea bass, and sculpin (scorpion fish), as well as numerous golden garibaldi damselfish, the state marine fish. It's common to see hundreds of beautiful (and harmless) leopard sharks schooling at the north end of the cove, near La Jolla Shores, especially in summer.

Off the south end of Black's Beach, the rim of Scripps Canyon lies in about 60 feet of water and comprises the Marine Life Refuge. The canyon plummets more than 900 feet in some sections.

DIVE TOURS AND OUTFITTERS

Ocean Enterprises Scuba Diving. Stop in for everything you need to plan a diving adventure, including equipment, advice, and instruction. ✉ *7710 Balboa Ave., Suite 101, Clairemont* ☎ *858/565–6054* 🌐 *www.ocean-enterprises.com.*

Scuba San Diego. This center is well regarded for its top-notch instruction and certification programs, as well as for guided dive tours. Trips include dives to kelp reefs in La Jolla Cove, and night diving at La Jolla Canyon. They also have snorkeling tours to La Jolla's Sea Caves, plus evening kayaking tours under the firework-lit sky on Mission Bay (in summer only). ✉ *San Diego Hilton Hotel, 1775 E. Mission Bay Dr., Mission Bay* ☎ *619/260–1880* 🌐 *www.scubasandiego.com* 🎫 *From $70.*

FISHING

San Diego's waters are home to many game species; you never know what you'll hook. Depending on the season, a half- or full-day ocean charter trip could bring in a yellowfin, dorado, sea bass, or halibut. Longer trips to Mexican waters can net you bigger game like a marlin or a bigeye tuna. Pier fishing doesn't offer as much excitement, but it's the cheapest ocean fishing option available. No license is required to fish from a public pier, which includes those at Ocean Beach, Imperial Beach, and Oceanside.

Public lakes are frequently stocked with a variety of trout and largemouth bass, but also have resident populations of bluegill and catfish.

California Department of Fish and Game. A fishing license, available at most bait-and-tackle and sporting-goods stores, is required for fishing from the shoreline. Nonresidents can purchase an annual license or a 10-day, 2-day, or 1-day short-term license. Licenses can also be purchased online through the department's website or at the San Diego headquarters. Children younger than 16 do not need a license. Note that some city reservoirs no longer sell snacks, drinks, bait, or fishing licenses, nor do they rent pedal boats or electric motors. They also accept payment by credit card or check only for day-use fees. Make sure to check updated concession availability for your specific destination, or obtain a fishing license in advance. **■ TIP→ You do not need a license to fish from public piers.** ✉ *3883 Ruffin Rd.* ☎ *858/467–4201* 🌐 *www.wildlife.ca.gov.*

GO FISH

The California Department of Fish and Game (🌐 *www.wildlife.ca.gov*) issues "Fishing Passports" showing 150 different species of fresh and saltwater fish and shellfish found throughout the state. In San Diego County fishing aficionados can catch (and, hopefully, release) many of the species listed, receiving a stamp for each species caught.

13

FRESHWATER FISHING

There are three freshwater lakes—Dixon, Hodges, and Wohlford—that surround the North County city of Escondido.

Lake Jennings. County-operated Lake Jennings is stocked with trout in winter and catfish during the summer; it's a popular fly-fishing spot and also offers camping and great picnicking. ✉ *9535 Harritt Rd., Lakeside* ☎ *619/443–2510* 🌐 *www.lakejennings.org* 🎫 *$8.*

Lake Morena. This spot near the Pacific Crest Trail is popular for fishing, camping, and hiking. The lake is stocked with trout in the winter, and you're likely to catch bass and catfish year round. ✉ *2550 Lake Morena Dr., Campo* ☎ *619/579–4101, 619/478–5473 recorded information* 🌐 *www.sdparks.org* 🎫 *Parking $3; fishing $7; camping from $22.*

SALTWATER FISHING

Fisherman's Landing. You can book space on a fleet of luxury vessels from 57 feet to 124 feet long and embark on multiday trips in search of yellowfin tuna, yellowtail, and other deep-water fish. Half-day fishing and whale-watching trips are also available. ✉ *2838 Garrison St., Point Loma* ☎ *619/221–8500* 🌐 *www.fishermanslanding.com* 🎫 *From $45.*

H&M Landing. Join one of the West's oldest sportfishing companies for year-round fishing trips plus whale-watching excursions from December through March. ✉ *2803 Emerson St., Point Loma* ☎ *619/222–1144* 🌐 *www.hmlanding.com* 🎫 *From $24.*

Helgren's Sportfishing. Your best bet in North County, Helgren's offers fishing and whale-watching trips from Oceanside Harbor. ✉ *315 Harbor Dr. South, Oceanside* ☎ *760/722–2133* 🌐 *www.helgrensportfishing.com* 🎫 *From $30.*

FRISBEE GOLF

Disc golf is a popular local sport that's like golf, except it's played with Frisbees.

Brengle Terrace Park Disc Golf Course. Just inland from Oceanside, the city of Vista has an 18 "hole" disc golf course that's free of charge. The course is spread across hilly Brengle Terrace Park, home to a playground, walking trails, an amphitheater, and botanical gardens. An on-site pro shop next to the baseball field rents free discs Thursday–Sunday, 9–5; simply leave your ID during store hours. ✉ *1200 Vale Terrace Dr., Vista* ☎ *760/639–6151* 🌐 *www.cityofvista.com.*

Morley Field Disc Golf Course. Located in Balboa Park, the Morley Field course is open daily from dawn to dusk. Frisbees are available to rent for a small fee, and there's also a small fee for using the course (it's first come, first serve). Rules are posted for those new to the sport. ✉ *3090 Pershing Dr., Balboa Park* ☎ *619/692–3607* 🌐 *www.morleyfield.com* 🎫 *$5.*

GOLF

San Diego's climate—generally sunny, without a lot of wind—is perfect for golf, and there are some 90 courses in the area, appealing to every level of expertise. Experienced golfers can play the same greens as PGA-tournament participants, and beginners or rusty players can book a week at a golf resort and benefit from expert instruction. You'd also be hard-pressed to find a locale that has more scenic courses—everything from sweeping views of the ocean to verdant hills inland.

During busy vacation seasons it can be difficult to get a good tee time. Call in advance to see if it's possible to make a reservation. You don't necessarily have to stay at a resort to play its course; check if the one you're interested in is open to nonguests. Most public courses in the area provide a list of fees for all San Diego courses.

COURSES

Below are some of the best courses in the area. The adult public's greens fees for an 18-hole game are included for each course, as well as the courses' championship (blue) yardage; carts (in some cases mandatory), instruction, and other costs are additional. Rates go down during twilight hours, and San Diego residents may be able to get a better deal. Prices change regularly, so check with courses for up-to-date greens fees and deals.

Balboa Park Golf Course. San Diego's oldest public course is five minutes from Downtown in the heart of Balboa Park and offers impressive views of the city and the bay. The course includes a 9-hole executive course and a challenging 18-hole course that weaves among the park's canyons with some tricky drop-offs. Finish off your round with biscuits and gravy and a mimosa at Tobey's 19th Hole Cafe, a greasy spoon that's also Balboa Park's best-kept secret. ✉ *2600 Golf Course Dr., Balboa Park* ☎ *619/235–1184* ⊕ *www.sandiego.gov* 🎫 *$40 weekdays, $50 weekends* ⛳ *27 holes, 6339 yards, par 72.*

Fodor's Choice ★ **Coronado Municipal Golf Course.** Spectacular views of Downtown San Diego and the Coronado Bridge as well as affordable prices make this public course one of the busiest in the world. Bordered by the bay, the trick is to keep your ball out of the water. Wind can add some difficulty, but otherwise this is a leisurely course and a good one to walk. It's difficult to get on unless you reserve a tee time 3 to 14 days in advance. The course's Bayside Grill restaurant is well-known for its Thursday and Sunday night prime rib dinner. Reservations are recommended. ✉ *2000 Visalia Row, Coronado* ☎ *619/522–6590* ⊕ *www.golfcoronado.com* 🎫 *$37 weekdays, $42 weekends* ⛳ *18 holes, 6590 yards, par 72.*

13

Cottonwood Golf Club. This peaceful public golf club 20 minutes from Downtown San Diego is set among rolling hills and offers two 18-hole courses—the Lakes, aptly name for the eight lakes that dot the course, and the not-too-challenging Ivanhoe course. Both are good walking courses with nice practice putting greens. ✉ *3121 Willow Glen Rd., El Cajon* ☎ *619/442–9891* ⊕ *www.cottonwoodgolf.com* 🎫 *Ivanhoe: $37 weekdays, $57 weekends. Lakes: $27 weekdays, $41 weekends* ⛳ *Ivanhoe: 18 holes, 6831 yards, par 72. Lakes: 18 holes, 6610 yards, par 71.*

Eastlake Country Club. Ted Robinson designed this fun public course a few miles from the Olympic Training Center in Chula Vista. Eastlake offers great views of Mount Miguel, and despite the water hazards and sandtraps, it's good for players of all skill levels. It's also a pretty course with waterfalls, six lakes, and hundreds of trees. Reservations can be made up to seven days in advance and you can save quite a bit by taking advantage of the club's Twilight rates. ✉ *2375 Clubhouse Dr., Chula Vista* ☎ *619/482–5757* ⊕ *www.eastlakecountryclub.com* 🎫 *$69 Mon.–Thurs., $79 Fri., $89 weekends* ⛳ *18 holes, 6606 yards, par 72.*

Encinitas Ranch Golf Course. See the Pacific Ocean from virtually every vantage point at this course on bluffs in North County. Local golfers love it because low scores aren't that hard to come by. It's a forgiving course with wide-open fairways. Encinitas Ranch also has a 6,000-square-foot clubhouse with a bar and café. The adjoining patio has a stone fireplace and great ocean views. ✉ *1275 Quail Gardens Dr., Encinitas* ☎ *760/944–1936* ⊕ *www.jcgolf.com* 🎫 *$81 Mon.–Thurs., $87 Fri., $103 weekends (cart included)* ⛳ *18 holes, 6587 yards, par 72.*

Mission Bay Golf Course and Practice Center. Making sure people have fun is the number-one goal at this city-run golf course. San Diego's only night-lighted course, the final tee time is at 7:45 pm for 9 holes, and the executive course with par 3 and 4 holes isn't too challenging. The golf course's scenic and breezy location next to Mission Bay helps keep it comfortably cool. They also have a foot golf course, in which a player kicks a soccer ball into a cup in as few shots as possible. ✉ *2702 N. Mission Bay Dr., Mission Bay* ☎ *858/581–7880* ⊕ *www.sandiego.gov/golf* 🎫 *$17 for 9 holes weekdays, $22 weekends; $29 for 18 holes weekdays, $36 weekends* ⛳ *18 holes, 2715 yards, par 58.*

Torrey Pines Golf Course has fantastic views to go along with its challenging holes.

Mount Woodson Golf Club. This beautiful, heavily wooded club in a hilly area off Highway 67 is set amid a grove of ancient oak trees and granite boulder-strewn hillsides with spectacular views of the historic Woodson Castle, a private residence built in 1921 that is now one of San Diego's most popular wedding venues. The course features some challenging holes like the par 5 Windinface, a deep, three-tiered green, where accuracy is a must. The course also features wooden bridges and good views, particularly from Hole 17. There is a pro shop and a small café. This is a popular local tournament site. ✉ *16422 N. Woodson Dr., Ramona* ☎ *760/788–3555* 🌐 *www.mtwoodsongolfclub.com* 🎫 *$45 weekdays, $65 weekends* 🏌 *18 holes, 6004 yards, par 70.*

Riverwalk Golf Club. With three different 9-hole layouts that can be combined in a variety of ways, this course near the Fashion Valley shopping center is sort of a "choose your own adventure" one. The layouts, designed by Ted Robinson Sr. and Jr., feature natural terrain and oak and eucalyptus trees throughout. There are also a variety of water features including four lakes and the San Dieguito River. This course is challenging but suitable for players of all skill levels with multiple tees on each hole. ✉ *1150 Fashion Valley Rd.* ☎ *619/296–4653* 🌐 *www.riverwalkgc.com* 🎫 *9 holes: $30 Mon.–Thurs., $35 Fri.–Sun. 18 holes: $89 Mon.–Thurs., $99 Fri.–Sun.* 🏌 *Presidio: 9 holes, 3397 yards, par 36. Mission: 9 holes, 3153 yards, par 36. Friars: 9 holes, 3230 yards, par 36.*

Fodor's Choice ★ **Torrey Pines Golf Course.** Due to its clifftop location overlooking the Pacific and its classic championship holes, Torrey Pines is one of the best public golf courses in the United States. The course was the site of the 2008 U.S. Open and has been the home of the Farmers Insurance Open since 1968. The par-72 South Course, redesigned by Rees Jones in 2001, receives rave reviews from touring pros; it is longer, more challenging, and more expensive than the North Course. Tee times may be booked from 8 to 90 days in advance (858/522–1662) and are subject to an advance booking fee ($45). ✉ *11480 N. Torrey Pines Rd., La Jolla* ☎ *858/452–3226, 800/985–4653* 🌐 *www.torreypinesgolfcourse.com* 🎫 *South: $192 weekdays, $240 weekends. North: $105 weekdays, $131 weekends; $40 for golf cart* ⛳ *South: 18 holes, 7227 yards, par 72. North: 18 holes, 6874 yards, par 72.*

RESORTS

Fodor's Choice ★ **Barona Creek Golf Club.** Rated among the top five courses nationwide, this 7,392-yard course won accolades from day one for its challenging slopes, strategically placed boulders, and native grass landscaping. Barona Creek golf course offers four tees to accommodate golfers of all skills and abilities. For those looking to be challenged at the expert level, the course provides a championship layout with four T configurations. ✉ *1000 Wildcat Canyon Rd., Ramona* ☎ *619/328–3742* 🌐 *www.barona.com* 🎫 *$120 weekdays, $160 weekends* ⛳ *Black: 18 holes, 7092 yards, par 72. Gold: 18 holes, 6632 yards, par 72. Silver: 18 holes, 6231 yards, par 72. Burgundy: 18 holes, 5296 yards, par 70.*

Carlton Oak Country Club. Many prestigious qualifying events—including the U.S. Open and U.S. Amateur qualifiers—have been held at this difficult course that was built in 1958 and designed by Pete Dye. The historic course is considered a local landmark and has a picturesque setting, with sycamore and eucalyptus trees, several lakes, and a creek. The Oaks Bar and Grill serves sandwiches and wraps and offers good happy hour specials between 4 and 7. ✉ *9200 Inwood Dr., Santee* ☎ *619/448–4242* 🌐 *www.carltonoaksgolf.com* 🎫 *$55 Mon.–Thurs., $65 Fri., $85 weekends* ⛳ *18 holes, 6700 yards, par 72.*

Omni La Costa Resort and Spa. One of the premier golf resorts in Southern California, La Costa over the years has hosted many of the best professional golfers in the world as well as prominent politicians and Hollywood celebrities. The Dick Wilson–designed Champions course has Bermuda fairways and bunkers. The more spacious Legends Course received a complete makeover in 2013 including a redesign of all 18 greens, as well as new bunkers and turfgrass plantings. After a day on the links you can wind down with a massage, steam bath, and dinner at the resort. ✉ *2100 Costa del Mar Rd., Carlsbad* ☎ *760/438–9111* 🌐 *www.omnihotels.com* 🎫 *$210 Mon.–Thurs., $230 Fri.–Sun.* ⛳ *Champions: 18 holes, 6747 yards, par 72. Legends: 18 holes, 6587 yards, par 72.*

Fodor's Choice ★ **Park Hyatt Aviara Golf Club.** This golf course consistently ranks as one of the best in California and is the only course in San Diego designed by Arnold Palmer. The course features gently rolling hills dotted with native wildflowers and views of the protected adjacent Batiquitos Lagoon and the Pacific Ocean. There are plenty of bunkers and water features for those looking for a challenge, and the golf carts, included in the cost, come fitted with GPS systems that tell you the distance to the pin. The two-story Spanish colonial clubhouse has full-size lockers, lounge areas, a bar, and a steak house. ✉ *7447 Batiquitos Dr., Carlsbad* ☎ *760/603–6900* 🌐 *www.golfaviara.com* 🎫 *$235 Mon.–Thurs., $255 Fri.–Sun.* 🏌 *18 holes, 7007 yards, par 72.*

Rancho Bernardo Inn Golf Course. Designed by William Francis Bell in 1962, this 18-hole course has a traditional layout, but renovations in 2014 have kept it feeling fresh and new. New bunkers were even added in 2013. The course has hosted both PGA and LPGA events and offers an oasis in Rancho Bernardo, with its tree-lined fairways and various water features. A challenging 18th hole requires an approach shot over a creek. Located at the esteemed Rancho Bernardo Inn, the property offers great amenities like a spa and several restaurants, including AVANT, where gourmet mustards are served on tap. ✉ *17550 Bernardo Oaks Dr., Rancho Bernardo* ☎ *858/675–8470* 🌐 *www.ranchobernardoinn.com/golf* 🎫 *$105 Mon.–Thurs., $119 Fri., $144 weekends* 🏌 *18 holes, 6631 yards, par 72.*

Sycuan Golf Resort. With its three courses originally designed by Cecil B. Hollingsworth, this resort offers something for every golfer. Due to flooding in the late 1970s, the courses had to be redesigned by golf course architect Ted Robinson Sr., who added elevation changes and lakes to increase the difficulty. Hackers will love the executive par-3 course, while seasoned golfers can play the championship courses. Sycuan Golf Resort hosts a variety of tournaments, including the Junior World Golf Championships, U.S. Public Links Qualifying site, and the San Diego Junior Amateur. ✉ *3007 Dehesa Rd., El Cajon* ☎ *619/219–6028, 800/457–5568* 🌐 *www.sycuanresort.com* 🎫 *Willow Glen and Oak Glen: $119; Pine Glen: $31* 🏌 *Willow Glen: 18 holes, 6687 yards, par 72. Oak Glen: 18 holes, 6682 yards, par 72. Pine Glen: 18 holes, 2508 yards, par 54.*

HANG GLIDING AND PARAGLIDING

Torrey Pines Gliderport. Perched on the cliffs overlooking the ocean north of La Jolla, this is one of the most spectacular spots to hang glide in the world. It's for experienced pilots only, but hang gliding and paragliding lessons and tandem rides for inexperienced gliders are available. Those who'd rather just watch can grab a bite at the Cliffhanger Cafe, which offers incredible views of the Pacific and of the paragliders taking off. During the summer, there's live music on weekends. ✉ *2800 Torrey Pines Scenic Dr., La Jolla* ☎ *858/452–9858* 🌐 *www.flytorrey.com* 🎫 *From $175.*

HIKING AND NATURE TRAILS

From beachside bluffs and waterfront estuaries to the foothills and trails of the nearby Laguna Mountains and the desert beyond, San Diego County has several vegetation and climate zones—and plenty of open space for hiking. Even if you lack the time to explore the outskirts, a day hike through the canyons and gardens of Balboa Park or the canyons and hills of Mission Trails Park is a great way to escape to nature without leaving the city.

Guided hikes are conducted regularly through Los Peñasquitos Canyon Preserve and the Torrey Pines State Beach and Reserve.

OVER-THE-LINE

A giant beach party as much as a sport, Over-the-Line is a form of beach softball played with two teams of just three people each. Every July, over two weekends that include wild beer drinking and partying, the world championships are held on Fiesta Island. Admission is free, but parking is impossible (shuttle buses are available). Check the Old Mission Beach Athletic Club's website (🌐 *www.ombac.org*) for more information.

HIKING

Fodor's Choice ★ **Bayside Trail at Cabrillo National Monument.** Driving here is a treat in itself, as a vast view of the Pacific unfolds before you. The view is equally enjoyable on Bayside Trail (2 miles round-trip), which is home to the same coastal sagebrush that Juan Rodriguez Cabrillo saw when he first discovered the California coast in the 16th century. After the hike, you can explore nearby tide pools, the monument statue, and the Old Point Loma Lighthouse. Don't worry if you don't see everything on your first visit; your entrance receipt ($10 per car) is good for 7 days. ✉ *1800 Cabrillo Memorial Dr., Point Loma* ✣ *From I–5, take Rosecrans exit and turn right on Canon St. then left on Catalina Blvd. (also known as Cabrillo Memorial Dr.); follow until end* ☎ *619/557–5450* 🌐 *www.nps.gov/cabr* 🎫 *Parking $10.*

Los Peñasquitos Canyon Preserve. Trails at this inland park north of Mira Mesa accommodate equestrians, runners, walkers, and cyclists as well as leashed dogs. Look at maps for trails specific to bikes and horses. A small waterfall among large volcanic rock boulders is one of the park's most popular sites—it's an unexpected oasis amid the arid valley landscape. ✉ *12020 Black Mountain Rd., Rancho Peñasquitos* ✣ *From I–15, exit Mercy Rd,. and head west to Black Mountain Rd.; turn right then left at first light; follow road to Ranch House parking lot* ☎ *858/484–7504* 🌐 *www.sandiego.gov.*

Mission Trails Regional Park. This park 8 miles northeast of Downtown encompasses nearly 5,800 acres of wooded hillsides, grasslands, chaparral, and streams. Trails range from easy to difficult; they include one with an impressive view of the city from Cowles Mountain and another along a historic missionary path. The park is also a popular place for rock climbing and camping (the Kumeyaay Lake Campground is open on weekends). Lake Murray is at the southern edge of the park, off Highway 8. ✉ *1 Father Junípero Serra Trail, Mission Valley* ☎ *619/668–3281* 🌐 *www.mtrp.org.*

Torrey Pines State Reserve. Hikers and runners will appreciate this park's many winning features: switch-back trails that descend to the sea, an unparalleled view of the Pacific, and a chance to see the Torrey pine tree, one of the rarest pine breeds in the United States. The reserve hosts guided nature walks as well. All food is prohibited at the reserve, so save the picnic until you reach the beach below. Parking is $12–$15, depending on day and season. ✉ *12600 N. Torrey Pines Rd., La Jolla*

⊕ Exit I–5 at Carmel Valley Rd. and head west toward Coast Hwy. 101 until you reach N. Torrey Pines Rd.; turn left. ☎ *858/755–2063* 🌐 *www.torreypines.org* 🎫 *Parking $12–$15.*

NATURE TRAILS

San Dieguito River Park. This 55-mile corridor begins at the mouth of the San Dieguito River in Del Mar and heads from the riparian lagoon area through coastal sage scrub and mountain terrain to end in the desert, which is east of Volcan Mountain near Julian. It's open to hikers, bikers, and horses. The expansive park is also home to the Sikes Adobe Farmhouse, an 1880s farmstead that was almost completely destroyed by wildfire in 2007. After painstaking restoration it reopened in 2010 and is now home to a museum. The restored adobe creamery reopened in 2014. ✉ *18372 Sycamore Creek Rd., Escondido* ☎ *858/674–2270* 🌐 *www.sdrp.org* 🎫 *Adobe parking $3.*

Tijuana Estuary. Mostly contained within Border Field State Park, this estuary is one of the last riparian environments in Southern California. The freshwater and saltwater marshes shelter migrant and resident waterfowl. Horse-riding trails fringe the south end of the Tijuana Estuary in Border Field State Park. The visitor center is open Wednesday through Sunday, but the trails are open daily. ✉ *301 Caspian Way, Imperial Beach* ⊕ *Exit I–5 at Coronado Ave., head west to 3rd St., turn left onto Caspian, which leads into estuary parking lot.* ☎ *619/575–3613* 🌐 *www.trnerr.org* 🎫 *Southern entrance parking $5.*

HORSEBACK RIDING

The Ranch at Bandy Canyon. At this historic ranch in Escondido, you can ride horseback by taking group or private lessons. Trail rides go past old dairy farms and orange groves. ✉ *16251 Bandy Canyon Rd., Escondido* ☎ *760/871–6494* 🌐 *www.bandycanyon.com* 🎫 *From $75.*

Fodor's Choice ★ **San Diego Beach Rides at Pony Land.** This family-owned business south of Imperial Beach has been operating for 30 years and offers private rides by appointment. The quarter and painted horses are carefully matched to each person for rides that can include a jaunt through the Tijuana River Valley Preserve, a sunset ride along the beach, or a swimming adventure, where your horse actually goes with you into the water. ✉ *2606 Hollister St.* ☎ *619/947–3152* 🌐 *www.ponylandsandiego.com* 🎫 *From $75.*

JET SKIING

Jet Skis can be launched from most ocean beaches, although you must ride beyond surf lines, and some beaches have special regulations governing their use.

California Watersports. Waveless Carlsbad Lagoon, east of the intersection of Tamarack Avenue and I–5, is easy to reach from this water recreation center, which has a private beach and landing ramp. You can rent ski boats, WaveRunners, Jet Skis, canoes, aqua cycles, and stand-up paddleboards. ✉ *4215 Harrison St., Carlsbad* ☎ *760/434–3089* 🌐 *www.carlsbadlagoon.com* 🎫 *From $20.*

San Diego Jet Ski. The shop is open daily in spring, summer, and fall; in winter, call ahead for a reservation. In addition to Jet Skis the outfitter rents jet boats, kayaks, and paddleboards. ✉ *4275 Mission Bay Dr., Pacific Beach* ☎ *858/272–6161* 🌐 *www.sdjetski.com* 🎫 *From $60.*

Seaforth Boat Rentals. You can rent Yamaha WaveRunners and explore San Diego Bay or Mission Bay from Seaforth Boat Rentals' four different San Diego locations. On most Fridays and weekends you can join a two-hour WaveRunner tour of La Jolla's coast, departing from the Mission Bay location (April–September only). ✉ *1715 Strand Way, Coronado* ☎ *888/834–2628* 🌐 *www.seaforthboatrental.com* 🎫 *From $99.*

13

JOGGING

Running is a very popular San Diego pastime and organized races like the Rock'n'Roll Marathon (🌐 *runrocknroll.competitor.com*) and La Jolla Half (🌐 *www.lajollahalfmarathon.com*) bring thousands of visitors to San Diego each year. You don't have to sign up for one of these races, though, to get in on the action. Just get out and pound the pavement by going for an easy jog along the San Diego Waterfront (do as the locals do and add in a stair workout at the Convention Center), or hit the trails in Balboa Park.

Fodor'sChoice ★ **Balboa Park.** Balboa Park offers 65 miles of hiking, biking, and running trails of various difficulty. Joggers can start out from any parking lot, but it's probably easiest to start anywhere along the 6th Avenue side. Entry to the numerous lots is best where Laurel Street connects with 6th Avenue. Trails are clearly marked and color coded and if you really want to follow a designated "route" that informs you of the distance you've gone start from one of five gateways in the park: Golden Hill, Marston Point, Morley Field, Park Boulevard, and Sixth and Upas. ✉ *1549 El Prado* 🌐 *www.balboapark.org.*

Embarcadero. Extending from the marina to the Maritime Museum, this popular Downtown run along the Embarcadero stretches for 2 miles along the bay. ✉ *N. Harbor Dr., Downtown.*

Mission Bay. There are several great runs around Mission Bay including an 8.4-mile inner loop around WHERE? and a 5.4-mile trail around Fiesta Island. For serious runners, there's a 12-mile flat route that frames the interior of the bay. ✉ *1590 E. Mission Bay Dr.*

Mission Beach Boardwalk. Spanning about 3 miles from north Pacific Beach to south Mission Beach, this beachfront boardwalk is a great place to run while soaking up the scenery and beach culture. ✉ *3146 Mission Blvd., Ocean Front Walk.*

KAYAKING

There are several places to kayak throughout San Diego. You can spend an especially memorable afternoon exploring the Seven Caves off La Jolla Cove, where you can often see seals, sea lions, and even dolphin.

Bike & Kayak Tours. La Jolla's location of Bike & Kayak Tours offers a Leopard Shark Encounter snorkeling tour ($39 a person), where adventuresome travelers can see the shy spotted creatures up close. The Coronado location has you embarking on a kayak tour ($49 per person) underneath the Coronado Bridge at dusk to enjoy incredible views of Downtown San Diego. The Coronado location also offers stand-up paddleboards for as little as $29 a person. ✉ *1201 1st St., #215, Coronado* ☎ *858/454–1010* 🌐 *www.bikeandkayaktours.com* 🎫 *From $39.*

Everyday California. This action-on-the-water sports company also has its own clothing line offering beach casual styles inspired by La Jolla. Tours with expert guides, many of which are former college-level athletes, include a sunset kayak tour, where wildlife to see includes sea lions, seals, pelicans, and dolphin; the tour combines kayaking and snorkeling. Leopard shark migration tours are offered May–August, and whale watching tours December–March. If you'd rather go out on your own, Everyday California rents kayaks, stand-up paddleboards, surfboards, snorkel equipment, and bodyboards. ✉ *2261 Ave. De La Playa, La Jolla* ☎ *858/454–6195* 🌐 *www.everydaycalifornia.com* 🎫 *From $40.*

Hike Bike Kayak Adventures. This shop offers several kayak tours, from easy excursions in Mission Bay that are well suited to families and beginners to more advanced jaunts. Tours include kayaking the caves off La Jolla coast, whale-watching (from a safe distance) December through March, moonlight and sunset trips, and a cruise into the bay to see SeaWorld's impressive fireworks shows over the water in the summer. Tours last two to three hours and require a minimum of four people. ✉ *2222 Ave. de la Playa, La Jolla* ☎ *858/551–9510* 🌐 *www.hikebikekayak.com* 🎫 *From $65.*

La Jolla Kayak. This family-owned company offers kayak tours of the Seven Caves of La Jolla as well as snorkel and biking adventures. Several guides have extensive backgrounds in marine biology and ecology. ✉ *2199 Ave. De La Playa, La Jolla* ☎ *858/459–1114* 🌐 *www.lajollakayak.com* 🎫 *From $39.*

SAILING AND BOATING

The city's history is full of seafarers, from the ships of the 1542 Cabrillo expedition to the America's Cup that once had a home here. Winds in San Diego are fairly consistent, especially in winter. You can rent a slip at one of several marinas if you're bringing your own boat. If not, you can rent vessels of various sizes and shapes—from small paddleboats and kayaks to Hobie Cats—from various vendors. In addition, most bayside resorts rent equipment for on-the-water adventures. Kayaks are one of the most popular boat rentals, especially in La Jolla, where people kayak around the Underwater Park and Ecological Reserve at the cove. Most of what's available from these outlets is not intended for the open ocean—a dangerous place for the inexperienced.

For information, including tips on overnight anchoring, contact the **Port of San Diego Mooring Office** (☎ *619/686–6227* 🌐 *www.portofsandiego.org*).

For additional information contact the **San Diego Harbor Police** (☎ *619/686–6272*).

BOAT CHARTERS

California Cruisin'. Contact California Cruisin' for sailboat or powerboat charter excursions and dinner cruises. The company also provides dockside accommodations aboard a private luxury yacht or houseboat on San Diego Bay. ✉ *1450 Harbor Island Dr., Downtown* ☎ *619/296–8000* 🌐 *www.californiacruisin.com* 🎫 *From $350.*

Flagship Cruises & Events. Get on board here for harbor tours, two-hour dinner and brunch cruises, and a ferry to Coronado. ✉ *990 N. Harbor Dr., Embarcadero* ☎ *619/234–4111, 800/442–7847 reservations* 🌐 *www.flagshipsd.com* 🎫 *From $25.*

The Gondola Company. You don't have to travel to Venice to be serenaded by a gondolier. This company features authentic Venetian gondola rides that depart daily from the picturesque Coronado Cays. ✉ *503 Grand Caribe Causeway,, Suite C, Coronado* ☎ *619/429–6317* 🌐 *www.gondolacompany.com* 🎫 *From $95 for 2 people.*

Harbor Sailboats. You can rent sailboats from 22 to 45 feet long here for open-ocean adventures. The company also offers skippered charter boats for whale-watching, sunset sails, and bay tours. ✉ *2040 Harbor Island Dr., Harbor Island* ☎ *619/291–9568* 🌐 *www.harborsailboats.com* 🎫 *From $75.*

Hornblower Cruises and Events. This outfit operates harbor cruises, sunset cocktail and dining cruises, whale-watching excursions, and yacht charters. ✉ *970 N. Harbor Dr., Embarcadero* ☎ *619/686–8700, 619/686–8715 ticket booth* 🌐 *www.hornblower.com* 🎫 *From $19.*

BOAT RENTALS

Action Sport Rentals. From its facility at Bahia Resort Hotel and its sister location, the **Catamaran Resort Hotel** (*3999 Mission Blvd., Mission Beach 858/488–2582*), Action Sport Rentals has paddleboats, kayaks, powerboats, and sailboats from 14 to 22 feet. Thanks to their location on the calm waters of Mission Bay, both are great places for beginners to try paddleboarding. ✉ *998 W. Mission Bay Dr., Mission Bay* ☎ *619/241–4794* 🌐 *www.actionsportrentals.com* 🎫 *From $25.*

Seaforth Boat Rentals. You can book charter tours and rent kayaks, Jet Skis, fishing skiffs, powerboats and sailboats at Seaforth's five locations around town. The outfitter also can hook you up with a skipper for a deep-sea fishing trip. Seaforth also rents paddleboards at their Mission Bay and Coronado locations. ✉ *1715 Strand Way, Coronado* ☎ *888/834–2628* 🌐 *www.seaforthboatrental.com* 🎫 *From $25.*

SURFING

If you're a beginner, consider paddling in the waves off Mission Beach, Pacific Beach, Tourmaline Surfing Park, La Jolla Shores, Del Mar, or Oceanside. More experienced surfers usually head for Sunset Cliffs, La Jolla reef breaks, Black's Beach, or Swami's in Encinitas. All necessary equipment is included in the cost of all surfing schools. Beach-area Ys offer surf lessons and surf camp in the summer months and during spring break.

Menehune Surf School. This surf school provides surf lessons as well as paddleboard and surfboard rentals. Private or family lessons can be arranged (from $70 per person for one hour). Menehune Surf also offers popular surf camps for kids every summer from June through August at La Jolla Shores and Del Mar. ✉ *La Jolla Shores Beach, La Jolla* ✣ *Blue canopy at La Jolla Shores Beach located north of parking lot at Kellogg Park in front of 4th–5th house on sand as you walk toward Scripps Pier* ☎ *866/425–2925* 🌐 *www.menehunesurf.com* 🎫 *From $70.*

San Diego Surfing Academy. Choose from private and group lessons and customizable surf camps for teens, kids, adults, and families. Instructional videos are also available online. The academy, which has been running since 1995, is based near Oceanside Harbor and meets for lessons near Tower 10. Students are given a keepsake GoPro video of their surf lesson. The Surfing Academy also offers surf trips to Costa Rica and Nicaragua for beginners. ✉ *Oceanside* ✣ *Near Oceanside Harbor at Tower 10* ☎ *760/230–1474, 800/447–7873* 🌐 *www.sandiegosurfingacademy.com* 🎫 *From $90.*

Fodor's Choice ★ **Surf Diva Surf School.** Check out clinics, surf camps, and private lessons especially formulated for girls and women. Most clinics and trips are for women only, but there are some coed options. Guys can also book private lessons from the nationally recognized staff. Surf Diva is also home to a boutique that sells surf and stand-up paddleboard equipment. They also offer surf retreats in Costa Rica. ✉ *2160 Ave. de la Playa, La Jolla* ☎ *858/454–8273* 🌐 *www.surfdiva.com* 🎫 *From $85.*

SURF SHOPS

Cheap Rentals. Many local surf shops rent both surf and bodyboards. Cheap Rentals is right off the boardwalk, just steps from the waves. It rents wet suits, bodyboards, and skimboards in addition to soft surfboards and long and short fiberglass rides. It also has good hourly to weekly pricing on paddleboards and accessories. ✉ *3689 Mission Blvd., Mission Beach* ☎ *858/488–9070, 800/941–7761* 🌐 *www.cheap-rentals.com* 🎫 *From $5/hour.*

Hansen's. A short walk from Swami's beach, Hansen's is one of San Diego's oldest and most popular surf shops. It has an extensive selection of boards, wet suits, and clothing for sale, and a rental department as well. ✉ *1105 S. Coast Hwy. 101, Encinitas* ☎ *760/753–6595* 🌐 *www.hansensurf.com* 🎫 *$20/day.*

CLOSE UP

Longboarding vs. Shortboarding

Longboarders tend to ride boards more than 8 feet long with rounded noses. Shortboarders ride lightweight, high-performance boards from 5 to 7 feet long with pointed noses. (Funboards are a little longer than shortboards, with broad, round noses and tails that make them good for beginners who want something more maneuverable than a longboard.) A great longboarder will have a smooth, fluid style and will shuffle up and down the board, maybe even riding on the nose with the toes of both feet on the very edge ("hanging 10"). Shortboarders tend to surf faster and more aggressively. The best shortboarders surf perpendicular to the wave face and may even break free of the wave—known as "aerials" or "catching air." Nonsurfers are often most impressed and amused by the mistakes. "Wipeouts," the sometimes spectacular falls, inevitably happen to all surfers.

13

STAND-UP PADDLEBOARDING

The popularity of stand-up paddleboarding, or SUP, has grown tremendously in recent years. Devotees love the excellent core workout it provides, while newcomers appreciate how much quicker it is to master than traditional surfing. You can paddleboard pretty much anywhere and many local surf breaks are popular for those with experience, but the calmer waters of Mission Bay and Glorietta Bay in Coronado offer more stability for beginners.

In addition to Seaforth Boat Rentals, Surf Diva, and Action Sport Rentals (see Sailing and Boating), Cheap Rentals (see Surf Shops) these are good places to try out your skills.

VOLLEYBALL

Ocean Beach, South Mission Beach, Del Mar Beach, and Moonlight Beach are major congregating points for beach volleyball enthusiasts. These are also the best places to find a pickup game.

WHALE-WATCHING CRUISES

Whale-watching season peaks in January and February, when thousands of gray whales migrate south to the warm weather, where they give birth to their calves. Head to Cabrillo National Monument's Whale Overlook to see the whales pass through Point Loma. If you want a closer look, charter boats and cruises host whale-watching excursions.

Flagship Cruises & Events. Join one of the twice-daily whale-watching trips during the season from December through April. Tours are led by naturalists from Birch Aquarium at Scripps. ✉ *990 N. Harbor Dr., Embarcadero* ☎ *619/234–4111, 800/442–7847 reservations* 🌐 *www.flagshipsd.com* 🎫 *From $40.*

Hornblower Cruises and Events. Yachts take passengers to catch a glimpse of gray whales and perhaps an occasional school of dolphins. Live narration is provided by experts from the San Diego Natural History Museum. ✉ *970 N. Harbor Dr., Embarcadero* ☎ *619/686–8700, 619/686–8715 ticket booth* 🌐 *www.hornblower.com* 🎟 *From $46.*

WINDSURFING

Also known as sailboarding, windsurfing is a sport best practiced on smooth waters, such as Mission Bay. More experienced windsurfers will enjoy taking a board out on the ocean. Wave jumping is especially popular at the Tourmaline Surfing Park in La Jolla and in the Del Mar area, where you can also occasionally see kiteboarders practice their variation on the theme.

SPECTATOR SPORTS

BASEBALL

Fodor's Choice ★ Long a favorite spectator sport in San Diego, where games are rarely rained out, baseball gained even more popularity in 2004 with the opening of PETCO Park, a stunning 42,000-seat facility in the heart of Downtown. The ballpark underwent a huge effort to improve dining in the park, and local food vendors and craft breweries now dominate the dining options. Although the Padres have not had the winning record many fans had hoped for over the years, PETCO is a great place to spend an afternoon win or lose.

Fodor's Choice ★ **San Diego Padres.** From April into October, the Padres slug it out for bragging rights in the National League West. Home games are played at PETCO Park. Tickets are usually available on game day, but rival matchups against the Los Angeles Dodgers and the San Francisco Giants often sell out quickly. For an inexpensive day at the ballpark, go for "The Park at the Park" tickets ($10 and up, depending on demand; available for purchase at the park only) and have a picnic on the grass while watching the game on one of several giant-screen TVs. You also get access to the full concourse. Head to the fifth floor to find a Stone Brewing outdoor beer garden with sweeping views of Downtown and the San Diego Bay. ✉ *100 Park Blvd., East Village* ☎ *619/795–5000, 877/374–2784* 🌐 *sandiego.padres.mlb.com* 🎟 *From $10.*

HORSE RACING

Del Mar Thoroughbred Club. The racetrack attracts the best horses and jockeys in the country—Seabiscuit even won a much-talked-about race here in 1938. Spectators can enjoy 11 weeks of racing annually at the historic Del Mar Racetrack. The summer season starts in mid-July and runs through early September and includes a summer concert series and opening and closing day celebrations. The fall season lasts for a month starting in November. The track, which opened in 1937, was founded in part by singer and actor Bing Crosby. ✉ *2260 Jimmy Durante Blvd., Del Mar* ⊕ *Take I–5 north to Via de la Valle exit* ☎ *858/792–4242* 🌐 *www.dmtc.com* 🎟 *From $10.*

macy's
JESSOP'S
TEAVANA
TEAVANA
THE ART OF SHAVING
BANANA REP

SHOPPING

Updated by Kai Oliver-Kurtin

San Diego's retail landscape has changed radically in recent years with the opening of several new shopping centers—some in historic buildings—that are focused more on locally owned boutiques than national retailers. Where once the Gaslamp was the place to go for urban apparel and unique home decor, many independently owned boutiques have decided to set up shop in the charming neighborhoods east of Balboa Park known as North Park and South Park. Although Downtown is still thriving, any shopping trip to San Diego should include venturing out to the city's diverse and vibrant neighborhoods. Not far from Downtown, Little Italy is the place to find contemporary art, modern furniture, and home accessories.

Old Town is a must for pottery, ceramics, jewelry, and handcrafted baskets. Uptown is known for its mélange of funky bookstores, offbeat gift shops, and nostalgic collectibles and vintage stores. The beach towns offer the best swimwear and sandals. La Jolla's chic boutiques offer a more intimate shopping experience, along with some of the classiest clothes, jewelry, and shoes in the county. The new La Plaza La Jolla is an open-air shopping center with boutiques and galleries in a Spanish-style building overlooking the cove. Point Loma's Liberty Station shopping area in the former Naval Training Center has art galleries, restaurants, and home stores. Trendsetters will have no trouble finding must-have handbags and designer apparel at the world-class Fashion Valley mall in Mission Valley, a haven for luxury brands such as Hermès, Gucci, and Jimmy Choo.

Enjoy near-perfect weather year-round as you explore shops along the scenic waterfront. The Headquarters at Seaport is a new open-air shopping and dining center in the city's former Police Headquarters building. Here there are some big names, but mostly locally owned boutiques selling everything from gourmet cheese to coastal-inspired home accessories. Just next door, Seaport Village is still the place to go for trinkets and souvenirs. If you don't discover what you're looking for in the boutiques, head to Westfield Horton Plaza, the Downtown mall with more than 120 stores. The sprawling mall completed a major restoration project in 2016 to include a new public plaza, amphitheater, and fountains.

Most malls have free parking in a lot or garage, and parking is not usually a problem. Westfield Horton Plaza and some of the shops in the Gaslamp Quarter offer validated parking or valet parking.

SHOPPING PLANNER

Shops near tourist attractions and the major shopping malls tend to open early and close late. Standard hours are typically 10 to 9 on weekdays and 10 to 10 on weekends. Smaller shops may close as early as 5 on weekdays and Sunday. It's best to call ahead to confirm hours if you have your heart set on visiting a particular shop.

The city's major attractions have gift shops with more than just stuffed animals and T-shirts. The museum shops at Balboa Park (☎ *619/239–0512*) brim with affordable treasures. The Zoo Store and Ituri Forest Outpost (☎ *619/231–1515*) at the San Diego Zoo carry international crafts, world music, and hats, while the San Diego Zoo Safari Park's Bazaar (☎ *760/738–5055*) sells authentic African artifacts, books, home-decor items, and apparel. The Big Shop (☎ *760/918–5346*) at LEGOLAND is great for collectors and collectors-in-training, with the largest selection of LEGO sets in the nation.

Some hotels offer free shuttles to shopping centers, outlet malls, and nearby casinos. Check with the concierge for schedules.

Carlsbad Premium Outlets. A 40-minute drive north of Downtown San Diego, this outdoor shopping center contains more than 90 outlet stores, including designer brands like Coach, Cole Haan, Kate Spade New York, and Michael Kors. ✉ *5620 Paseo del Norte, Ste. 100, Carlsbad* ☎ *760/804–9000* 🌐 *www.premiumoutlets.com.*

Las Americas Premium Outlets. A 20-minute drive south of Downtown San Diego near the international border crossing, this outdoor outlet mall in San Ysidro has about 125 shops. The usual brand names are here, including Banana Republic, Calvin Klein, J. Crew, Nike, and Tommy Bahama. Visit a duty-free shop to save on sales tax, or take a break to refuel in the food court. ■ **TIP→ Shuttle service to Las Americas is available from many San Diego area hotels, and the San Diego Trolley's San Ysidro stop is a five-minute walk from the mall.** ✉ *4211 Camino de la Plaza, off I–5, San Ysidro* ☎ *619/934–8400* 🌐 *www.premiumoutlets.com.*

FAMILY **Viejas Outlet Center.** About 30 miles east of the city on Viejas Indian Reservation, this outlet mall in the community of Alpine is situated across from the Viejas Casino & Resort. Major brands represented here include Coach, Guess, Levi's, Polo Ralph Lauren, and Wilsons Leather. ■ **TIP→ Free entertainment is offered year-round at the Show-Court. Kids enjoy the FunZone Arcade, bowling, and ice rink (open late October through January).** ✉ *5000 Willow Rd., off I–8, Exit 33, Alpine* ☎ *619/659–2070* 🌐 *www.viejasoutletcenter.com.*

SHOPPING BY NEIGHBORHOOD

DOWNTOWN

The city's ever-changing Downtown offers a variety of shopping venues including the open-air Westfield Horton Plaza, a traditional mall; the eclectic-to-mainstream shops of the Gaslamp Quarter; and the upscale shopping at the Headquarters at Seaport. Within easy walking distance of the Convention Center and Downtown hotels, the area is a shopper's delight.

GASLAMP QUARTER

The mix of retailers in the historic heart of San Diego changes frequently, but there are always boutiques in the Victorian buildings and renovated warehouses along 4th and 5th avenues. Also in the quarter are the usual mall stores and gift shops. Some stores close early, starting as early as 5 pm, and many are closed Sunday or Monday.

CLOTHING AND ACCESSORIES

Blends. Minimalist decor provides a perfect backdrop for the wild colors and patterns featured on original sneakers from Adidas, Nike, Vans, and other in-demand brands. Prices are steep, but many of the urban styles are unique. ✉ *719 8th Ave., Gaslamp Quarter* ☎ *619/233–6126* 🌐 *blendsus.com.*

Dolcetti Boutique. With everything from flirty dresses to casual daytime outfits and a full-service hair salon on-site, this Gaslamp Quarter boutique is a one-stop shop for getting ready for a night on the town. The lofty space with exposed brick walls is owned by style-savvy sisters, and also carries accessories, jewelry, menswear, and children's clothing. ✉ *635 5th Ave., Gaslamp Quarter* ☎ *619/501–1559* 🌐 *www.dolcettiboutique.com* ⏲ *Closed Mon.*

Goorin Bros. Hats. Established in Pittsburgh in 1895, this company has helped make hats hip again with its stylish takes on fedoras, bowlers, and Panama hats. The San Diego location occupies the first floor of the historic Yuma building, a former brothel in the red light district. ✉ *631 5th Ave., Gaslamp Quarter* ☎ *619/450–6303* 🌐 *www.goorin.com.*

Quiksilver Boardriders Club. This surf shop carries Quiksilver's full line of bathing suits, wet suits, accessories, and famous surfboards. ✉ *402 5th Ave., Gaslamp Quarter* ☎ *619/234–3125* 🌐 *www.quiksilver.com.*

HOME ACCESSORIES AND GIFTS

Bubbles Boutique. Budget-conscious fashionistas will love this eclectic Gaslamp Quarter spot, where many items, including boho-chic dresses, floppy hats, and fringe handbags are priced under $100. The boutique also stocks studded belts, wrap bracelets, and other jewelry designed by local designers. ✉ *226 5th Ave., Gaslamp Quarter* ☎ *619/236–9003* 🌐 *www.bubblesboutique.com.*

TOP SHOPPING EXPERIENCES

Fashion Valley: Bloomingdale's, Nordstrom, Neiman Marcus, and haute boutiques are all under one roof.

Gaslamp Quarter: Gaslamp's trendy shops carry everything from vintage clothing to antiques and art.

La Jolla: At the ocean-side enclave of the rich and famous, prices might leave your credit card reeling—but browsing is free.

North Park: Transform yourself from tourist into hipster in no time with finds from this neighborhood's edgy boutiques.

Old Town: No need for a passport. Mexico's finest crafts, artwork, and jewelry are all in this neighborhood north of the border.

The Headquarters: Locally owned boutiques rule at this new shopping center in a former police headquarters.

Gaslamp Garage. Crammed floor to ceiling with merchandise and decorated to look like a 1950s auto repair shop, the city's largest souvenir shop is the place to head for Padre's gear and San Diego mementos. The store also stocks a wide variety of sportswear and sandals from brands like Reef, Roxy, and Volcom, and the Kidz Garage has toys, electronics, and apparel from infant to size 12. ✉ *301 5th Ave., Gaslamp Quarter* ☎ *619/241–4240.*

SHOPPING CENTERS

Westfield Horton Plaza. Macy's, Regal Cinemas, and natural foods grocer Jimbo's ... *Naturally!* anchor this multilevel complex that has more than 120 stores, plus fast-food and sit-down dining. Adjacent to the mall, Horton Plaza Park opened in 2016 as an urban outdoor space with an amphitheater, fountains, and more than 200 events a year. The parking garage is a maze, so make sure to note which level you parked. Horton Plaza offers one hour of free parking between the hours of 5 am and 8 pm, but select retailers offer extended validation. Validation machines are dispersed throughout the mall (no purchase necessary). ✉ *324 Horton Plaza, Gaslamp Quarter* ☎ *619/239–8180* 🌐 *www.westfield.com/hortonplaza.*

LITTLE ITALY

With more than 33,500 square feet of retail, Little Italy is an especially fun place to visit during holiday celebrations and special events like ArtWalk in April and Taste of Little Italy in June. The weekly Saturday farmers' market is one of the city's best, and brings people from all over the county to the neighborhood (🌐 *www.sdweekly-markets.com*). Many shops have a strong European ambience, and shoppers will find enticing wares that include colorful ceramics, hand-blown glassware, modern home accents, and designer shoes. Kettner Boulevard and India Street north of Grape Street are considered the North Little Italy Art and Design District. The website Little Italy San Diego (🌐 *www.littleitalysd.com*) has detailed info about neighborhood shops and events.

CLOTHING AND ACCESSORIES

Azzurra Capri. Walking into this white shop with blue trim will transport you instantly to Italy's stylish and sophisticated Amalfi Coast. Inspired by the island of Capri, this upscale boutique stocks swimsuits, resort wear, cashmere scarves, and handmade Italian leather sandals adorned with things like Swarovski crystals and turquoise. ✉ *1840 Colombia St., Little Italy* ☎ *619/230–5116* 🌐 *azzurracapri.com.*

Kapreeza. Owner Renata Carlseen stocks her elegant boutique with upscale lingerie, bras, and sexy swimwear from European designers. Take advantage of customized bra fittings and free gift wrapping. ✉ *1772 Kettner Blvd., Little Italy* ☎ *619/702–6355* 🌐 *www.kapreeza.com.*

Rosamariposa. This charming jewelry shop specializes in necklaces, earrings, and bracelets crafted by Indonesian artists using natural fibers, wood, seeds, and recycled glass. It also stocks dream catchers, handbags and specialty key rings. ✉ *611 W. Fir St., Little Italy* ☎ *619/237–8064* 🌐 *www.rosamariposasd.com* ⏲ *Closed Mon. and Tues.*

Vocabulary Boutique. A local favorite for its friendly vibe and stylish inventory, this cozy boutique often stars in regional fashion shoots. It's known for unique, affordable outfits for women, men, and kids, as well as accessories, home decor, paper, and gift items. ✉ *414 W. Cedar St., Little Italy* ☎ *619/544–1100* 🌐 *www.vocabularyboutique.com.*

FOOD AND WINE

Bottlecraft Beer Shop. This boutique beer shop and tasting room stocks the best craft beer from San Diego and around the world, from double IPAs and pale ales to saisons and wheat beers. Owner Brian Jensen offers a wealth of knowledge on the local craft beer scene. Bottlecraft now has additional locations in North Park and Liberty Station. ✉ *2252 India St.* ☎ *619/487–9493* 🌐 *bottlecraftbeer.com.*

HOME ACCESSORIES AND GIFTS

Architectural Salvage of San Diego. If you have any interest in home design and renovation, this shop that specializes in reusing old materials should be top of your list. The warehouse space is filled with unusual building and decorative materials, as well as items that come from various time periods throughout the 1900s. Products range from stained-glass windows and light fixtures to cabinets and doors in styles ranging from Victorian to Craftsman. ✉ *2401 Kettner Blvd., Little Italy* ☎ *619/696–1313* 🌐 *www.architecturalsalvagesd.com.*

Blick Art Materials. Besides supplying local artists with their tools, Blick also carries art books, fine stationery and pens, ornate gift wrap, and beautiful leather-bound journals. ✉ *1844 India St., Little Italy* ☎ *619/687–0050* 🌐 *www.dickblick.com.*

Boomerang for Modern. This well-curated furniture store in the North Little Italy Design District is a shrine to mid-century modern design. Discover now-classic furniture, lighting and accessories like George Nelson star clocks, abstract oil paintings, Swedish rugs, and chairs by legendary designers Charles and Ray Eames. The store itself has become quite a fixture in San Diego—it celebrated its 30th anniversary in 2015, and there's even a coffee-table book published on the store's history. ✉ *2475 Kettner Blvd., Little Italy* ☎ *619/239–2040* 🌐 *www.boomerangformodern.com* ⏲ *Closed Sun.*

Casa Artelexia. This colorful shop specializing in Mexican gifts and art started as a booth at a farmers' market by a father-daughter team, but has since evolved into a large retail space with its own art gallery and event space. Products—handpicked and imported from different parts of Mexico—include hand-blown glassware, Sacred Heart wall hangings, books and paintings depicting Frida Kahlo, and Dia de Los Muertos-themed items. Casa Artelexia also offers weekly art classes, and has a second store located in North Park. ✉ *2400 Kettner Blvd., No. 102, Little Italy* ☎ *619/544–1011* 🌐 *www.artelexia.com.*

Masquerade Art of Living. Masquerade's collection includes fine art and wearable art, as well as gifts, mirrors, lamps, and other home accessories. The gallery/boutique also carries handbags, Italian jewelry, and Venetian masks. ✉ *1608 India St., No. 105, Little Italy* ☎ *619/235–6564* ⏲ *Closed Mon.*

Vitreum. The Japanese artist Takao owns this gallery-like shop that sells beautifully handcrafted home-decor items—tableware, glass vases, tea sets, and decorative gifts. ✉ *619 W. Fir St., Little Italy* 🌐 *www.vitreum-us.com.*

MARKETS

Little Italy Mercato. This festive Saturday market sells products from more than 175 farmers and vendors; it's one of the largest and liveliest in San Diego. Enjoy a panini or Italian pastry as you stroll the aisles, shopping for handcrafted gifts, cheese, fresh produce, honey, and olive oil. ✉ *Cedar St., between Kettner Blvd. and Front St., Little Italy* 🌐 *www.littleitalymercato.com.*

EMBARCADERO

The new Headquarters at Seaport shopping district is breathing new life into the somewhat touristy San Diego waterfront. Spanning 14 acres and offering more than 50 shops and 17 restaurants, Seaport Village remains popular for souvenirs and entertainment.

SHOPPING CENTERS

Fodor's Choice ★ **The Headquarters at Seaport.** This new upscale shopping and dining center is in the city's former Police Headquarters, a beautiful and historic Mission-style building featuring an open courtyard with fountains. Restaurants and shops, many locally owned, occupy former jail facilities and offices. Pop into **Urban Beach House** for coastal-inspired fashion from popular surf brands for men and women, including accessories and home decor. Swing by **Madison San Diego** for a great selection of leather goods and accessories, from apparel and handbags to belts and travel accessories. **Dallmann Fine Chocolates** sells truffles in flavors like banana's foster and coconut curry. **Venissimo Cheese** dishes up the best cheese from around the world, from goat milk chevre filled with Italian truffle salt to French triple creme brie topped with tangy cranberries. **Geppetto's** has been a San Diego staple for more than 40 years, offering classic toys and games that inspire creativity for the entire family. ✉ *789 W. Harbor Dr., Downtown* ☎ *619/235–4014* 🌐 *theheadquarters.com.*

Seaport Village. If you're looking for trinkets and souvenirs, this is the place. This complex of kitschy shops and waterfront restaurants has upped its hip factor with boutiques like **San Pasqual** wine bar;

Old Town is the place to go for colorful Mexican wares.

bamboo clothing–maker **Cariloha**; and **Frost Me Gourmet Cupcakes,** the bakery known for its win on Cupcake Wars Season 9. While there, keep an eye out for **Urban Girl Accessories** to find an eclectic mix of clothing and gifts from name brands and local artisans, and stop by **Village Hat Shop** to browse their collection of 50,000 fedoras, bowlers, cowboy, and custom embroidered hats. In addition to shopping, the village has views of the bay, fresh breezes, and great strolling paths. A hand-carved historic carousel and frequent public entertainment are among the attractions. Seaport Village is within walking distance of hotels, the San Diego Convention Center, and the San Diego Trolley. ✉ *849 W. Harbor Dr., at Pacific Hwy., Downtown* ☎ *619/235–4014* 🌐 *www.seaportvillage.com/shopping.*

BALBOA PARK

As the country's largest urban cultural park, Balboa Park is one of San Diego's most frequented attractions. Encompassing 15 museums, the San Diego Zoo, and performing arts venues, Balboa Park is a hub of activity. Visit the visitor center gift shop for souvenirs or stop by any of the museum stores for specialty items related to current and past exhibits.

HOME ACCESSORIES AND GIFTS

Mingei International Museum Store. The Collectors' Gallery shop at the Mingei showcases an international collection of textiles, jewelry, apparel, and home decor items. Artwork is displayed on a rotating basis in the store's gallery, and there's a nice selection of books on craft and folk art. If you're in San Diego during the first part of the year, watch out for the store's annual Treasures Art Sale, when some items that have been donated to the museum are put on sale, from African baskets to handmade jewelry. ✉ *1439 El Prado, Balboa Park* ☎ *619/239–0003* 🌐 *www.mingei.org/store* ⏲ *Closed Mon.*

OLD TOWN AND UPTOWN

OLD TOWN

Tourist-focused Old Town, north of Downtown off I–5, has festival-like ambience that also makes it a popular destination for locals. At Old Town San Diego State Historic Park, you may feel like a time traveler as you visit shops housed in restored adobe buildings. Farther down the street are stores selling Mexican blankets, piñatas, and glassware. Old Town Market offers live entertainment, local artists selling their wares from carts, and a market crammed with unique apparel, home-decor items, toys, jewelry, and food. Dozens of stores sell San Diego logo merchandise and T-shirts at discounted prices, and there are great deals on handcrafted jewelry, art, and leather accessories. When you've tired of shopping, there are plenty of Mexican restaurants where you can dine, down a margarita, or both.

14

FOOD AND WINE

Cousin's Candy Shop. Sample homemade fudge made in 16 flavors and taffy that's been cooked, stretched, and wrapped on-site at this old-fashioned confectionery shop. The old-time candies in nostalgic tins make thoughtful gifts. ✉ *2711 San Diego Ave., Old Town* ☎ *619/297–2000* 🌐 *www.cousinscandy.net.*

HOME ACCESSORIES AND GIFTS

Tafoya & Son Pottery. This shop in a historic adobe building specializes in Mexican Talavera pottery and Turkish porcelain. Look for sterling silver jewelry designed by owner Chris Tafoya. ✉ *2769 San Diego Ave., Old Town* ☎ *619/574–0989* 🌐 *www.tafoyaandson.com.*

Tienda de Reyes. This festive "store of the kings" stocks Old Town's largest selection of Day of the Dead art, and carries sculpture, handbags, and glassware from Mexico and Peru. ✉ *2754 Calhoun St., Old Town* ☎ *619/491–0611* 🌐 *www.tiendadereyes.com.*

Variations Imports. Shop here for wall art, clocks, medieval decor, Asian figurines, and unusual imports from around the world. ✉ *3975 Twiggs St., Old Town* ☎ *619/260–1008* 🌐 *www.variationsimports.com.*

Ye Olde Soap Shoppe. The mere scent of Ye Olde's hand-fashioned soaps conjures up a relaxing bath. If you want to craft your own soaps, you'll find a full line of supplies, as well as soaps and lotions from around the world. ✉ *2497 San Diego Ave., Old Town* ☎ *800/390–9969* 🌐 *www.soapmaking.com.*

JEWELRY

The Diamond Source. Specializing in fashionable diamond and precious gemstone jewelry, this shop showcases the creations of master jeweler Marco Levy. There's a second location in La Jolla Cove. ✉ *2474 San Diego Ave., Old Town* ☎ *619/299–6900* 🌐 *www.thediamondsource.com* ⏲ *Closed Mon.*

MARKETS

OFF THE BEATEN PATH

Kobey's Swap Meet. Not far from Old Town, San Diego's premier flea market seems to expand every week. Sellers display everything from art and gifts to fresh flowers and futons at the open-air event, which is held Friday through Sunday. The back section, with secondhand goods, is great for bargain hunters. ✉ *Valley View Casino Center parking lot, 3500 Sports Arena Blvd.* ☎ *619/226–0650* 🌐 *www.kobeyswap.com* 🎟 *$2 weekends, $1 Fri.*

Old Town Market. The atmosphere is colorful, upbeat, and Mexico-centric at this eclectic market. Local artisans create some of the wares for sale, including everything from dolls and silver jewelry to gourmet foods, home-decor items, and apparel. ✉ *4010 Twiggs St., Old Town* ☎ *619/278–0955* 🌐 *www.oldtownmarketsandiego.com.*

Old Town Saturday Market. San Diego's largest weekend artisan market presents live music and local artists selling jewelry, paintings, photography, handblown glass, apparel, pottery, and decorative items. The San Diego Trolley's Old Town stop is two blocks north of the market. ✉ *Harney St. and San Diego Ave., Old Town* ☎ *858/272–7054* 🌐 *www.oldtownsaturdaymarket.com* 🎟 *Free.*

SHOPPING CENTERS

Fodor's Choice ★

Bazaar del Mundo Shops. With a Mexican villa theme, the Bazaar hosts riotously colorful gift shops such as **Ariana,** for ethnic and artsy women's fashions; **Artes de Mexico,** which sells handmade Latin American crafts and Guatemalan weavings; and **The Gallery,** which carries handmade jewelry, Native American crafts, collectible glass, and original silk-screen prints. The **Laurel Burch Gallerita** carries the complete collection of its namesake artist's signature jewelry, accessories, and totes. ✉ *4133 Taylor St., at Juan St., Old Town* ☎ *619/296–3161* 🌐 *www.bazaardelmundo.com.*

Fiesta de Reyes. Within the Old Town San Diego State Historic Park, Fiesta de Reyes exudes the easy feel of Old California. Friendly shopkeepers dressed in period attire host a collection of boutiques and eateries around a flower-filled square with a design reminiscent of Old Town circa the 1850s. Many of the shops stock items reminiscent of that era. Visit **Silver Lily** for one-of-a-kind silver pieces with semi-precious stones, **Fiesta Cocina** for festive kitchenware, and **Temecula Olive Oil Company** for local olive oils and artisan foods. The **Tile Shop** carries hand-painted Mexican tiles, **Geppetto's** specializes in classic toys, and **La Panaderia** sells Mexican-style baked goods and ice cream. Two restaurants, **Casa de Reyes** and the **Barra Barra Saloon,** serve Mexican food and provide daily musical entertainment. ✉ *2754 Calhoun St., Old Town* ☎ *619/297–3100* 🌐 *www.fiestadereyes.com.*

HILLCREST

The Uptown neighborhood of Hillcrest has many avant-garde apparel shops alongside gift, thrift, and music stores.

MARKETS

Hillcrest Farmers Market. One of the city's best farmers' markets, Hillcrest features 175 vendors that sell farm-fresh produce, handmade clothing, jewelry, and other types of handicrafts every Sunday. Browse the market and plan to stay for lunch: there are several vendors selling top-notch ready-to-eat food, from fresh-made crepes and tamales to African and Indian cuisine. ✉ *3960 Normal St., between Lincoln St. and Normal Ave., Hillcrest* 🌐 *www.hillcrestfarmersmarket.com.*

MISSION HILLS

The shops and art galleries in Mission Hills, west of Hillcrest, have a modern and sophisticated ambience that suits the trendy residents.

CLOTHING AND ACCESSORIES

Le Bel Age Boutique. A neighborhood staple for more than 30 years, this charming boutique carries maxi dresses, capri pants, and handbags, as well as jewelry designed by the owner, Valerie. Just down the street, sister boutique **Chateau Bel Age** features hard-to-find French designers and exotic-looking kaftans. ✉ *1607 W. Lewis St., Mission Hills* ☎ *619/297–7080* ⏲ *Closed Sun. and Mon.*

HOME ACCESSORIES AND GIFTS

Maison en Provence. This adorable little shop located in a Mission Hills bungalow is the place for Francophiles to get their French fix in San Diego. The French proprietors Pascal and Marielle Giai stock linen tablecloths and dishes from Provence. There are also fine soaps, antique postcards, and the most elegant of pocket knives. **■ TIP→ For French inspiration and information about French events in San Diego, check the store's great blog.** ✉ *820 Ft. Stockton Dr., Mission Hills* ☎ *619/298–5318* 🌐 *maisonenprovence.skynetblogs.be* ⏲ *Closed Mon.*

JEWELRY

Taboo Studio. This upscale gallery displays and sells the handcrafted jewelry of more than 75 artists from around the world. The stars here are the limited-edition pieces that incorporate precious metals and gemstones. The shop will also repurpose your old jewelry into something new. ✉ *1615½ W. Lewis St., Mission Hills* ☎ *619/692–0099* 🌐 *www.taboostudio.net* ⏲ *Closed Sun. and Mon.*

MUSIC

M-Theory Music. This locally owned record store in Mission Hills carries new and used vinyl and CDs. They regularly host in-store performances. ✉ *915 W. Washington St., Mission Hills* ☎ *619/220–0485* 🌐 *www.mtheorymusic.com.*

MISSION VALLEY

Northeast of Downtown near I–8 and Route 163, Mission Valley holds two major shopping centers and a few smaller strip malls. Fashion Valley hosts an impressive roster of high-end department stores—among them Neiman Marcus, Nordstrom, and Bloomingdale's—and a passel of luxury boutiques. Westfield Mission Valley is home to mainstays like Macy's and Old Navy, plus bargain-hunter favorites like Marshall's and Nordstrom Rack. The San Diego Trolley and city buses stop at both centers.

CLOTHING AND ACCESSORIES

Saks Off 5th. Across from Westfield Mission Valley, **Saks Off 5th** sells bargain-priced fashions by Ralph Lauren, Armani, and Burberry that are past season. ✉ *1750 Camino de la Reina, Mission Valley* ☎ *619/296–4896* 🌐 *www.saksoff5th.com.*

SHOPPING CENTERS

Fodor's Choice ★ **Fashion Valley.** More than 18 million shoppers visit Fashion Valley each year. That's more than the combined attendance of SeaWorld San Diego, LEGOLAND California, the San Diego Padres, the San Diego Chargers, and the San Diego Zoo. San Diego's best and most upscale mall has a contemporary Mission theme, lush landscaping, and more than 200 shops and restaurants. Acclaimed retailers like Nordstrom, Neiman Marcus, Bloomingdale's, and Tiffany & Co. are here, along with boutiques from fashion darlings like Michael Kors, Jimmy Choo, Tory Burch, and James Perse. H&M is a favorite of fashionistas in search of edgy and affordable styles. Free wireless Internet service is available throughout the mall. Select "Simon WiFi" from any Wi-Fi–enabled device to log onto the network. ■ **TIP→ If you're visiting from out of state, are a member of the military, or have a AAA membership, you can pick up a complimentary Style Pass at Simon Guest Services (located on the lower level beneath AMC Theaters near Banana Republic), which can get you savings at more than 70 of Fashion Valley's stores and restaurants.** ✉ *7007 Friars Rd., Mission Valley* ☎ *619/688–9113* 🌐 *www.simon.com/mall/fashion-valley.*

FAMILY **Westfield Mission Valley.** Among the 124 shops at this sprawling outdoor mall, you'll find Macy's, American Eagle Outfitters, DSW Shoe Warehouse, and Victoria's Secret. Car- and truck-themed Smarte Carte strollers provide a fun and safe shopping experience for kids, while offering plenty of room for parents to stow purchases. Find them near Target. ✉ *1640 Camino del Rio North, Mission Valley* ☎ *619/296–6375* 🌐 *www.westfield.com/missionvalley.*

NORTH PARK

North Park, east of Hillcrest, is a hipster's paradise, with resale shops, trendy boutiques, and stores that sell mostly handcrafted items.

CLOTHING AND ACCESSORIES

Fodor's Choice ★ **Aloha Sunday Supply Co.** This carefully curated boutique with high ceilings and blonde-wood accents carries no Billabong or Quicksilver, but make no mistake, this is a surf shop. The store sells only handcrafted pieces like Matuse wet suits, Thorogood leather boots, and the store's own brand of tailored men's clothing designed by co-owner and former pro surfer Kahana Kalama. ✉ *3039 University Ave., North Park* ☎ *619/269–9838* 🌐 *www.alohasunday.com.*

Maven. Shop hard-to-find clothing, accessories, and home decor at this locally owned store focused on handmade goods. ✉ *2946 Adams Ave., Normal Heights* ☎ *619/280–2474* 🌐 *www.mavensd.com.*

Mimi & Red Boutique. Laid-back ambience, friendly service, and racks full of moderate to high-end women's fashions have made this shop a favorite with cool San Diegans. Nixon and Everly are here along with RVCA, Free People, and handcrafted bath and body products. ✉ *3041 University Ave., North Park* ☎ *619/298–7933* 🌐 *www.mimiandred.com.*

Overload. Get the latest brands of footwear, streetwear, skateboards, and accessories at this edgy skate shop. ✉ *3827 30th St., North Park* ☎ *619/296–9018* 🌐 *www.shopoverload.com.*

Rufskin. The flagship menswear boutique for the namesake denim line sells sexy jeans, casual and dress shirts, swimwear, bold accessories, and custom leather items. ✉ *3944 30th St., North Park* ☎ *619/564–7880* 🌐 *www.rufskin.com* ⏲ *Closed Sun.*

Simply Local. This shop carries merchandise from more than 55 local artisans, including jewelry, home decor, bath products, and specialty foods like almond butter and local honey. ✉ *3013 University Ave., North Park* ☎ *619/756–7958* 🌐 *www.simplylocalsandiego.com.*

HOME ACCESSORIES AND GIFTS

Fodor's Choice ★ **Pigment.** This beautifully styled shop carries a wide variety of design-conscious goods for the home, including geometric print pillows, outdoor bistro chairs, and home bar accessories. In Pigment's plant lab, you can build your own terrariums, which make great souvenirs. ✉ *3801 30th St., North Park* ☎ *619/501–6318* 🌐 *www.shoppigment.com.*

14

SOUTH PARK

South Park's 30th, Juniper, and Fern streets have everything from eco-friendly fashions to craft supplies and home decor.

CLOTHING AND ACCESSORIES

Graffiti Beach. This indie boutique in South Park's historic 30th & Fern building is filled with quirky art, jewelry, gifts, and clothing from emerging designers and artists using recycled or repurposed materials. This is a great place to pick up souvenirs if you're into supporting local: 75% of the designers are from California. ✉ *2220 Fern St., South Park* ☎ *858/433–0950* 🌐 *www.shopgraffitibeach.com.*

HOME ACCESSORIES AND GIFTS

Gold Leaf. This home decor shop is run by a husband-and-wife duo. There's furniture, kitchenware, jewelry, greeting cards, and a kid's section. ✉ *2225 30th St., South Park* ☎ *619/738–8120* 🌐 *www.goldleafsouthpark.com.*

JUNC. This funky shop stocks unique gifts, men's and women's clothing, accessories, and housewares. ✉ *2209 Fern St., South Park* ☎ *619/283–2611* 🌐 *www.shop-junc.com.*

Tend Living. This trendy plant shop and boutique stocks succulents, ferns, and cacti that make great home decor gifts. ✉ *1925 30th St., South Park* ☎ *858/876–8363* 🌐 *www.tendliving.com.*

West Grove Collective. Find books, kitchenware, fair-trade items, and travel gear at this shop that was completely remodeled in 2015. Also here are organic clothing, children's apparel, and a vinyl music selection. ✉ *3010 Juniper St., South Park* ☎ *619/795–3780* 🌐 *www.westgrove-southpark.com* ⏲ *Closed Mon.*

MISSION BAY AND THE BEACHES

Mission Boulevard and Grand and Garnet Avenue are the big shopping thoroughfares in the beach towns. Souvenir shops are scattered up and down the boardwalk, and along Mission Boulevard there are surf, skate, and bike shops, bikini boutiques, and stores selling hip T-shirts, jeans, sandals, and casual apparel. Garnet Avenue is the hot spot for resale boutiques, thrift stores, and pawn shops. The Ocean Beach Antique District in the 4800 block of Newport Avenue invites browsing with several buildings housing multiple dealers under one roof. Independent stores showcase everything from vintage watches and pottery to linens and retro posters.

MISSION BEACH

CLOTHING AND ACCESSORIES

Gone Bananas Beachwear. This store can be a bit overwhelming with its more than 15,000 pieces of swimwear lining the walls from floor to ceiling. To make shopping a bit easier, swimsuits have been arranged by color. Browse through mix-and-match pieces from the most fashion-forward swimwear designers like Mikoh, San Lorenzo, and Vitamin A. It's worth taking the time to peruse what is simply San Diego's best swimwear selection. ✉ *3785 Mission Blvd., Mission Beach* ☎ *858/488–4900* 🌐 *www.gonebananasbeachwear.com.*

LA JOLLA

San Diego's answer to Rodeo Drive in Beverly Hills, La Jolla has chic boutiques, art galleries, and gift shops lining narrow, twisty streets that attract well-heeled shoppers and celebrities. Prospect Street and Girard Avenue are the primary shopping stretches, and North Prospect is packed with art galleries *(see Chapter 11: Performing Arts, for information on art galleries)*. The Upper Girard Design District stocks home decor accessories and luxury furnishings. Store hours vary widely, so it's wise to call in advance though most shops on Prospect Street stay open until 10 pm on weeknights to accommodate evening strollers. If you're driving, there's free parking in the La Jolla Cove or garages along Prospect Street, between Wall and Silverado, or along Herschel, Girard, and Fay. Rates range from $1.50 for 20 minutes to a maximum of $15 per day. After 4 pm, there's a flat rate of $10.

BOOKS

Warwick's. This family-owned-and-operated bookstore has been a La Jolla fixture since 1939, and often hosts big-name author signings. They also carry stationery, calendars, and other gifts. ✉ *7812 Girard Ave., La Jolla* ☎ *858/454–0347* 🌐 *www.warwicks.com.*

CLOTHING AND ACCESSORIES

Ascot Shop. The classic Ivy League look is king in this traditional haberdashery that sells menswear by Hugo Boss, Robert Talbott, and Peter Miller. In-house same-day tailoring is available. ✉ *7750 Girard Ave., La Jolla* ☎ *858/454–4222* 🌐 *www.ascotshop.com* ⊗ *Closed Sun.*

Fresh Produce. Sunny and spirited Fresh Produce sells beach-inspired clothing made with comfy fabrics. The boutique's easy-to-wear pieces are perfect for vacations and weekend getaways. ✉ *1147 Prospect St., La Jolla* ☎ *858/456–8134* 🌐 *www.freshproduceclothes.com.*

La Jolla Surf Systems. One block from La Jolla Shores beach, this local institution stocks hip beach and resort wear, plus top-brand surfboards, bodyboards, and wet suits. The shop also rents surf and stand-up paddleboards, beach chairs, umbrellas, kayaks, and snorkel gear. ✉ *2132 Avenida de la Playa, La Jolla* ☎ *858/456–2777* 🌐 *www.lajollasurfsystems.com.*

Rangoni Firenze. The shoe shop carries its own house brand as well as other, mostly Italian, men's and women's footwear labels including Icon and Pele Moda. ✉ *7870 Girard Ave., La Jolla* ☎ *858/459–4469* 🌐 *www.rangonistore.com.*

Sauvage. This luxurious boutique sells sexy and sophisticated swimsuits, beachwear, jewelry, and accessories for women, as well as swim trunks, surf shorts, and workout gear for men. ✉ *1025 Prospect St., Suite 140, La Jolla* ☎ *858/729–0015* 🌐 *www.sauvageswimwear.com.*

HOME ACCESSORIES AND GIFTS

Africa and Beyond. This La Jolla art gallery has been selling traditional and contemporary African art for more than 25 years. Find Shona stone sculptures and ceremonial masks as well as ceramics, fair trade gifts, and furniture. Not everything at the shop comes from Africa—look for oceanic art from Papa New Guinea, and sterling and gold-plated jewelry from across the world. ✉ *1250 Prospect St., La Jolla* ☎ *858/454–9983* 🌐 *www.africaandbeyond.com.*

La Jolla Cove Gifts. Located one block from the ocean, this gift shop sells T-shirts, souvenirs, seashells, jewelry, and nautical items. ✉ *8008 Girard Ave., No. 120, La Jolla* ☎ *858/454–2297* 🌐 *www.lajollacovegifts.com.*

Muttropolis. Dogs (and their owners) love the chic chew toys sold here. They also love the accessories, such as high-fashion coats and hoodies for strutting La Jolla's sun-splashed streets. There's haute cat-ture for felines here as well, and lots of catnip toys. ✉ *7755 Girard Ave., La Jolla* ☎ *858/459–9663* 🌐 *www.muttropolis.com.*

JEWELRY

CJ Charles. An exquisitely appointed shop selling designer and estate jewelry, CJ Charles specializes in Bulgari watches and Cartier, along with stunning fine jewelry, Baccarat crystal, and gift items. ✉ *1135 Prospect St., La Jolla* ☎ *858/454–5390* 🌐 *www.cjcharles.com.*

Pomegranate. In La Jolla for more than 33 years, Pomegranate pairs contemporary and antique jewelry with fashions by American, European, and Asian designers. ✉ *1152 Prospect St., La Jolla* ☎ *858/459–0629* 🌐 *www.pomegranatelajolla.com.*

SHOPPING MALLS

Westfield UTC. This popular outdoor mall on the east side of I–5 has more than 150 shops and 40 eateries, plus an ArcLight Cinemas and a children's play area. **Nordstrom, Macy's,** and **Sears** anchor the center, and specialty stores of note include **Madewell** (*858/458–0012*) for high-quality basics; **Pottery Barn Kids** (*858/453–1249*) for children's bedding and accessories; **Crate & Barrel** (*858/558–4545*) for kitchenware, china dishes, and furniture; and an **Apple Store** (*858/795–6870*) for the latest igadget. One of the country's greenest shopping centers, UTC has lush gardens, open-air plazas, and pedestrian-friendly walkways. Additional eco-friendly cred: Tesla Motors, maker of electric vehicles, shows off its latest models here. ✉ *4545 La Jolla Village Dr., between I–5 and I–805, La Jolla* ☎ *858/546–8858* 🌐 *www.westfield.com/utc.*

POINT LOMA AND CORONADO

POINT LOMA

The laid-back Point Loma Peninsula offers incredible views of Downtown San Diego, and some great shopping away from the large crowds often seen in Downtown and at Fashion Valley.

CLOTHING AND ACCESSORIES

Men's Fashion Depot. San Diego insiders head to this warehouse-style men's store for discounted suits and affordable tuxedos. Browse their inventory of more than 12,000 suits, as well as shoes, belts, and ties. Speedy alterations are available. ✉ *3730 Sports Arena Blvd., Point Loma* ☎ *619/222–9570* 🌐 *www.mensfashiondepot.com.*

HOME ACCESSORIES AND GIFTS

Fodor's Choice ★ **SCOUT at Quarters D.** Located in the former naval base commander's quarters at Liberty Station, Scout at Quarters D feels more like a private home than a retail space. The home-furnishing and design store specializes in artifact-style items, including vintage maps, bungalow-modern furniture, and rich-hued Farrow & Ball paint. A local icon, the historic Hotel San Diego sign is a permanent fixture in the garden. ✉ *2675 Rosecrans St., Point Loma* ☎ *619/225–9925* 🌐 *www.scout-home.com.*

SHOPPING CENTERS

Liberty Station. San Diego's former Naval Training Center is now a mixed-use development with shops, restaurants, and art galleries. With its large grassy areas and Spanish colonial revival–style architecture, it's a great place to take a stroll. The section on Truxton Road between Womble and Roosevelt includes a **Trader Joe's, Vons,** and restaurants like **Tender Greens** and **Sammy's Woodfired Pizza.** To the north are more locally owned businesses lining the arcades in the area known as the Arts District. **Casa Valencia Galeria** features art exclusively from Baja; **Moniker General** sells homewares, custom furniture, and craft beer and coffee; and **Chi Chocolat** carries handmade chocolates and truffles. New in 2016, **Liberty Public Market** is San Diego's only food hall, open daily with 30 eclectic vendors selling artisanal goods. If you're in town on the first Friday of the month, check out Liberty Station's **Friday Night Liberty** (5 to 9 pm), a free art walk featuring refreshments and entertainment. ✉ *2640 Historic Decatur Rd., Point Loma* ☎ *619/573–9300* 🌐 *www.libertystation.com.*

OCEAN BEACH

CLOTHING AND ACCESSORIES

Noon Design Shop. Affordable handmade jewelry and American-made home accessories like tea towels, candles, and glassware fill the shelves at this whimsical boutique and design studio in Ocean Beach. Noon also stocks fresh-smelling soaps, lotions, and perfumes, as well as letterpress greeting cards. ✉ *4993 Niagra Ave., #105, Ocean Beach* ☎ *619/523–1744* 🌐 *www.noondesignshop.com.*

Teeter. Products made by local artisans are featured at this modern shop. Browse home decor and artwork, jewelry, plants, greeting cards, unique gifts, and children's toys. ✉ *5032 Niagara Ave., Ocean Beach* ☎ *619/550–8993* 🌐 *www.shopteetersd.com.*

HOME ACCESSORIES AND GIFTS

Ocean Gifts & Shells. This huge beach-themed store is filled with seashells of every size and shape, nautical decor items, wind chimes, swimwear and accessories, toys, and souvenirs. ✉ *4934 Newport Ave., Ocean Beach* ☎ *619/224–6702* 🌐 *www.oceangiftsandshells.com.*

MARKETS

Ocean Beach Farmers' Market. This bustling midweek market features live music, fresh produce, samples from local restaurants, crafts, and more. Other popular offerings include handmade apparel and accessories, holistic products, and a bouncy house for kids. ✉ *4900 Newport Ave., between Cable and Bacon Sts., Ocean Beach* 🌐 *oceanbeachsandiego.com/attractions/annual-events/farmers-market-wednesdays.*

CORONADO

Coronado's resort hotels attract tourists in droves, but somehow the town has managed to avoid being overtaken by chain stores. Instead, shoppers can browse through family-owned shops, dine at sidewalk cafés along Orange Avenue, stroll through the historic Hotel del Coronado, and take in the specialty shops at Coronado Ferry Landing. Friendly shopkeepers make the boutiques lining Orange Avenue, Coronado's main drag, a good place to browse for clothes, home decor, gift items, and gourmet foods.

BOOKS

FAMILY **Bay Books.** This independent bookstore is the spot to sit, read, and sip coffee on an overcast day by the sea. Great for international travelers, there's a large selection of foreign-language magazines and newspapers, and for youngsters, there's a section in the back devoted to children's books and games. Because of its close proximity to the Navy bases on Coronado, the shop has a large stock of books dedicated to military history. Bay Books also has regular book-signing events; it has hosted a wide array of authors, from Newt Gingrich to Captain Chesley "Sully" Sullenberger. ✉ *1029 Orange Ave., Coronado* ☎ *619/435–0070* 🌐 *www.baybookscoronado.com.*

CLOTHING AND ACCESSORIES

Dale's Swim Shop. All things beachy catch your eye in this shop crammed full of swimsuits, hats, sunglasses, and sunscreen. ✉ *1150 Orange Ave., Coronado* ☎ *619/435–1757.*

Island Birkenstock. Do your feet a favor and check out the comfy sandals, clogs, slippers, and walking shoes sold here. All the latest Birkenstock styles are available in sizes to fit men, women, and children. ✉ *1350 Orange Ave., Coronado* ☎ *619/435–1071* 🌐 *www.birkenstocksd.com.*

FOOD AND WINE

Wine A Bit. Part store and part wine bar, the popular Wine A Bit carries hundreds of boutique wines, along with craft beers, appetizers, and decadent desserts. Cigars, gifts, and wine-related accessories are also for sale. ✉ *928 Orange Ave., Coronado* ☎ *619/365–4953* 🌐 *www.wineabitcoronado.com.*

HOME ACCESSORIES AND GIFTS

The Attic. Modern and vintage home-decor items and accessories are The Attic's specialties. The shop also sells stylish Will Leather Goods bags, as well as jewelry and affordable gifts. ✉ *1011 Orange Ave., Coronado* ☎ *619/435–5432* 🌐 *www.theatticcoronado.com.*

Celtic Corner Scottish Treasures. Get in touch with your Celtic roots with imported apparel, gifts, tableware, and jewelry from Ireland, Scotland, England, and Wales. You can rent or order a custom-made kilt. ✉ *916 Orange Ave., Coronado* ☎ *619/435–1880* 🌐 *www.celticcorner.net.*

Seaside Papery. Customize your correspondence with products from Seaside Papery, including high-end wedding invitations, greeting cards, luxury personal stationery, and wrapping papers. ✉ *1162 Orange Ave., Coronado* ☎ *619/435–5565* 🌐 *www.seasidepapery.com.*

JEWELRY

D Forsythe Jewelry. Stepping into D Forsythe is like taking a quick spin around the world. The one-of-a-kind jewelry sold here features sapphires, emeralds, moonstones, and baroque pearls from such faraway places as Denmark, Cambodia, Turkey, Bali, India, England, and Thailand. ✉ *1136 Loma Ave., Coronado* ☎ *619/435–9211* 🌐 *www.dforsythe.com* ⏲ *Closed Sun. and Mon.*

SHOPPING CENTERS

Coronado Ferry Landing. A staggering view of San Diego's Downtown skyline across the bay and a dozen boutiques make this a delightful place to shop while waiting for a ferry. **La Camisa** (*619/435–8009*) is a fun place to pick up kitschy souvenirs, T-shirts, fleece jackets, and postcards. **The French Room** (*619/889–4325*) specializes in comfy women's shoes and affordable casual wear. **House of Soles & Shades** (*619/437–0546*) sells sandals and designer eyewear. There's a farmers' market every Tuesday from 2:30–6, and some restaurants offer a daily late-afternoon happy hour. ✉ *1201 1st St., Coronado* ☎ *619/435–8895* 🌐 *www.coronadoferrylandingshops.com.*

Fodor's Choice ★ **Hotel Del Coronado.** At the gift shops within the peninsula's main historic attraction, you can purchase sportswear, designer handbags, jewelry, and antiques. **Babcock & Story Emporium** carries an amazing selection of home decor items, garden accessories, and classy gifts. **Blue Octopus** is a children's store featuring creative toys, gifts, and apparel. **Spreckels Sweets & Treats** offers old-time candies, freshly made fudge, and decadent truffles. **Kate's** has designer fashions and accessories, while **Brady's for Men,** with its shirts and sportcoats, caters to well-dressed men. **Crown Jewels Coronado** features fine jewelry, some inspired by the sea. ✉ *1500 Orange Ave., Coronado* ☎ *619/435–6611* 🌐 *www.hoteldel.com/coronado-shopping.*

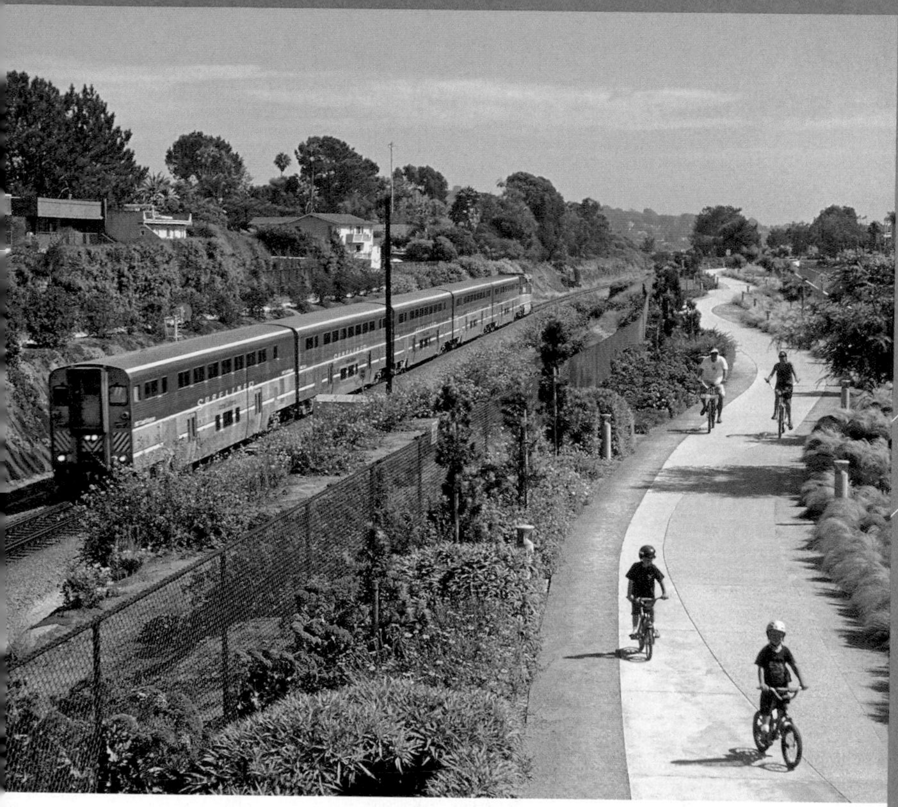

15

NORTH COUNTY AND AROUND

WELCOME TO NORTH COUNTY AND AROUND

TOP REASONS TO GO

★ **Talk to the animals:** Get almost nose to nose with giraffes, lions, tigers, and rhinos at the San Diego Zoo Safari Park in Escondido.

★ **Build a dream at LEGOLAND California Resort:** Explore model cities built with LEGO bricks, including New Orleans, Washington, D.C., and New York City.

★ **Be a beach bum:** Surf Swami's for towering blue-water breaks, tiptoe through the sand at Moonlight Beach, cruise the coast in a sailboat, or spot a whale spouting.

★ **Tour SoCal-style wineries:** Savor the red and white wines while touring in Temecula, home to more than 35 wineries as well as boutique lodging and classy restaurants.

★ **Step back in time:** Sink your teeth into sweet apple pie in the historic mining town of Julian where the Cuyamuca Mountains meet the Colorado Desert.

1 North Coast. From Del Mar to Oceanside the quintessential beach towns march north along I–5. These coastal cities offer sophisticated shopping, art galleries, dining, and accommodations, but there are also great beaches where you can watch surfers testing the breaks in winter. LEGOLAND and other attractions are just east of I–5.

2 Inland North County and Temecula. Historically this is the citrus- and avocado-growing belt of San Diego County. Since the opening of the San Diego Zoo Safari Park in Escondido and expansion of the winemaking industry in Temecula Valley more than 20 years ago, visitors have added inland North County to their must-see lists.

3 The Backcountry and Julian. The backcountry consists of the mountain ranges that separate metropolitan San Diego and the North Coast from the desert. It's where San Diegans go to hike, commune with nature, share a picnic, and study the night sky. Julian, the only real community within these mountains, is famous for its apple pies and Fourth of July parade.

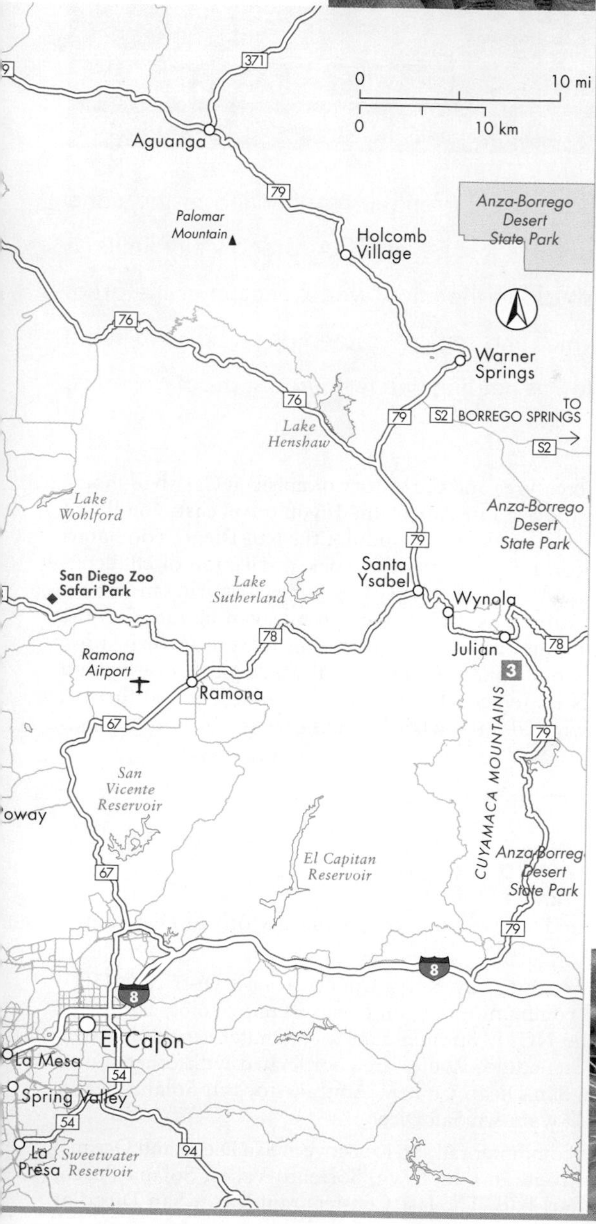

GETTING ORIENTED

San Diego's North County, encompassing the portion of San Diego County that lies north of the metro area from the ocean to the desert, has some of the same attractions of the city to the south: perpetual sunshine, great beaches, and entertainment, including LEGOLAND and the San Diego Zoo's Safari Park. A visit to North County offers a chance to escape the metro area and find a little quiet in the backcountry, serious wine tasting and good eating in Temecula, several luxury resorts and golf courses, some world-class destination spas, art and historic centers, a bit of gold rush–era history, and a more laid-back lifestyle.

Updated by Marlise Kast-Myers

A whole world of scenic grandeur, fascinating history, and scientific wonder lies just beyond San Diego's city limits. If you travel north along the coast, you'll encounter the great beaches for which the region is famous, along with some sophisticated towns holding fine restaurants, great galleries, and museums.

Learn about sea creatures and the history of music in Carlsbad, home of LEGOLAND and Sea Life Aquarium. If you travel east, you'll find art hubs and organic farms in Escondido, the San Diego Zoo Safari Park, a pair of world-class destination spas, a selection of challenging golf courses, and nightlife in bucolic settings. Inspiring mountain scenery plus beautiful places to picnic and hike can be found in the Cuyamaca Mountains and in the surrounding areas near the historic gold-rush-era town of Julian (known for its apple pies). Just beyond the county limits in Temecula you can savor Southern California's only developed wine country, where dozens of wineries offer tastings and tours.

PLANNER

GETTING HERE AND AROUND

BUS AND TRAIN TRAVEL

The Metropolitan Transit System covers the city of San Diego up to Del Mar.

Buses and trains operated by North County Transit District (NCTD) serve all coastal communities in San Diego County, going as far east as Escondido; the NCTD Sprinter runs a commuter service between Oceanside and Escondido. Routes are coordinated with other transit agencies serving San Diego County. Amtrak stops in Solana Beach, Oceanside, and Downtown San Diego.

Coaster operates commuter rail service between San Diego and Oceanside, stopping en route in Old Town, Sorrento Valley, Solana Beach, Encinitas, and Carlsbad. The last Coaster train leaves San Diego at about 7 each night. NCTD's bus system, Breeze, serves North County; for on-demand service they offer Flex, and door-to-door paratransit service on Lift.

Bus and Train Contacts Amtrak. ✉ *235 S. Tremont St., Oceanside* ☎ *760/722-4622 in Oceanside, 800/872-7245* 🌐 *www.amtrak.com.* **Coaster.** ☎ *760/996-6500* 🌐 *www.gonctd.com.* **Metropolitan Transit System.** ☎ *619/233-3004* 🌐 *www.sdmts.com.* **North County Transit District.** ☎ *760/966-6500* 🌐 *www.gonctd.com.*

CAR TRAVEL

Interstate 5 is the main freeway artery connecting San Diego to Los Angeles, passing just east of the beach cities from Oceanside south to Del Mar. Running parallel west of I–5 is Route S21, also known and sometimes indicated as historic Highway 101, Old Highway 101, or Coast Highway 101, which never strays too far from the ocean. An alternate, especially from Orange and Riverside counties, is I–15, the inland route through Temecula, Escondido, and eastern San Diego County.

A loop drive beginning and ending in San Diego is a good way to explore the backcountry and Julian area. You can take the S1, the Sunrise National Scenic Byway (sometimes icy in winter) from I–8 to Route 79 and return through Cuyamaca Rancho State Park (also sometimes icy in winter). If you're only going to Julian (a 75-minute trip from San Diego in light traffic), take either the Sunrise Byway or Route 79, and return to San Diego via Route 78 past Santa Ysabel to Route 67; from here I–8 heads west to Downtown.

Escondido sits at the intersection of Route 78, which heads east from Oceanside, and I–15, the inland freeway connecting San Diego to Riverside, which is 30 minutes north of Escondido. Route 76, which connects with I–15 north of Escondido, veers east to Palomar Mountain. Interstate 15 continues north to Temecula.

RESTAURANTS

Dining in North County tends to reflect the land where the restaurant is located. Along the coast, for example, there is one fine-dining spot after another. Most have dramatic water views and offer platters of exquisite fare created by graduates of the best culinary schools. Right next door you can wander into a typical beach shack or diner for the juiciest hamburger you've ever tasted. Locally sourced food can be found at restaurants throughout the area, although a few chefs have adopted molecular gastronomic techniques. Farm-to-table cuisine is most common in Rancho Sante Fe, Del Mar, and Escondido. Backcountry cuisine east of Escondido toward Julian is generally served in huge portions and tends toward home-style cooking, steak and potatoes, burgers, and anything fried.

HOTELS

Like the restaurants, hotels in the North County reflect the geography and attractions where they are set. There are a number of luxury resorts that offer golf, tennis, entertainment, and classy service. For those who want the ultimate pampered vacation, the North County holds two world-class spas: Cal-a-Vie and the Golden Door. Along the beach, there are quite a few stand-alone lodgings that attract the beach crowd; while some lack in appeal and service, they still charge a big price in summer. Lodgings in the Carlsbad area are family-friendly, some with their own water parks. In Temecula, some of the best and most delightful lodgings are tied to wineries; they offer a whole experience: accommodations, spa, dining, and wine. One-of-a-kind bed-and-breakfasts are the rule in the Julian area. Some hotels charge resort fees up to $35 per night.

Hotel and restaurant reviews have been shortened. For full information, visit Fodors.com.

WHAT IT COSTS

	$	$$	$$$	$$$$
Restaurants	under $18	$18–$27	$28–$35	over $35
Hotels	under $161	$161–$230	$231–$300	over $300

Restaurant prices are for a main course at dinner, excluding 8% tax. Hotel prices are for a standard double room in high (summer) season, excluding 9% to 10.5% tax.

FLOWERS

The North County is a prolific flower-growing region. Nurseries, some open to the public, line the hillsides on both sides of I–5 in Encinitas, Leucadia, and Carlsbad. Most of the poinsettias sold in the United States get their start here. If you're visiting in spring, don't miss the ranunculus bloom at the Flower Fields at Carlsbad Ranch.

San Diego Botanic Gardens in Encinitas displays native and exotic plants year-round. The gardens at the San Diego Zoo Safari Park attract nearly as many people as the animals do.

Visitor Information San Diego Tourism Authority. ☎ *619/232–3101* 🌐 *www.sandiego.org.*

NORTH COAST: DEL MAR TO OCEANSIDE

Once upon a time, to say that the North Coast of San Diego County was different from the city of San Diego would have been an understatement. From the northern tip of La Jolla up to Oceanside, a half-dozen small communities developed separately from urban San Diego—and from one another. Del Mar, because of its 2 miles of wide beaches, splendid views, and Thoroughbred horse-racing complex, was the playground of the rich and famous. Up the road, agriculture played a major role in the development of Solana Beach and Encinitas.

Carlsbad, too, rooted in the old Mexican rancheros, has agriculture in its past, as well as the entrepreneurial instinct of a late-19th-century resident, John Frazier, who promoted the area's water as a cure for common ailments and constructed a replica of a European mineral-springs resort. Oceanside was a beachside getaway for inland families in the 19th century; its economic fortunes changed considerably with the construction of Camp Pendleton as a Marine Corps training base during World War II. Marines still train at the huge base today.

What these towns shared was at least a half-century's worth of Southern California beach culture—think Woodies (wood-bodied cars), surfing, the Beach Boys, alternate lifestyles—and the road that connected them. That was U.S. Highway 101, which nearly passed into oblivion when I–5 was extended from Los Angeles to the Mexican border.

DID YOU KNOW?

San Diego County consists of 18 incorporated cities and several unincorporated communities, and is about the same size as the state of Connecticut.

Then began an explosion of development in the 1980s, and the coast north of San Diego has come to resemble a suburban extension of the city itself. Once-lovely hillsides and canyons have been bulldozed and leveled to make room for bedroom communities in Oceanside, Carlsbad, and even such high-price areas as Rancho Santa Fe and La Jolla.

If you venture off the freeway and head for the ocean, you can discover remnants of the old beach culture surviving in the sophisticated towns of Del Mar, Solana Beach, Cardiff-by-the-Sea, Encinitas, Leucadia, Carlsbad, and Oceanside, where the arts, fine dining, and elegant lodgings also now rule. As suburbanization continues, the towns are reinventing themselves—Carlsbad, for instance, has morphed from a farming community into a tourist destination with such attractions as LEGOLAND California, several museums, and an upscale outlet shopping complex. Oceanside, home of one of the longest wooden piers on the West Coast (its first pier was built in the 1880s), promotes its beach culture with a yacht harbor and beachside resort hotels.

DEL MAR

23 miles north of Downtown San Diego on I–5, 9 miles north of La Jolla on Rte. S21.

Del Mar comprises two sections: the small historic village adjacent to the beach west of I–5 and a growing business center surrounded by multimillion-dollar tract housing east of the freeway. Tiny Del Mar village, the smallest incorporated city in San Diego County, holds a population of 4,500 tucked into a 2.1-square-mile beachfront. It's known for its quaint half-timbered Tudor-style architecture, 2 miles of accessible beaches, and the Del Mar racetrack and San Diego County Fairgrounds complex. The village attracted rich and famous visitors from the beginning; they still come for seclusion and to watch the horses run. The Del Mar Gateway business complex has high-rise hotels and fast-food outlets east of the interstate at the entrance to Carmel Valley. Both Del Mars, old and new, hold expensive homes belonging to staff and scientists who work in the biotech industry and at UC San Diego in adjacent La Jolla. Access to Del Mar's beaches is from the streets that run east–west off Coast Boulevard; access to the business complex is via Highway 56.

TOUR OPTIONS

San Diego Air Tours conducts excursions aboard restored 1920s-vintage open-cockpit biplanes. Flights are from Montgomery Field and start at $199 per couple for 20 minutes. Civic Helicopters gives whirlybird tours of the area along the beaches, starting at $300 for 30 minutes aboard a Robinson R-44.

Tour Contacts Civic Helicopters. ✉ *2206 Palomar Airport Rd., Suite H, Carlsbad* ☎ *760/438–8424* 🌐 *www.civichelicopters.com.* **San Diego Air Tours.** ✉ *3750 John J. Montgomery Dr., Suite D, San Diego* ☎ *760/930–0903, 800/359–2939* 🌐 *www.sandiegoairtours.com.*

EXPLORING

TOP ATTRACTIONS

FAMILY **Del Mar Fairgrounds.** The Spanish Mission–style fairground is the home of the **Del Mar Thoroughbred Club** (*www.dmtc.com*). Crooner Bing Crosby and his Hollywood buddies—Pat O'Brien, Gary Cooper, and Oliver Hardy, among others—organized the club in the 1930s, and the racing here (usually July through September, Wednesday through Monday, posttime 2 pm) remains a fashionable affair. Del Mar Fairgrounds hosts more than 100 different events each year, including the San Diego County Fair, the Del Mar National Horse Show in April and May, and the fall Scream Zone that's popular with local families. ✉ *2260 Jimmy Durante Blvd.* ☎ *858/755–1161* 🌐 *www.delmarfairgrounds.com.*

WORTH NOTING

Del Mar Plaza. Along with its collection of high-end shops, the tiered plaza contains outstanding restaurants and fountain courtyards with Pacific views. Some businesses validate parking, which is underground. ✉ *1555 Camino del Mar* 🌐 *www.delmarplaza.com.*

FAMILY **Free Flight Exotic Bird Sanctuary.** This small exotic-bird aviary adjacent to the Del Mar Fairgrounds houses a collection of parrots and other exotic birds—a guaranteed child pleaser. ✉ *2132 Jimmy Durante Blvd.* ☎ *858/481–3148* 🌐 *www.freeflightbirds.org* 🎟 *$7.*

Seagrove Park (*Powerhouse Park*). Picnics and weddings make this coastal park popular on weekends. For free summer evening concerts and beach access, head to Powerhouse Park at the north end of this small stretch of grass overlooking the ocean. ✉ *15th St. and Coast Blvd.* ☎ *858/755–1524.*

WHERE TO EAT

The neighborhood just north of La Jolla is well-known for its posh, ocean-view homes and the famed Del Mar racetrack. It's also known for the numerous restaurants that line the main drag of Camino Del Mar; there's even a few worthwhile spots tucked into upscale shopping centers and beachside locales.

$$$$ FRENCH Fodor's Choice ★ ✕ **Addison.** Indulge in the finer things in life at this AAA 5-Diamond restaurant by acclaimed chef William Bradley who serves up haute French flavors in his 4- and 10-course prix-fixe dinners. Beyond the swanky bar and wine cave is a sophisticated Tuscan-style dining room with intricately carved dark-woods, marble pillars, and arched windows draped

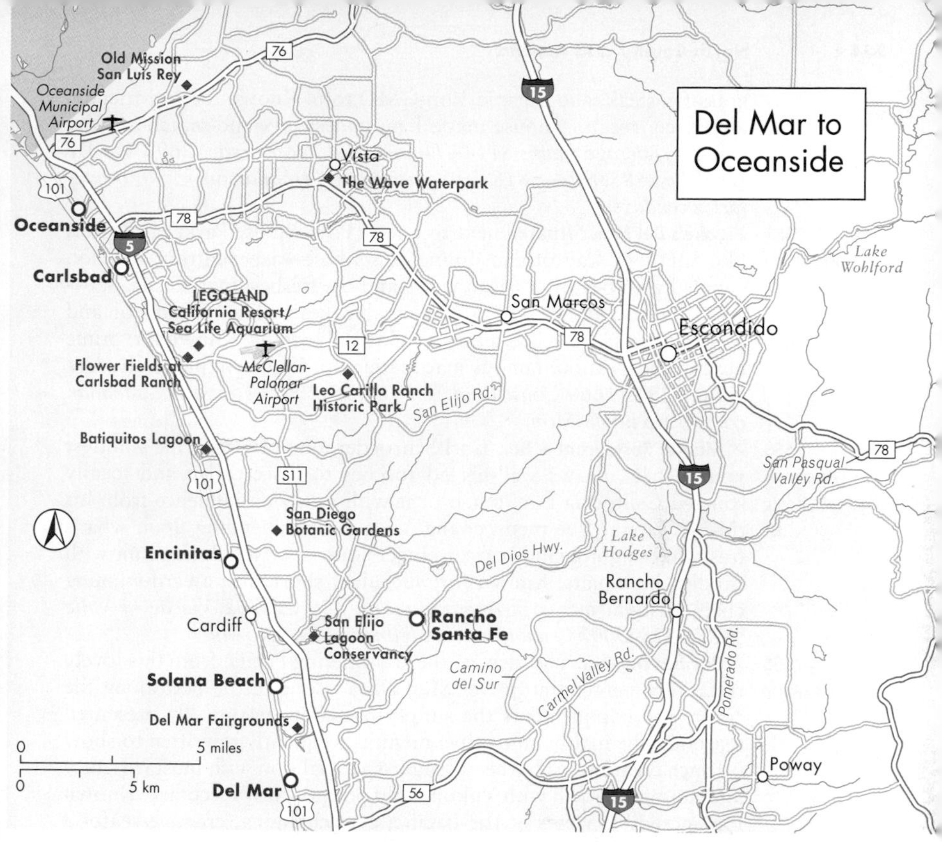

in red velvet. **Known for:** decadent tasting menus; the ultimate fine-dining experience; impeccable service. *Average main: $110 5200 Grand Del Mar Way 858/314–1900 www.addisondelmar.com Closed Sun. and Mon. No lunch.*

$$ MODERN ITALIAN **Cucina Enoteca.** An off-shoot of Bankers Hill's Cucina Urbana, Enoteca occupies a grand two-story space in the Flower Hill Promenade shopping center and is as notable for its whimsical decor—antler chandeliers, burlap-wrapped chairs, and more than 400 horse figurines honor the restaurant's proximity to the Thoroughbred Club—as it is for its beloved Italian food. There are many familiar favorites from Cucina Urbana like the creamy polenta board and pizzas, as well as unique Enoteca plates, including a "chef's whim" risotto and a surf and turf riff that features rib eye, sausage, shrimp, sweet peppers, and mascarpone potato. **Known for:** wines at retail; daily deals 4:30–6; buffet-style antipasti during Sunday brunch; garden-like second-floor seating area. *Average main: $25 Flower Hill Promenade, 2730 Via de la Valle 858/704–4500 www.cucinaenoteca.com No lunch Mon.*

$ MODERN AMERICAN FAMILY **Flower Child.** Fast-casual takes a healthy spin at this cheery spot—think Technicolor peace sign, floral wallpaper in the bathroom, and yoga mat "parking" for those dining postworkout. The menu evokes the same colorful vibe with salads mixed with fresh ingredients like organic kale, lemon tahini vinaigrette, and proteins that include sustainable salmon, grass-fed steak, and organic, non-GMO tofu. **Known for:** kid-friendly ambience; rotating house-made lemonades; mix-and-match healthy sides. *Average main: $11 Flower Hill Promenade, 2690 Via De La Valle 858/314–6818 www.iamaflowerchild.com No breakfast weekdays.*

$$$ AMERICAN **Jake's Del Mar.** Situated next to grassy Powerhouse Park, Jake's feels like Southern Californian dining at its best—a beachfront location coupled with beautiful ocean views and the freshest ingredients. Starters include ocean-inspired fare like crab cakes with tamarind aioli and pineapple salsa as well as a tangy yellowtail tostada. **Known for:** prime beachfront location; famous macadamia nut ice cream pie. *Average main: $29 1660 Coast Blvd. 858/755–2002 www.jakesdelmar.com No lunch Mon.*

$$$ AMERICAN Fodor's Choice ★ **Market Restaurant + Bar.** Carl Schroeder, one of California's hottest young chefs, draws well-heeled foodies to his creative and locally sourced California fare, much of it with an Asian influence from his time in Japan. The menu changes regularly depending upon what's fresh, but might include carrot-ginger soup or crispy duck confit with candied kumquats. **Known for:** succulent short ribs; award-winning chef; seasonal menu. *Average main: $30 3702 Via de la Valle 858/523–0007 www.marketdelmar.com No lunch.*

$$$ SEAFOOD **Pacifica Del Mar.** The view of the shimmering Pacific from this lovely restaurant perched atop Del Mar Plaza is one of the best along the coast, and complements the simply prepared, beautifully presented seafood. The highly innovative menu is frequently rewritten to show off such creations as barbecue sugar-spice salmon with mustard sauce and mustard catfish with Yukon Gold potato–corn succotash. **Known for:** incredible views of the Pacific; ever-changing, creative seafood menu; upscale dining with a clientele to match. *Average main: $30 Del Mar Plaza, 1555 Camino del Mar 858/792–0476 www.pacificadelmar.com.*

$$ AMERICAN **Prepkitchen Del Mar.** This snug Del Mar restaurant is like stepping into the home of your most fashionable friend who has an industrial-meets-vintage dining room edged in books, antiques, wines, and rustic wooden posts. Come hungry, in fact skip lunch, because there are way too many exceptional dishes to limit yourself to just one. **Known for:** one of the best burgers in San Diego; small starter plates for sharing; handmade pasta. *Average main: $23 1201 Camino Del Mar 858/792–7737 www.prepkitchendelmar.com.*

WHERE TO STAY

$$$$ RESORT FAMILY Fodor's Choice ★ **Fairmont Grand Del Mar.** Mind-blowing indulgence in serene surroundings, from drop-dead gorgeous guest accommodations to myriad outdoor adventures, sets the opulent Mediterranean-style Fairmont Grand Del Mar apart from any other luxury hotel in San Diego. **Pros:** ultimate luxury; secluded, on-site golf course; enormous rooms; has most acclaimed fine-dining restaurant in San Diego. **Cons:** floor plan may be confusing; hotel is not on the beach. *Rooms from: $415 5200 Grand Del Mar Ct., San Diego 858/314–2000, 855/314–2030 www.fairmont.com/san-diego Greens fees $250; 18 holes, 7160 yards, par 72 249 rooms No meals.*

$ HOTEL **Hilton Garden Inn San Diego Del Mar.** The corporate crowd—and anyone wanting to reach San Diego's attractions within 15 minutes—select this Hilton property conveniently located where Highways 5–805 and 56 merge. **Pros:** great location; friendly staff; spa and in-house deli. **Cons:** parking lot views; no in-room safes. *Rooms from: $159* *3939 Ocean Bluff Ave.* *858/720–9500* *www.sandiegodelmar.hgi.com* *84 rooms* *No meals.*

$$$$ HOTEL **L'Auberge Del Mar.** Rooms at this oceanfront luxury hotel underwent a full renovation in 2017, each now reminiscent of an airy beach cottage with plantation shutters, a fireplace, and vintage coastal artwork. **Pros:** beach casual meets upscale chic; excellent service; dogs welcomed with gift bags. **Cons:** occasional train noise; adult atmosphere; ground-level rooms have no privacy. *Rooms from: $450* *1540 Camino del Mar* *858/259–1515, 800/245–9757* *www.laubergedelmar.com* *121 rooms* *No meals.*

15

SHOPPING

In Del Mar, browse the cute boutiques in Del Mar Village or head to Flower Hill Promenade, an outdoor shopping center that has become one of San Diego's most thriving retail destinations with an eclectic mix of locally owned retailers. If you're headed to the Del Mar Racetrack, be sure to pick up a glamorous hat to wear while cheering on the ponies—a racetrack tradition.

HOME ACCESSORIES AND GIFTS

Fair Trade Decor. This home store in Del Mar Village stocks only fair trade items from more than 40 countries, including goat wool rugs from Mexico, colorful telephone wire baskets from South Africa, and throws made from recycled saris. *1412 Camino Del Mar* *858/461–1263* *www.fairtradedecor.com.*

SHOPPING CENTERS

Flower Hill Promenade. At first glance, this open-air shopping center anchored by a **Whole Foods Market** (*858/436–9800*) might look like your typical upscale SoCal mall, but take a closer look, because there's way more to it than meets the eye. There's not only some great shopping—much of it locally owned and eco-minded—but also some of San Diego's best restaurateurs like Tracy Borkum and Steven Molina have opened restaurants here (CUCINA enoteca and Flower Child, respectively). **Sweetpea** (*858/481–0683*) stocks children's clothing from brands like Burberry, Petit Bateau, and Monnalisa. **Van de Vort** (*858/720–1059*) sells the latest boho-chic fashions, including floral prints, fringe and maxi dresses. **Lone Flag** (*858/793–0712*) stocks functional, modern fashion and accessory staples. **Pink Soul Boutique** (*858/888–0142*) carries vegan leather jewelry and hand-painted yoga pants and tops. *2720 Via De La Valle, Del Mar* *858/481–2904* *www.flowerhill.com.*

SOLANA BEACH

1 mile north of Del Mar on Rte. S21, 25 miles north of Downtown San Diego on I–5 to Lomas Santa Fe Dr. west.

Once-quiet Solana Beach is *the* place to look for antiques, collectibles, and contemporary fashions and artwork. The Cedros Design District, occupying four blocks south of the Amtrak station, contains shops, galleries, designers' studios, restaurants, and a popular music venue, the Belly Up Tavern. The town is known for its excellent restaurants, but most area lodging is in adjacent Del Mar and Encinitas.

WHERE TO EAT

$ BAKERY FAMILY Fodor's Choice ★ ✕ **Claire's on Cedros.** Breakfast foodies religiously line up for a table at this cheerful A-frame restaurant for the chance to dig in to wholesome food made from scratch. Built from reclaimed wood and salvaged bricks, the eatery has a green roof, solar panels, and is insulated with recycled denim—all of which helped it earn platinum LEED status. **Known for:** scratch kitchen; California-style comfort food; generous portions. *Average main: $13 ✉ 246 N. Cedros Ave., across from Solana Beach Transit Center ☎ 858/259–8597 🌐 www.clairesoncedros.com ⏲ No dinner Sun.–Thurs.*

$$ SEAFOOD FAMILY ✕ **The Fish Market.** In 1976, a fisherman and captain teamed up to deliver fresh, quality seafood at a decent price. Today, they run six restaurants across California including this North County branch that lacks an ocean view but makes up for it with perfectly cooked fish and simple preparations from a menu that changes daily. **Known for:** delicious clam chowder; crisp fish-and-chips; fish smoked with hickory and sugar maple woods; happy hour 11–4 on weekends. *Average main: $25 ✉ 640 Via de la Valle ☎ 858/755–2277 🌐 www.thefishmarket.com.*

$$$$ FRENCH ✕ **Pamplemousse Grille.** One of North County's best restaurants, across the street from the Del Mar Fairgrounds and racetrack, offers French cuisine with California flare. Chef-proprietor Jeffrey Strauss brings a caterer's sensibilities to the details, like a mix-or-match selection of sauces—such as wild mushroom, grain mustard, or peppercorn—to complement the simple but absolutely top-quality grilled meats and seafood. **Known for:** exceptional service; comprehensive wine list; traditional French sauces to accompany entrées. *Average main: $36 ✉ 514 Via de la Valle ☎ 858/792–9090 🌐 www.pgrille.com ⏲ No lunch Sat.–Thurs.*

$ PIZZA FAMILY ✕ **Pizza Port.** Local families flock here for great pizza and handcrafted brews. Pick a spot at one of the long picnic-type tables, choose traditional or whole-grain beer crust for your pie and any original topping—such as the Monterey, with pepperoni, onions, mushrooms, and artichoke hearts—and tip back a brew from one of the longest boutique lists in San Diego. **Known for:** handcrafted beer; whole-grain beer crust. *Average main: $17 ✉ 135 N. Hwy. 101 ☎ 858/481–7332 🌐 www.pizzaport.com.*

$$$ STEAKHOUSE ✕ **Red Tracton's.** Across the street from the Del Mar racetrack, this classic old-fashioned steak and seafood house is a high-roller's heaven and a perennial favorite with jockeys celebrating their wins. Everyone from the pianist to the waitresses is well aware that smiles and prompt service can result in tips as generously sized as the gigantic Australian lobster tails that the menu demurely lists at "market price." The food is simple but good,

Legoland California's Miniland USA has scenes from San Francisco, Washington, D.C., New Orleans, New York, and Las Vegas.

and the menu highlights roasted prime rib in addition to filet mignon, panfried scallops, and such starters as lobster bisque and "jumbo" shrimp on ice. **Known for:** lively piano music; juicy steaks, prime rib, and shrimp; supper club atmosphere. *Average main: $31 ✉ 550 Via de la Valle ☎ 858/755–6600 🌐 www.redtractonssteakhouse.com.*

NIGHTLIFE

Belly Up. A fixture on local papers' "best of" lists, Belly Up has been drawing crowds since it opened in the mid-'70s. Its longevity attests to the quality of the eclectic entertainment on its stage. Within converted Quonset huts, critically acclaimed artists play everything from reggae and folk to—well, you name it. *✉ 143 S. Cedros Ave. ☎ 858/481–8140 🌐 www.bellyup.com.*

SHOPPING

Aaron Chang Ocean Art Gallery. On the south end of Cedros Design District, the Ocean Art Gallery features works by award-winning surf photographer, Aaron Chang. On display are photographic prints with ocean themes and several striking surfboard sculptures. *✉ 415 S. Cedros Ave., No. 110 ☎ 858/345–1880 🌐 www.aaronchang.com.*

Antique Warehouse. More than 100 dealers carry American, European, and Asian furniture, mid-century items, folk and country art. *✉ 212 S. Cedros Ave. ☎ 858/755–5156.*

FAMILY **Cedros Design District.** A collection of more than 85 shops, along a two-block stretch of S. Cedros Avenue, this district specializes in interior design, apparel, jewelry, and gifts. You won't find chain restaurants here, as they are not allowed, but you will find local chefs shopping at the Sunday Farmers' Market (1 to 5 pm). There's also free parking along this dog-friendly strip. ✉ *District office, 444 S. Cedros Ave.* 🌐 *www.cedrosavenue.com.*

House Vintage. Inside this tiny 1920s cottage are funky, handmade treasures including repurposed furniture and craft kits for DIY projects. The owner also hosts monthly on-site art classes like furniture painting 101 and DIY paint class. ✉ *315 S. Cedros Ave.* ☎ *858/222–2989* 🌐 *www.debisdesigndiary.com* ⏲ *Closed Mon.–Wed.*

Solo. Operated by eight creative women, this upscale collective is a highlight of Cedros. Shoppers are lured in by the restored warehouse and won over by antiques, artwork, home furnishings, and books on cooking, industrial design, and everything in between. ✉ *309 S. Cedros Ave.* ☎ *858/794–9016* 🌐 *www.solocedros.com.*

RANCHO SANTA FE

4 miles east of Solana Beach on Rte. S8, Lomas Santa Fe Dr., 29 miles north of Downtown San Diego on I–5 to Rte. S8 east.

Groves of huge, drooping eucalyptus trees cover the hills and valleys of this affluent and exclusive town east of I–5. Rancho Santa Fe and the surrounding areas are primarily residential, where there are mansions at every turn. It's also common to see entire families riding horses on the many trails that crisscross the hillsides.

Modeled after a Spanish village, the town was designed by Lilian Rice, one of the first women to graduate with a degree in architecture from the University of California. Her first structure, a 12-room house built in 1922, evolved into the Inn at Rancho Santa Fe, which became a gathering spot for celebrities such as Bette Davis, Errol Flynn, and Bing Crosby in the 1930s and 1940s. The challenging Rancho Santa Fe Golf Course, the original site of the Bing Crosby Pro-Am, is considered one of the best courses in Southern California.

WHERE TO EAT AND STAY

$$$$ FRENCH

✕ **Mille Fleurs.** From its location in the heart of wealthy, horsey Rancho Santa Fe to the warm Gallic welcome extended by proprietor Bertrand Hug and the talents of chef Martin Woesle, Mille Fleurs is a winner. The quiet dining rooms are decorated like a French villa. **Known for:** exotic produce from neighboring Chino Farms; flawless seasonal dining; soft jazz in the piano bar Wednesday–Saturday; authentic French desserts. 💲 *Average main: $38* ✉ *Country Squire Courtyard, 6009 Paseo Delicias* ☎ *858/756–3085* 🌐 *www.millefleurs.com* ⏲ *No lunch Sat.–Wed.*

$$$ AMERICAN Fodor's Choice ★

✕ **Morada.** Loyal locals frequent this classy farm-to-fork restaurant, where black-and-white photos of Santa Fe's history provide a glimpse into the storied past of The Inn at Rancho Santa Fe. Cozy up to the fireplace and partake of locally sourced California cuisine that leans heavily on comfort food like 72-hour braised short ribs, root vegetable potpie, baked macaroni-and-cheese, and Jidori chicken with buttermilk biscuits and collard greens. **Known for:** elevated comfort food; California inspired menu. 💲 *Average main: $33* ✉ *The Inn at Rancho Santa Fe, 5951 Linea Del Cielo* ☎ *858/381–8289* 🌐 *www.theinnatrsf.com.*

$$$$ MEDITERRANEAN **Veladora.** Setting the stage for your dining journey at Veldora are open wood beams, iron chandeliers, and a Damien Hirst butterfly wing art piece valued at $1.1 million—this place is refined without being stuffy. There are nearly 900 wines and 120 tequilas on the menu giving you more than enough options to pair with the foie gras, ahi tartar, and oysters on the half shell. **Known for:** attentive service; extensive wine list; menu for small dogs; remarkable slow poached Maine lobster and pan-roasted filet mignon. *Average main: $38* *5921 Valencia Circle* *858/756–1123* *www.ranchovalencia.com* *Closed Mon.*

$$$ HOTEL **The Inn at Rancho Santa Fe.** Understated elegance is the theme of this genteel old resort, designed in 1923 by Lilian Rice, who was known for her architectural works reflecting Spanish colonial style. **Pros:** charming historic hotel; excellent service; country comfort. **Cons:** dim lighting in the rooms; cold pool; some rooms close to the road. *Rooms from: $275* *5951 Linea del Cielo* *858/756–1131, 800/843–4661* *www.theinnatrsf.com* *88 rooms* *No meals.*

15

$$$$ RESORT FAMILY Fodor's Choice ★ **Rancho Valencia Resort & Spa.** Elegant, two-level, hacienda-style casitas—appointed with corner fireplaces, luxurious bathrooms, and shuttered French doors leading to private patios—are nestled among 45 acres in one of Southern California's most affluent neighborhoods. **Pros:** complimentary four-hour use of new Porsches; impeccable personalized service; minibar and fitness classes included in rate; one of nation's top tennis resorts. **Cons:** $30 daily resort fee; very expensive; far from San Diego attractions. *Rooms from: $868* *5921 Valencia Circle* *858/756–1123, 866/233–6708* *www.ranchovalencia.com* *49 suites* *No meals.*

SHOPPING

The Country Friends. Operated by a nonprofit foundation, The Country Friends is a great place for unusual gifts and carries collectibles, silver, furniture, and antiques donated or consigned by community residents. *6030 El Tordo* *858/756–1192* *www.thecountryfriends.org* *Closed Sun. and Mon.*

The Spa at Rancho Valencia. The Spa at Rancho Valencia Resort invites couples (and everyone else) to relax, romance, and renew. Massages include Thai, relaxation, deep tissue, hot stone, and prenatal, but the Lovers Ritual begins with a couples bath, followed by a Duet Massage in a cabana for two. Treatment rooms have private Jacuzzis, fireplaces, and outdoor showers. Day access to the spa amenities—plunge circuit, sauna, relaxation room, saline pool, fitness classes—is included when you book a treatment. Discounted rates are offered Monday–Thursday. **Price:** Massages $185–$380; facials $195–$355; body therapies $140–$445; couples $380–$730. *5921 Rancho Valencia Cir.* *858/759–6490* *www.ranchovalencia.com.*

Vegetable Shop at Chino Farm. This is the place to buy the same premium (and very expensive) fruits, micro greens, edible flowers, and rare vegetables that the Chino Family Farm grows for many of San Diego's upscale restaurants, and for such famed California eateries as Chez Panisse in Berkeley and George's in La Jolla. *6123 Calzada del Bosque* *858/756–3184* *www.chinofamilyfarm.com* *Closed Mon.*

ENCINITAS

6 miles north of Solana Beach on Rte. S21, 7 miles west of Rancho Santa Fe on Rte. S9, 28 miles north of Downtown San Diego on I–5.

Flower breeding and growing has been the major industry in Encinitas since the early part of the 20th century. The city, which encompasses the coastal towns of Cardiff-by-the-Sea and Leucadia as well as inland Olivenhain, is home to Paul Ecke Poinsettias (open only to the trade), and today is the largest producer and breeder of the Christmas blossom in the world. The golden domes of the Self-Realization Fellowship Retreat mark famed Swami's Beach and the southern entrance to downtown Encinitas.

The vibe is laid-back, with surfing and yoga as top priorities for residents. Expect to see flip-flop clad locals crossing the boulevard with surfboards in tow, and signs of historic California alive and well. Lining the main drag are plenty of cafés, bars, and restaurants to hold your attention, as well as the 1928 La Paloma Theater that still shows cult classics, foreign films, and music performances nightly.

GETTING HERE AND AROUND

From San Diego, head north on I–5. If you're already on the coast, drive along Route S21. Lodgings, restaurants, and the beach pop up along Route S21 (Old Highway 101) west of the freeway. The San Diego Botanic Gardens lie to the east of the freeway.

EXPLORING

TOP ATTRACTIONS

FAMILY **San Diego Botanic Gardens.** More than 3,300 rare, exotic, and endangered plants are on display on 37 landscaped acres. Displays include plants from Central America, Africa, Australia, the Middle East, the Mediterranean, the Himalayas, Madagascar, and more; the most diverse collection of bamboo in North America; California native plants; and subtropical fruits. The park contains the largest interactive children's garden on the West Coast, where kids can roll around in the Seeds of Wonder garden, explore a baby dinosaur forest, discover a secret garden, or play in a playhouse. An Under the Sea Garden displays rocks and succulents that uncannily mimic an underwater environment. ✉ *230 Quail Gardens Dr.* ☎ *760/436–3036* 🌐 *www.sdbgarden.org* 🎫 *$14.*

WORTH NOTING

FAMILY **San Elijo Lagoon Conservancy.** Between Solana Beach and Encinitas, this is the most complex of the estuary systems in San Diego North County. A 7-mile network of trails surrounds the 979 reserve, where more than 700 species of plants, fish, and birds (many of them migratory) live. Be sure to stop by the San Elijo Lagoon Nature Centre. The center, open 9 to 5 daily, offers museum-quality exhibits about the region and a viewing deck overlooking the estuary. Docents offer free public walks every Saturday at 10 am. ✉ *2710 Manchester Ave., Cardiff-by-the-Sea* ☎ *760/436–3944 conservancy, 760/634–3026 nature center* 🌐 *www.sanelijo.org* 🎫 *Free.*

WHERE TO EAT

$ SEAFOOD Fodor's Choice ★ **Fish 101.** The line out the door—especially during happy hour—is a clear sign you're at the best place in North County to find locally sourced, sustainably caught fish at a great price. Owned by surfer-diver-fisherman, John Park, the vibe is SoCal at its best, with a chill staff serving fresh-shucked oysters, thick clam chowder, and fish sandwiches grilled to perfection; a chalkboard menu displays the day's catch and what's been shucked on ice. **Known for:** happy hour with $1 oysters, $3 tacos, and $4 beers; fresh and healthy seafood; seasonal, sustainable ingredients. *Average main: $13* *1468 N. Coast Hwy. 101* *760/943–6221* *fish101restaurant.com/* *Closed Mon.*

$$ VEGETARIAN **Ki's Restaurant.** Veggies with a view could be the subtitle for this venerable Cardiff-by-the-Sea restaurant that grew from a simple juice shack. Ki's is well known for heart-healthy, gluten-free, vegan, locally sourced, ovo-lacto, vegetarian-friendly dishes like huevos rancheros, filling tofu scrambles, taco plates, chopped salads with feta and nuts, watermelon juice, and carrot ice-cream smoothies. **Known for:** healthy vegan and gluten-free menu; yummy Asian-inspired dishes; popular post-surfing spot across from the beach; heaping Açai bowls. *Average main: $20* *2591 S. Coast Hwy. 101, Cardiff-by-the-Sea* *760/436–5236* *www.kisrestaurant.com.*

$$$$ SEAFOOD **Pacific Coast Grill.** This casual beachy-style eatery offers a sweeping ocean view and seasonal Pacific Coast fare that reflects California's Mexican and Asian influences. Lunch in the spacious dining room or on the dog-friendly sunny patio brings sashimi ahi salad with greens, seaweed and mango, plum-ginger–braised short ribs, or perfect fried-fish tacos washed down with a margarita that sings with fresh lime and lemon juice. **Known for:** romantic waterfront dining; fresh oysters, sushi rolls, and black mussels; stunning sunsets; rich lobster carbonara. *Average main: $37* *2526 S. Hwy. 1010, Cardiff-by-the-Sea* *760/479–0721* *www.pacificcoastgrill.com.*

$$ AMERICAN **Solace & The Moonlight Lounge.** The modern American cuisine, patio overlooking historic Highway 101, and industrial setting—garage doors that retract on sunny days and exposed spiral ductwork— at this downtown Encinitas restaurant draws a beach-fresh clientele. Cocktails like the cucumber mule, pair well with the warm cheddar-and-chive biscuit topped with orange honey butter or the $1 oysters served daily 3–6. **Known for:** weekend brunch; cinnamon roles and cheddar biscuits; cocktails and $1 oysters. *Average main: $20* *25 East E St.* *760/753–2433* *www.eatatsolace.com.*

WHERE TO STAY

$ B&B/INN **Cardiff by the Sea Lodge.** Opened in 1990, this quirky hotel oozes with character from its rooftop garden complete with fire pits and Jacuzzi to its uniquely themed rooms that range from Hawaiian paradise to French country. **Pros:** great rates; friendly staff; close to beach. **Cons:** dated rooms; some train noise. *Rooms from: $139* *142 Chesterfield Ave., Cardiff-by-the-Sea* *760/944–6474* *www.cardifflodge.com* *17 rooms* *Breakfast.*

15

SHOPPING

Souvenir items are sold at shops along South Coast Highway 101 and in the Lumberyard Shopping Center.

Encinitas Seaside Bazaar. For art, clothing, jewelry, antiques, and leather goods, this open-air craft market on Highway 101 has more than 50 booths selling local crafts at reasonable prices. It's open weekends 9–5. ✉ *459 S. Coast Hwy. 101* ☎ *760/753–1611* ⏲ *Closed weekdays.*

Hansen's. One of San Diego's oldest surfboard manufacturers is owned by Don Hansen, surfboard shaper extraordinaire, who came here from Hawaii in 1962. The store also stocks a full line of surf and snowboard apparel, wet suits, surf cams, and casual wear. ✉ *1105 S. Coast Hwy. 101* ☎ *800/480–4754, 760/753–6596* 🌐 *www.hansensurf.com.*

CARLSBAD

6 miles from Encinitas on Rte. S21, 36 miles north of Downtown San Diego on I–5.

Once-sleepy Carlsbad, lying astride I–5 at the north end of a string of beach towns extending from San Diego to Oceanside, has long been popular with beachgoers and sunseekers. On a clear day in this village you can take in sweeping ocean views that stretch from La Jolla to Oceanside by walking the 2-mile-long sea walk running between the Encina Power Station and Pine Street. En route, you can get closer to the water via several stairways leading to the beach; quite a few benches are here as well.

East of I–5 is LEGOLAND California and other attractions like two of the San Diego area's most luxurious resort hotels, one of the last remaining wetlands along the Southern California coast, a discount shopping mall, golf courses, the cattle ranch built by movie star Leo Carrillo, and colorful spring-blooming Flower Fields at Carlsbad Ranch. Until the mid-20th century, when suburban development began to sprout on the hillsides, farming was the main industry in Carlsbad, with truckloads of vegetables shipped out year-round. Some agriculture remains. Area farmers develop and grow new varieties of flowers, including the ranunculus that transform a hillside into a rainbow each spring, and Carlsbad strawberries are among the sweetest in Southern California; in spring you can pick them yourself in fields on both sides of I–5.

GETTING HERE AND AROUND

LEGOLAND California Resort, off Cannon Road east of I–5, is surrounded by the Flower Fields, hotels, and the Museum of Making Music. On the west side of the freeway is beach access at several points and quaint Carlsbad village shops.

ESSENTIALS

Visitor Information Carlsbad Convention and Visitors Bureau. ✉ *400 Carlsbad Village Dr.* ☎ *760/434–6093, 800/227–5722* 🌐 *visitcarlsbad.com.*

EXPLORING

TOP ATTRACTIONS

Batiquitos Lagoon. While development destroyed many of the saltwater marsh wildlife habitats that once punctuated the North County coastline, this 610-acre lagoon was restored in 1997 to support fish and bird populations. Today, there are 185 species of birds here. A stroll along the 2-mile trail from the Batiquitos Lagoon Foundation Nature Center along the north shore of the lagoon reveals nesting sites of the red-winged blackbird, lagoon birds such as the great blue heron, the great egret, and the snowy egret; and life in the mud flats. This is a quiet spot for contemplation or a picnic. ✉ *7380 Gabbiano La.* ✣ *Take Poinsettia La. exit off I–5, go east, and turn right onto Batiquitos Dr., then right again onto Gabbiano La.* ☎ *760/931–0800* 🌐 *www.batiquitosfoundation.org.*

DID YOU KNOW?

Carlsbad village owes its name to John Frazier, who dug a well for his farm here in the 1880s. The water bubbling from it was soon found to have the same properties as water from the mineral wells of Karlsbad, Bohemia (now Karlovy Vary, Czech Republic, but then under the sway of the Austro-Hungarian Empire). When Frazier and others went into the business of luring people to the area with talk of the healing powers of the local mineral water, they changed the name of the town from Frazier's Station to Carlsbad, to emphasize the similarity to the famous Bohemian spa.

15

FAMILY Fodor'sChoice ★ **Flower Fields at Carlsbad Ranch.** The largest bulb production farm in Southern California has hillsides abloom here each spring, when thousands of Giant Tecolote ranunculus produce a stunning 50-acre display of color against the backdrop of the blue Pacific Ocean. Other knockouts include the rose gardens—with examples of every All-American Rose Selection award-winner since 1940—and a historical display of Paul Ecke poinsettias. Open to the public during this time, the farm offers family activities that include wagon rides, panning for gold, and a kids' playground. ✉ *5704 Paseo del Norte, east of I–5* ☎ *760/431–0352* 🌐 *www.theflowerfields.com* 🎫 *$14* ⏲ *Closed mid-May–Feb.*

FAMILY Fodor'sChoice ★ **LEGOLAND California Resort.** The centerpiece of a development that includes resort hotels, a designer discount shopping mall, an aquarium, and a water park, LEGOLAND has rides and diversions geared to kids ages 2 to 12. Fans of *Star Wars*, and building Legos in general, should head straight to *Star Wars* **Miniland,** where you can follow the exploits of Yoda, Princess Leia, Obi-Wan, Anakin, R2, Luke, and the denizens of the *Star Wars* films. There's also **Miniland U.S.A.,** which features a miniature, animated, interactive collection of U.S. icons that were constructed out of 34 million LEGO bricks! **LEGO Heartlake City,** features LEGO Friends and Elves, and you can test your ninja skills in **LEGO NINJAGO WORLD.**

If you're looking for rides, **NINJAGO The Ride** uses hand gesture technology to throw fire balls, shock waves, ice, and lightning to defeat villains in this interactive 4-D experience. Journey through ancient Egyptian ruins in a desert roadster, scoring points as you hit targets with a laser blaster at **Lost Kingdom Adventure.** Or, jump on the **Dragon Coaster,** an indoor/outdoor steel roller coaster that goes through a castle. Don't let the name frighten you—the motif is more humorous than scary. Kids ages 6 to 13 can stop by the **Driving School** to drive speed-controlled cars (not on rails) on a miniature road; driver's licenses are awarded after the course. Junior Driving School is the pint-size version for kids 3 to 5.

Bring bathing suits—there are lockers at the entrance and at Pirate Shores—if you plan to go to **Soak-N-Sail**, which has 60 interactive features, including a pirate shipwreck–theme area. You'll also need your swimsuit for **LEGOLAND Water Park,** where an additional $30 gives you access to slides, rides, rafts, and the CHIMA Water Park, as well as Surfer's Bay with competitive water raceways and a "spray ground" with water jets.

Be sure to try Granny's Apple Fries, Castle Burgers, and Pizza Mania for pizzas and salads. The Market near the entrance has excellent coffee, fresh fruit, and yogurt. The LEGOLAND Hotel is worth a visit even if you're not staying overnight. There are activities and a LEGO pit in the lobby that will entertain kids while parents recover with a cocktail. **■ TIP→ The best value is one of the Hopper Tickets that give you one admission to LEGOLAND plus Sea Life Aquarium and/or the LEGOLAND Water Park for $119. These can be used on the same day or on different days. Purchase tickets online for discounted pricing. Go midweek to avoid the crowds.** ✉ *1 Legoland Dr.* ✥ *Exit I–5 at Cannon Rd. and follow signs east ¼ mile* ☎ *760/918–5346* 🌐 *www.legoland.com/california* 🎟 *LEGOLAND $95 adults, $89 children; parking $15; water park additional $30; hopper ticket $119* ⏲ *Closed Tues. and Wed. Sept.–Feb.*

WORTH NOTING

Carlsbad Mineral Water Spa. Remnants from late 1800s, including the original well dug by John Frazier and a monument to him, are found here. The elaborately decorated stone building houses a small day spa and the Carlsbad Water Company, a 21st-century version of Frazier's waterworks, where the Carlsbad water is still sold. Spa treatment packages range from one hour to three hours; treatments include combinations of wraps, alkaline mineral baths, mud facials, and full-body massages at prices from $99 to $249. ✉ *2802 Carlsbad Blvd.* ☎ *760/434–1887* 🌐 *www.carlsbadmineralspa.com.*

Leo Carrillo Ranch Historic Park. This was a real working ranch with 600 head of cattle owned by actor Leo Carrillo, who played Pancho in the *Cisco Kid* television series in the 1950s. Before Carrillo bought the spread, known as Rancho de Los Kiotes, in 1937, the rancho was the home of a band of Luiseno Indians. Carrillo's hacienda and other buildings have been restored to reflect the life of the star when he hosted his Hollywood friends for long weekends in the country. Four miles of trails take visitors through colorful native gardens to the cantina, washhouse, pool and cabana, barn, and stable that Carrillo used. You can tour these buildings on weekends when guided tours are offered twice daily. After Carrillo's death in 1961, the ranch remained in the family until 1979, when part of the acreage was acquired by the city for a park. ✉ *6200 Flying Leo Carrillo La.* ☎ *760/476–1042* 🌐 *www.carrillo-ranch.org* 🎟 *Free* ⏲ *Closed Mon.*

FAMILY **Museum of Making Music.** Take an interactive journey through 100 years of popular music with displays of more than 500 vintage instruments and samples of memorable tunes from the past century. Hands-on activities include playing a digital piano, drums, guitar, and more. ✉ *5790 Armada Dr., east of I–5* ☎ *760/438—5996* 🌐 *www.museumofmaking-music.org* 🎟 *$10* ⏲ *Closed Mon.*

The spring blooms at the Flower Fields at Carlsbad Ranch are not to be missed.

FAMILY **Sea Life Aquarium.** Offering an educational and interactive underwater experience, the walk-through exhibits focus on creatures found in local waters including California lakes and streams and the cold water marine animals that live along the California coast. Other exhibits include an underwater acrylic tunnel that affords a deep sea (but dry) look at sharks, fish, and invertebrates. There's a seahorse kingdom, interactive tide pools, jelly fish discovery and a chance for kids to build a LEGO coral reef. This park has a separate admission from LEGOLAND, although one- and two-day tickets including both venues are available. ✉ *1 LEGOLAND Dr.* ☎ *760/918–5346* 🌐 *www.visitsealife.com/california* 🎫 *$22* ☞ *Strollers not permitted June–Aug.*

WHERE TO EAT

$$$$ STEAKHOUSE ✕ **Argyle Steakhouse.** Even if you don't play golf, the elegant Argyle, occupying the Aviara Golf clubhouse, is an excellent choice for some of the finest cuts of locally sourced prime and Wagyu beef. The 18th green, Batiquitos Lagoon, and the Pacific Ocean create beautiful vistas from nearly every table, whether you are inside at the clubby bar or outside on the deck. **Known for:** excellent locally sourced prime and Wagyu beef; menu concierge; amazing lagoon views. $ *Average main: $46* ✉ *7447 Batiquitos Dr.* ☎ *760/603–9608* 🌐 *www.argylesteakhouse.com* ⏲ *No breakfast.*

$$ AMERICAN ✕ **Bistro West.** This busy spot, part of the West Inn complex, might be called the boisterous bistro, especially if you get there during happy hour, when it appears that all of Carlsbad is tipping back a few. The bistro specializes in comfort food; a huge chicken potpie tops the list that also includes rotisserie chicken, beef Stroganoff, and house-made pastas, burgers, and pizza. **Known for:** elevated comfort food; popular happy hour; great list of California wines. $ *Average main: $27* ✉ *4960 Ave. Encinas* ☎ *760/930–8008* 🌐 *www.bistrowest.com* 🧥 *Jacket required.*

$$ BARBECUE Fodor's Choice ★ **Campfire.** Paying tribute to community around the campfire, it's all about connecting here, both with the cool crowd and with the distinctive cocktail and dinner menus. Throughout the restaurant, subtle hints of the camping theme—canvas-backed booths, servers in flannels, leather menus branded with the Campfire log—are visible, but it's the food that will leave you setting up camp, as chefs work their magic behind glass walls grilling, roasting, and smoking almost every dish including the shrimp with pumpkin chili butter. **Known for:** smoky cocktails; wood-fired American fare. *Average main: $23* *2725 State St.* *760/637–5121* *www.thisiscampfire.com* *No lunch Mon.*

WHERE TO STAY

$$$ HOTEL **Beach Terrace Inn.** One of only four SoCal hotels directly on the sand, this former 1960s Best Western was remodeled in 2011 as a boutique inn with plantation shutters, luxurious linens, and open floor plans. **Pros:** in-room spa services; no resort fees; enormous rooms. **Cons:** lots of stairs; no kitchenettes; no restaurant or bar. *Rooms from: $269* *2775 Ocean St.* *760/729–5951* *www.beachterraceinn.com* *48 rooms* *Breakfast.*

$$ HOTEL FAMILY **Cape Rey Carlsbad.** Sea and sand loom large at this Hilton property, where the fitness center has an ocean view and guest rooms have sitting areas so you can easily enjoy the sea views and breezes when you're not exploring South Carlsbad State Park nearby. **Pros:** afternoon coastal breezes; 150 steps from the beach; shuttle service to nearby sites. **Cons:** on main highway; resort fee; some rooms face the parking lot. *Rooms from: $229* *1 Ponto Rd.* *760/602–0800* *www.caperey.com* *215 rooms* *No meals.*

$$ HOTEL FAMILY **Carlsbad Inn Beach Resort.** On the main drag and with direct access to the beach, this sprawling inn and time-share condominium complex is popular with families and has a variety of rooms, ranging from cramped to large, including many with ocean views, balconies, and kitchenettes, and some with fireplaces and hot tubs. **Pros:** on the beach; walking distance to shops and restaurants; warm ambience. **Cons:** lots of kids; can be noisy; tiny pool. *Rooms from: $209* *3075 Carlsbad Blvd.* *760/434–7020, 800/235–3939* *www.carlsbadinn.com* *61 rooms* *No meals.*

$$ HOTEL FAMILY **Legoland Hotel.** This is the place for the family that eats, sleeps, and lives LEGOs. **Pros:** ocean views from some rooms; dive-in movies at the pool; tempting hands-on activities throughout the hotel. **Cons:** frequently sells out; no romance here. *Rooms from: $179* *5885 The Crossings Dr.* *887/534-6526* *www.legoland.com/california* *250 rooms* *Breakfast.*

$$ HOTEL FAMILY Fodor's Choice ★ **Ocean Palms Beach Resort.** Just 40 steps from the sand, bring your kids (furry or not) to this delightful pet- and family-friendly hotel where the staff go out of their way to please guests. **Pros:** no resort fees; helpful staff; full kitchens; near shops and restaurants. **Cons:** some rooms face the street; inconsistent Wi-Fi in some rooms. *Rooms from: $169* *2950 Ocean St.* *760/729–2493* *www.oceanpalms.com* *52 rooms* *Breakfast.*

$$$$ RESORT FAMILY **Omni La Costa Resort & Spa.** This chic Spanish colonial oasis on 400 tree-shaded acres has ample guest rooms, two golf courses, and is known for being family-friendly, with plenty of kids activities (including a kids' club, a game room, eight swimming pools, three waterslides, and a water play

zone). **Pros:** adult-only pool; excellent kids' facilities; spa under the stars. **Cons:** very spread out, making long walks necessary; lots of kids; $30 daily resort fee. *Rooms from: $349 2100 Costa del Mar Rd. 760/438–9111, 800/439–9111 www.lacosta.com 748 rooms No meals.*

$$$$ RESORT FAMILY Fodor's Choice ★ **Park Hyatt Aviara Resort.** This former Four Seasons hilltop retreat is one of the most luxurious hotels in San Diego, boasting an Arnold Palmer–designed golf course, a tennis club, two pools, six restaurants, and views overlooking Batiquitos Lagoon and the Pacific among it's 250 acres. **Pros:** unbeatable location; best golf course in San Diego; surrounding nature trails. **Cons:** $25 resort fee and $35 parking; expensive; breakfast not included. *Rooms from: $309 7100 Aviara Resort Dr. 800/233–1234, 760/448–1234 www.parkhyattaviara.com Greens fees $255; 18 holes, 7007 yards, par 72 327 rooms No meals.*

$$ B&B/INN FAMILY **West Inn and Suites.** Coastal luxury meets Cape Cod practicality at this warm and friendly inn near the beach. **Pros:** full buffet breakfast; great service; guest shuttle service for Carlsbad area; near beaches. **Cons:** adjacent to railroad tracks and freeway; no water views. *Rooms from: $189 4970 Av. Encinas 760/448–4500, 866/431–9378 www.westinnandsuites.com 86 rooms Breakfast.*

15

SHOPPING

FAMILY **Carlsbad Premium Outlets.** With 90 stores, this outlet center is one of two designer factory outlets in the San Diego area. Within this attractively landscaped complex you can find Brooks Brothers, Nike, Tahari, Le Creuset, Coach, and Polo Ralph Lauren plus a few spots to grab a quick bite. *5620 Paseo Del Norte 760/804–9000, 888/790–7467 www.premiumoutlets.com/carlsbad.*

OCEANSIDE

8 miles north of Carlsbad on Rte. S21, 37 miles north of Downtown San Diego on I–5.

The beach culture is alive and well in Oceanside with surf shops, casual restaurants, museums, and a boardwalk that leads to the pier and harbor where surfers line up to catch the next wave. Numerous hotels are within walking distance of the city's best swimming and surfing beaches: Harbor Beach, brimming with beach activities and fun, and Buccaneer Beach, home to some of the best surfing in North County. And Camp Pendleton, the sprawling U.S. Marine base, lies at the north end of the city. **TIP→ If you'd like to see the base, visitors must be sponsored and vetted, with forms filled out four days in advance.**

Oceanside is also home to Mission San Luis Rey, the largest and one of the best-preserved California missions. The town's history extends back to the 1700s, when the Spanish friars walked along the California coast founding missions as they went. Today it celebrates its historic culture with the regionally exciting Oceanside Museum of Art, which displays the works of San Diego area artists. Residents and visitors gather weekly at the farmers' market and Sunset Market on Main Street, where shopping for fresh-picked produce is a pleasant pastime.

GETTING HERE AND AROUND

The northernmost of the beach towns, Oceanside, lies 8 miles north of Carlsbad via I–5; exit the freeway on Mission Avenue. If you go west, you'll come to the redeveloped downtown and harbor where you'll find most of the restaurants, lodgings, and attractions. Downtown Oceanside is quite walkable from the Transportation Center, where Amtrak, the Coaster, and Sprinter stop. Buses and taxis are also available at the Transportation Center.

ESSENTIALS

Visitor Information Oceanside Welcome Center. ✉ *928 N. Coast Hwy., Suite A* ☎ *760/721–1101, 800/350–7873* 🌐 *www.visitoceanside.org.*

EXPLORING

TOP ATTRACTIONS

California Surf Museum. A large collection of surfing memorabilia, going back to the earliest days of the sport, is on display here, along with old black-and-white photos, vintage boards, apparel, and accessories. ✉ *312 Pier View Way* ☎ *760/721–6876* 🌐 *www.surfmuseum.org* 🎟 *$5; free 1st Tues. of month.*

Oceanside Pier. At 1,954 feet, this is one of the longest piers on the West Coast. The water surrounding it is known for its surf breaks and good fishing. A restaurant, Ruby's Diner, stands at the end of the wooden pier's long promenade. ✉ *Pier View Way.*

FAMILY Fodor's Choice ★ **Old Mission San Luis Rey.** Known as the King of the Missions, the 18th, the largest, and the most prosperous of California's missions was built in 1798 by Franciscan friars under the direction of Father Fermin Lasuen to help educate and convert local Native Americans. The *sala* (parlor), the kitchen, a friar's bedroom, a weaving room, and a collection of religious art and old Spanish vestments convey much about early mission life. A location for filming Disney's 1950's *Zorro* TV series, the well-preserved mission is still owned by the Franciscans. ✉ *4050 Mission Ave.* ☎ *760/757–3651* 🌐 *www.sanluisrey.org* 🎟 *$7.*

WORTH NOTING

Oceanside Harbor. With 1,000 slips, this is North County's fishing, sailing, and water-sports center. On the south end of the harbor, the Oceanside Harbor Village has oyster bars, fish-and-chip shops, and an ice cream parlor where you can linger and watch the boats coming and going. If you fancy a day at sea, Helgren's Sportfishing can arrange whale-watching and harbor tours. ✉ *1540 Harbor Dr. N* ☎ *760/435–4000* 🌐 *www.oceansideharborvillage.com.*

Oceanside Museum of Art. Housed in side-by-side buildings designed by two Southern California modernist architects—Irving Gill and Frederick Fisher—the museum showcases contemporary art exhibitions including paintings, photography, sculptures, furniture, quilts, and architectural glass by San Diego area artists. ✉ *704 Pier View Way* ☎ *760/435–3720* 🌐 *www.oma-online.org* 🎟 *$8; free 1st Sun. of every month* ⊙ *Closed Mon.*

The Wave Waterpark. A 3-acre water park in the neighboring city of Vista is one of the few places in the country with a flowrider, a type of standing wave that allows riders on bodyboards to turn, carve, and slash almost as though they were surfing on a real wave. If you haven't learned how to do that, you can tube down the park's own river or slip down the 35-foot waterslide. There's even a lap pool for serious swimmers. ✉ *101 Wave Dr., Vista* ☎ *760/940–9283* 🌐 *www.thewave-waterpark.com* 🎟 *$20* ⏱ *Closed Oct.–May 26.*

WHERE TO EAT

$ SEAFOOD ✕ **Harbor Fish & Chips.** Pick up a basket of fresh-cooked fish-and-chips at this dive and you're in for a treat. The shop has been serving clam chowder, shrimp cocktail, and fish sandwiches since 1969. **Known for:** fresh coleslaw made from scratch; great prices; affordable daily specials; flavorful battered fish. $ *Average main: $12* ✉ *276 S. Harbor Dr.* ☎ *760/722–4977* 🌐 *www.harborfishandchips.net.*

$$ AMERICAN FAMILY Fodor's Choice ★ ✕ **Flying Pig Pub & Kitchen.** This meat-focused eatery fills bellies with farm-to-table artisanal cuisine like buttermilk-breaded calamari, Prince Edward Island mussels, and a pork cutlet with a side of mash and grits. Add a sunny-side up farm egg to your burger, chop, shank, or house-made pasta, and if you're into sauces, chef is on-point with lick-your-plate gravies based with garlic, onions, and herbs. **Known for:** rustic American cuisine; craft beers on tap; house-made pasta, bread, and bacon; natural prime-grade steaks seared in cast-iron skillet. $ *Average main: $18* ✉ *626 S. Tremont St.* ☎ *760/453–2940* 🌐 *www.flyingpigpub-kitchen.com* ⏱ *No breakfast or lunch.*

$$$ SEAFOOD ✕ **333 Pacific.** Directly across from Oceanside Pier you'll find Oceanside's most upscale restaurant which specializes in seafood dishes in an elegant, art deco setting. It's worth visiting for the ocean views and appetizers and sides like cayenne-honey Brussels sprouts, rosemary-truffle fries, and coconut lime risotto. **Known for:** martinis; weekly dinner specials. $ *Average main: $35* ✉ *333 N. Pacific St.* ☎ *760/433–3333* 🌐 *www.333pacific.com* ⏱ *No breakfast. No lunch Mon.–Thurs.*

WHERE TO STAY

$ HOTEL Fodor's Choice ★ 🏨 **Courtyard Marriott Oceanside.** Close proximity to the beach and train, coupled with plenty of modern amenities, make this SoCal-style Marriott Oceanside's best lodging. **Pros:** convenient location; five wheelchair-accessible rooms; quality amenities. **Cons:** breakfast not included; no ocean views. $ *Rooms from: $139* ✉ *3501 Seagate Way* ☎ *760/966–1000* 🌐 *www.courtyardoceanside.com* *142 rooms* 🍴 *No meals.*

$ HOTEL 🏨 **Oceanside Marina Suites.** Come for the proximity to water: these unusually large rooms and one- and two-bedroom suites, with fireplaces and expansive balconies in many, are on a spit of land, surrounded by water and cool ocean breezes on all sides. **Pros:** water views; spacious rooms; free parking. **Cons:** marina location noisy and busy on weekends; standards are timeworn; minimal breakfast. $ *Rooms from: $109* ✉ *2008 Harbor Dr. N* ☎ *760/722–1561, 800/252–2033* 🌐 *www.omihotel.com* *57 rooms* 🍴 *Breakfast.*

SHOPPING

Sunset Market. Every Thursday night 5–9 pm, Oceanside's Main Street comes alive with food stalls, a farmers' market, live music, and an arts and crafts fair. ✉ *316 Mission Ave.* ✣ *Corner of Pier View Way and S. Tremont St.* ☎ *760/754–4512* 🌐 *www.mainstreetoceanside.com.*

INLAND NORTH COUNTY AND TEMECULA

Long regarded as San Diego's beautiful backyard, replete with green hills, quiet lakes, and citrus and avocado groves, inland San Diego County and the Temecula wine country are among the fastest-growing areas in Southern California. Subdivisions, many containing palatial homes, now fill the hills and canyons around Escondido and Rancho Bernardo. As the premium winemaking region of Southern California, Temecula's Mediterranean climate produces award-winning blends, ideal for those who want to tour local vineyards after a stroll through historic Old Town center or a round of golf on any one of Temecula's championship courses. Growth notwithstanding, inland San Diego County still has such natural settings as the San Diego Zoo Safari Park, Rancho Bernardo, and the destination spas like the renowned Golden Door Spa and Cal-a-Vie Health Spa.

RANCHO BERNARDO

23 miles northeast of Downtown San Diego on I–15.

Rancho Bernardo straddles a stretch of I–15 between San Diego and Escondido and is technically a neighborhood of San Diego. Originally sheep- and cattle-grazing land, it was transformed in the early 1960s into a planned suburban community, one of the first, and a place where many wealthy retirees settled down. It's now home to a number of high-tech companies, the most notable of which is Sony. If you want to spend some time at the nearby San Diego Zoo Safari Park, this community, home of the Rancho Bernardo resort, makes a convenient and comfortable headquarters for a multiday visit.

WHERE TO EAT

$$$ AMERICAN Fodor's Choice ★

✕ **AVANT.** The appropriately named AVANT—meaning stylistically advanced and original—delivers contemporary California cuisine in an upscale setting. Dark woods, leather chairs, and pillar-candle chandeliers adorn the mission-style dining room where live music is performed Thursday–Saturday night. **Known for:** grass-fed rib eye; their own double-barrel reposado tequila; live music Thursday–Saturday nights. *Average main: $35 ✉ Rancho Bernardo Inn, 17550 Bernardo Oaks Dr. ☎ 866/990–6845 ⊕ www.avantrestaurant.com ⊙ No breakfast or lunch.*

$$ EUROPEAN

✕ **The Barrel Room.** A refined-English pub ambience and a European-inspired menu set the tone for the unpretentious creations of chef Trevor Chappell. Shareable plates include charcuterie boards, lamb chops with red chimichurri, and pistachio-crusted sea bass with cipollini risotto, while the Farro shrimp salad is a meal in itself. **Known for:** wine-tasting events; plates to share. *Average main: $24 ✉ The Plaza, 16765 Bernardo Center Dr. ☎ 858/673–7512 ⊕ www.tbrsd.com.*

WHERE TO STAY

$$$ RESORT FAMILY

Rancho Bernardo Inn. The gorgeous, flower-decked 265-acre grounds draw a sophisticated clientele looking for a golf and spa getaway. **Pros:** excellent service; popular golf course; website offers great packages and specials. **Cons:** walking required in spacious grounds;

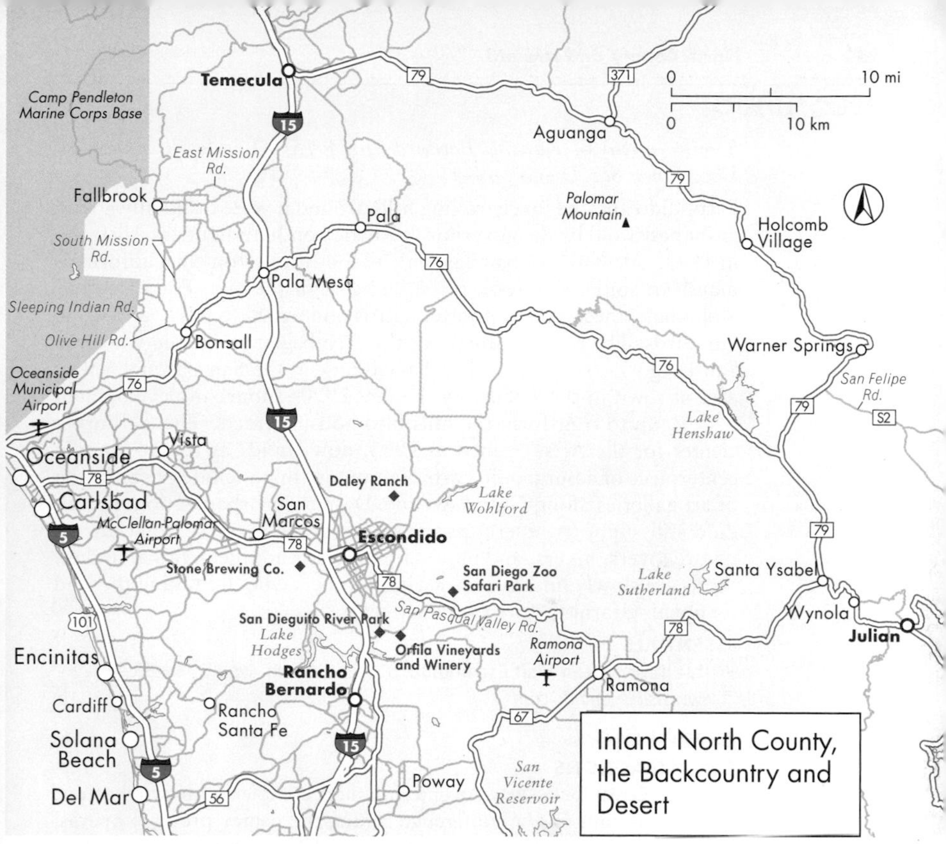

sections of hotel are showing signs of age; day use of spa amenities costs extra. *Rooms from: $289* ✉ *17550 Bernardo Oaks Dr., San Diego* ☎ *858/675–8500, 888/476–4417* 🌐 *www.ranchobernardoinn.com* *Greens fees $103, 18 holes, 6631 yards, par 72* *287 rooms* *No meals.*

SHOPPING

Bernardo Winery. A trip to the oldest operating winery in Southern California, founded in 1889 and run by the Rizzo family since 1928, feels like traveling back to early California days; some of the vines on the former Spanish land-grant property have been producing grapes for more than 100 years. Most of the grapes now come from other wine-growing regions. A collection of quaint shops surrounds the winery. V's Coffee Shoppe has fresh pastries and charcuterie plates and Cafe Merlot serves lunch daily except Monday. Shops sell cold-pressed olive oil and other gourmet goodies, as well as apparel, home-decor items, and arts and crafts. A farmers' market is held Friday 9 am–1 pm, and there's live music on the Tasting Room Patio Sunday 2–5 pm. ✉ *13330 Paseo Del Verano N, San Diego* ☎ *858/487–1866* 🌐 *www.bernardowinery.com* *Winery free, tastings $10.*

ESCONDIDO

8 miles north of Rancho Bernardo on I–15, 31 miles northeast of Downtown San Diego on I–15.

Escondido and the lovely rolling hills around it were originally a land grant bestowed by the governor of Mexico on Juan Bautista Alvarado in 1843. The Battle of San Pasqual, a bloody milestone in California's march to statehood, took place just east of the city. For a century and a half, these hills supported citrus and avocado trees, plus large vineyards. The rural character of the area began to change when the San Diego Zoo established its Safari Park in the San Pasqual Valley east of town in the 1970s. By the late 1990s suburban development had begun to transform the hills into housing tracts. The California Center for the Arts, opened in 1993, now stands as the downtown centerpiece of a burgeoning arts community that includes a collection of art galleries along Grand Avenue. Despite its urbanization, Escondido still supports several pristine open-space preserves that attract nature lovers, hikers, and mountain bikers. And, the area's abundant farms are slowly luring award-winning chefs who are taking the lead on opening farm-to-fork establishments.

ESSENTIALS

Visitor Information Visit Esconidido. ✉ *235 E. Grand Ave.* ☎ *760/839–4777* 🌐 *www.VisitEscondido.com.*

EXPLORING

TOP ATTRACTIONS

FAMILY **California Center for the Arts.** An entertainment complex with two theaters, an art museum, and a conference center, the center presents operas, musicals, plays, dance performances, and symphony and chamber-music concerts. Performers conduct free workshops for children; check the website for dates. The museum, which focuses on 20th-century art, occasionally presents blockbuster exhibits that make a side trip here worthwhile. ✉ *340 N. Escondido Blvd.* ☎ *800/988–4253 box office, 760/839–4138 museum* 🌐 *artcenter.org* 🎫 *Museum $8* ⏲ *Closed Mon.*

FAMILY **Daley Ranch.** A 3,058-acre conservation area and historic ranch site is laced with more than 20 miles of multipurpose trails for hikers, mountain bikers, and equestrians. The 2.4-mile Boulder Loop affords sweeping views of Escondido, and the 2.5-mile Ranch House Loop passes two small ponds, the 1928 Daley family ranch house, and the site of the original log cabin. Private cars are prohibited on the ranch, but there's free parking just outside the entrance. Free naturalist-guided hikes are offered on a regular basis; call for schedule. Leashed dogs permitted. ✉ *3024 La Honda Dr.* ☎ *760/839–4680* 🌐 *www.daleyranch.org* 🎫 *Free.*

FAMILY Fodor's Choice ★ **San Diego Zoo Safari Park.** A branch of the San Diego Zoo, 35 miles to the north, the 1,800-acre preserve in the San Pasqual Valley is designed to protect endangered species from around the world. Exhibit areas have been carved out of the dry, dusty canyons and mesas to represent the animals' natural habitats in various parts of Africa and Asia.

The best way to see these preserves is to take the 25-minute, 2½-mile Africa tram safari, included with admission. As you pass in front of the large, naturally landscaped enclosures, you can see animals bounding across prairies and mesas as they would in the wild. More than 3,500 animals of more than 400 species roam or fly above the expansive grounds. Predators are separated from prey by deep moats, but only the elephants, tigers, lions, and cheetahs are kept in enclosures. Good viewpoints are at the Elephant Viewing Patio, African Plains Outlook, Kilmia Point. ■ **TIP→ Prepare for summer heat. Wear a hat, cool clothing, and drink plenty of water; water refills are free. Also walk in the shade whenever possible. In summer, when the park stays open late, the trip is especially enjoyable in the early evening, when the heat has subsided and the animals are active and feeding. When the tram travels through the park after dark, sodium-vapor lamps illuminate the active animals. Photographers with zoom lenses can get spectacular shots of zebras, gazelles, and rhinos.**

For a more focused view of the park, you can take one of several other safaris that are well worth the additional charge. You can choose from several behind-the-scenes safaris, fly above it all via the zip-line safari, or get up close to giraffes and rhinos on a Caravan safari.

The park is as much a botanical garden as a zoo, serving as a "rescue center" for rare and endangered plants. Unique gardens include cacti and succulents from Baja California, a bonsai collection, a fuchsia display, native plants, and protea.

The **Lion Camp** gives you a close-up view of the king of beasts in a slice of African wilderness complete with sweeping plains and rolling hills. As you walk through this exhibit, you can watch the giant cats lounging around through a 40-foot-long window. The last stop is a research station, where you can see them all around you through glass panels.

The ticket booths at **Nairobi Village,** the park's center, are designed to resemble the tomb of an ancient king of Uganda. Animals in the **Petting Kraal** here affectionately tolerate tugs and pats and are quite adept at posing for pictures with toddlers. At the **Congo River Village** 10,000 gallons of water pour each minute over a huge waterfall into a large lagoon. **Hidden Jungle,** an 8,800-square-foot greenhouse, is a habitat for creatures that creep, flutter, or just hang out in the tropics. Gigantic cockroaches and bird-eating spiders share the turf with colorful butterflies and hummingbirds and oh-so-slow-moving two-toed sloths. **Lorikeet Landing** holds 75 of the loud and colorful small parrots—you can buy a cup of nectar at the aviary entrance to induce them to land on your hand. The park's newest project is the **Tull Family Tiger Trail,** a Sumatran tiger habitat opened in 2014, where you can get face-to-face (with a glass between) with the gorgeous cats. The 5-acre exhibit features a waterfall and swimming hole, and addresses poaching and other environmental threats to the species.

All the park's walk-to exhibits and animal shows (included in admission) are entertainingly educational. The gift shops are well worth a visit for their limited-edition items. There are lots of restaurants, snack bars, and some picnic areas. Rental lockers, strollers, and wheelchairs are available. You can also arrange to stay overnight in the park in summer on a Roar and Snore Sleepover ($140 and up, plus admission). ✉ *15500 San Pasqual Valley Rd.* ✥ *Take I–15 north to Via Rancho Pkwy. and follow signs for 6 miles* ☎ *760/747–8702* 🌐 *www.sdzsafaripark.org* 🎟 *$52 one-day pass including Africa tram ride; multipark and multiday passes are available; special safaris are extra starting at $50 per person; parking $12.*

WORTH NOTING

Escondido Arts Partnership Municipal Gallery. This gallery showcases works by local artists, with regular exhibitions and year-round special events. ✉ *262 E. Grand Ave.* ☎ *760/480–4101* 🌐 *www.escondidoarts.org* 🎟 *Free* 🕒 *Closed Sun., Mon., and Wed.*

Escondido History Center. This outdoor museum adjacent to the California Center for the Arts in Grape Day Park consists of several historic buildings moved here to illustrate local development from the late 1800s, when grape growing and gold mining supported the economy. Exhibits include the 1888 Santa Fe Depot, Escondido's first library, the Bandy Blacksmith shop, a furnished 1890 Victorian house, and other 19th-century buildings. **■ TIP→ Download their app, Explore Escondido, for a self-guided tour of the historic district, organic farms, wineries, museums, and more.** ✉ *321 N. Broadway* ☎ *760/743–8207* 🌐 *www.escondidohistory.com* 🎟 *$3 suggested donation* 🕒 *Closed Fri., Sun., and Mon.*

Orfila Vineyards & Winery. Visitors here can taste award-winning Syrah, Sangiovese, and Viognier produced from grapes harvested from the 10,000-acre vineyard. The Rose Arbor has a picnic area, and there's a gift shop with wine-related merchandise. There's also a tasting room on Main Street in Julian. ✉ *13455 San Pasqual Rd.* ☎ *760/738–6500* 🌐 *www.orfila.com* 🎟 *Tastings $12.*

FAMILY **San Dieguito River Park.** The park maintains several hiking and walking trails in the Escondido area. These are part of an intended 70-mile-long Coast to Crest Trail that will eventually link the San Dieguito Lagoon near Del Mar with the river's source on Volcan Mountain, north of Julian. Among the existing trails are three that circle Lake Hodges: the **North Shore Lake Hodges Trail;** the **Piedras Pintadas Trail,** which informs about native American Kumeyaay lifestyles and uses for native plants; and the **Highland Valley Trail,** the first mile of which is the Ruth Merrill Children's Walk. Three trails in **Clevenger Canyon** lead to sweeping views of the San Pasqual Valley. **■ TIP→ Visit the website for a list of upcoming free guided hikes and pay attention to signs warning against leaving valuables in your car.** ✉ *18372 Sycamore Creek Rd.* ☎ *858/674–2275* 🌐 *www.sdrp.org* 🎟 *Free.*

FAMILY **Stone Brewing Co.** One of the fastest-growing companies in the United States, Stone staked out a hilltop overlooking Escondido to create, brew, and sell its beloved craft beer. It's a gorgeous, solar-run facility, filled with massive stainless steel tanks used in beer-making. You can take a tour to see how the beer is made and get a taste, dine on farm-to-table fare at the on-site bistro, and purchase signature items in the company store. Thirty-six craft and specialty beers are always on tap in the tasting bar and the bistro, which has indoor and garden seating for lunch and dinner. ■**TIP→ Check their website for weekly events, including live music on the lawn during summer months.** ✉ *1999 Citracado Pkwy.* ☎ *760/294–7866* 🌐 *www.stonebrewing.com* 🎫 *Tours $3.*

WHERE TO EAT

It might not have coastal views and ocean breezes, but Escondido has recently lured several top chefs capitalizing on the surrounding farms in this untapped market. Don't be surprised to find an elegant French restaurant next to a hole-in-the-wall taco stand, along with a clientele as mixed as the area's cuisine. Despite the inland location, Grand Avenue has a string of charming downtown eateries, with local chefs serving farm-to-table dishes at a fraction of what you'd pay along the coast.

$$$ FRENCH FUSION ✕ **Bellamy's Restaurant.** Californian-French fare comes to Escondido at this fine-dining restaurant by French master chef Patrick Ponsaty. Live piano music, crystal chandeliers, and leather tufted chairs set the stage for a six-course tasting menu ($75) of market oysters, scallops with cauliflower mousse, and poached pear foie gras. **Known for:** California-French cuisine; upscale dining. $ *Average main: $28* ✉ *417 W. Grand Ave.* ☎ *760/747–5000* 🌐 *www.bellamysdining.com* ⏲ *No lunch Sat. Closed Sun.*

$$$ FRENCH ✕ **Vincent's.** This French restaurant is an excellent choice for dinner before an event at the nearby California Center for the Arts. Original paintings decorate the walls and crisp white tablecloths cover the tables, adorned with fresh flowers. **Known for:** half-off wine Wednesdays; weekly prix fixe menu; delicious tender beef cheeks; warm artesian breads with rich sauces. $ *Average main: $30* ✉ *113 W. Grand Ave.* ☎ *760/745–3835* 🌐 *www.vincentsongrand.com* ⏲ *Closed Sun. and Mon. No breakfast or lunch.*

$$$ MODERN AMERICAN ✕ **Vintana.** Don't let its location above the Lexus dealership dissuade you; this swanky restaurant is part of the Cohen Restaurant empire and it's designed as three restaurants in one: a formal glass-walled dining room; a lively patio with fire pits and cabanas; and the lobby bar with leather couches and a wine shop. No matter where you dine, try the macadamia-crusted sea bass or the skirt steak with blue cheese quesadillas, followed with a cocktail using one of the more than 140 vodkas. **Known for:** weekend brunch; nightly specials; large portions. $ *Average main: $30* ✉ *The Centre at Lexus Escondido, 1205 Auto Park Way* ☎ *760/745–7777* 🌐 *www.dinevintana.com.*

$$ AMERICAN Fodor's Choice ★ ✕ **The Wooden Spoon.** Former fine-dining chef Jesse Paul—who oversaw kitchens at Four Seasons Aviara, L'Auberge Del Mar, and Via Italia Trattoria—left it all behind to bring redefined comfort food to Escondido. In this casual mom-and-pop restaurant, it starts with seasonal produce gathered daily from eight local farms, followed by preparation and service from a tight-knit family-like staff. **Known for:** comfort food; supporting local farms; root beer floats. $ *Average main: $20* ✉ *805 E. Valley Pkwy.* ☎ *760/745–0266* 🌐 *www.woodenspoonsd.com* ⏲ *No dinner Mon. and Tues.*

With more than 40 wineries, most along Rancho California Road, Temecula is Southern California's premier winemaking region.

WHERE TO STAY

With the exception of the Welk Resort, which is now primarily a time-share property, Escondido has little to offer in the way of accommodations. The neighboring towns of Vista and San Marcos are home to two of the most luxurious destination spas in the nation.

$$$$ RESORT **Cal-a-Vie Health Spa.** At this destination spa—celebrities like Julia Roberts and Oprah Winfrey escape here for some serious R&R—you'll feel like you've died and gone to a pampering Provençal village heaven. **Pros:** exclusive spa haven; on 500 private acres; customized to health and fitness goals. **Cons:** no children under 16; three-day minimum stay; no TVs or alcohol might be an issue for some. *Rooms from: $4,675* *29402 Spa Havens Way, Vista* *760/945–2055* *www.cal-a-vie.com* *32 rooms* *All meals.*

$$$$ RESORT Fodor's Choice ★ **Golden Door.** Considered by many to be the world's best destination spa, the venerable Golden Door takes you on a journey to tranquillity, transformation, and self-realization during a seven-night stay; day passes are available. **Pros:** peaceful sanctuary; customized programs; luxury camp forms sisterhood; largest collection of Japanese art in the country. **Cons:** no alcohol, sugar, or salt; mostly appeals to women; expensive. *Rooms from: $8,850* *777 Deer Springs Rd., San Marcos* *760/744–5777* *www.goldendoor.com* *40 rooms* *All meals.*

$$ RESORT FAMILY **Welk Resort.** Built by bandleader Lawrence Welk in the 1960s, the property sprawls over 600 acres of rugged, oak-studded hillside and is family-friendly, with abundant children's activities. **Pros:** excellent theater; popular golf course; near the Safari Park. **Cons:** located outside the city; very spread-out; rooms may not always be available due to

time-sharing; time-share pitch. *Rooms from: $198* *8860 Lawrence Welk Dr.* *760/749–3000, 800/932–9355* *www.welkresorts.com* *714 rooms* *No meals.*

SHOPPING

Although farmland began to give way to suburbs in the 1990s, and the area's fruit, nut, and vegetable bounty has diminished, you can still find overflowing farm stands in the San Pasqual Valley and in Valley Center, just east of the city.

FAMILY **Bates Nut Farm.** Home of San Diego's largest pumpkin patch each fall, this family farm is where you might find a 200-pound squash. It also sells locally grown pecans, macadamia nuts, and almonds. On the 100 acres, there's a farm zoo, a picnic area, and a gift shop. *15954 Woods Valley Rd., Valley Center* *800/642–0348* *www.batesnutfarm.biz* *$5 parking fee in Oct. on weekends.*

Canterbury Gardens. Occupying an old winery, this shop specializes in giftware and seasonal decorative accessories for the home, plus it has a year-round selection of Christmas ornaments and collectibles by Christopher Radko, Mark Robert's Fairies, and Department 56. *2402 S. Escondido Blvd.* *760/746–1400* *www.canterburygardens.com* *Closed Sun.*

15

TEMECULA

29 miles from Escondido, 60 miles from San Diego on I–15 north to Rancho California Rd. east.

Once an important stop on the Butterfield Overland Stagecoach route and a market town for the huge cattle ranches surrounding it, Temecula (pronounced teh- *mec*-yoo-la) is now a developed wine region, designated the South Coast region, which also includes some wineries in San Diego County. Known for its gently rolling hills, the region is studded with ancient oak trees and vernal pools. French and Italian grapes thrive in the valley's hot climate, which has turned Temecula's wine route into a tourist attraction and weekend escape for San Diegans. Today there are more than 40 wineries open to the pubic, with plans to double that number by 2019. Winemakers are creating luscious blended reds and whites that resemble rich Rhones and Tuscan vintages. Because most of the wineries sell their bottles only at the wineries, it pays to stock up if you find something you especially enjoy.

Most of the wineries that line both sides of Rancho California Road offer tours and tastings (for a fee) daily and have creatively stocked boutiques, picnic facilities, and restaurants on the premises. Some wineries have opened luxury boutique lodgings and fine-dining restaurants. For shopping, restaurants, and museums, Old Town runs along historic Front Street on the west side of I–15. In addition to its visitor appeal, Temecula is also a suburban bedroom community for many who work in San Diego's North County. Between hot-air balloon rides over vineyards and wine tours by horse-drawn carriage, this romantic destination has plenty to offer for the wine lover, and everyone else.

TOUR OPTIONS

Several companies offer individual and group tours of the Temecula wine country with departures from San Diego and Temecula. Some include lunch or refreshments as part of the package.

Limousine Tours **Destination Temecula.** ✉ *28475 Old Town Front St., Suite F* ☎ *951/695–1232, 800/584–8162* 🌐 *www.destem.com.* **Grapeline Wine Tours.** ✉ *Office, 27286 Via Industria, Suite A* ☎ *951/693–5755* 🌐 *www.gogrape.com.* **Temecula Carriage Company.** ☎ *858/205–9161* 🌐 *www.temeculacarriageco.com.*

ESSENTIALS

Visitor Information **Visit Temecula Valley.** ✉ *28690 Mercedes St., Suite A* ☎ *951/491–6085* 🌐 *www.visittemeculavalley.com.* **Temecula Valley Winegrowers Association.** ✉ *29377 Rancho California Rd., Suite 203* ☎ *951/699–6586, 800/801–9463* 🌐 *www.temeculawines.org.*

EXPLORING

TOP ATTRACTIONS

Fodor's Choice ★ **Old Town Temecula.** Once a hangout for cowboys, Old Town has been updated and expanded to include boutique shops, good restaurants, a children's museum, and a theater, while retaining its Old West appearance. A walking tour put together by the **Temecula Valley Historical Society,** starting at the Temecula Valley Museum, covers some of the old buildings; most are identified with bronze plaques. **■ TIP→ Free maps can be downloaded from their website (www.temeculahistoricalsociety.org). Guided walking tours are hosted every Saturday (10 am–noon; $5) by the Temecula Valley Museum.** ✉ *Temecula* 🌐 *www.oldtowntemecula.com.*

WORTH NOTING

FAMILY **Pennypickle's Workshop** (*Temecula Children's Museum*). This is the imaginary home of Professor Phineas Pennypickle, where kids accompanied by parents enter a time machine that carries them through six rooms of interactive exhibits demonstrating perception and illusion, music making, flight and aviation, chemistry and physics, plus power and electricity. The shop stocks an array of educational toys, games, and books. Reservations are not taken, so be sure to get their early, especially during school vacations. ✉ *42081 Main St.* ☎ *951/308–6376* 🌐 *www.pennypickles.org* 🎫 *$5* ⏲ *Closed Mon.*

FAMILY **Santa Rosa Plateau Ecological Reserve.** This 9,000-acre wooded preserve provides a glimpse of what this countryside was like before the developers took over. Trails wind through ancient oak forests and past seasonal, vernal pools and rolling grassland. A visitor and operations center has interpretive displays and maps; some of the reserve's hiking trails begin here. There are designated trails for leashed dogs, horses, and mountain bikers. ✉ *39400 Clinton Keith Rd., Murrieta* ✣ *Take I–15 south to Clinton Keith Rd. exit and head west 5 miles* ☎ *951/677–6951* 🌐 *www.santarosaplateau.org* 🎫 *$4 per person; $1 for each horse or dog* ⏲ *Closed Mon.*

FAMILY **Temecula Valley Museum.** Adjacent to Sam Hicks Monument Park, this museum focuses on Temecula Valley history, including early Native American life, Butterfield stage routes, and the ranchero period. A hands-on interactive area for children holds a general store, photographer's studio, and ride-a-pony station. Outside there's a playground and picnic area. **■TIP→ A walking tour ($5) of Old Town Temecula is given every Saturday 10–noon.** ✉ *28314 Mercedes St.* ☎ *951/694–6450* 🌐 *www.temeculavalleymuseum.org* 🎟 *$5 suggested donation.*

Europa Village. You'll find three tasting rooms here, reflecting three European-style wineries: French Cabernet Sauvignon; Spanish Tempranillo; and Italian Pinot Grigio. You can walk through lush gardens and enjoy weekend entertainment. The Inn at Europa Village, perched on an adjacent hilltop, offers 10 guest rooms. ✉ *3347 La Serena Way* ☎ *951/216–3380* 🌐 *www.europavillage.com* 🎟 *Tastings $15 weekdays; $20 weekends.*

Fodor's Choice ★ **Hart Family Winery.** A perennial crowd-pleaser, this winery specializes in well-crafted red wines made by father-son winemakers Joe and Jim Hart. Joe, who started the winery in the 1970s with his wife, Nancy, focuses on growing grapes suited to the Temecula region's singular climate and soils—syrah, cabrenet Franc, and cabernet sauvignon might be expected, but they also produce little known varietals such as Aleatico, used in the winery's marvelous dessert wine. The reds are the stars, though, along with the amiable Hart family members themselves. ✉ *41300 Ave. Biona* ☎ *951/676–6300* 🌐 *www.hartfamilywinery.com* 🎟 *Tasting $12.*

Leoness Cellars. Rhone-style blends—along with killer views—are the specialties of this mountaintop facility. Winemaker Tim Kramer and his staff produce about a dozen and a half wines each year, of which you can select six. If you like reds, be sure to try the syrahs, which are almost always winners. Winery tours take in the vineyards and the winemaking areas. The tours require a reservation, as do wine-and-food pairing sessions that might include fruits and cheeses or, in the case of dessert wines, some chocolates. They have a large gift shop with country keepsakes, and a French restaurant open weekends. **■TIP→ Bring a jacket, as this tasting room can get chilly.** ✉ *38311 DePortola Rd.* ☎ *951/302–7601* 🌐 *www.leonesscellars.com* 🎟 *Tasting $16–$20; tours with tasting $22–$85.*

Miramonte Winery. At Temecula's hippest winery, perched on a hilltop, listen to Spanish-guitar recordings while sampling the slightly pricy opulente meritage, a supple Roussanne, or the sultry syrah. Owner Cane Vanderhoof's wines have earned dozens of awards. While you're enjoying your wine on the deck, order an artisan cheese plate. On Friday and Saturday night from 7 to 10, the winery turns into a local hot spot with tastings of signature wines ($20) and beer, live music, and dancing that spills out into the vineyards. ✉ *33410 Rancho California Rd.* ☎ *951/506–5500* 🌐 *www.miramontewinery.com* 🎟 *Tastings $15–$17, tours $75 (reservations required weekends).*

Mount Palomar Winery. One of the original Temecula Valley wineries, opened in 1969, Mount Palomar introduced Sangiovese grapes, a varietal that has proven perfectly suited to the region's soil and climate. New owners have transformed the homey winery into a grand Mediterranean villa with acres of gardens and trees. Some of the wines are made from grapes brought from Italy nearly 50 years ago. Try the dry Sangiovese or Bordeaux-style meritage. Annata's Bistro, open for lunch daily and for dinner Friday through Sunday, presents live entertainment on Friday nights. ✉ *33820 Rancho California Rd.* ☎ *951/676–5047* 🌐 *www.mountpalomar.com* 🎟 *Winery free, tasting $16 Mon.–Thurs., $20 Fri.– Sun.*

Wiens Family Cellars. A visit to this serious winery can be an enlightenment; request information cards for a full description of each vintage you taste, combinations of Cabernet Sauvignon, Cabernet Franc, Petite Syrah, Zinfandel, and Pinot Noir. The winery is known for its so-called Big Reds, which include Crowded, a four-grape blend; lighter Infinite Perspective, a three-grape blend; and a jammy Zinfandel. ✉ *35055 Via Del Ponte* ☎ *951/694–9892* 🌐 *www.wienscellars.com* 🎫 *Tastings $20.*

Fodor'sChoice ★ **Wilson Creek Winery & Vineyards.** One of Temecula's busiest tasting rooms sits amid inviting, parklike grounds. Wilson is known for its award-winning Petite Syrah and Almond Champagne, but the winery also produces appealing still wines. The viognier, reserve syrah, reserve zinfandel, and late-harvest zinfandel all merit a taste. The on-site Creekside Grill Restaurant serves sandwiches, salads, and seasonal entrées such as Mexican white sea bass. Dine inside or select a picnic spot, and the servers will deliver your meal to you. As a certified gluten-free restaurant, they have some incredible dishes including a vegetable potpie. For casual to-go items, they have the Courtyard Bar & Grill, and for overnight guests, the Wilson Creek Manor has nine suites within a luxurious 12,000 square-foot retreat. ✉ *35960 Rancho California Rd.* ☎ *951/699–9463* 🌐 *www.wilsoncreekwinery.com* 🎫 *Tasting $20.*

WHERE TO EAT

$ MEDITERRANEAN Fodor'sChoice ★ ✕ **The Goat & Vine.** At this vintage-meets-industrial style restaurant, don't be surprised to see a line outside the door, as patrons wait to partake of Mediterranean–Italian–American dishes made from scratch in the stone hearth kitchen. Nearly everything is produced in house, including the sauces, dressings, and breads baked with a sourdough starter dating back 120 years. **Known for:** stone hearth kitchen; house Sangria; sourdough pretzels. 💲 *Average main: $13* ✉ *41911 5th St.* ☎ *951/695–5600* 🌐 *www.thegoatandvine.com* ⏲ *No breakfast.*

$$ TUSCAN ✕ **Trattoria Toscana.** Don't be thrown off by the strip mall location or the simple 10-table setting; the food at Trattoria Toscana is about as authentic as it gets. The owners—California native Blythe Wilson and Sardinian-born chef Pietro Cinus—met while Wilson was exploring the Tuscan countryside and together they brought all things Italian to Temecula. **Known for:** dishes from Tuscany and Sardinia; special three-course dinners. 💲 *Average main: $20* ✉ *Palm Plaza, 26485 Ynez Rd. , between Overland and Winchester Dr.* ☎ *951/296–2066* 🌐 *www.trattoriatoscanaintemecula.com* ⏲ *Closed Tues.*

WHERE TO STAY

$$$ HOTEL Fodor'sChoice ★ 🏨 **Carter Estate Winery and Resort.** Enter by way of a long driveway lined with olive trees, past the automatic gates, and suddenly you're in a Mediterranean-inspired neighborhood of freestanding bungalows that overlook the vineyards and mountains. **Pros:** welcome bottle of wine; pool-side restaurant; use of facilities at South Coast Winery Resort. **Cons:** slow Wi-Fi; breakfast not included; rose gardens attract bees. 💲 *Rooms from: $250* ✉ *34450 Rancho California Rd.* ☎ *844/851–2138* 🌐 *www.carterestatewinery.com* 🛏 *60 rooms* 🍽 *No meals.*

$$ B&B/INN 🏨 **The Inn at Europa Village.** Offering a lovely hillside setting for an escape to the wine country, this 10-room bed-and-breakfast delights guests

with old-world charm and modern amenities, while providing the perfect spot to unplug (there are no TVs) and watch the world—and hot-air balloons—go by. **Pros:** privacy and scenery; delicious home-cooked breakfast; 2-fo-1 wine tasting at Europa Village. **Cons:** long walk to wineries; no TVs; two-night minimum stay on weekends. *Rooms from: $220 ✉ 33350 La Serena Way ☎ 877/676–7047 🌐 www.europa-village.com/inn 10 rooms Breakfast.*

$$$ HOTEL **Ponte Vineyard Inn.** Comfortable and relaxed digs offer vineyard and garden views and have an Old California feel, with lots of dark wood, leather furnishings, and open spaces. **Pros:** fire pits in garden; excellent service; live music on weekends. **Cons:** many weekend weddings. *Rooms from: $250 ✉ 35001 Rancho California Rd. ☎ 951/587–6688 🌐 www.pontevineyardinn.com 60 rooms No meals.*

$$ HOTEL **South Coast Winery Resort & Spa.** At Temecula's largest winery, this full-service resort offers richly appointed and highly private rooms surrounded by 38 acres of vineyards. **Pros:** elegantly appointed rooms; full-service resort; pool and spa. **Cons:** spread out property requires lots of walking; poor service; $19 resort fee. *Rooms from: $199 ✉ 34843 Rancho California Rd. ☎ 951/587–9463, 866/994–6379 🌐 www.southcoastwinery.com 132 rooms No meals.*

15

$ RESORT **Temecula Creek Inn.** Sprawling over 360 acres, this spacious property boasts rooms with private patios or balconies overlooking the championship golf course. **Pros:** beautiful grounds; top golf course; great views. **Cons:** simple furnishings; shows its age; location away from Old Town and wineries. *Rooms from: $149 ✉ 44501 Rainbow Canyon Rd. ☎ 951/694–1000, 888/976–3404 🌐 www.temeculacreekinn.com Green fees $60–$85, 27 holes, 6800 yards, par 36 130 rooms, 1 guesthouse No meals.*

SPORTS AND THE OUTDOORS

A Grape Escape Balloon Adventure. Enjoy a morning hot-air balloon lift-off from Europa Village Winery. *✉ 33475 La Serena Way ☎ 951/699–9987, 800/965–2122 🌐 www.hotairtours.com $159.*

California Dreamin'. Leave on a hot-air balloon ride from a private Temecula vineyard. Rates range from $148 to $178. *✉ 33133 Vista Del Monte Rd. ☎ 800/373–3359 🌐 www.californiadreamin.com.*

SHOPPING

Temecula Lavender Co. Owner Jan Schneider offers an inspiring collection of the herb that fosters peace, purification, sleep, and longevity. Bath salts, hand soaps, essential oil, even dryer bags to freshen up the laundry—she's got it all. *✉ 28561 Old Town Front St. ☎ 951/676–1931 🌐 www.temeculalavenderco.com.*

FAMILY **Temecula Olive Oil Company.** Ranch tours and complimentary tastings of locally pressed olive oil are offered at the Temecula Olive Oil Company, where you can find a selection of oils seasoned with garlic, herbs, and citrus. This Old Town shop has dipping and cooking oils, locally crafted oil-based soaps and bath products, and a selection of preserved and stuffed olives. *✉ 28653 Old Town Front St. ☎ 951/693–4029 🌐 www.temeculaoliveoil.com.*

THE BACKCOUNTRY AND JULIAN

The Cuyamaca and Laguna mountains to the east of Escondido—sometimes referred to as the backcountry by county residents—are favorite weekend destinations for hikers, bikers, nature lovers, stargazers, and apple-pie fanatics. Most of the latter group head to Julian, a historic mining town now better known for apple pie than for the gold once extracted from its hills.

JULIAN

62 miles from San Diego to Julian, east on I–8 and north on Rte. 79.

Gold was discovered in the Julian area in 1869, and gold-bearing quartz a year later. More than $15 million worth of gold was taken from local mines in the 1870s. Many of the buildings along Julian's Main Street and the side streets today date back to the gold-rush period; others are reproductions.

When gold and quartz became scarce, the locals turned to growing apples and pears. During the fall harvest season you can buy fruit, sip apple cider (hard or soft), eat apple pie, and shop for local original art, antiques, and collectibles. But spring is equally enchanting (and less congested), as the hillsides explode with wildflowers—thousands of daffodils, lilacs, and peonies. More than 50 artists have studios tucked away in the hills surrounding Julian; they often show their work in local shops and galleries. The Julian area comprises three small crossroads communities: Santa Ysabel, Wynola, and historic Julian. You can find bits of history, shops, and dining options in each community. Most visitors come to spend a day in town, but the hillsides support small bed-and-breakfast establishments for those who want to linger longer.

It's worth a side trip to Cuyamaca Rancho State Park, 15 miles south of Julian. Spread over more than 25,000 acres of meadows and forests, the park offers a beautiful outdoor experience with a lake, camps, picnic areas, and more than 100 hiking trails. For an inspirational desert view, stop at the lookout about 2 miles south of Julian on Route 79. The Sunrise Highway, passing through the Cleveland National Forest is the most dramatic approach to Julian.

ESSENTIALS

Visitor Information Julian Chamber of Commerce. ✉ *Town Hall, 2129 Main St.* ☎ *760/765–1857* 🌐 *www.visitjulian.com.*

EXPLORING

TOP ATTRACTIONS

FAMILY **Julian Pioneer Museum.** When the gold mines in Julian played out, the mobs of gold miners who had invaded it left, leaving behind discarded mining tools and empty houses. Today the Julian Pioneer Museum, a 19th-century brewery, displays remnants of that time, including pioneer clothing, a collection of old lace, mining tools, and original photographs of the town's historic buildings and mining structures. ✉ *2811 Washington St.* ☎ *760/765–0227* 🌐 *julianpioneermuseum.org* 🎟 *$3* 🕒 *Closed Mon.–Wed.*

Hot-air ballooning is available daily, year-round, in Temecula and flights typically last 60–75 minutes.

FAMILY **Observer's Inn.** One of the best ways to see Julian's star-filled summer sky is by taking a sky-tour at Mike and Caroline Leigh's observatory, with research-grade telescopes. The hosts guide you through the star clusters and galaxies, pointing out planets and nebulae. The guides also offer solar tours at 11 am, when you can get a good look at the sun using a telescope designed for this purpose. It's also an inn, if you wish to stay the night. Reservations are necessary for tours and lodging. ✉ *3535 Hwy. 79* ☎ *760/765–0088* 🌐 *www.observersinn.com* 🎟 *$30* ✍ *Reservations essential.*

Volcan Mountain Wilderness Preserve. The Volcan Mountain Foundation and San Diego Parks and Recreation manage this 3,000-acre preserve, where hikes challenge your stamina and views are stunning. A 5-mile trail through the preserve passes through Engelmann oak forest, native manzanita, and rolling mountain meadows to a viewpoint where the panorama extends north all the way to Palomar Mountain. On a clear day you can see Point Loma in San Diego. At the entrance you pass through gates designed by James Hubbell, a local artist known for his ironwork, wood carving, and stained glass. You can see splendid views from the Volcan Summit. Guided hikes on the Sky Island Trail and the Oak Walk Trail are offered regularly. ✉ *1209 Farmer Rd. (trailhead), north of Julian Town* ✥ *From Julian take Farmer Rd. to Wynola Rd., go east a few yards, and then north on continuation of Farmer Rd.* ☎ *760/765–2300* 🌐 *www.volcanmt.org* 🎟 *Free.*

WORTH NOTING

FAMILY Fodor's Choice ★ **Eagle Mining Company.** Five blocks east of the center of Julian you can take an hour-long tour of an authentic family-owned gold mine from 1870. Displays along the route include authentic tools and machinery, gold extraction process, and gold quartz–bearing veins. A small rock shop and gold-mining museum are also on the premises. ✉ *2320 C St.* ☎ *760/765–0036* 🌐 *www.theeaglemining.com* 🎫 *$10.*

WHERE TO EAT

$$ MODERN AMERICAN FAMILY Fodor's Choice ★ **✕ Jeremy's on the Hill.** For a quiet dinner, pleasant surroundings, and some of the best burgers around, Jeremy's is the place to go. Although the menu features grilled steak and locally grown pork and veggies, the stars are rack of lamb and bison meat loaf. **Known for:** great burgers; flash-fried Brussels sprouts; on-site sommelier. $ *Average main: $27* ✉ *4354 Hwy. 78* ☎ *760/765–1587* 🌐 *www.jeremysonthehill.com.*

$ CAFÉ **✕ Julian Pie Company.** The apple pies that made Julian famous come from the Smothers family bakery in a one-story house on Main Street. In pleasant weather you can sit on the front patio and watch the world go by while savoring a slice of hot pie—from Dutch apple to apple mountain berry crumb—topped with homemade cinnamon ice cream. **Known for:** sweet Dutch apple pie; frozen uncooked pies to go; flaky crust. $ *Average main: $8* ✉ *2225 Main St.* ☎ *760/765–2449* 🌐 *www.julianpie.com.*

$ CAFÉ FAMILY **✕ Julian Tea & Cottage Arts.** Sample finger sandwiches, scones topped with whipped cream, and lavish sweets, which are served during afternoon tea inside the Clarence King House, built by Will Bosnell in 1898. Regular sandwiches, soups, salads, and a children's tea are also available. **Known for:** homemade lemon curd and scones; bottomless tea; charming turn-of-the-century home. $ *Average main: $15* ✉ *2124 3rd St.* ☎ *760/765–0832, 866/765–0832* 🌐 *www.juliantea.com* ⏲ *Closed Tues. and Wed. No breakfast or dinner.*

$ BAKERY FAMILY Fodor's Choice ★ **✕ Moms Pie House.** In 1984, "Mom" (aka Anita Nichols) opened her first pie shop in the old Julian Café building. People lined the streets for a slice of the guilty pleasure, known for its buttery crust, not-too-sweet filling with local apples, and commitment to quality. **Known for:** pressed apple cider; cinnamon ice cream; baking classes. $ *Average main: $8* ✉ *2119 Main St.* ☎ *760/765–2472* 🌐 *www.momspiesjulian.com* ⏲ *No dinner.*

$$ SICILIAN **✕ Romano's Restaurant.** You can gorge on huge portions of antipasto, pizza, pasta, sausage sandwiches, and seafood in a cozy old house. Start with the generous antipasto platter that's big enough for the whole table. **Known for:** thin crust pizza; cozy setting; old-school Italian cooking. $ *Average main: $20* ✉ *2718 B St.* ☎ *760/765–1003* 🌐 *www.romanosrestaurantjulian.com.*

$ CAFÉ **✕ Soups 'n Such Cafe.** It's worth the wait for breakfast or lunch at this cozy café, where everything is fresh and made to order. The breakfast standout is eggs Benedict, both classic and vegetarian. **Known for:** combo soup, salad, and sandwich for $12; great BLT, homemade soups. $ *Average main: $15* ✉ *2000 Main St.* ☎ *760/765–4761* ⏲ *No dinner.*

$ PIZZA FAMILY ✕ **Wynola Pizza & Bistro.** Locals and San Diegans come to this quaint and casual indoor-outdoor restaurant for delicious, single-portion pies, such as pesto pizza, Thai chicken pizza, vegan pizza, and pulled pork pizza. Other items include chili, lasagna, seared Cajun salmon, and a killer fire-roasted artichoke dip served with homemade buffalo crackers. **Known for:** gourmet wood-fired pizza; summer Sunday barbecues from 11–4; weekday specials. *Average main: $15 4355 Hwy. 78, Santa Ysabel 760/765–1004 www.wynolapizza.com.*

JULIAN'S BLACK HISTORY

According to local history and old photos, the Julian area had a large population of African Americans in the years following the Civil War. Indeed, it was a black man, Fred Coleman, who discovered gold in Julian, and the Julian Hotel was founded and operated by Albert and Margaret Robinson, also black. Headstones recognizing the contributions of Julian's black pioneers continue to be placed in the old section of the Pioneer Cemetery.

WHERE TO STAY

$$ B&B/INN **Butterfield Bed and Breakfast.** This beautifully landscaped inn on a 3-acre hilltop is cordial and romantic, with knotty-pine ceilings, Laura Ashley accents, and rooms with nice touches, such as fireplaces or woodstoves and private entrances. **Pros:** great food that's dietary need–friendly; interesting and helpful hosts; secluded. **Cons:** very quiet; no room phones. *Rooms from: $185 2284 Sunset Dr. 760/765–2179, 800/379–4262 www.butterfieldbandb.com 5 rooms Breakfast.*

$ B&B/INN **Julian Gold Rush Hotel.** Built in 1897 by freed slave Albert Robinson and his wife, Margaret, this old hotel is Julian's only designated national landmark and offers antiques-filled rooms and cottage accommodations with private entrances and fireplaces. **Pros:** genuine historic hotel; convivial atmosphere; afternoon tea. **Cons:** small rooms; no TV. *Rooms from: $155 2032 Main St. 760/765–0201, 800/734–5854 www.julianhotel.com 16 rooms Breakfast.*

$ HOTEL **Julian Lodge.** Near shops, this small hotel is a replica of a late-19th-century inn and has rooms and public spaces furnished with antiques. **Pros:** in-town location; free parking; reasonable rates. **Cons:** simple appointments; mediocre breakfast; no view. *Rooms from: $125 2720 C St. 760/765–1420, 800/542–1420 www.julianlodge.com 23 rooms Breakfast.*

$$ HOTEL **Viejas Casino & Resort Hotel.** The last thing you expect to find at a hotel in the backcountry (albeit one steps from the casino and its restaurants) is sophisticated art and furnishings created by local artists. **Pros:** attentive service; well-appointed rooms; modern, clean resort. **Cons:** close to freeway; not great for kids. *Rooms from: $179 5000 Willows Rd., Alpine 619/445–5400, 800/938–2532 www.viejas.com 237 rooms No meals.*

$$ B&B/INN **Wikiup Bed and Breakfast.** Best known for its herd of llamas, this contemporary cedar-and-brick inn is decorated with romantic furnishings and offers guest rooms with fireplaces and outdoor hot tubs for stargazing. **Pros:** private entrances; pleasant surroundings. **Cons:** limited

facilities; decor may be a bit much for some; two-night minimum. *Rooms from: $185* *1645 Whispering Pines Dr.* *800/694–5487* *www.wikiupbnb.com* *5 rooms* *Breakfast.*

NIGHTLIFE

Nickel Beer Company. Some of the best brew in San Diego is served at this little beer bar that occupies an old jail in Julian. Owner Tom Nickel is considered one of the most creative brewers in the region and is always cooking up new recipes that win accolades from judges and fans. There are 16 taps and contents change regularly. On the weekends there's entertainment, and the patio is dog-friendly. *1458 Hollow Glen Rd.* *760/765–2337* *www.nickelbeerco.com.*

SHOPPING

The Julian area has a number of unique shops that are open weekends, but midweek hours vary considerably. In autumn locally grown apples, pears, nuts, and cider are available in town and at a few roadside stands. The best apple variety produced here is a Jonagold, a hybrid of Jonathan and Golden Delicious.

Birdwatcher. Wild-bird lovers can shop for birdhouses, birdseed, hummingbird feeders, guidebooks for serious birding, and bird-theme accessories, such as jewelry, apparel, and novelties. *2775 B St.* *760/765–1817* *www.thebirdwatcher.net.*

Santa Ysabel Art Gallery. On display here are works of fine art, including paintings, stained glass, sculptures, fiber, and other creations by local artists. *30352 Hwy. 78, Santa Ysabel* *760/765–1676* *www.santaysabelartgallery.com* *Closed Tues. and Wed.*

TRAVEL SMART SAN DIEGO

GETTING HERE AND AROUND

When traveling in the San Diego area, consider the big picture to avoid getting lost. Water lies to the west of the city. To the east and north, mountains separate the urban areas from the desert. If you keep going south, you'll end up in Mexico.

Downtown San Diego is made up of several smaller communities, including the Gaslamp Quarter and Balboa Park that you can easily explore by walking, driving, riding the bus or trolley, or taking a taxi. In the heart of the city, numbered streets run west to east and lettered streets run north to south. The business district around the Civic Center, at 1st Avenue and C Street, is dedicated to local government and commerce.

AIR TRAVEL

Flying time to San Diego is 5 hours from New York, 4 hours from Chicago, 3 hours from Dallas, and 45 minutes from Los Angeles.

AIRPORT

The major airport is San Diego International Airport (SAN), formerly called Lindbergh Field. All airlines depart and arrive at Terminal 1 and Terminal 2. Free, color-coded shuttles loop the airport and match the parking lot they serve: Lot 1 (green) on Harbor Drive is for long-term parking, and Economy Lot (blue) on Pacific Highway is for short-term parking. With only one runway serving two main terminals, San Diego's airport is too small to accommodate the heavy traffic of busy travel periods. Small problems including fog and rain can cause congested terminals and flight delays. Delays of 20–30 minutes in baggage claim aren't unusual.

Major construction in 2013 resulted in improved traffic flow, better parking, expanded waiting areas, additional gates, more shopping and dining options, and a public art collection that changes regularly. Shopping and dining options include these popular spots: Einstein Bros. Bagel, Best Buy Express, Brighton Collectibles, Be Relax Spa, Phil's Barbecue, and Stone Brewing. In addition, if you have a flight delay, consider catching a 10-minute cab ride to the Gaslamp Quarter for last minute shopping or a stroll around Downtown.

If you need travel assistance at the airport, Airport Ambassadors are stationed at the information centers in both terminals.

Airports San Diego International Airport. ✉ *3225 N. Harbor Dr., off I–5* ☎ *619/400–2400* 🌐 *www.san.org.*

GROUND TRANSPORTATION

San Diego International Airport is 3 miles from Downtown. Shuttle vans, buses, and taxis run from the Transportation Plaza, reached via the skybridges from Terminals 1 and 2. The cheapest and sometimes most convenient shuttle is the Metropolitan Transit System's Flyer Route 992, red-and-white-stripe buses that serve the terminals at 10- to 15-minute intervals between 5 am and 11 pm. These buses have luggage racks and make a loop from the airport to Downtown along Broadway to 9th Avenue and back, stopping frequently within walking distance of many hotels; they also connect with the San Diego Trolley and Amtrak. The $2.25 fare includes transfer to local transit buses and the trolley, and you should have exact fare (in coins or bills) handy. Information about the Metropolitan Transit System's shuttles and buses, the San Diego Trolley, and Coaster commuter train can all be found on the joint transit website 🌐 *www.transit.511sd.com.*

If you're heading to North County, the Flyer can drop you off across from the Santa Fe Depot, where you can take the Coaster commuter train as far north as Oceanside for $5.50.

Of the various airport shuttles, only SuperShuttle has tie-downs for wheelchairs.

Ground shuttle service is available between LAX and San Diego, but can be prohibitively expensive, with rates for the two-hour trip starting at $296, so a car rental may be a more economical option. All the shuttles listed at the end of this section offer the service.

Taxis departing from the airport are subject to regulated fares—($2.80 initial fee, $3 per mile). Taxi fare is about $20 plus tip to most Downtown hotels. The fare to Coronado runs about $30 plus tip. Limousine rates vary and are charged per hour, per mile, or both, with some minimums established.

Contacts Advanced Shuttle. ✉ *4350 Palm Ave., La Mesa* ☎ *800/719–3499, 619/466–6885* 🌐 *www.advancedshuttle.com.* **San Diego Transit.** ☎ *619/233–3004* 🌐 *transit.511sd.com.* **SuperShuttle.** ✉ *123 Caminio de la Riena* ☎ *800/974–8885* 🌐 *www.supershuttle.com.*

BOAT TRAVEL

Many hotels, marinas, and yacht clubs rent slips short term. Call ahead, because available space is limited. The San Diego and Southwestern yacht clubs have reciprocal arrangements with other yacht clubs.

Flagship Cruises takes you between Downtown and Coronado in a nostalgic, old-school ferry every hour from 9 am to 10 pm. The ride lasts about 15 minutes and costs $4.75 each way; bicycles and Segways are free.

San Diego SEAL Tours, operated by Old Town Trolley, combine the best of land and sea, departing from Seaport Village daily. After exploring picturesque San Diego neighborhoods, the bus-boat hybrid rolls right into the water for a cruise around the bay. The $42 tour is narrated with fun facts, too.

Ferry Contacts Flagship Cruises. ✉ *990 N. Harbor Dr.* ☎ *800/442–7847* 🌐 *www.flagshipsd.com.* **San Diego SEAL Tours.** ☎ *866/955–1677* 🌐 *www.sealtours.com.*

Marinas Best Western Island Palms Hotel & Marina. ✉ *2051 Shelter Island Dr.* ☎ *619/222–0561* 🌐 *www.islandpalms.com.* **The Dana on Mission Bay.** ✉ *1710 W. Mission Bay Dr.* ☎ *619/225–2141* 🌐 *www.thedana.com.* **Kona Kai Resort & Spa.** ✉ *1551 Shelter Island Dr.* ☎ *619/224–7547* 🌐 *www.resortkonakai.com.* **San Diego Marriott Marquis & Marina.** ✉ *333 W. Harbor Dr.* ☎ *619/230–8955* 🌐 *www.marriott.com.* **San Diego Yacht Club.** ✉ *1011 Anchorage La.* ☎ *619/221–8400* 🌐 *www.sdyc.org.* **Southwestern Yacht Club.** ✉ *2702 Qualtrough St.* ☎ *619/222–0438* 🌐 *www.southwesternyc.org.*

BUS AND TROLLEY TRAVEL

Under the umbrella of the Metropolitan Transit System, there are two major transit agencies in the area: San Diego Transit and North County Transit District (NCTD). You will need to buy a $2 compass card, available when you board for the first time, on which are loaded your destinations to use MTS. Day passes, available for 1 to 30 days and starting at $5, give unlimited rides on nonpremium regional buses and the San Diego Trolley. You can buy them from most trolley vending machines, at the Downtown Transit Store, and at Albertsons markets. A $14 Regional Plus Day Pass adds Coaster service and premium bus routes.

The bright-red trolleys of the San Diego Trolley light-rail system operate on three lines that serve Downtown San Diego, Mission Valley, Old Town, South Bay, the U.S. border, and East County. The trolleys operate seven days a week from about 5 am to midnight, depending on the station, at intervals of about 15 minutes. The trolley system connects with San Diego Transit bus routes—connections are posted at each trolley station. Bicycle lockers are available at most stations and bikes are allowed on buses and trolleys though space is limited. Trolleys can get crowded during morning and evening rush hours. Schedules are posted at each stop; on-time performance is excellent.

NCTD bus routes connect with Coaster commuter train routes between Oceanside and the Santa Fe Depot in San Diego. They serve points from Del Mar north to San Clemente, inland to Fallbrook, Pauma Valley, Valley Center, Ramona, and Escondido, with transfer points within the city of San Diego. NCTD also offers special express-bus service to Qualcomm Stadium for select major sporting events. The Sprinter light rail provides service between Oceanside and Escondido, with buses connecting to popular North County attractions.

San Diego Transit bus fares range from $2.25 to $5; North County Transit District bus fares are $4. You must have exact change in coins and/or bills. Pay upon boarding. Transfers are not included; the $5 day pass is the best option for most bus travel and can be purchased on board.

San Diego Trolley tickets cost $2.50 and are good for two hours, but for one-way travel only. Round-trip tickets are double the one-way fare.

Tickets are dispensed from self-service machines at each stop; exact fare in coins is recommended, although some machines accept bills in $1, $5, $10, and $20 denominations and credit cards. Ticket vending machines will return up to $10 in change. For trips on multiple buses and trolleys, buy a day pass good for unlimited use all day.

Bus and Trolley Information North County Transit District. ☎ *760/966-6500* 🌐 *www.gonctd.com.* **San Diego Transit.** ☎ *619/233-3004* 🌐 *transit.511sd.com.* **Transit Store.** ✉ *102 Broadway* ☎ *619/234-1060* 🌐 *www.sdmts.com.*

CAR TRAVEL

A car is necessary for getting around greater San Diego on the sprawling freeway system and for visiting the North County beaches, mountains, and desert. Driving around San Diego County is pretty simple: most major attractions are within a few miles of the Pacific Ocean. Interstate 5, which stretches north–south from Oregon to the Mexican border, bisects San Diego. Interstate 8 provides access from Yuma, Arizona, and points east. Drivers coming from the Los Angeles area, Nevada, and the mountain regions beyond can reach San Diego on I–15. During rush hours there are jams on I–5 and on I–15 between I–805 and Escondido.

There are a few border inspection stations along major highways in San Diego County, the largest just north of Oceanside on I–5 near San Clemente. Travel with your driver's license, and passport if you're an international traveler.

Gas is widely available in San Diego County, except in rural areas. Outlets are generally open 24 hours and accept major credit cards that can be processed at the pump. Full service is not available, but you will usually find window-washing tools next to a pump; water and air are available somewhere on the property. All fuel in California is unleaded and sold at three price levels. Pricing is per gallon pumped and varies widely by season, location, and oil company provider. In San Diego gas tends to cost about 15% more than it does in many other California cities.

PARKING

Meters in Downtown usually cost $1 to $2.50 an hour; enforcement is 10–8 every day but Sunday. **■TIP→ If you are headed to Horton Plaza, the mall validates for one hour with no purchase required.** Be extra careful around rush hour, when certain on-street parking areas become tow-away zones. Violations in congested areas can cost you $45 or more. In the evening and during events in Downtown, parking spaces are hard to find. Most Downtown hotels offer valet parking service. The Convention Center has nearly 2,000 spaces that go for $15 to $35 for event parking. On game day at PETCO Park, expect to pay $10 to $35 for a parking space a short walk from the stadium. Other Downtown lots cost $10–$45 per day.

Balboa Park and Mission Bay have huge free parking lots, and it's rare not to find a space, though it may seem as if you've parked miles from your destination.

Old Town has large lots surrounding the transit center, but parking spaces are still hard to find. Parking is more of a problem in La Jolla and Coronado, where you generally need to rely on hard-to-find metered street spots or expensive by-the-hour parking lots.

ROAD CONDITIONS

Highways are in good condition in the San Diego area. From 6 to 8:30 am and 3:30 to 6 pm, traffic is particularly heavy on I–5, I–8, I–805, and I–15. Before venturing into the mountains, check on road conditions; mountain driving can be dangerous. Check Caltrans or listen to radio traffic reports for information on the length of border waits from Mexico. For roadside assistance, dial 511 from a mobile phone.

RENTAL CARS

In California you must be 21 to rent a car, and rates may be higher if you're under 25. Some agencies will not rent to those under 25; check when you book. Children up to age eight or under 4'9" in height must be placed in safety or booster seats. For non–U.S. residents an international license is recommended but not required.

Rates fluctuate with seasons and demand, but generally begin at $39 a day and $250 a week for an economy car with air-conditioning, automatic transmission, and unlimited mileage. This doesn't include an 8.75% tax.

TAXI TRAVEL

Fares vary among companies. If you are heading to the airport from a hotel, ask about the flat rate, which varies according to destination; otherwise you'll be charged by the mile (which works out to $20 or so from any Downtown location). Taxi stands are at shopping centers and hotels; otherwise you must call and reserve a cab. For on-demand private transportation, Uber is readily available throughout San Diego County with competitive rates up to 40% less than that of a taxi. Travelers with the Uber app can submit a trip request through their smartphone. The companies listed *below* don't serve all areas of San Diego County. If you're going somewhere other than Downtown, ask if the company serves that area.

Taxi Companies Orange Cab. ☎ *619/223–5555* 🌐 *www.orangecabsandiego.net.* **Silver Cabs.** ☎ *619/280–5555* 🌐 *www.sandiegosilvercab.com.* **Yellow Cab.** ☎ *619/444–4444* 🌐 *www.driveu.com.*

TRAIN TRAVEL

Amtrak serves Downtown San Diego's Santa Fe Depot with daily trains to and from Los Angeles, Santa Barbara, and San Luis Obispo. Connecting service to Oakland, Seattle, Chicago, Texas, Florida, and points beyond is available in Los Angeles. Amtrak trains stop in San Diego North County at Solana Beach and Oceanside. You can obtain Amtrak timetables at any Amtrak station, or by visiting the Amtrak website.

Coaster commuter trains, which run daily between Oceanside and San Diego, stop at the same stations as Amtrak as well as others. The frequency is about every half hour during the weekday rush hour, with four trains on Saturday (with additional Friday and Saturday night service in spring and summer). One-way fares are $4 to $5.50, depending on the distance traveled. The Oceanside, Carlsbad, and Solana Beach stations have beach access. The Sprinter runs between Oceanside and Escondido, with many stops along the way.

Metrolink operates high-speed rail service ($17) between the Oceanside Transit Center and Union Station in Los Angeles.

Train vending machines accept all major credit cards. Reservations, which you can make online, are suggested for trains running on weekends between San Diego and Santa Barbara. Make your reservations early to get the best fares. For security reasons, Amtrak requires ticket holders to provide photo ID.

Information Coaster. ☎ *760/966–6500* 🌐 *www.gonctd.com/coaster.* **Metrolink.** ☎ *800/371–5465* 🌐 *www.metrolinktrains.com.*

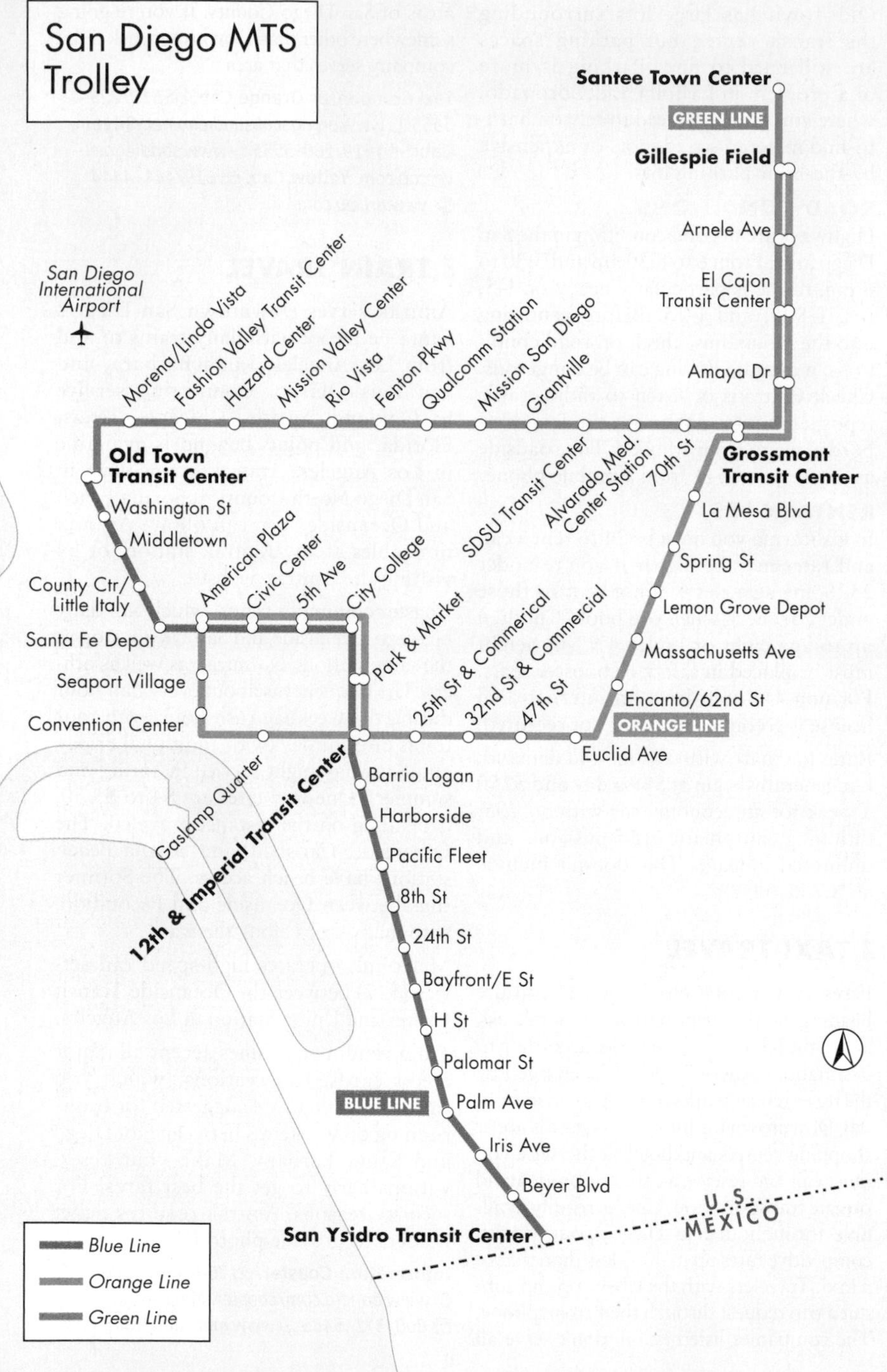
San Diego MTS Trolley
San Diego International Airport
Santee Town Center
GREEN LINE
Gillespie Field
Arnele Ave
El Cajon Transit Center
Amaya Dr
Grossmont Transit Center
La Mesa Blvd
Spring St
Lemon Grove Depot
Massachusetts Ave
Encanto/62nd St
ORANGE LINE
Euclid Ave
Morena/Linda Vista
Fashion Valley Transit Center
Hazard Center
Mission Valley Center
Rio Vista
Fenton Pkwy
Qualcomm Station
Mission San Diego
Grantville
Alvarado Med. Center Station
70th St
SDSU Transit Center
Old Town Transit Center
Washington St
Middletown
County Ctr/ Little Italy
Santa Fe Depot
Seaport Village
Convention Center
American Plaza
Civic Center
5th Ave
City College
Park & Market
25th St & Commercial
32nd St & Commercial
47th St
Gaslamp Quarter
12th & Imperial Transit Center
Barrio Logan
Harborside
Pacific Fleet
8th St
24th St
Bayfront/E St
H St
Palomar St
BLUE LINE
Palm Ave
Iris Ave
Beyer Blvd
San Ysidro Transit Center
U.S.
MEXICO
Blue Line
Orange Line
Green Line

ESSENTIALS

CUSTOMS AND DUTIES

Customs officers operate at the San Ysidro border crossing, at San Diego International Airport, and in the bay at Shelter Island.

You're always allowed to bring goods of a certain value back home without having to pay any duty or import tax. But there's a limit on the amount of tobacco and liquor you can bring back duty-free. If the total value of your goods is more than the duty-free limit, you'll have to pay a tax (most often a flat percentage) on the value of everything beyond that limit.

MONEY

With the mild climate and proximity to the ocean and mountains, San Diego is popular with tourists and conventioneers and, accordingly, is a relatively expensive place to visit. Three-star rooms average between $200 and $280 per night in high season, but there is also a good variety of modest accommodations available. Meal prices compare to those in other large cities, and you can usually find excellent values by dining in smaller, family-run establishments. Admission to local attractions can cost anywhere from $10 to $90. Thankfully, relaxing on one of the public beaches or meandering through the parks and neighborhoods is free—and fun. ■ **TIP→ To save money on restaurants, spas, and boutiques, scour the coupon section at www.sdreader.com or visit www.groupon.com.**

Prices here are given for adults. Substantially reduced fees are almost always available for children, students, and senior citizens. Most museums in Balboa Park offer free admission to residents on Tuesdays.

ITEM	AVERAGE COST
Cup of Coffee	$3
Glass of Wine	$11
Sandwich	$12
One-Mile Taxi Ride	$3
Museum Admission	$19

PACKING

San Diego's casual lifestyle and year-round mild climate set the parameters for what to pack. You can leave formal clothes and cold-weather gear behind.

Plan on warm weather at any time of the year. Cottons, walking shorts, jeans, and T-shirts are the norm. Pack bathing suits and shorts regardless of the season. Few restaurants require a jacket and tie for men. Women may want to also bring something a little dressier than their sightseeing garb.

Evenings are cool, even in summer, so be sure to bring a sweater or a light jacket. Rainfall in San Diego isn't usually heavy; you won't need a raincoat except in winter, and even then, an umbrella may suffice.

Be sure you have comfortable walking shoes. Even if you don't walk much at home, you will probably find yourself covering miles while sightseeing on your vacation. Also bring a pair of sandals or water shoes for the beach.

Sunglasses and sunscreen are a must in San Diego. Binoculars can also come in handy, especially if you're in town during whale-watching season, from December through mid–April, or planning to stargaze in the desert in the summer. If you plan on surfing, consider packing or renting a wet suit or rashguard depending on the season. In winter, water temperatures drop into the 50s and average around 72 degrees in the summer.

RESTROOMS

Major attractions and parks have public restrooms. In the Downtown San Diego area, you can usually use the restrooms at major hotels and fast-food restaurants.

TIPPING

TIPPING GUIDELINES FOR SAN DIEGO	
Bartender	$1 to $5 per round of drinks, depending on the number of drinks
Bellhop	$1 to $5 per bag, depending on the level of the hotel
Hotel Concierge	$5 or more, if he or she performs a service for you
Hotel Doorman	$1 to $2 if he helps you get a cab
Hotel Maid	$1 to $3 a day (either daily or at the end of your stay, in cash)
Hotel Room-Service Waiter	$1 to $2 per delivery, even if a service charge has been added
Porter at Airport or Train Station	$2 per bag
Skycap at Airport	$1 to $3 per bag checked
Taxi Driver	15% to 20%, but round up the fare to the next dollar amount
Tour Guide	10% of the cost of the tour
Valet Parking Attendant	$2 to $5, but only when you get your car
Waiter	15% to 20%, with 20% being the norm at high-end restaurants; nothing additional if a service charge is added to the bill

SAFETY

San Diego is generally a safe place for travelers who observe all normal precautions. Dress inconspicuously (this means removing badges when leaving convention areas) and know the routes to your destination before you set out. At the beach, check with lifeguards about any unsafe conditions such as dangerous riptides or water pollution. The San Diego Tourism Authority offers a print and Web version of Visitor Safety Tips, providing sensible precautions for many situations, *see Visitor Information.*

TOURS

BIKE TOURS

Biking is very popular in San Diego. You can find trails along the beach, in Mission Bay, and throughout the mountains. Pedal your way around San Diego with The Bike Revolution, which delivers and rents bikes. Where You Want To Be Tours offers walking tours as well as tours on bike.

Contacts The Bike Revolution. ✉ *522 6th Ave.* ☎ *619/564–4843* 🌐 *www.thebikerevolution.com.* **Where You Want to Be Tours** (*Secret San Diego*). ✉ *611 K St., #B224* ☎ *619/917–6037* 🌐 *www.wheretours.com.*

BOAT TOURS

Flagship Cruises and Events and Hornblower Cruises & Events both operate one- and two-hour harbor cruises departing from the Broadway Pier. No reservations are necessary for the tours, which cost $24–$31.04; both companies also do dinner cruises ($96) and brunch cruises. These companies also operate during whale-watching season, from December to mid-April. Fishing boats that also do whale watches in season include H&M Landing and Seaforth Boat Rentals.

Contacts Flagship Cruises and Events. ✉ *990 N. Harbor Dr., Embarcadero* ☎ *619/234–4111* 🌐 *www.flagshipsd.com.* **H&M Landing.** ✉ *2803 Emerson St.* ☎ *619/222–1144* 🌐 *www.whalewatchingathmlanding.com.* **Hornblower Cruises & Events.** ✉ *970 N. Harbor Dr.* ☎ *619/234–8687, 800/668–4322* 🌐 *www.hornblower.com.* **San Diego SEAL Tours.** ✉ *500 Kettner Blvd., Embarcadero* ☎ *619/298–8687* 🌐 *www.sealtours.com.* **Seaforth Boat Rentals.** ✉ *1641 Quivira Rd., Mission Bay* ☎ *888/834–2628* 🌐 *www.seaforthboatrental.com.*

BUS AND TROLLEY TOURS

Old Town Trolley Tours takes you to 10 sites, including Old Town, Seaport Village, Horton Plaza, and the Gaslamp Quarter, Coronado, Little Italy, and El Prado in Balboa Park. The tour is narrated, and for the price of the ticket ($40) you can get on and off as you please at any stop. The trolley leaves every 30 minutes, operates daily, and takes two hours to make a full loop.

DayTripper, San Diego Scenic Tours, and Five Star Tours do one-day or multiple-day bus tours of attractions in Southern California.

DayTripper Tours. Single- and multiday trips throughout Southern California, the Southwest, and Baja depart from San Diego year-round. Popular day trips include the Getty Museum, and theater performances in Los Angeles. Call or check website for pickup locations. ☎ *619/299–5777, 800/679–8747* 🌐 *www.daytripper.com* 🎫 *From $75.*

Five Star Tours. Private and group sightseeing bus tour options around San Diego and beyond include everything from the San Diego Zoo to Brewery tours and trips to Baja, Mexico. ✉ *1050 Kettner Blvd.* ☎ *619/232–5040* 🌐 *www.fivestartours.com* 🎫 *From $48.*

Old Town Trolley Tours. Combining points of interest with local history, trivia, and fun anecdotes, this hop-on, hop-off trolley tour provides an entertaining overview of the city and offers easy access to all the highlights. The tour is narrated, and you can get on and off as you please. Stops include Old Town, Seaport Village, the Gaslamp Quarter, Coronado, Little Italy, and Balboa Park. The trolley leaves every 30 minutes, operates daily, and takes two hours to make a full loop. ✉ *San Diego* ☎ *619/298–8687* 🌐 *www.trolleytours.com/san-diego* 🎫 *From $40.*

San Diego Scenic Tours. Half- and full-day bus tours of San Diego and Tijuana depart daily, and some include a harbor cruise. Tours depart from several hotels around town. ✉ *San Diego* ☎ *858/273–8687* 🌐 *www.sandiegoscenictours.com* 🎫 *From $38.*

GO CAR TOURS

These miniature talking cars offer the benefits of a guided tour, but taken at your own pace. Tour the city in a bright yellow three-seater, equipped with GPS navigation and accompanying narration. Go Car Tours offers two routes: choose from Downtown, Balboa Park, Uptown, and Old Town or Point Loma, Cabrillo National Monument, and Ocean Beach. The tours can be driven straight through, or visitors can park and explore any of the sights en-route. Rentals are $58 for the first hour, $220 for five hours. There is a maximum daily charge of five hours if you want to keep the car for the entire day.

Contacts Go Car Tours. ✉ *2100 Kettner Blvd.* ☎ *800/914–6227* 🌐 *www.gocartours.com.*

WALKING TOURS

Several fine walking tours are available on weekdays or weekends; upcoming walks are usually listed in the *San Diego Reader.*

Balboa Park Offshoot Tours. On Saturday at 10 am, free, hour-long walks start from the Balboa Park Visitor Center. The tour's focus rotates weekly, covering topics such as the park's history, palm trees, and desert vegetation. Reservations are not required, but no tours are scheduled between Thanksgiving and the New Year. ✉ *Balboa Park Visitor Center, 1549 El Prado, Balboa Park* ☎ *619/239–0512* 🌐 *www.balboapark.org* 🎫 *Free.*

Coronado Walking Tours. Departing from the Glorietta Bay Inn at 11 am Tuesday, Thursday, and Saturday, this 90-minute stroll through Coronado's historic district takes in the island's mansions, old Tent City, the Hotel del Coronado, and the castles and cottages that line the beautiful beach. Reservations are recommended. ✉ *1630 Glorietta Blvd.* ☎ *619/435–5993* 🌐 *coronadowalkingtour.com* 🎫 *$12* ☞ *Cash only.*

Gaslamp Quarter Historical Foundation. Two-hour walking tours of the Downtown historic district depart from the William Heath Davis House at 11 am on Saturday. ✉ *410 Island Ave.* ☎ *619/233–4692* 🌐 *www.gaslampquarter.org* 🎟 *$20.*

Urban Safaris. Led by longtime San Diego resident Patty Fares, these two-hour Saturday walks through diverse neighborhoods like Hillcrest, Ocean Beach, and Point Loma are popular with tourists and locals alike. The tours, which always depart from a neighborhood coffeehouse, focus on art, history, and ethnic eateries, among other topics. Reservations are required, and private walks can be arranged during the week. ☎ *619/944–9255* 🌐 *www.walkingtoursofsandiego.com* 🎟 *$10.*

VISITOR INFORMATION

For general information and brochures before you go, contact the San Diego Tourism Authority, which publishes the helpful *San Diego Visitors Planning Guide*. When you arrive, stop by one of the local visitor centers for general information.

Citywide Contacts San Diego Tourism Authority. ✉ *750 B St., Suite 1500* ☎ *619/232–3101* 🌐 *www.sandiego.org.* **San Diego Visitor Information Center.** ✉ *996 N. Harbor Dr., Downtown* ☎ *619/236–1242* 🌐 *www.sandiego.org.*

San Diego County Contacts Borrego Springs Chamber of Commerce. ✉ *786 Palm Canyon Dr., Borreo Springs* ☎ *760/767–5555* 🌐 *www.borregospringschamber.com.* **California Welcome Center Oceanside.** ✉ *928 N. Coast Hwy., Oceanside* ☎ *760/721–1101, 800/350–7873* 🌐 *www.visitoceanside.org.* **Carlsbad Visitors Center.** ✉ *400 Carlsbad Village Dr., Carlsbad* ☎ *800/227–5722* 🌐 *www.visitcarlsbad.com.* **Coronado Visitor Center.** ✉ *1100 Orange Ave., Coronado* ☎ *619/435–7242* 🌐 *www.coronado-visitorcenter.com.* **Encinitas Chamber of Commerce.** ✉ *535 Encinitas Blvd., Suite 116, Encinitas* ☎ *760/753–6041* 🌐 *www.encinitaschamber.com.* **Julian Chamber of Commerce.** ☎ *760/765–1857* 🌐 *www.visitjulian.com.*

Statewide Contacts Visit California. ☎ *916/444–4429, 800/462–2543* 🌐 *www.visitcalifornia.com.*

INSPIRATION

Check out these books for further San Diego reading. The novel *Drift* by Jim Miller explores San Diego's boom time through the eyes of a college professor in the year 2000. *Leave Only Paw Prints: Dog Hikes in San Diego* offers myriad walking spots that are dog-friendly, along with smart travel tips for your furry friend. *San Diego Legends: Events, People and Places That Made History* goes beyond the typical history-book material to reveal little-known stories about San Diego.

San Diego has a rich film history, thanks to the city's unique geography and proximity to Los Angeles. Some of the better-known films made here include *Some Like it Hot, Top Gun, Traffic,* and *Almost Famous*. The bar scene in *Top Gun* was filmed at a local restaurant, Kansas City BBQ, on the corner of Kettner Boulevard and West Harbor Drive. And, of course, don't forget to take *Anchorman* Ron Burgundy's advice, and "Stay classy, San Diego."

ONLINE RESOURCES

For a dining and entertainment guide to San Diego's most popular nightlife district, check out Gaslamp.org. For insider tips from a local perspective, try Local Wally's San Diego Tourist Guide. For information on the birthplace of California, search the Old Town San Diego organization's site. Browse the website of San Diego's premier upscale lifestyle magazine, *Ranch and Coast. San Diego Magazine* also has a useful site. Search the site of ArtsTix for half-price show tickets. For a comprehensive listing of concerts, performances, and art exhibits, check out the local alternative paper

San Diego Reader. For edgier arts and culture listings, pick up the *San Diego Citybeat* alt-weekly.

Websites ArtsTix. 🌐 *www.sdartstix.com.* **Gaslamp Info.** 🌐 *www.gaslamp.org.* **Local Wally.** 🌐 *www.localwally.com.* **Old Town San Diego.** 🌐 *www.oldtownsandiego.org.* ***Ranch and Coast.*** 🌐 *www.ranchandcoast.com.* ***San Diego Citybeat.*** 🌐 *www.sdcitybeat.com.* ***San Diego Magazine.*** 🌐 *www.sandiegomagazine.com.* ***San Diego Reader.*** 🌐 *www.sandiegoreader.com.* ***San Diego Union-Tribune.*** 🌐 *www.sandiegouniontribune.com.*

INDEX

PHOTO CREDITS

Cover credit: Nadia Borisevich / Shutterstock [Description: Panda, San Diego Zoo, San Diego, California]. 1, Irene Chan/Alamy. 2-3, Christopher Penler / Shutterstock. 5, Matthew Field/wikipedia.org. **Chapter 1: Experience San Diego:** 8-9, Brett Shoaf/Artistic Visuals. 18 (left), mlgb, Fodors.com member. 18 (top center), SuperStock/age fotostock. 18 (top and bottom right), San Diego CVB/Joanne DiBona. 19 (top left and right), San Diego CVB. 19 (bottom left), Epukas/wikipedia.org. **Chapter 2: Downtown:** 29, Stevegould | Dreamstime.com. 31, Lowe Llaguna/Shutterstock. 32, Steve Snodgrass/Flickr. 35, Neilld | Dreamstime.com. 37, Brett Shoaf/Artistic Visuals. **Chapter 3: Balboa Park and San Diego Zoo:** 39 and 41, Brett Shoaf/Artistic Visuals. 42, Irina88w | Dreamstime.com. 47, Appalachianviews | Dreamstime.com. 51, Ambient Images/Alamy. 53 (top), Dreyer Peter/age fotostock. 53 (bottom), Epukas/wikipedia.org. 54, Robert Holmes. 55, Steve Snodgrass/Flickr. 56 (left and top center), fPat/Flickr. 56 (bottom center), Matthew Field/wikipedia.org. 56 (top right), Jim Epler/Flickr. 56 (bottom right), Philippe Renault/age fotostock. 57, lora_313/Flickr. 58 (left), Cburnett/wikipedia.org. 58 (right), Susann Parker/age fotostock. 59 (top), George Ostertag/age fotostock. 59 (bottom right), Sally Brown/age fotostock. 59 (bottom left), Stefano Panzeri / Shutterstock. **Chapter 4: Old Town and Uptown:** 61, Kongomonkey | Dreamstime.com. 63, dichohecho/Flickr. 64, Sbphotog | Dreamstime.com. 65, ZUMA Press Inc / Alamy. 69, Kongomonkey | Dreamstime.com. **Chapter 5: Mission Bay and the Beaches:** 71, Brett Shoaf/Artistic Visuals. 73, SD Dirk/Flickr. 74, San Diego CVB. 76, Andreas Hub/Visit California. **Chapter 6: La Jolla:** 79, Brett Shoaf/Artistic Visuals. 81, Roger Isaacson. 82, Jason Pratt/Flickr. 84, Brett Shoaf/Artistic Visuals. **Chapter 7: Point Loma and Coronado:** 87, Radius Images / Alamy. 89, Brett Shoaf/Artistic Visuals. 90, San Diego CVB. 91 (top), jamesbenet/iStockphoto. 91 (bottom), Cass Greene/iStockphoto. 92, Sborisov | Dreamstime.com. **Chapter 8: Where to Eat:** 97, Lorena Whiteside. 98, Amy K. Fellows. **Chapter 9: Where to Stay:** 131, Hotel del Coronado. 132, Andaz San Diego. **Chapter 10: Nightlife:** 145, Sandy Huffaker/ALTITUDE Sky Lounge. 146, David H. Collier/Visit California. **Chapter 11: Performing Arts:** 159, Lamb's Players Theatre / J.T. MacMillan. 160, Lynn Susholtz. **Chapter 12: Beaches:** 167 and 168, Brett Shoaf/Artistic Visuals. 169 (top), San Diego CVB. 169 (bottom), Dija/Shutterstock. 170, alysta/Shutterstock. 171 (top), Lowe Llaguno/Shutterstock. 171 (bottom), San Diego CVB. 172, sburel/iStockphoto. 178, Brett Shoaf/Artistic Visuals. **Chapter 13: Sports and the Outdoors:** 185, Brett Shoaf/Artistic Visuals. 186, Sebastien Burel/Shutterstock. 187 (top), Janet Fullwood. 187 (bottom), Sebastien Burel/iStockphoto. 188, Stas Volik/Shutterstock. 196, Sebastien Burel/Shutterstock. **Chapter 14: Shopping:** 207, Sepavo | Dreamstime.com. 208, Ggoodrow | Dreamstime.com. 214, Brett Shoaf/Artistic Visuals. **Chapter 15: North County and Around:** 255, Brett Shoaf/Artistic Visuals. 227 (top), Ken Bohn, San Diego Zoo. 227 (bottom), Alan Vernon/Flickr. 228, Adeliepenguin | Dreamstime.com. 237, Aguina | Dreamstime.com. 245, ZuMa Press, Inc / Alamy. 256, Msurdin | Dreamstime.com. 263, Kitleong | Dreamstime.com. Back cover, from left to right: Joelle Gould/iStockphoto; Leandro Neumann Ciuffo/Flickr, [CC BY 2.0]; Yi Fan/iStockphoto. Spine: Randy Miramontez / Shutterstock.

NOTES

ABOUT OUR WRITERS

Veteran traveler **Claire Deeks van der Lee** feels lucky to call San Diego home. An East Coast transplant, she never takes the near-perfect weather for granted. Claire loves playing tourist in her own city, exploring San Diego's cultural attractions as well as its myriad neighborhoods and Balboa Park—so it was a perfect fit for her to work on the Experience and Exploring chapters of this book. Claire has contributed to *Everywhere* magazine and several Fodor's guides.

Based in Vista, California, journalist and author **Marlise Kast-Myers** lives on a small farm with her husband. She's contributed to more than 50 publications including *Surfer, San Diego Magazine*, and *Union Tribune*, as well as more than 20 Fodor's guides. Her travels have taken her to more than 80 countries—mostly for surfing, snowboarding, and hiking expeditions. She updated the Beaches, Sport and Outdoors, North County, and Travel Smart chapters.

Kai Oliver-Kurtin is a San Diego-based freelance writer who loves covering the people, places, culture and events that embody the city's distinct charm and energy. She contributes to various publications including *San Diego Magazine, Modern Luxury San Diego*, and *USA Today Travel*, as well as her blog, San Diego Sights & Bites. Kai updated the Shopping chapter.

After writing for *Entertainment Weekly* in New York, **Archana Ram** took a 13-month backpacking trip around the world before landing in San Diego in 2013. The East Coast native has been writing about her adopted city for *Travel + Leisure, Sunset, Afar* and other outlets. She updated the Where to Eat chapter.

A self-confessed hotel addict, **Juliana Shallcross** has been reporting on hotels around the world for more than a decade, most recently for *Condé Nast Traveler*, Rand McNally's *Getaway*, and *Hotels Magazine*. A native of New Jersey, Juliana has lived in Los Angeles since 2002 and has yet to get bored of taking road trips in California. She updated the Where to Stay chapter.

Jeff Terich is a culture seeker and night owl who is most at home on a barstool, watching live music. He's the music editor at San Diego CityBeat and a freelance arts and music writer with 17 years of experience writing for publications like *American Songwriter, ALARM, Paste and Chord*. When he's not breaking in his earplugs at shows in San Diego, he's often traveling with his wife Candice or in search of a good bourbon cocktail. Jeff updated the Nightlife and Performing Arts chapters.